Mechanisms of Immigration Control

Mechanisms of Immigration Control: A Comparative Analysis of European Regulation Policies

Edited by
Grete Brochmann
and
Tomas Hammar

Oxford • New York

First published in 1999 by
Berg
Editorial offices:
150 Cowley Road, Oxford OX4 1JJ, UK
70 Washington Square South, New York, NY 10012, USA

Berg is the imprint of Oxford International Publishers Ltd.

Library of Congress Cataloging-in-Publication Data

A catalogue record for this book is available from the Library of Congress

British Library Cataloguing-in-Publication Data

A catalogue record for this book is available from the British Library

ISBN 1 85973 267 4 (Cloth)
1 85973 272 0 (Paper)

Typeset by JS Typesetting, Wellingborough, Northants.
Printed in the United Kingdom by WBC Book Manufacturers, Mid Glamorgan.

Contents

Contents

Acknowledgements

This book is the second part of a research programme 'Migration, Population and Poverty', primarily financed by the Swedish Council for Social Research (SFR – Socialvetenskapliga Forskningsrådet), a programme that has also received financial grants from the Norwegian Research Council (NFR – Norges Forskningsråd). The initiative came from the editors of this book, Grete Brochmann and Tomas Hammar, together with one of the contributing authors, Kristof Tamas. The research programme has been based at the Stockholm University Centre for Research in International Migration and Ethnic Relations (Ceifo).

The first part of the programme resulted in a book 'International Migration, Immobility and Development, Multidisciplinary Perspectives', which was published by Berg (Oxford) in 1997, edited by Tomas Hammar, Grete Brochmann, Kristof Tamas, and Thomas Faist. The approach is primarily theoretical and multidisciplinary, and several questions, basic in research about international migration, are raised, such as: 'why do people not migrate?' 'does migration from less developed countries stimulate or obstruct development?' 'what are the dynamics of a migration process?' – Experts from geography, economics, political science, sociology and social anthropology contributed to the analysis.

In this second book from the programme, attention is turned from the emigration countries of the South and the East to the immigration countries of the North. The theme is immigration control and the mechanisms by which European immigration policies have been shaped and practised during the 1980s and 1990s, a period of increasingly tight restrictions against immigration from the outside world but also of gradually closer cooperation within the European Union. In this book eight European countries are analysed and compared by a qualified team of social scientists (from the fields of geography, economics, political science and sociology), specializing in international migration.

This second project has also received most of its financial support from the Swedish Council for Social Research (SFR). The Norwegian research Council (NFR) has also made valuable funding available. The Institute for Social Research (ISF) in Oslo has supported the project by entering a

Acknowledgements

generous cooperation agreement with Ceifo in Stockholm. In addition, a number of people and institutions have spent valuable time to lend assistance to the project at various stages. Thanks to the generosity of the Institute for Migration and Ethnic Studies (IMES) at the university of Amsterdam, Hans van Amersfoort has found the precious time needed for writing a chapter on the control policy of the Netherlands. The Institut d'Études Politiques de Paris has through Georges Tapinos hosted one of the project meetings. The Instituto Cattaneo has made the same honour to the project at a meeting in Bologna and so has, finally, the Institute for Social Research (ISF) at two other meetings in Oslo. Fondazione Cariplo per le Iniziative e lo Studio sulla Multietnicita (ISMU) has funded research time for Giuseppe Sciortino, author of the Italian chapter. As editors we are most grateful for this support.

Grete Brochmann and Tomas Hammar
Oslo and Stockholm
September 1998

Notes on Contributors

Hans van Amersfoort gained his PhD in geography and is professor at the Institute of Social Geography and senior researcher at the Institute for Migration and Ethnic Studies at the University of Amsterdam, Netherlands; recent books on immigration and the formation of minority groups, and on the nationality question in Europe; special interest in ethnic residential patterns.

Rainer Bauböck has a PhD in sociology and is assistant professor at the department of political science, Institute for Advanced Studies in Vienna, Austria. In 1998–99 he is a visiting member at the Institute for Advanced Studies, Princeton, USA; recent books: *Transnational citizenship, membership and rights in international migration* and *Blurred Boundaries. Migration, Ethnicity and Citizenship* (co-editor).

Grete Brochmann gained her PhD in sociology and is research director at the Institute for Social Research, Oslo, associate professor at the University of Oslo, Norway and author of a book on women's migration to the Middle East. She has regional interests in East Africa, Sri Lanka, the Gulf states and Mozambique, and has written recent books on migration policies and the European Community, and on Bosnian refugees in the Nordic countries.

Tomas Hammar has a PhD in political science, professor emeritus at the Centre for Research in International Migration and Ethnic relations (Ceifo), Stockholm University, Sweden. He was director of the Centre from 1982 until 1993. He is a specialist in the political analysis of migration, and has written books on European immigration policy, democracy and the nation-state.

James F. Hollifield gained his PhD in political science. He is Arnold Professor of political economy and director of international studies in Southern Methodist University, Dallas, and has served as associate director of research at the CNRS in Paris and at Harvard Center for International

Affairs. He recently wrote *Immigrants, Markets and States*, and is co-editor of *Controlling Immigration, A Global Perspective.*

Giuseppe Sciortino has a PhD in sociology, and is professor of sociology in Trieste. He has served in the Trento Instituto di Cultura and is affiliated to the Istituto Carlo Cattaneo in Bologna: he is also a specialist on immigration and labour market policies, and on Italian immigration policy.

Kristof Tamas, MA and doctoral candidate in political science, special adviser in the division for migration and asylum policy of the Swedish Ministry for Foreign Affairs, and researcher at the Centre for Research in International Migration and Ethnic Relations (Ceifo), Stockholm University, Sweden. He has a special interest in international migration politics in Sweden and Europe and in policies addressing the causes of migration.

Dietrich Thrädhardt gained his PhD in political science in the Westphalian Wilhelms University of Münster, Germany. He has served as dean at the University of Münster, and as professor at a university in Tokyo, Japan. He recently wrote about politics and history of the Federal Republic of Germany, on local politics, migration, and European integration, social integration, and European integration, social integration, and naturalization of immigrants in Germany.

The Mechanisms of Control
Grete Brochmann

People move. This is a fact, historically speaking, in most social contexts throughout the world. The reasons for moving have been and still are highly varied. Whether people move out of necessity to escape violence or persecution, whether they move for joyful purposes, or whether they change environment to improve their economic conditions and their chances in life, can broadly speaking be seen as symptoms or indicators of societal conditions: the economic viability of a society, the level of democratic development, minority politics, trust and expectations in relation to the authorities and so forth. The kind of *barriers* to movement prospective and actual migrants confront at various stages of a migration process is another litmus test of social processes and politics, nationally and internationally. Whether control is imposed at the place of origin, by the migrant himself/herself or at the receiving end, is a reflection of the global state of affairs at the time.

The current project deals with control policies in destination countries – more precisely in Europe in the late 1980s and the 1990s. We have selected eight receiving countries to enable a comparative analysis of the generation and implementation of immigration control policies in the late twentieth century.

Receiving countries have various preconditions for controlling immigration, and control policies have taken different forms, historically speaking. These policies are expected to satisfy social, economic and security needs for immigration regulation, without violating international treaties and conventions for asylum and human rights protection, and without violating the public sense of fair treatment of human beings. When studying immigration control in a comparative perspective, it is relevant to ask under which condition and in which ways modern nation states find it necessary to control various flows of migrants. Usually there will be both national and international parameters influencing the formation of a concrete national policy.

The Growing Salience of International Migration

Migration to Western Europe, both from the 'East' and from the 'South' has increased since the second half of the 1980s. Many governments have expressed fear that the so-called 'migration pressure' (see Tapinos, 1992; Straubhaar, 1993) might increase even more. Large inflows of migrants and refugees have been seen as burdens adding economic recession, leading to problems on labour markets and for social welfare systems. Massive immigration might also have an impact on national security and national identity, on the ethnic and religious composition of the people and on political stability in receiving countries (Weiner, 1993). The fall of the Soviet Union and the creation of new states, the conflicts in former Yugoslavia, the wars and civil wars in the Middle East and in Africa, have all been seen as potential causes of migration to Europe.

With this alarm at immigration from the east and the south, immigration policies in the Western European countries have been heavily focused on *control*. State borders are reinforced, refugee categories redefined, internal surveillance is increased and more deportations are effectuated. Having been a marginal political topic, immigration has developed into one of the most central and complicated issues within Western Europe.

In theories of international migration, economic factors tend to prevail and far too little attention is paid to the role of the state. However, in periods of strict immigration control, such as the present, the significance of state policies is on trial. It may probably be shown that states' control policies, more than any other factor, can explain direction, volume and composition of international migration. Although some receiving countries may be less efficient in this control, states are generally able to construct more-or-less effective control policies such as those that characterise the international migration of the 1990s (see Freeman, 1994).

Control systems are not perfect, though, and clandestine migration and illegal trafficking of migrants are unavoidable problems. Since the door was closed for labour migrants in the beginning of the 1970s, the main legal forms of entry have been through the asylum 'door', the humanitarian 'door' or through family reunification. Increasingly more immigrants are non-Europeans and the number of asylum seekers has escalated. Having minute chances of success through legal means, many entered by clandestine channels. The traditional distinction between 'economic' and 'political' migrants (labour migrants and refugees), has become increasingly problematic in the 1980s and the 1990s. Efforts are made by the states, alone and in co-operation, to establish efficient control policies and to avoid misuse of the asylum system as well as of the other options made available for refugees.

The Major Dilemma

Considering the mounting increase in mobility, brought about by the international revolution in transportation and communication, a basic assumption of this project is that efficient immigration control is necessary in today's Europe. Free immigration under the current global situation could undermine state regulation of labour and housing markets and make planning virtually impossible. It could also alter conditions in welfare states like those built up in Western Europe after World War II. Nonetheless, immigration control carries with it various forms of *costs* – social, economic and political – for the state and for society, some of which are visible in the short run, others only traceable over a longer time perspective. Some costs are easily connected to the control system: border police budgets, expenses attached to public administration of immigration/ asylum policies, budgets for international co-operation, and so forth. Other costs are more subtle or ambiguous, and difficult to relate directly to immigration control, like the price attached to a more 'controlled' society generally speaking, and possible xenophobic reactions towards 'visible' foreigners who are believed to be unwanted. Strict control may also unintentionally serve to decrease tourism, hamper business exchanges or restrict favourable or necessary immigration.

Besides, what is a cost for some might be a benefit for others, and *vice versa*. The most obvious counterpart to the controlling states is the migrants themselves. The steadily increased immigration control of the last twenty years in Western Europe has imposed a major barrier to prospective migrants, and limited the scope of *choice*. The barriers are, however, differentiated, in the sense that nationality determines the degree to which one is subject to control. Generally speaking nationals from the so-called OECD countries face less severe scrutiny, let alone citizens of member countries of the European Union, who are qualified for free movement across internal EU (and EEA) borders.

Apart from costs, there are obligations that present receiving countries with limitations as to the formulation of control policies. Such obligations may be international or domestic ones, and they may be supported by ethical considerations or by positive law. Some rather weak international constraints on immigration control are specified in international law (such as the International Covenant on Civil and Political Rights, the European

Convention on Human Rights and the Geneva Refugee Convention). Compliance with these norms is often merely supported by international opinion; in some areas it is, however, surveyed by international commissions or even enforced by judiciary bodies such as the European Court for Human Rights. Other international obligations result from bilateral and multilateral treaties between sending and receiving countries that regulate, for example, visa-free entry, readmission in case of deportations, or social welfare entitlements of resident aliens. Domestically, constitutional rights have become quite important constraints on deportations and, to a lesser degree, also on denial of family reunion. National courts have often gained an important role in challenging government policies of immigration control. Even where they are not based on positive law, normative obligations may become relevant in the formulation of control policies. Some governments want a reputation for respecting humanitarian principles or egalitarian norms of democratic welfare states. More often, however, these latter norms serve as a justification for strictly controlling and limiting first admissions in order to maintain basic levels of social equality among the whole resident population.

A number of authors have also argued for international moral obligations to open borders for immigrants from poorer countries, but such ideas have clearly had little impact on the formulation of policies. Generally speaking, international moral obligations tend to become more relevant as motivations for government action when they coincide with some state or party interest. Admission of refugees is, for example, often influenced by foreign policy interests. Interests may, however, also combine with international moral obligations to justify restrictive immigration control. Some Western governments seem, for example, willing to increase certain types of international assistance if they expect that this will help in reducing emigration pressure.

To formulate and implement immigration control policies that correspond to normative obligations, while at the same time taking care of the 'interest of the state' – all within a context of uncertain prognoses and insufficient information – may be said to constitute the current major dilemma of European governments. Studying this dilemma, as reflected in the various preconditions for, types of, and implementation of control policies in European countries, is one of the aims of this project.

It is the *policies* that form the most basic unit of analysis in our context, although *consequences* of policies – intended and unintended – as well as central factors *influencing* policies, bring in the perspective of other actors and institutions as well.

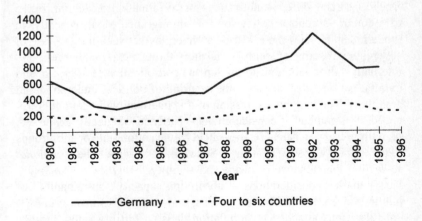

Figure 1.1a Inflows of Foreign Resident Population into the Project Countries
(in thousands)

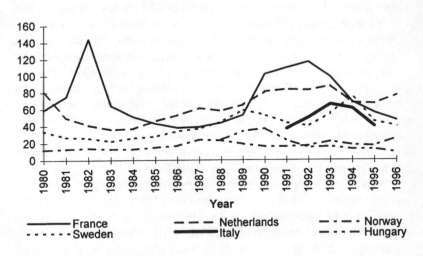

Figure 1.1b Inflows of Foreign Resident Population into six Project Countries
(in thousands)

Rationale of Control Policies

One may sort out different motivations for the formation and legitimization of a country's control policy towards immigrants. Most basically, in modern democracies there will be an interplay between the exercise of sovereignty in terms of control of territory through external borders, and internally – the continuous formation and consolidation of the social and cultural national distinctions – the securing of political integration and continuity. The tangible expression of this interplay will again be influenced by a number of considerations – partly ideologically expressed, partly representing actual *interests* held by the nation state or sub-groups of the economy or society at large. Such dimensions could be a) *national security* – maintenance of peace and stability; b) *national economy* – labour market considerations – 'absorption capacity', sustainability of public budgets for welfare provisions, and so forth; c) *demography* – considerations attached to population density, fertility rates, the age pyramid, and so forth; d) *social and cultural cohesion* – preservation of national identity, religious traditions, social integration, etc.

A selection or combination of these factors will by and large constitute the basis for a state's legitimization of its national control policy towards immigrants. The instruments that are available for the government depend on a complex web of elements. This will be influenced by administrative and management systems; traditions in relation to immigration; national history generally speaking, particularly with respect to civic and political culture, collective identity and ideology of nationhood. This web of factors is again strongly influenced by the international context at any given point in time. Other states' national policies, international agreements, conventions and organizations as well as the migrant flows themselves, contribute to form a state's immigration policies. Besides, in today's Europe a 'meta-level' constitutes its own dynamic: people's *perception* of reality in terms of immigration pressure.

This 'meta' – or psychological – element has come to play an increasingly important part in the European setting lately. The events in 1989 created a 'crisis atmosphere' in relation to immigration in Western Europe, as the prospective immigration from the newly opened eastern countries was expected to come on top of the increased flows from the south. This atmosphere was further aggravated by the catastrophe in former Yugoslavia. More than anything, this sudden new situation underlined the unpredictability in the migration field, a factor that seems to have triggered xenophobic reactions, and put the various authorities into an even more defensive mode. What comes first in this respect – popular perceptions or official restriction – is an object for concrete analysis in the various national contexts.

Some Definitions

A number of concepts will be used in the framework of this project. Some of the more important of these will be defined here.

Immigration and emigration are population movements across national boundaries. Individuals who migrate to a country and then reside there for longer than a short period of time (for instance more than three months), are immigrants from the perspective of the receiving country, and at the same time emigrants in relation to the country of origin (sending country). Immigrants/emigrants may be citizens or non-citizens (aliens). Non-citizens with a legal and permanent residence status and several socio-economic or even some political rights, may be called *denizens*.

There are a great number of possible categorizations of immigrants/immigration, which have implications for control policy formulation. The motivation for individuals to migrate is often mixed. Governments never-theless base their policies on a differentiation according to assumed motive of the migrant; economic (such as migrants workers, professionals, business people); political (asylum seekers, refugees, war refugees); family reunification (spouses, minor and adult children, parents, siblings, other relatives). Immigration may be *legal /regular* if all permits are in order, or *illegal/irregular* if some or all permits are missing. The latter type includes those who have entered illegally, those who have overstayed a legal period and those who work without permission. In the admission of refugees we may distinguish between active policies of taking in groups fleeing from persecution, war or famine, and situations where destination states are rather passively exposed to refugees producing crises in neighbouring countries and become a natural target for those seeking shelter. In both kinds of admission, receiving countries will generally try to establish systems of control that make sure that only the welcome and 'deserving' refugees can benefit from asylum.

Immigration may be *temporary* (renewable or not) or permanent (revoc-able or not). These are the basic categories we are dealing with in this project, and we will, for reasons of convenience, label them *migrants* or *immigrants* as a collective term when there is no analytical reason for making a further distinction.

Migration control policy of receiving states is exercised at different points along a path that leads from origin to permanent settlement and naturalization in a destination country. For documented labour migration

Table 1.1 Foreign Resident Population and Labour Force 1983–1995

Country/ Population 1995	Foreign Resident Population in thousands and per cent				Foreign Labour in 1995	
	1983	*1988*	*1993*	*1995*	*Thousands*	*Per cent*
Austria 8.055	297 *4%*	344 *5%*	690 *9%*	724 *9%*	317	10%
France 58.265	3,714 *7%*	...	3,597 *6%*	...	1,573	6%
Germany 81.539	4,535 *7%*	4,513 *7%*	6,878 *9%*	7,174 *9%*	2,569	7%
Hungary 10.212	...	...	186* *2%*	140 *1%*	21	0%
Italy 57.333	381 *1%*	490 *1%*	649 *2%*	991 *2%*	436	2%
Netherlands 15.494	552 *4%*	624 *4%*	780 *5%*	725 *5%*	221	4%
Norway 4.370	95 *2%*	136 *3%*	162 *4%*	161 *4%*	52	5%
Sweden 8.838	397 *5%*	421 *5%*	508 *6%*	532 *5%*	220	5%

* 1992 data.
Source: SOPEMI 1994 and 1996. French data are based on the census of 1982 and of 1990; Italian data from the Home Office. Council of Europe, Recent demographic developments in Europe 1996. OECD International Migration Statistics 1998.

we may identify five major points: first, policies at origin aimed at influencing the build-up of an emigration *potential* (generally the aim is to reduce the potential, only in very rare cases will receiving states try to create a potential for wanted emigration); second, policies at origin in order to control the size of an emigration *flow* (promotion of immigration by recruitment, control of flows by visa requirements, deterrence of unwanted immigrants by information campaigns); third, control at admission to the territory (visa, border checks, residence permits); fourth, control at access to the labour market and employment (work permits); fifth, return migration policies (by financial incentives or by enforcement of return in case of unemployment or lack of independent income).

What is Meant by 'Control'?

The two most basic components of immigration control are external and internal alien control. The term 'immigration control' is often used synonymously with the more frequent term 'immigration regulation'. We use both terms in this text, but 'control' according to our use, is defined more broadly. Studies of immigration control often concentrate on policy generation, content, implementation, outcome as well as evaluations. We will also cover these dimensions, yet the main target for our analysis will be the *mechanisms* operating in the interplay or the grey zone between external and internal control, as will be discussed more in depth below. We will investigate the varying conditions under which a number of European countries attempt to regulate the size and composition of immigration and to control aliens already in the country. We also use the term control rather than regulation to demonstrate that our perspective is broader in another sense. Whereas state policy is the dependent variable and the main *actor* in our system, a number of other actors in society – non-governmental organizations like trade unions and employers organiz- ations, other actors in the labour and housing market, political parties, humanitarian organizations and civil society at large (including anti- immigrant groups) and of course the migrants themselves – serve to reinforce, maintain or obstruct state policies, thereby also influencing preconditions for control.

A country's public immigration control refers to the rules and proc- edures governing the selection, admission and deportation of foreign citizens. It also includes rules that control foreign citizens (aliens) once they visit or take residence in the immigration country, including control of their employment. The intensity of this control is, however, variable. Under certain conditions hardly any public control is exercised. Employers may be allowed to recruit labour directly, or the states may negotiate bilateral agreements with sending countries to the same effect. Agreements about free movements of people, decided by states under specific conditions, should also be considered a type of immigration regulation. The EU and the Nordic Area have for example both decided that migration between member countries should be exempted from control. Free move- ment and residence is one extreme on a spectrum of levels of control where the other extreme, theoretically, is complete control, namely the capacity to stop any movement or terminate the residence of all aliens at any time.

Immigrants can go through three different *gates*, regulating entrance into European states. The first is through the receiving of work or residence permit for shorter periods and becoming temporary migrant workers. This first, temporary, status can also apply to asylum seekers and foreigners who receive temporary settlement on humanitarian grounds. The second status is as *denizens,* receiving work or residence permits without time restrictions, or permanently, often receiving social and legal rights, and even some limited political rights. The third and last gate passed gives the status of a naturalized citizen, with all political rights. By and large, some form of immigration regulation is conducted on all levels, and foreign citizens remain under aliens control until they become naturalized citizens with full political rights (Hammar, 1990). This study shall include all these levels of control.

Table 1.2 Naturalizations by all Means of Acquisition: total amount and naturalization rate* 1998 and 1995

| Year | 1988 | | 1995 | |
Country	n	Rate	n	Rate
Austria	8,200	2.3	15,300	2.1
France	74,000	3.0	92,400	2.6
Germany	46,800	1.0	313,600	4.5
Hungary	13,200	7.1	10,700	7.6
Italy	4,225	0.9	7,400	0.8
Netherlands	9,100	5.7	71,400	9.2
Norway	3,400	3.6	11,800	7.2
Sweden	18,000	8.5	32,000	5.9

Source: SOPEMI 1993–98.
* Naturalizations per year divided by size of foreign population.

Integration policy refers to the conditions provided to resident immigrants. It consists of all aspects that influence the situation for immigrants in a receiving country. These include legal rights as well as social opportunities and political and cultural participation in the wider society. Legal integration is a process that provides individual immigrants with a gradually improved status moving towards equal citizenship. It is at the same time a gradual attenuation of their subjection to internal immigration control. Aliens are subject to stronger forms of control because their residence can be more easily terminated than that of denizens; denizens are partly exempted from immigration control but generally only naturalized citizens enjoy the full basket of rights associated with free movement (security of residence and non-deportability, unconditional readmission from abroad, family reunification entitlements). Regulating legal integration at the second gate and third gate is therefore a major policy instrument in immigration control. Restrictive policies of internal control keep a large part of the immigrant population in a temporary status and provide the state with a legal capacity to reduce their numbers by enforcing remigration.

Whereas the links between legal integration and immigration control are direct and explicit, they are more indirect and implicit for social and cultural integration. Work and housing conditions, social benefits and social services, educational opportunities and language training, opportunities to participate in ethnic communities, in politics and trade union activities, and so forth, may have an impact on the size and composition of immigration. Sometimes generous conditions can work as pull factors for immigrants, and sometimes the lack of, or poor, integration facilities can deter migrants from trying to enter a particular country, or from trying to settle for good. The concentration of ethnic groups in certain urban areas, the formation of ethnic communities with their own religious and cultural institutions and an official policy of cultural segregation, assimilation or pluralism may also influence immigration patterns and the duration of residence of immigrants. Often, the initial integration of newcomers takes place within ethnic networks facilitated by the resources they can provide for their members. The emergence of such networks facilitates chain migration. In overseas immigration countries ethnic groups also organize politically, and often lobby the government with regard to admission and integration policies.

Different kinds of state systems engender different models for incorporation or integration of foreigners. The degree of proclaimed and actual openness in terms of liberal entry control; the 'political culture' related to the granting of citizenship and the tolerance for ethnic and religious diversity will influence the way individuals and groups of foreigners relate and adjust within their new environment. This again will have important implications for the kind of status immigrants can hope for; whether they will constitute ethnic communities within a multi-cultural society; whether they will intermingle to the degree that distinctions are no longer significant or whether they will form ethnic minorities – marginalized and excluded from the main body of society. The outcome of the various policy tracks combined with public 'interpretations' of these tracks will feed back into the formulation of external control policies. Beyond these interconnections with external control systems, the integration of foreigners in a broad sense may serve as a control mechanism in its own right: integrated individuals (foreign or national) are more easily controlled as 'good citizens'; as taxpayers, as house tenants, as child educators and so forth.

We will, in this project, only deal with the integration dimension as far as it is relevant for the discussion on the external/internal control mechanisms.

External versus Internal Control

The discussion of control policies is often limited to a question of admittance or non-admittance. The analysis needs to be broadened by calling into attention more subtle and indirect aspects of control. First and foremost there is an interplay between external and internal control dimensions, as indicated above. Furthermore, there are both explicit and implicit aspects of a country's total 'control regime'.

External control consists of the more visible measures undertaken by states to control entry before departure or arrival through such measures as visa restrictions at borders and at airports, or through legislation against illegal trafficking and clandestine immigration. Over the last few years, European states have strengthened and diversified their external control by introducing *preventive* measures. Information campaigns have been designed in emigration regions in order to inform potential migrants of the minimal chances of entering immigration countries, flows have been halted by supporting UN supervised safe zones in refugee producing areas, or aid has been used within the framework of bilateral agreements with emigration or transit countries to prevent migrants from reaching the borders of Western European countries.

Internal control of aliens may be exercised from their first entry to their possible fulfilment of citizenship. The types of internal control can include measures during evaluation of asylum applications, the requirement of residence and work permits, the use of ID cards, employer sanctions, inspection of work sites or of private or public housing, inspection at language classes, in school, hospitals and so forth, wherever immigrants encounter welfare authorities. Yet control policies might be influenced or modified by the conduct of non-governmental actors such as unions, humanitarian organizations, employers, and other interest groups.

Immigration control is mostly a mixture of external and internal control, and the mixture can differ greatly from country to country. Some states, being traditional immigration countries (US, Canada and Australia), have emphasized external control, and made relatively little use of internal controls. In Europe, this is also true for the British system of immigration control. Intercontinental migrants who travel by ship or by aeroplanes are easier to inspect than those who come over land, crossing borders

Table 1.3 Asylum Seekers and Temporary Protected by Countries 1985–97
(in thousands)

Country	1980	1982	1985	1988	1991	1992	1993	1994	1995	1996	1997
Austria	9	6	7	16	27	16	5	5	6	7	7
France	19	23	29	34	47	29	28	26	20	17	21
Germany	108	37	74	103	256	438	323	127	128	116	104
Hungary	...	...	...	13	53	16	5	3	6	1	2
Italy	n.a.	...	5	1	36	12	28	26	18	1	2
Netherlands	1	1	6	8	22	20	35	53	29	23	34
Norway	...	0	1	7	5	5	13	3	2	2	2
Sweden	5	7	15	20	27	84	38	19	9	6	10

Source: Eurostat, Migration Statistics 1995, and Statistics in Focus 1996:1, Asylum-seekers in Europe 1985–1995; OECD International Migration Statistics 1998, and SOPEMI 1996–98; Italian data from Home Office; Hungarian data from Office of Refugee Affairs; 1997 data from Intergovernmental Consultations on Asylum, Refugee and Migration Policies in Europe (IGC), Data Summary June 1998.

between states, as for instance on the European continent. Many European countries prefer external control, not only for its efficiency, but also out of dislike for ID cards, ID numbers and other measures that are perceived as violations of the personal integrity of individuals, and as threats to the liberties of a democratic state. German immigration control has for instance been hampered both by Germany's geographical position in the middle of Europe, and by its strong commitment to the protection of the individual's personal integrity. The Scandinavian countries, which have used ID numbers for a long time as a basis for their population register, also employ them for internal control of non-citizens in the countries. This is one reason why it is much more difficult to overstay without permits or to work illegally in these countries. Another reason may be that the countries are relatively small and sparsely populated, and that social control in general therefore tends to be strong. A third reason may be that at least those aliens working in large enterprises are well controlled by strong trade unions.

Control (external and internal) may be intended to regulate the size of immigration, and a country may decide upon a maximum number that should not be surpassed. The US decides on the number of immigrants to be admitted per year, while Switzerland has set a global ceiling aiming at a balance between the size of the Swiss and the foreign populations. Canada and Australia predetermine the optimum level of immigration that the authorities should aim for during the year. If it is hard to make good forecasts of future immigration, it may, however, be equally hard to

Table 1.4 A Framework for the Analysis of Control Policy

	Direct/explicit	*Indirect/implicit*
External	Entry restrictions/Border control Visa schemes Carrier liability for transporting undocumented migrants Computerized data bases on 'unwanted persons' Legislation against illegal trafficking Preventive measures abroad: safe havens, information campaigns, readmission agreements	Erratic handling of entry restrictions/ elements of arbitrariness Indistinct definitions of 'needs of the nation' Preventive measures abroad: Development aid, direct foreign investment, reducing trade barriers
Internal	Deterrent measures during periods of application and examination Internal surveillance; Regulated access to ID-cards Regulated access to housing, social benefits, health care, education Temporary residence, denizenship, naturalization 'Amnesties' Employer sanctions Remigration incentives Repatriation and deportation	No Non-enforcement of deportation/ tolerated illegal status – administrative discretion in deciding on residence and employment permits, etc.; ethnic community formation and cultural recognition; policies and opinion building that facilitates initial integration and durable settlement, or conversely, social segregation or discrimination.

effectuate decisions about the number of immigrants to be admitted. Some observers claim that no regulation can do this effectively; others agree that it cannot be done with absolute efficiency, but they still believe that the impact of regulation is considerable.

It is an empirical question whether external or internal control is more efficient, in general or under certain circumstances. Comparing countries may be one way to approach this question. Another interesting empirical question is how European immigration countries perceive their own 'absorption capacity' – the factors that have an impact on their interest in and ability to admit foreign citizens. Are evaluations of this capacity based, for example, solely on the short-term admittance conditions?

Other relevant questions are how and with what consequences external and internal control are linked to and combined with each other in practice. When states over the last few years have reinforced their control, did they first of all rely on external or internal control? Several preventive measures have been taken, among them the establishment of UN supervised safe zones, as mentioned above, or bilateral aid agreements with emigration or transit countries to prevent migration flows from emerging or reaching Western European countries. To what extent are such preventive measures complementing or replacing internal control?

Both the internal and the external control complex might be seen as continua. For the sake of clarity, we may divide each complex in an *explicit/ direct* and an *implicit/indirect* dimension: *explicit* meaning public policy, and *implicit* meaning hidden or subdued control mechanisms, and more or less systematic malpractices of public policies. The explicit dimension is by definition *public*, whereas the implicit one might be either concealed or occasionally be given explicit or public expressions.

As usual the distinctions are not clearcut. As indicated, there are grey areas in between the boxes, as well as important interactions across the spheres. There are different laws enacted to regulate each policy area. Different administrative agencies are responsible for policy implement- ation, and different professions are involved.

Integration policy, as a part of a country's internal control policy, can have both explicit and implicit functions. The same is true for the general welfare policy of a country, relating both to immigrants and citizens. The welfare state brings a dual dimension into the migration context: on the one hand it becomes pertinent to control the limited resources of the welfare societies, yet on the other hand the welfare aspect makes it more attractive to enter from 'the other side'.

Generally speaking there is an important interplay between the immi- gration policy of a state and its welfare regime. We may call this the immigration/welfare paradox. On the one hand, internal social redistrib- ution and high levels of equality or of basic social protection for all require more closure and restrictive external control. Admitting immigrants who will then be subjected to unequal and discriminatory treatment may create lasting marginalization, which will undermine the state's or the trade unions' capacity to maintain high standards for wages, work conditions and social benefits. 'Equal standards for all' is a costly strategy, which gives an extra sharpness to immigration restrictions in times of recession. On the other hand, these standards may also be pull factors for further immigration and they may require some relaxation of immigration control. Immigrants can only fully integrate in society when they are able to bring in their close family members and to travel between countries of origin and residence. Moreover, highly restrictive systems of internal control with massive police checks in workplaces, private homes and streets may also undermine the liberal features of democratic welfare states and increase the social stigmatization of certain ethnic groups.

Parameters Influencing Policy Outcomes

If we view this external/internal complex as a dynamic system with significant cross linkages and substantial interplay, there is nonetheless no simple causal relationship as many other factors also influence the outcome. Control and regulation policies of a state reflect tensions and dilemmas related to sometimes contradictory interests and considerations concerning immigration. A number of national and international actors, processes and events provide background premises and represent central forces when it comes to influencing policy outcome in each single state. The web of these factors will be specific in time and space, yet the most central ones will appear in different contexts in all our project countries.

First, and most generally speaking, the control a sovereign state exercises over the entry of immigrants and their subsequent access to residence, employment or social benefits will always be influenced by historical precedents and traditional patterns of behaviour – the history of immigration (magnitude and length of experience) and the state's 'control culture' as it were. Within this 'control culture' there are normative elements; traditions in terms of humanitarian values, cultural openness towards the outside world, legitimacy as to using economic conditions as a premise for policy-making in relation to immigration control, and so forth.

Secondly, labour unions may be influential both directly and indirectly in the field of immigration control, and also both related to the external and the internal dimension of the control complex. Unions may try to influence policymakers directly to restrict entry control to avoid abundance on the supply side in the labour market, or they may indirectly control access to labour markets through structural means: by acting as gate-keepers to organized branches, and through the general grip unions may have on working life and work politics, depending on the degree to which a state can be characterized as a corporatist regime.

Thirdly, parliamentary parties are certainly of importance. The various parties' stands on immigration control both ideologically and in practice play a role in their own right (by influencing legislation and administrative practice) and, besides, have an impact on the general climate in society. The policy that is actually implemented will again represent a forceful parameter and provide the context for further policymaking through feedback mechanisms from society. Thus political parties hold a dual position – both representing (parts of) the population and, at the same time, exercising a considerable influence on the attitudes of the very same population.

Fourthly, non-governmental organisations (NGOs), associations and social movements may exert influence on policy making, depending on the general strength of civil society and the relative strength of its agencies dealing with questions related to immigration. Such agencies may work both for and against the interests of actual or potential immigrants. Civil society constitutes itself both as a multiplicity of associations and as a sphere of public discourse, strongly shaped by the mass media. It is in the context of civil society that the climates for tolerance and communication – or xenophobia and racism – develop and feed back into politics.

The International Context

Beyond all these *national* forces, the international context – other states' policies and the character of the international flows in themselves increasingly constitute a pressing frame of reference for national policymaking. Migration has for quite some time had strong implications for interstate relations. In a situation where, according to the public definition, (unskilled) immigration is (with a few exceptions) not wanted in European countries, and the outside pressure is considerable, each and every state will have to look to other countries' control policies to ensure that its own belongs in the most restrictive flank. This political behaviour is based on the theoretical assumption that the 'magnet effect' will serve to channel the flows to the easiest accessible country. Besides, the establishment of the European Single Market in 1993 has reduced the autonomy of each state in shaping its own immigration policy even further.

In Western Europe, the Internal Market, with the dismantling of internal border controls, gives every single memberstate a clear interest in the immigration policies of its fellow memberstates. Each state is vulnerable to the policies of the others.[1] One might think that this vulnerability would make immigration issues prime candidates for transference to supranational decision making. Harmonization of the immigration policy of the EU has, however, been an arduous task. This probably has to do with what Paul Kapteyn calls 'the European dilemma': 'fear of their weak national position leads these countries to join forces, yet it is the same fear which holds them back' (Kapteyn, 1992).

---

1. Immigration issues have also ranked high in negotiations between the European Union and some of the states seeking entry. Swiss negotiations with the Union have, for example, involved extensive discussions about Swiss seasonal labour policy (Tomasi and Miller, 1993). Migration is, as we will see, also a central parameter in Hungary's relationship with the EU.

Historically, states have had to rely on control of national frontiers for their own security. Border control has been seen as a shield against terrorism, international crime, drug trafficking, illegal weapon trading – and unwanted immigration. The prospects of removing this national instrument have triggered calls for compensatory measures, both in terms of reinforced controls at the Community's external borders, and through strengthened *internal* (national) control mechanisms.

Immigration of third country nationals is not covered by the 1957 Treaty of Rome, which fosters free movement of persons *within* the EU area, but excludes non-EU citizens. In the 1987 revision of the Treaty of Rome, article 8a reads: 'The internal market shall comprise an area without internal frontiers in which the free movement of goods, persons, services and capital is ensured in accordance with the provisions of this Treaty'.

The lack of consensus on the interpretation of this article has represented a major barrier to a common immigration policy in the Community. Some member countries, particularly the UK and Denmark, have interpreted 'free movement of persons' to mean EU citizens only. The European Commission, on the other hand, has stated the general application of the article: 'The phrase "free movement of . . . persons" in Article 8a refers to all persons, whether or not they are economically active and irrespective of their nationality. The internal market could not operate under conditions equivalent to those in a national market if the movement of individuals within this market were hindered by controls at internal frontiers' (Commission, 1992a).

Immigration of third-country nationals in a way disturbs the basic philosophy of the Community. Free movement of labour is one of the constituting elements of the EEC Treaty, yet third-country nationals are *de facto* not yet included in this basis. The legal status of third-country nationals living in an EU memberstate (resident aliens) was not contained in the Single European Act, even though this group now constitutes the majority of the immigrant population in Western Europe. In 1994, around 17 million immigrants lived in the 15 EU countries. Approximately 11 million of these were third-country nationals (Eurostat).

A senior official in the European Commission, G. Callovi, asks: 'Will not firms' competitiveness in a free economic and trade area be threatened if third-country labour does not enjoy, in all member states, equality of treatment with national labour?' (Callovi, 1992: 368). Others have argued that it would be.

'against economic rationality to have a single European market with 12 [now 15] different policies towards non-EU residents, limiting their labour mobility to within the territory of one single member state and requiring them to apply for entry visas and work permits for other member-states. This would result in the inefficient use of manpower and would give rise to problems such as the case of firms having to provide services or operating in two or more member-states. This would, moreover, aggravate the discrimination between Community and non-Community nationals, thus reinforcing the already tarnished image of a Community with second or even third class citizens which is contrary to the democratic values which member-states purport to uphold' (Cruz, 1991: 14).

The core of the matter concerning Article 8a (later changed to 7a in the Maastricht Treaty) is how to control the movements of non-EU residents without simultaneously controlling those of EU nationals. The immigration issue illustrates a general dilemma facing the EU countries in the inter-section between the national and the inter-(supra-) national level: new structures are to be formed in a field that is touchy at the national level. On the one hand, the EU countries want to establish a common internal market, removing internal borders in order to promote competition and growth. On the other hand, the nationstates also cling to sovereignty in connection with control of their own conditions, in this case their own frontiers.

Despite the heated discussions over Article 7a, and the reluctance to transfer competence to the supra-national level in the area of immigration, enhanced freedom of movement with the Single Market has stimulated a tendency towards greater cooperation and coordination between EU member countries in this field. This tendency was further reinforced at the Amsterdam Summit in 1997, where the Schengen Accord was inte-grated into the EU structure, and parts of the immigration policy transferred to the supra-national institutional framework of the Union (albeit with a five-year transitional period without qualified majority rule).

Mechanisms of Control

To facilitate the analysis of the external/internal control complex, it can be useful to sort out a set of distinctions or *mechanisms* by which the various parameters play together to decide policy outcome. By empha-sizing the mechanism approach, we also signal in what terms we aim at theory building. Mechanisms, according to Jon Elster, help grasp the 'dynamic aspect of scientific explanation' (Elster, 1989: 7; also Hedström and Swedberg, 1995 and Stinchcombe, 1991) and imply a focus on a delimited number of phenomena that are believed to be significant for the understanding of external/internal control dynamics.

Firstly, we are dealing with *intentional politics*, in which the overriding concern is *efficiency* in achieving the aim of selective control with minimal immigration of non-OECD citizens. The sometimes competing aims of abiding by normative obligations or humanitarian principles is important for democratic welfare states, yet it is clearly a secondary concern in the actual practice of their governments. To achieve this overriding aim – control of immigration – authorities establish a system of instrumental policies.

Secondly, authorities are confronted with a number of mechanisms that produce *unintended consequences*. All immigration control operates in a context of high uncertainty and interdepedence of strategies pursued by different agents: there can be unforeseen consequences – and there can be foreseen consequences with unforeseen costs, which in the process appear as dilemmas or trade-offs. These consequences will in turn constitute a part of the context for further decisionmaking. The concrete make-up of this contradictory state of affairs will be analysed in the following chapters.

Another mechanism relevant for current policymaking in Europe is the relationship between an *individual approach* and a *flow approach* to immigration control. Most Western European countries have basically had an individual approach to immigrants: asylum seekers have been treated as individual cases, as have applications for family reunion. As the number of cases increased immensely, particularly from the mid-1980s, the processing costs and the time involved have made authorities search for collective means to rationalize procedures and to reduce the numbers able to arrive at the borders in the first place. Thresholds, quotas, the definition of 'safe third countries', visa schemes and so forth are all measures aiming at reducing immigration, by means of a *flow approach*. These measures embody serious dilemmas when it comes to protection of human rights. The various chapters will scrutinize which policy measures the individual countries have utilized in this realm.

The phenomenon of *xenophobia* is contradictory as a mechanism. Xenophobia *might* be a result of immigration – or the perception that immigration is a threat to national identity or traditional culture, to jobs for nationals, to the general social order, and so on. On the other hand, anti-immigrant sentiments may also be a result of images produced by a rigid control policy. Immigrants have in many countries become synony-mous with 'unwanted', a fact that feeds back into the attitude towards the immigrants who are already legitimately integrated. Public opinion becomes confused as to 'who is whom'? Various tensions, social unrest, xenophobia and more explicit racism are related to immigration in today's Europe. Even though these social concerns or fears may have other causes, immigration has *de facto* become a public target for dissent. This in turn pushes politicians into a constituency trap.

The *political actor* mechanism is closely related to this dynamics of xenophobia. The interplay between voters and politicians is intricate. Being responsive to the expectations of their constituency, politicians may serve as 'reinforcers' of the hostile tendencies, thus inducing new calls for control. It is also symbolically important for governments to appear to have control of their borders. The population must have confidence that protection against uncontrollable influxes is effective, otherwise the climate for tolerance will deteriorate, and the government's capability will be called into question. The need for significant symbols, and the need to win elections can certainly go both ways in this respect, as we will see in the respective cases, yet in times of recession the construction of migration as a threat seems to win more easily. However that may be, these mechanisms are relevant for explanations as to how politicians adapt norms and change policies.

Amnesties also serve as a contradictory mechanism in our context. As a major aim of immigration policies in today's Europe is to selectively manage inflows as well as their consequences, illegal immigrants represent the 'worst case' in terms of administration and planning. Amnesties both reflect a defensive symbol of a failed external control, and at the same time represent an active internal control mechanism. By legalizing illegals, the authorities bring them out into the open, making them targets for policies of incorporation in various fields in society. On the other hand, amnesties may have serious behavioural implications in terms of stimulating new flows by signalling legalization prospects for potential irregular migrants. As irregular migrants more often come as single individuals leaving their families behind, amnesties may also strongly increase the potential for legal family reunification migration.

The *labour market* as such is another central mechanism with strong repercussions on control issues. The efficiency of the state in controlling immigration is largely a question of the ability to supervise the labour market – the state's ability to prevent employers from hiring undocumented workers, and its ability to maintain generally high standards of employment conditions. Illegal immigration represents the most obvious disturbance to any regulated labour market. On the other hand, access to work is a central attraction in relation to the establishment and the maintenance of irregular immigration. The capacity to control inflows depends to a large degree on how the labour market is organized and structured.

A striking mechanism producing unintended consequences is what we can call *counter-control* or rather *circumvention* of control. Control strategies imposed by the authorities of receiving countries tend to give rise to circumvention strategies by actual or potential migrants. Immigrants are *actors* who will react to restrictive policies by utilizing whatever channels available when the want or need to migrate is strong enough. There exist today a plethora of methods to bypass European control policies, from the trafficking of migrants, destruction of personal documents to hamper identification, to 'overstaying' tourist or other kinds of visa. Perhaps the most powerful mechanisms in this respect are located in the network dimension. Where people have settled, more seem to follow. The network potential for the circumvention of control may range from friendly advice and assistance to falsification of documents or manipulation of migrants by organized crime. Thus, we may differentiate between individual circumvention, the use of informal networks, and more organized circumvention when it comes to the counter-mechanism. Circumvention is probably one of the most difficult problems for the authorities to adress, due to the inventiveness and the subtleties involved, and not least because of constraints on how far control policies can go before threatening basic liberties in the receiving society.

This latter point brings us back to the fundamental dilemma of the modern European states: The utmost price of a distorted control policy might be the undermining of the welfare system for all citizens. The norms and values that define the democratic welfare state may be violated by excluding immigrants either at the border or internally by not giving access to social, economic and political benefits. On the other hand, their inclusion could imply a challenge to people's sense of fairness when it comes to the division of burdens and rights among 'those who struggled to construct the collective bargains represented by the welfare state' (Heisler and Heisler 1990).

Limits of control may become manifest in an even more obvious way. It is likely that the restrictionist policies may conflict with national economic interests in the receiving states, in terms of reduced competitiveness and hampered growth rates; mismatch in the labour market, dwindling tourism, obstacles to business and so forth. It is furthermore likely that restrictions will collide with interests of individual citizens 'in maintaining life-styles often made possible by immigrant service providers and producers of low-cost goods' (Cornelius et al., 1994: 36).

Within this exposition of intentional policies and unintended consequences of control policies, there are implicit hypotheses and assumptions about national/international tendencies. Let us now formulate the most basic questions and important hypotheses on which we will base our national case studies.

Structuring Hypotheses

We assume that the coming years will witness a reinforcement and diversification of internal control systems whereas the external controls will grow in sophistication and effectiveness. Increased co-operation within the Schengen and EU context will contribute further to this tendency. There is a risk, however, that the more restrictions are imposed on migration, the more clandestine and criminal will be the traffic that can be expected.

With stronger pressure in a restrictive period – and considering the time-consuming and imperfect individual approach to entry control – the tendency to *externalize* regulation is believed to become stronger. Externalization refers to preventive measures (such as aid, economic transfers, 'early warning systems'), long-distance control through visa schemes, economic and humanitarian aid in the proximity of conflicts, the establishment of 'safe areas' in relation to refugee crises, carrier liabilities, and attempts to encourage sending states to reduce emigration levels.

We also hypothesize that higher pressure will bring with it a stronger emphasis on the *flow approach* at the expense of individual processing of migrants.

We assume that there will be significant variation between our case countries with regard to the relationship between effective control and the structure of the labour market. The role and strength of labour unions will be important in this respect. Another modification of the increased efficiency hypothesis would be the tendency towards *deregulation* in the labour market. If this tendency is consolidated, it will constitute a major challenge to the authorities, and undermine the preconditions for efficiency.

We furthermore think that the need for extra manpower at least in some of our case countries may lead to a gradual opening up to increased immigration from Eastern Europe. This process will depend on an eventual integration of Central and Eastern European states into the European Union framework. Full integration with free movement across the old Iron Curtain line can hardly be expected in the near future, however.

Two other major hypotheses will be dealt with throughout the cases. The first is that there is a relationship between economic performance and tolerance for immigration. A publicly acknowledged 'pull' in terms of labour demand tends to go along with a more positive attitude of national populations towards immigration and immigrants. The second indicates that, in the institutional setting of present welfare democracies, tolerance and ability or willingness to incorporate foreigners in society depends on a restrictive and well-functioning entry control.

These and more detailed hypotheses that will be formulated along the way, constitute the backbone of our comparative study.

Methodology

Having set the theoretical agenda, we have to explain our general method-ology and the selection of countries. The financial resources at our disposal have set limits to the number of countries but so also has our wish to keep the group of researchers reasonably small, while still covering the great diversity and variation in control policies as well as in traditions, legislation and recent experience with international migration. Our choice among old and new immigration countries in the north and in the south of Europe has partly been preconditioned by rather prosaic factors. Three countries were almost given as the initiative came from Sweden and Norway, and as one member of the original team is a second generation Hungarian. Special funding was offered for the Dutch participation. But other, more scientific considerations were also taken. In sum, we have chosen the eight project countries in such a way that they together provide us with a high degree of variation in the control of immigration and immigration policy; in terms of size of country, geographical location, history of immigration and degree of restrictiveness traditionally speaking.

The two major immigration countries in Europe – *France* and *Germany* – were obvious choices when undertaking a European comparative study. *Sweden* – as a traditional liberal welfare state with an inclusive policy towards immigrants – was a pioneer country when it comes to the formulation of a specific immigration policy. *Norway* is included partly as a contrast to Sweden – being similar in many respects as a strongly regulated welfare state, with high standard of living and influential unions, yet having a different history of immigration and partly a different approach to the field. *Italy* was included as a 'late-comer' in the field of immigration, yet with now substantial numbers arriving on its doorstep. Italy is also interesting due to its geographical location – close to a major 'sending' area (the Maghreb region in northern Africa). *The Netherlands* has the combined characteristic of being a major immigration country in Europe and, at the same time, representing a culturally pluralist country with strong emphasis on an 'ethnic minority' policy. *Austria*, seldom included in comparative studies, has been an entrance gate to Western

Europe for large numbers of refugees and migrants. Its borders cover a major stretch of the European Union's external frontier towards the Central Eastern European states and it provides an example of a guestworker policy framework maintained over more than 30 years. Finally, *Hungary* – although not (yet) a part of politically defined 'Western Europe' – nevertheless belongs in our group of countries. With the events in 1989 Hungary all of a sudden became a leading *transit* country for east–west migration. Since then Hungary has also become an immigration country in its own right, at the same time being a country in rapid transition – building democracy and expanding the market economy. Adding Hungary's aspirations of joining the European Union, the country constitutes an interesting and important case.

Each national report has covered (as far as possible) the empirical and analytical questions agreed upon within the group. Data have been collected from official documents, published statistics, from interviews with key persons, from published or ongoing research and from other primary and secondary sources. Mass media reporting and central political debates have also provided significant material. The project group has met four times during the project period in order to co-ordinate its work within the same framework of questions and methods. Major revisions have taken place in between the meetings. The method used in this project has been far more integrative and comparative than could be achieved in publications based on edited conference papers, as the national reports, based on the same grid of hypotheses and analytical questions, are read, revised and analysed in several sessions by all project participants in co-operation. According to our experience, this method is well adapted to comparative social research in which data are not directly comparable, and where terms and concepts are based in local traditions and in national legislation, which cannot be directly translated. In each country, social science in general is to a large extent focused on the national society. Scholars tend to write and think about issues such as immigration and control policy on the basis of their own national experience. The purpose of our project design is to give an international group of scholars, with expertise in our research field, resources to undertake a comparative and integrated study.

In terms of the comparative analysis, we need to explain both difference and convergence. Concerning political and legislative systems and what we have called 'control culture', the countries in question can be placed in different categories historically speaking. The national distinctions in this respect are highly relevant when we are aiming to explain outcomes of immigration control policies. As we hypothesize that policy convergence is the prevalent tendency within our sample of countries, we need to explain how this is possible taking into consideration the marked differences that have existed between the countries in recent history. We hope to accomplish this by various national case analyses, guided by the common theoretical ground spelled out in this introductory chapter.

References

Callovi, G. (1992), 'Regulation of immigration in 1993: pieces of the European Community jig-saw puzzle', *International Migration Review*, 26: 98.

Commission of the EC (1992), *Commission communication to the Council and to Parliament on abolition of border controls,* Brussels: SEC (92) 877 final.

Cornelius, W.A., Martin, P.L., and Hollifield, J.F. (eds) (1994) Controlling Immigration A Global Perspective, Stanford: Stanford University Press.

Cruz, A. (1991), '*Community competence over third-country nationals residing in an EC member state*', Brussels: Briefing paper 5, Churches Committee for Migrants in Europe.

Elster, J. (1989), *Nuts and Bolts for Social Sciences.* New York: Cambridge University Press.

Freeman, G.P. (1994), 'Can Liberal States Control Unwanted Migration?', In *The Annals of the American Academy of Political and Social Science*, 534. Beverly Hills: Sage.

Hammar, T. (1990), Democracy and the Nation State, Aldershot: Avebury.

Hedström, P. and Swedberg, R. (1995), *Social Mechanisms: Their Theoretical Status and use in Sociology,* Department of Sociology, Working Paper no. 27, Stockholm: University of Stockholm.

Heisler, M.O. and Heisler, B. (1990), 'Citizenship – old, new and changing', in H. Fijalkowski et al. (eds), *Dominant National Cultures and Ethnic Identities*, Berlin: Free University.

Kapteyn, P. (1992), 'A stateless market. National civilizations and European integration. Two examples: EC fraud and the Treaty of Schengen', Sociology. Amsterdam: University of Amsterdam.

Stinchcombe, A. (1991), 'The Conditions of Fruitfulness of Theorizing About Mechanisms in Social Science'. *Philosophy of the Social Sciences,* 21: 3.

Straubhaar, T. (1993), 'Migration Pressure', *International Migration,* 31: 5–41.

Tapinos, G. (1992), 'Migratory Pressure: An Expression of Concern or an Analytical Concept?', in Tapinos, G.P. and Keely, C.B., *Migration*

and Population: Two Views on International Migration, Working
Paper, World Employment Programme Research. Geneva: ILO.

Tomasi, L. and Miller, M.J. (1993), 'Post Cold-War International Migrat-
ion to Western Europe: Neither Fortress nor Invasion'. In Rocha-
Trindade, M. B. (ed.) *Recent migration trends in Europe,* 15–33,
Instituto de Estudos para o Desenvolvimento, Lisboa: Universidade
Aberta.

Weiner, M. (ed.) (1993) *International Migration and Security,* Boulder:
Westview.

2

Germany's Immigration Policies and Politics
Dietrich Thränhardt

The End of the Provisoire and a New Migration Regime

Migration and loss of control stood at the origins of the new Germany. The East Germans fled an oppressive regime and brought it down in a dialectical process of *exit, voice, and disloyalty*. Since the 1950s, migration to West Germany had endangered the very existence of the Communist regime due to the magnetism of the West German state and society (Thränhardt, 1995: 60). To secure their sphere of influence, the German Democratic Republic (GDR) leaders built the Berlin wall in 1961, a symbol of state control and coercion, which for the following decades was largely recognized as unpleasant but definite proof of Communist Germany´s sovereignty and stabilization. West Germans proclaimed free movement as a cornerstone of freedom and democracy and every refugee coming from East Germany was received as a proof of the superiority of the free world. Clearly, the migration regime reflected the general political situation.

In the détente of the early 1970s, East Germany was acknowledged as a state, but with reservations about citizenship. East Germans leaving could claim West German citizenship. Despite protests, East Germany accepted this special relationship. Beginning in 1976, the Communist regime expelled opponents or let them go, to get rid of the nuclei of turmoil. Moreover, West Germany used its economic power to buy out political prisoners from East Germany and ethnic Germans from Poland, Romania and the Soviet Union. This reduced the totalitarian pressure and made it less dangerous to participate in the opposition in the GDR, as the worst consequence would be imprisonment and subsequent transfer to the West.

Courageous refugees were instrumental in the breakdown of the Communist regime. It came about in the summer of 1989, when the Hungarian borders were opened and tens of thousands took the roads to the West, via Budapest, Prague and Warsaw, until the regime opened the Wall. In the GDR crowds took to the streets, shouting *Wir bleiben hier* ('we stay here') and *Wir sind das Volk* ('we are the people') demanding a change of the regime itself.

In the next phase, migration had an impact on the rapid process of unification and the transfer of goods and capital to East Germany, symbolized in the Deutsche Mark (DM). *Kommt die DM, bleiben wir, kommt sie nicht, geh'n wir zu ihr* ('if the DM comes, we stay, if not, we leave for it'), was a slogan with which the East Germans put pressure on the West German government to bring about an early economic unification and a political union under the existing West German constitution. The slogan clearly formulated the economic underpinnings of the political slogan *Wir sind* ein *Volk* ('we are one people'). The subsequent Westernization of East Germany in all aspects of life has even been metaphorically described as a migration, making the East Germans strangers in their own country (Dieckmann, 1996).

On the other hand, the removal of the eastern border control led to a strengthening of the western control. From 1989 on, Germany changed the migration regime, downsizing and readjusting regulations and programmes, built up during the Cold War. As a first step, the Begrüssungsgeld was discontinued. This welcome allowance for every East German visitor to West Germany became too costly when millions could travel freely from 9 November 1989.

Free immigration for ethnic Germans from the communist bloc had formed another part of the post war immigration system. In Potsdam at the end of the war, the Allies had ruled that ethnic Germans from Eastern Europe and Germany's Eastern provinces were to be transferred to Germany, based on the criteria of ethnicity and regardless of their political record. After initial reluctance to accept twelve million people into a destroyed country, West Germany in 1953 provided for the legal admission of all Germans from Communist countries, including, in the logic of anti-Communism, Albania and China. The discrimination against ethnic Germans in the communist bloc and their wish to leave for Germany were seen as 'a living proof of the inhuman policies of the communist states, whose victims found refuge in the West' (Delfs, 1993: 5, my translation). Members of the Communist nomenclatura were excluded. When Gorbachev opened the Iron Curtain, hundreds of thousands of ethnic Germans began to move towards Germany. The German government, overwhelmed by this inflow, felt a need to limit their numbers, and step by step reduced all sorts of privileges and integration arrangements that had been built on the national and ideological commitments of the Cold War.

Additionally, the government in various ways slowed down the implement-ation of access for newcomers, while in principle upholding the right to move to Germany.

The German constitution, in article 16, grants political refugees an individual right of asylum. Many of the fathers and mothers of the constitution had themselves been in exile, and as Carlo Schmid argued in the Constitutional Council, to be 'generous' to refugees was considered an important part of the new democratic beginning. In the Cold War years, West Germany had been particularly hospitable to refugees from Communist countries, a policy that again proved the superiority of the 'free world', and reaffirmed the anti-totalitarian consensus. There was less unanimity, however, about generosity towards refugees arriving from other repressive regimes, beginning with Chile in 1973, and from Third World countries. Their arrival prompted a fierce controversy about the legitimacy of their claims for asylum (Wolken, 1988).

In the decades of the 'economic miracle', Germany recruited more than two million workers from southern Europe. The recruitment agree-ments stressed European co-operation as well as the provisional character of the recruitment and forsaw the eventual return as a result of economic development in the sending countries, backed by the immigrants' remit-tances. Turks were considered Europeans, in the framework of the association with the EEC of 1961. Most workers returned to the sending countries, but an immigrant community developed over the years. After the end of the recruitment in 1973, the immigrants settled down, adapting to German society and influencing it in many ways.

A consistent control policy is hampered by the mistrust against anything reminiscent of an authoritarian state. Checks and balances are the essence of the German 'semi-sovereign state' (Katzenstein). Every administrative decision and each law is subject to judicial controls, leading to an extremely legalistic political style. In the particularly sensitive area of data protection, the Constitutional Court has ruled that the protection of personal integrity has the status of a fundamental right. At the same time, social benefits are ensured to everybody who lives on German territory. Moreover, the agonizing soul-searching process following on the Nazi dictatorship has led to a devaluation of German national identity, bringing back the pre-nationalist, universalist traditions of the time of Kant and Goethe. Both checks and balances and mistrust from the public set severe limits to the efficiency of the explicit internal control, in contrast to the trust in the state in Scandinavia. Under these circumstances, the government is bound to rely heavily on external and implicit control – not visible to the public and therefore not disturbing it.

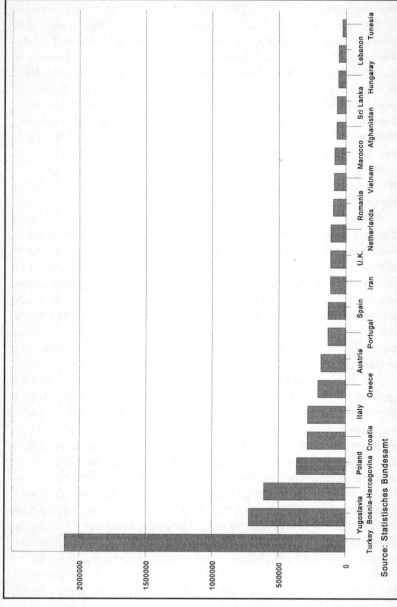

Figure 2.1 Foreigners in Germany (end 1997)

The German national identity problem has also hampered the natural-ization of foreigners, making it difficult to realize that citizenship could be an asset for immigrants. In the tradition of nationhood conceived as a cultural and historic matter, it was argued that any pressure to assimilate would be immoral and unjustified (Brubaker, 1992). Naturalization was facilitated only in 1991, and it is only since that time that the rate of naturalization has been rising. Even in 1997, Michael Glos, the leader of the CSU group in the parliament, argued that naturalization of immigrant children would imply a *Zwangsgermanisierung* (forced Germanization, *Süddeutsche Zeitung* (SZ) 24 March 1997). The immigrants themselves were largely reluctant to apply for a citizenship that did not give much practical advantage in daily life, especially as losing the old citizenship might have caused them problems in their country of origin. Exceptions here are refugee groups like the Vietnamese who disliked the government left behind and who naturalize in high numbers (Thränhardt, 1994: 219).

United Germany had to reconstruct the control system after 1989. Some immigration streams were discontinued or constrained, new ones were opened, while others continued. The immigration of ethnic Germans under-went, step-by-step, a cooling-down process. The government built paper walls and quota systems, but at the same time kept the promise of an open door, to avoid panicking. On the other hand, a new immigration chain was opened for Jews from the Soviet Union, or later the CIS, following a decision of the democratic East German government of 1990 and the lobbying of the German Jewish community (*Der Spiegel*, 22 and 27 May 1996; *Die Zeit*, 18 and 25 April 1997). Like the *Aussiedler* migration, this Jewish immigration was supported by public funding. Restrictions in relation to the neighbouring Eastern states were discont-inued, particularly visa requirements for Poles, Czechs, Slovaks and Hungarians. Extra quotas were created for workers from these and other countries further east. Even uncontroversial were some elements of European citizenship introduced in the Maastricht Treaty, especially the right to vote in local elections. These changes found neither opposition nor much interest, reflecting the dominant pro-European consensus. When the massacres in Bosnia had been shown on TV, a public outcry forced the reluctant government to accept 350,000 Bosnians in the summer of 1993.

Severe conflicts, however, arose around the asylum issue, until Chanc-ellor Kohl spoke of a 'state crisis'. Arson attacks and racist murders followed. This wave of open xenophobia came to an end in the winter of 1992/93, when people demonstrated in masses in what was called the

Lichterketten (light chains), while the major parties compromised on asylum restrictions and easier naturalization.

As a populous and prosperous country in the centre of Europe, Germany is bound to remain a magnet for immigration from Eastern Europe. Moreover, the German language is still important in countries like Russia, Poland, and the Ukraine. On the other hand, Germany did not have an important colonial tradition, losing her colonies in 1918. In contrast to the English, French, Spanish and Portuguese languages, German is therefore not a prominent language in the countries of the 'south'. There are few traditional links to these countries and immigration therefrom has been relatively insignificant, except for some asylum chains since the 1980s.

Political Contradictions

In spite of large immigration flows – second only to flows to the United States – and in spite of public organizing and financing of most of them, Germany officially still considers herself to be *kein Einwanderungsland* (not an immigration country). This is only one of several contradictions that create turbulence in the public debate in this country, where the socio-economic integration process has been rather successful in past decades. The dynamic political process, with ongoing constructions and decon-structions of stereotypes, creation of new outsider images and the inclusion of former outsiders as new insiders, changing laws, regulations and deregulations and so forth, is typical for this country in which the political agenda has been largely focussed on immigration. However, the waves of public excitement, of xenophobia as well as of solidarity, do not provide reliable indications of how important these developments and changes have been in relation to immigration control. Public awareness is often directed to minor incidents whereas important long-term developments may remain rather hidden.

Despite the grand debates between the left and the right and the ideological character of many discussions, the party positions are rather shaky and sometimes undergo erratic changes. Inside all the important parties and groups, basic differences of opinion can be found. Some examples are particularly striking. Within the governing majority, the FDP and a vocal group of 29 younger CDU MPs favour easier naturalization, sometimes even arguing that the Social Democrats' proposals are not groundbreaking enough. Together with the opposition, they clearly hold a majority for change, held back by coalition discipline and especially the staunch opposition of the Bavarian CSU (*SZ*, 17–22 May and 20 June

1996, 23 April 1997, 13–14 May 1997 and 18–29 October 1997). One of the outstanding hardliners, the Bavarian minister of the interior, has been co-opted as a member of the Lutheran synod of Bavaria where he tries to project a more decent outlook, offering, for instance, an extra quota for Church asylum, to provide an alternative to the Church sanctuary that is embarrassing to his political position, and to the relations between the churches and the 'Christian' party.

On the other hand, many Social Democrats favour a programme of planned immigration under a quota system, to balance the demographic gap developed since the early 1970s. At the party convention in the autumn of 1995, however, this position was challenged by a programme of 'integration first', submitted by vice chairman Herta Däubler-Gmelin, arguing that new immigrants should only be taken in when the old ones have been successfully integrated. Since 1996, rising unemployment figures have led to even more scepticism about the demographic argument, even from liberal figures like the former minister of the interior in North Rhine Westphalia (Schnoor, 1996).

The Free Democrats can look back at a respectable tradition of enlightened immigration policies, personalized in the *Ausländerbeauftragte* (Commissioner of Aliens), an office that has long been held by a member of their parliamentary party. However, on several occasions they did not dare to vote for their own ideas in the Bundestag when these were proposed by the opposition. In 1997 their new proposal has been ridiculed as a 'virtual draft bill' (*SZ*, 26–27 April 1997). The Greens have a pro-asylum and pro-immigration stand but do not offer an overall policy programme, having dropped the premature idea of opening the borders for everybody. Cohn-Bendit´s concept of creating new world-wide immigration quotas to provide an alternative to asylum, and thus separate immigration from asylum, has been widely discussed. However, most specialists and politicians have not been convinced.

The employers and industrialists oscillate between their traditional conservative leanings, ideas that immigration is an economic necessity in a time of demographic decline, and an interest in a cheap and motivated labour force. As one example of this rather uncommon alliance of planned openness, researchers from industrial economic institutes participate regularly in conferences organized by the social democratic Friedrich-Ebert-Stiftung (Hof, 1995).

The churches often bravely defy the government and defend numerous local parishes providing sanctuary for asylum seekers (Zentralkomitee, 1996; Ohne Papiere, 1997). On the other hand, they do not recruit personnel of immigrant origin for their broad range of tax based social activities, such as the kindergartens. Trade unions are the only organizations where foreigners enjoy full membership rights, and they are highly organized and equally protected. The trade unions have, however, only very few immigrants in leadership functions.

Restricting Aussiedler Inflows

The Aussiedler constitute the largest single state-organized migration flow in the world. In February 1996, in the context of the crisis of the welfare state and rising unemployment, a new debate about this migration began. The argument used by SPD chairman Oskar Lafontaine and other politicians was that the Aussiedler were bound to 'immigrate into unemployment' and to become a burden for the pension system and the taxpayers, and that such an amount of immigration could not go on in a country with four million unemployed. Moreover, Lafontaine argued that preference for the Aussiedler meant *Deutschtümelei* (*Germanishness*), a statement reminding one of his position in 1990, saying that endangered asylum seekers had a greater moral claim to immigrate than ethnic Germans who were no longer in imminent danger. These arguments are linked to an underlying political cleavage between those who say that Aussiedler are conservative and those who argue that asylum is a leftist cause. This originated in the passionate controversy over the *Ostpolitik*, which in the seventies patterned the party system. The Social Democrats and the Liberals were then defined as détente parties, whereas the Christian Democrats were seen as staunch anti-communists and defenders of Germany´s territorial heritage. The debate is connected to the arguments about nation and ethnicity, and the taboos against any form of German nationalism, resulting in vague ideas about 'post-national' identity and 'a multicultural society' (Radtke, 1996).

The government side argued that Aussiedler immigration would strengthen the social insurance systems, because most Aussiedler are of working age and have more children than the indigenous population, making up for the demographic deficit in Germany. This pro-immigration argument had previously been used by liberals, leftists and Church activists in favour of the immigrants from Southern Europe. The debate ended when the Social Democrats suffered heavy losses in the elections in Baden-Württemberg, Schleswig-Holstein and Rhineland-Palatinate in April 1996. They were not able to create the same sort of deep emotions as the conservatives had done against Turks and asylum seekers in 1982, 1987, 1989 and 1991–92 (Thränhardt, 1995). However, they also lost some moral credibility.

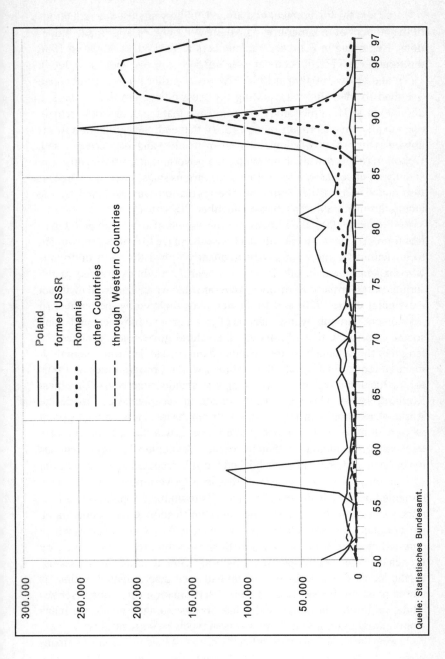

Figure 2.2 Aussiedler Immigration 1950–1997

Quelle: Statistisches Bundesamt.

Ironically the government first argued publicly against any reductions of the number of the immigrating Aussiedler, but thereafter made reductions. Beginning in February, the numbers were brought down. In 1996 the figure was 177,751, compared to 222,591 in 1994, about 140,000 in 1997, and below 100,000 in 1998. Five years earlier the government had operated in the same way, cutting the Aussiedler numbers by half to 220,000 in 1991, at the same time promising that the door would remain open to all ethnic Germans in the CIS. To that end, the application forms as well as the process of admission were made more and more complicated. Upholding the open door principle, the government could in this way silently regulate the admission process at various stags. The whole process was not visible inside Germany. The regulation was executed by the embassies in Kasakhstan, Russia and other CIS states.

In February 1996, the settlement process was also reorganized. Up to that time, Aussiedler were able to choose the place to which they wanted to go within Germany, and they frequently joined their kin or friends who had migrated in previous years. Hardly anybody moved to the former East Germany. Some local governments, which had tried to attract Aussiedler in the 1970s and 1980s, felt overwhelmed by the number of newcomers, particularly in a situation of growing unemployment and rising social security burdens. Moreover, the central government reduced the length of the language courses, excluded the Aussiedler from unemployment benefits, cut several other national welfare programmes and thus forced local and regional governments to shoulder the costs (Bommes/Rotthoff, 1994). This spoiled the climate of acceptance and made the Aussiedler a liability instead of an asset from the local government's point of view. It gave rise to rumours and arguments that the newcomers were less capable of integration than the earlier Aussiedler. The argument has never been systematically established but it is repeated again and again.

It is only in Eastern Germany that local government attitudes have remained positive because of the fear of a dwindling population and the effects of extremely low birth rates since unification. On the other hand, local opinions are particularly negative in those West German cities where Aussiedler have been placed into the empty quarters, abandoned by French or American troops. Aussiedlers are often regarded as 'Russians' by the locals, a shock for those who had been discriminated against as Germans in the USSR. Such double discrimination often characterizes ethnic migration, however, and it has not discouraged ethnic Germans from immigration. Life in Germany is so much easier regardless.

During the Cold War, it had officially been assumed that ethnic Germans were discriminated against in the Communist countries. After 1990,

German policies were readjusted. The government tried to secure legal equality and minority rights in Eastern Europe, thus stabilizing the German communities there. This policy was largely successful in Poland. In a treaty, minority rights were secured, and the new Polish democratic state no longer obstructed the public use of the German language. Consequently, it is no longer taken for granted that Germans are being persecuted in Poland, and they are therefore now only accepted in Germany under exceptional circumstances, and particularly for family reasons. The number of admissions has gone down from 200,000 in 1988 to 1,175 in 1996. On the other hand, people who held German citizenship before 1945 and their descendants are entitled to German passports. Thus 152,000 people in Upper Silesia now hold Polish as well as German nationality. They are free to travel to Germany and work there, but also to return to Poland. This has resulted in a situation where the Silesians can take the best of two worlds. They continue to live in Poland in their traditional environment, watching satellite TV programmes in German, and they sometimes work for a limited time in Germany, earning wages that are high by Polish standards. This is a policy of non-control, giving full rights to the people, and taking away the pull effects of integration assistance in Germany. The result is a stable environment.

The migration of Germans from Romania has decreased to a low of 4,284 in 1996. Most ethnic Germans already left, in an atmosphere of chaos and fear at the time of the collapse of the Ceausescu regime in 1991. For one of the two groups in Romania, the *Siebenbürger Sachsen* (Transsylvanian Saxons), living in the region since the thirteenth century, the Lutheran synod in 1990 recommended that emigration should proceed, although knowing that this would bring an end to a history of 600 years. Now only 50,000 Germans remain in Romania, most of them elderly people who could move to Germany under family reunification arrangements.

For the ethnic Germans in the CIS countries, however, stabilization has not been secured. The reestablishment of the autonomous German Volga republic failed because of Communist and local opposition. Two 'national counties' in Siberia enjoy cultural autonomy, and particularly that German is acknowledged as an official language besides Russian. On the other hand, Kazakhstan, Kirghistan, Uzbekistan, Tadzhikistan and Turkmenistan now promote their state languages, causing the Germans as well as the Russians to leave Central Asia. Thus most Aussiedler now come from Kazakhstan, once Stalin's dumping ground for deported minorities. Under an arrangement with Russia many of them first move to those bilingual counties which have become stepping stones as well as waiting rooms on the way to Germany. Since the German government has decided to hold language tests as a precondition for granting a visa, language instruction sponsored by the German government is now given in the counties and regions where many ethnic Germans reside. As the immigration questionnaire is very complicated, and many applicants need counselling and help to establish the necessary documents, it has become easier to obtain a visa in the regions where many Germans reside. In this way, a two-step flow has been created. The complications of paperwork, language tests, proof of German origin and culture, the intensified scrutiny, queuing at the embassies and consulates with limited staff, all lead to a limitation of the number of immigrants This is achieved in a complex process of explicit and implicit external control measures that largely give the government agencies a free hand to interpret the law.

All in all, this constitutes a step-by-step process of delegitimization of the ethnic Germans, coming from the countries of the East. The ideological commitment has ended after the breakdown of communism, and national commitment is not strong enough to produce solidarity in a period of high unemployment and with a 'post-national' generation. Therefore the German government proceeds with a cooling down policy, in various ways tightening its control practices step by step. At the same time, the public opinion is becoming more negative regarding further Aussiedler migration.

Open Borders for Jews from the CIS

Jewish immigrants have been classified as contingent refugees, and public assistance to them has been channelled through the Jewish welfare organization. Language and employment programmes, and other integration help was modelled along the lines of the Aussiedler and refugee programmes. Speedy implementation encouraged the inflow, resulting in 70,000 Jews immigrating up to 1997, while another 100,000 entitled to immigrate stayed in Russia and the Ukraine.

The immigration programme explicitly invited all CIS Jews. An implicit element was networking and encouragement, particularly from the local Jewish communities. They worked for adaptation, integration and the enlargement of their communities, despite emerging internal conflicts, as they themselves became more and more diverse and pluralistic. This immigration has largely been protected from those control measures, now curtailing the Aussiedler immigration. In the Jewish case already the idea of control is illegitimate. This 'sanctification' of the group also discourages all criticism. Non-cooperation is scandalized, as in the case of a tiny village in Brandenburg that did not want to have an immigration centre in the local manor. Officials who argued that Jewish immigration should be limited, like the Aussiedler immigration, were not backed by politicians. The only limit is given in the definition of being a 'Jew'. Thus a Jewish-born woman from Moscow was not accepted because she had converted to Protestantism. The Jewish *Zentralrat* in Germany has in this and other cases fulfilled the uncomfortable task of defining who is a 'Jew'. German diplomats in Moscow, St. Petersburg or Kiev are also bound to decide if an applicant has a Jewish identity. A common way to do that is to look into the old Soviet passports, issued at a time when Jewish identification did not carry any advantage.

Sending Bosnians back

Bosnian refugees in Germany have the same legal status as CIS Jews. However, they are treated differently. Whereas the Jewish immigration had started without any controversial debate, the flight of the Bosnian refugees occurred in an atmosphere of humanitarian activism, many people hosting Bosnian refugees, and others donating money, clothing or furniture. At the same time the problem of financial responsibility was never resolved. The *Länder* wanted the federal government to share the financial burden, but it did not contribute itself. The status of the refugees remained provisional.

Following the end of open war in Bosnia, a debate began about the return of the 350,000 Bosnian and 50,000 Croatian refugees. The conference of the Federal and *Länder* Ministers of the Interior declared that repatriation should begin on 1 July 1996, with single persons and childless couples returning first. This, however, proved to be impossible because of the devastation in Bosnia and the continuation of ethnic cleansing policies, particularly in the Serb and Croat held territories.

It took two years and a complex mixture of carrots and sticks until the majority of the Bosnian refugees in 1998 returned to their destroyed country. In the previous year, the *Länder* had reduced social security allowances by 20 per cent and invested the funds saved in rebuilding of houses in Bosnia. The governments of Bavaria and Berlin deported several families, raiding them in the morning without warning. This provoked passionate criticism from respected former government ministers Genscher, Geissler and Schwarz-Schilling (SZ 21 May 1997). North Rhine Westphalia initiated counselling programmes and orientation visits in Bosnia in cooperation with the IOM. They also tried to find individual solutions, for example, allowing children to finish the school year or a three year apprenticeship. The federal government appointed a central coordinator for resettlement and linked German financial assistance to a Bosnian policy of open doors for returning refugees. In sum, the remigration policy consisted of a combination of internal pressure, some of it arbitrary and a strong call for return. Even if tough measures were used by the police only in two of the sixteen *Länder* and in a few hundred cases, the impact on the refugees was strong. More important, however, was the constructive assistance given to enable people to live in Bosnia again.

Paying Vietnam to Take back Her People

Part of the Vietnamese community found themselves in an even worse situation. Whereas the 'boat people', in the 1970s rescued in the seas around Vietnam, had been remarkably well integrated (Kosaka-Isleif, 1991), the Vietnamese workers recruited by the former East Germany were marginalized and driven into a semi-legal existence. In particular, many of them had become involved in cigarette smuggling, competing gangs struggling for dominance, and a system of exploitation, repression, and murder. The German government's repatriation attempts have so far been unsuccessful, despite payment of huge amounts of 'development aid'. In the end, Vietnam signed an agreement on repatriation, but this was buried under paperwork, and only very few were allowed to return (up to 1998). Instead, more Vietnamese arrived via clandestine routes. With an unwilling government in the country of origin, it was impossible to deport people. The unclear legal situation created problems for both the community and the country at large, and of course for the Vietnamese in Germany. The financial transfers to a Communist government to facilitate deportations were of a particular historic irony, as Germany during the Cold War had bought people out from Communist countries, paying huge amounts of money.

Asylum

After the asylum crisis of 1991–93 and the asylum compromise, both sides in this controversy carefully watched the details, waiting for the decision of the Constitutional Court. In connection with several other controversial cases, conservative politicians tried to put pressure on the judges. In a decision on 14 May 1996 the Court demanded only minor changes, particularly an extended period of seven days, instead of only three, to appeal against negative decisions in 'urgent cases' at the airports. The three elements of the 1993 régime, which implied limitations of the right of asylum, remained intact: first country responsibility, safe country of origin and special airport procedures.

Following the attacks on foreigners in 1991–93, and the *Lichterketten* demonstrations against these assaults, the public remained on the alert. Hearing of an arson attack against an asylum seeker's hostel in Lübeck on 18 January 1996, many people at once suspected an extremist connection. Even Ignatz Bubis, the leader of the Jewish community, met protests when he insisted that it was still unclear who had committed the crime. In the end, there seems to be no sufficient evidence to try anybody. Once refugees have made it to the borders, the determination of the federal authorities to limit the number of asylum seekers is hampered by a watchful public and a powerful court system.

European Wage Dumping as a Source of Immigration

A critical discussion started in the mid 1990s about the forms of EU labour in Germany, particularly concerning Irish, British, Portuguese and Spanish construction workers. Whereas the numbers of non-EU contract workers, mostly from Poland, could largely be controlled and reduced in the downward trend of the economy (Hönekopp, 1997), the new immigration of EU workers was free. The migration dynamic and the political controversy, however, stems from the unregulated wage structure of this new labour immigration. In contrast to France and the Netherlands, which have integrated the EU workers into their regulation systems (Groenendijk and Hampsink, 1995), in Germany a conflict arose about the principle of equal payment. German construction workers earned about 20 DM and in all, they cost the employers about 40 DM per hour, including social security benefits, whereas temporary immigrant workers cost much less, since there is no minimum wage in Germany. This difference has attracted 210,000 EU workers to Germany, thus creating unemployment among German construction workers. Part of the immigrant labour is organized through various forms of subcontracting. IG BAU, the construction union, estimates that there are an additional 100,000–200,000 undocumented workers.

Inside Germany, there are winners and losers. Whereas the construction union, the construction companies, the Labour Minister and the Opposition tried to bring about wage agreements and legislation guaranteeing equal pay, the general employers' association has refused to consent. The employers want cheaper construction and a showpiece of deregulation, hoping to start breaking down the high cost system of regulated wages and social security. The conflict has deeply split the employers' associations. In September 1997, a temporary solution was found, on the basis of a minimum wage of 16 instead of 17 DM (West Germany). The context was a general crisis in those traditional bipartite and tripartite arrangements which used to be praised as the heart of the 'German model'. Moreover, this is the first debate on EU immigration since 1968. It concerns the relationship between that traditional, corporatist system of regulation that has protected the indigenous workforce against competition from outside. Lower wages for new immigrant workers make them succcessful competitors in the labour market and may thus result in a breakdown of the internal immigration control. The building sector thus follows the globalization of the merchant fleet, with the introduction of a *second register* not bound by the rules of the German wage system. The core engineering industries, however, were not targeted. In particular, IG Metall, the steel and engineering union, was able to uphold the standards.

Public Opinion's Blind Spots

It should be noted that – in contrast to other countries – there is almost no debate about 'illegals' in Germany. Part of the explanation is that asylum applications have functioned as a sort of overflow or protection mechanism for immigrants who have managed to enter the country, providing them with social assistance. Even under the new laws, more than half of all asylum seekers are tolerated in the country in various legal forms ('little asylum'), even if only a minority is granted official asylum status. There are indications, however, that the concept of 'illegals' may get more attention in the future. Firstly, after years of neglect and chaos, the government is now trying to get all the unresolved asylum cases decided. It will therefore be more difficult to use asylum applications as a means to stay in the country for some time. Secondly, the media are mentioning this group more often. And lastly, unemployment has become a feature of German life that will continue for the foreseeable future.

The German discussion on Europe and immigration usually focuses on burden sharing, with the idea that Germany's burden is too high. This is particularly underpinned by the figures for the Bosnian refugees and the asylum seekers. In contrast to France, there is no nervous discussion about Schengen.

The Immigration System

The justification of the new asylum regulations given in the 1996 judgement of the Constitutional Court was that these regulations were to be part of a European regime to be introduced. However, the liberal Vice President of the Bundestag and staunch supporter of asylum and migrants, Burkhard Hirsch (1996), criticized this, saying that a European regime was not in sight. So far, there is only a poor coordination between the countries, resulting in a 'competition of shabbiness', as Heribert Prantl has argued in the *Süddeutsche Zeitung*. Elements of a positive coordination are rare, although the High Commissioner for Refugees could serve as an institution for this purpose.

Germany has become accustomed to a mix of several immigration and control regime elements. This policy has not been created by a grand design but results from various origins and sources:

- the consequences of the wars, the cessation of territory and the resulting ethnic discrimination against ethnic Germans in Eastern Europe;
- the opening for Jews from CIS countries in remembrance of the Shoah;
- the asylum promise, written into the constitution as a symbol of a new beginning after the Nazi regime;
- the recruitment of workers from 1955 to 1973;
- the acceptance of refugee groups from Hungary, Czechoslovakia, Vietnam, Bosnia and other countries;
- the free movements inside the EU, the European Economic Area, and in practice also for professionals from North America and Japan;
- the German interest in open borders in relation to the neighbouring countries in Eastern Europe.

Current discussions about an immigration law (with a more rational and comprehensive approach in mind) are largely oriented to amendment of the existing immigration policy, reducing or increasing one element or the other. It seems impossible to close the doors totally, and in the present situation, it would also be quite difficult to open them for new inflows, be they bright young talent from all over the world or other world wide schemes. Thus the 'muddling-through' approach of the past seems set to continue into the future, and changes will only be implemented gradually.

Immigration control has, as discussed here, resulted in extremely distinct policies with regard to different groups, ranging from free and assisted immigration for CIS Jews (the only control perspective being their Jewishness), an assisting but in practice more restricted policy towards ethnic Germans from the CIS, a laissez-faire policy for EU citizens, regulation of family reunification, acceptance of Bosnian refugees for a limited period, and at the other end finally, a policy of excluding most groups from the Third World.

Regulatory Policies and Europeanization

The goal to open the country for European neighbours, for investors, and tourists, and so forth is quite contrary to the goal of closing it for unwanted newcomers. To a certain extent this sharp contradiction can be solved by an externalization of the control. A remote control management therefore functions in relation to all those who do not have membership or accession rights in Germany or are unable to cross the borders without government backing (for example the ethnic migrants from the CIS). It could also be used – if the government wanted this – to reduce the numbers of Jewish immigrants from the CIS who – mostly not speaking German – are even more dependent on government aid and have fewer family connections. Concerning these groups, the government can largely decide about the size of the inflows. The cool attitude towards Aussiedler, shared by large parts of the German left, makes these externalized problems less visible to the German public. Instead, any kind of internal control constitutes an explicit problem, involving the public and the courts.

In accordance with the Schengen agreement, visa requirements have been extended to all potential sources of immigration outside Europe. The embassies will follow restrictive lines in relation to countries like Turkey, Russia and Yugoslavia but even more so to African countries like Nigeria, suspected of drug trafficking, prostitution and fraudulent money schemes. Airlines and ships are fined for transporting people without passports and visas.

This has resulted in a re-Europeanization of the inflows, as non-Europeans are largely unable to overcome the barriers. Flows from Iraq and Iran via Turkey are important exceptions. This Europeanization of border controls has two faces. On the one hand, the flows across the inner-Schengen borders are largely free, and Western Europe has become a free space for citizens of member states. This deliberate policy has been successful to such an extent that the reimposition of an old-style person-by-person control is not feasible any more today. On the other hand, the outer borders of the Schengen territory have become more important – materially as well as symbolically. This has led the German government to pursue a stricter control policy at the Eastern borders to Poland and

Table 2.1 Germany: Decisions by Border Control Authorities in 1995

Bordering Country	No Admittance	Retransfer	Expulsion
Denmark	6,853	310	4
Poland	18,895	7,105	5,460
Czeck Republic	17,369	7,746	322
Austria	31,859	2,236	156
Switzerland	25,775	735	24
Schengen states*	17,051	1,512	218
Airports	4,809	10,008	30,255
Harbours	3,131	21	16

* France and Benelux
Source: German Home Ministry.

the Czech Republic, concentrating the control personnel there, and leaving only some mobile units at the Western and Southern borders.

Deportations are mostly executed by way of air transports. The complex treaty system, linking the EU and the intermediary states in East Central Europe, shields the West from inflows from the East and the South, making countries like Poland and the Czech republic agents of the EU countries' control system. To send unwanted migrants back through these countries would, however, necessitate complicated and costly administrative and legal procedures. Therefore, Germany as well as other states tries to deport people directly to the states of origin, and bilateral agreements including economic incentives have been concluded to further this goal.

After the asylum compromise of 1992/93, the number of asylum applications has gone down from 438,191 in 1992 to 104,300 in 1997. Still, however, it amounts to half of all applications in Europe. Turkey and Yugoslavia, repressing their ethnic minorities, have been the principal countries of origin. The number of applications made by Turkish citizens increased from 15.0 per cent in 1994 to 20.5 per cent in 1996. At the same time the inflow from non-European countries with severe internal repression was relatively low, due to the European barrier system of visa and control.

In 1996, the federal agency for refugees processed 194,451 asylum applications, reducing the amount of pending cases to a low record of 48,660. This drastic reduction in the possibility to stay in the country as an asylum seeker, waiting during a long decision process of several instances, ended the control crisis of the early 1990s. The duration of the process and the build-up of undecided cases had clearly been the main reason for the crisis. Only after the asylum compromise did the federal government employ sufficient personnel to deal with all the applications.

Table 2.2 Germany: Asylum Decisions in 1966

Decisions:	194,451	100%
Yes: Asylum is given	14,389	7%
Non refoulement	9,611	5%
('small asylum')		
No: the application is rejected	126,652	65%
Deportation is impossible	2,086	1%
Settled in other ways	43,799	22%

Source: German Home Ministry.

The speeding up was so effective that in 1996 some of the staff could be given new assignments. Some are now used to reconstruct the papers of the former East German secret service, papers which had been torn to pieces before the storming of its offices at the end of the GDR. On the other hand, it is clear that the quality of the fast track decisions has not been the best, and that available personnel resources have not been used to improve this quality. The decisions are taken by officials individually (*Einzelentscheider*), autonomous legal officers, comparable to judges, but under pressure to decide a high number of cases in a given time.

Thus, the explicit external control has been made more effective. Speeding up has been the decisive aspect, combined with a simplification of the process, which has also implied a limitation of access to the asylum process.

Germany's Attractiveness

We still have to give an explanation, however, why many people seek asylum in Germany, more than in most other countries. The per capita rate has been comparable only in Switzerland, Sweden, Austria and, after 1994, also in the Netherlands. Three pull factors seem to be important.

Firstly, and despite all critique about declining standards, the government services have functioned well even with an intake of more than 3,000 persons per day over more than two years. The government has been able to feed and house the newcomers, to provide the necessary medical and other services, and to pay social security allowances without delay. In particular, the quality of local government services and the even distribution of refugees around the country have made a difference compared to other countries. This sort of working machinery may have constituted an implicit pull factor.

Secondly, the opportunity to earn money, legally and informally, has been attractive. Of great importance is the fact that, in 1991, asylum seekers were again given the opportunity to work while waiting. Besides, high levels of social security payments and of wages have also resulted in relatively high wages in the informal sector in Germany, particularly compared with countries like the United States, Britain and Italy, where the informal sectors are larger and more complex. The attractiveness of small, full-employment states like Switzerland and Sweden until 1994, points in the same direction.

Thirdly, networks have played an important part, bringing many Turks and Yugoslavs to Germany, where refugees and others have received support from their countrymen. The very large immigrant populations of Turks, Croatians, Bosnians and Macedonians, have facilitated and encouraged significant new chain migration to the country.

Finally, the authorities' ability to control the inflows may have been somewhat reduced as a high percentage of the courts' decisions have been in favour of refugees. In comparison to some other states, the decision-making process in Germany is generally speaking highly formalized and this may also constitute an implicit factor working towards openness.

Limits to Deportations

There is no clear evidence about what happens to the bulk of those asylum seekers who are not accepted by the Federal Agency for the Recognition of Foreign Refugees or by the courts. One per cent does not possess the necessary papers, or is not reacknowledged by the authorities of the country of origin. Some forward a second asylum application. In the years before 1993, this opened an extended period of stay in Germany, and some people even made a third application. In critical cases sympathizers or officials have also encouraged refugees to apply again, to avoid hard decisions. In this way, the formal control system has been circumvented, at the expense of a growing number of unsettled applications.

Since the revision of the asylum laws in 1993, the number of deportations has risen sharply (Table 2.3). This number of deportations does

Table 2.3 Germany: Deportations 1987–1995

Year	1987	1988	1989	1990	1991	1992	1993	1994	1995
n	2,417	2,793	3,327	5,861	8,232	10,798	36,165	36,183	21,487

Source: German Home Minisry.

not correspond at all, however, to the number of asylum applications that have been turned down. When decisions are negative, the applicants either return to their country of origin, go elsewhere (which is quite difficult after the introduction of the first country rule), or stay on without legal status. The proportions are not known. The government, always busy informing the public about the newest number of asylum applications, has taken a blind eye, and researchers have scarcely been active in this difficult field. Many applicants leave the country, others stay illegally or go to third countries. A quarter of all applicants are officially reported to be 'settled otherwise', meaning that they are no longer visible to the officials who do not know where they have gone. Only a small percentage has been deported by the police.

Detention is the harshest measure of explicit control, used to ensure that people leave the country, and in order to avoid the regular jails, special detention centres for asylum seekers have been established. When the speed in the asylum process was accelerated in 1994, the number of detentions rose to a peak. According to information from the Ministries of Justice in the larger Länder, there had been no more than 51 detentions in 1991 but the number rose to 4,097 in 1994, and then fell to 3,117 in 1996. There is widespread criticism of these detentions, and it is widely argued that people with no other guilt than entering another country are not criminals. It is evident from an ethical as well as from a financial point of view that imprisonment should only be an instrument of last resort, used in relatively few cases.

Since 1994 the Church sanctuary movement has mounted a highly visible protest against excessive forms of control. When the asylum laws were changed, and the negative asylum rulings increased, this sanctuary movement wanted to protect some rejected refugees, and to publicly demonstrate that these women and men were in real danger if they returned to their country of origin. The Church sanctuary has been particularly strong in Bavaria where the Land government has taken a particularly harsh and uncompromising stand. In several cases a Church sanctuary has gone on for several months or even years in Bavaria, whereas in other German Länder positive solutions are found or in some cases the police is sent in. The conflict over Church sanctuary has been intense, with the Churches openly opposing a dominating 'Christian' party. According to a more cynical explanation, the open conflicts serve the agenda of just that party, which always has liked to play up asylum problems and xenophobia. On the whole, however, this situation shows the limits of explicit external control in a modern democracy, with an outspoken public opinion and concerned citizens, but also limited powers of the authorities and – in the case of Germany – a bad memory of state authorities enforcing harsh measures.

Limits of Internal Controls

As a complement to external control, the government has introduced explicit internal control mechanisms, mostly aimed at reducing or abolishing economic incentives to immigrate. The first idea was to prohibit employment, removing the opportunity to work during the asylum procedure. This was done in the early eighties. It had the disadvantage, however, of making the government responsible for the care of all the applicants, demotivating them, destroying social cohesion in the families and causing anger among the Germans who had to work and pay taxes. Whereas bona fide refugees were economically restricted, and their subsistence level lowered, bogus refugees escaped control and had leverage to do business. More problems arose when the applicants were later on obliged to live in special asylum centres, established as a form of internal explicit control, which would remove any attraction of coming to Germany. Again this system was expensive compared to private housing, and problematic for bona fide refugees, and especially their children. It created problems as people of diverse origins had to live together, and some refugees were subjected to the pressures of drug dealers, criminals or oppressive political activists who profited from the tense situation.

Tired of all these problems, Germany in 1991 again allowed asylum seekers to work, just at the time when France and Switzerland introduced a ban on gainful employment, combined with a fast-track decision process. In 1992 the number of asylum seekers in France decreased, as well as in Switzerland, Austria and Italy. But in Germany the number of applicants soared in 1992 and 1993 and a dramatic asylum crisis developed.

This then gave birth to the idea of reducing the level of welfare payments to asylum seekers, in order to discourage them economically. This idea gained momentum in the context of more general criticism of the welfare system. Another argument was that there were almost no welfare payments to asylum seekers in some other European countries, and that this fact created a pull effect towards Germany. Therefore, the level of transfer payments to asylum seekers was set 20 per cent below that of other recipients during the first year, and certain categories of expensive medical treatments (like complex dentures) were closed to them. In 1997, this reduction was extended to a period of three years. The government's cost for these payments were, however, still three times higher than in France, where in addition the time limit was only one year.

Special Relations with Turkey

Since 1964, Turkey has been associated with the EU. Although the goal of Turkish membership is not upheld any longer in the EU, and the customs union of 1996 seems to be the end of the road for the foreseeable future, the Association Treaty is a binding element of EU law. In a few important decisions, the Association Council has defined the special privileges, enjoyed by Turkish citizens already living inside the EU, granting them almost the same freedom of movement and work as that given to citizens of EU member states according to the articles 48, 49, and 50 of the EEC treaty. Moreover, acting in the spirit of an open Europe, the European Court has made authoritative interpretations of the Association Treaty and the decisions of the Association Council, thus providing Turkish citizens with a supra-national guarantee for their rights.

The repercussions have importance for the German control system. The European court has ruled that

- Turkish children may join their parents working in Germany up to the age of 21, whereas the age limit in German law is 16. After five years of legal residence, they acquire a right to work.
- Turkish students who have been working legally along with their studies are entitled to continue to work and stay.
- Sailors who have been working on German ships for four years are entitled to work on land.
- Contract workers, like speciality cooks, are entitled to a general work permit after one year (Gümrükcü, 1996: 17 f.).

More rulings in the same sense are to be expected. The Turkish lorry drivers working with EU companies may become such a particular case. If in the future this kind of gateway into Europe will be combined with other third-country contract systems, this development might become even more important. The German government is unhappy about these rulings and tries to limit the consequences, putting pressure on the German judge at the European Court, and implementing the decisions slowly and restrictively. On the other hand in the winter of 1996/97, the Turkish government started a campaign to explain in detail to Turkish citizens what their rights are in Germany.

In principle, all EU countries are subject to these same legal provisions. As most of Europe's Turkish citizens live in Germany, chain migration and family relations play a particularly important role in that country. A total of 2,045,060 Turkish citizens lived in the country at the end of the year 1996, by far the largest group within Germany's total foreign population of 7,314,046. Thus the rights given under explicit external control arrangements are made effective within the context of implicit private arrangements.

Rights, Control Limits and Denizen Perspectives

The open and inclusive system of socio-economic rights is a powerful implicit factor. According to the EEC equality rules, as incorporated into the *Betriebsverfassungsgesetz* (German law on industrial democracy) of 1972, and with the extension of these rules to non-EEC workers, equality has been largely guaranteed inside the factories. The foreign workers have a slightly higher union membership rate than the German workers, and the number of denizen factory councillors is rising year by year. The unions and the factory councils have a definite interest in the inclusion of the denizen workforce and in the implementation of the principles of non-discrimination laid down in the law mentioned above. These inclusive tendencies are also at work in the social welfare system, particularly for the large majority of denizens who have lived in Germany for many years, enjoying full rights in the social insurance system. They are thus members of society, and their residential status is safe, thanks to a mixture of explicit and implicit factors.

The system of judicial review is highly developed, it has powerful traditions in German history and it was again strengthened because of the experience of the arbitrary Nazi regime; human rights were given binding legal power, inscribed into the constitution. This judicial system provides a high level of human rights protection, including immigration rights, such as family re-unification, and protection against expulsion. The development of a whole new branch of judicial expertise on the rights and the status of denizens and on immigration (*Ausländerrecht* or aliens legislation) and the many rulings of the Constitutional Court, the labour courts, the social courts and other elements of the judicial system provide wide opportunities for immigration and for the achievement of a legal status in Germany. As the government is constrained by this judicial system, which limits its means of intervention, the explicit control aspects are weakened, while instead the implicit aspects are strengthened.

Moreover, given an informal or underground labour market in such branches as construction, hotel and restaurant industries, and domestic or household services, other labour regulations, for example with regard to immigrant students, may be easily circumvented.

Naturalization policy has long been exclusive. The laws were modified in 1991 and 1993, however, and there is now an established right to acquire German citizenship for the 'first generation' of immigrants as well as for the second and third. This has largely ended the traditional divergence of the French and the German traditions of naturalization, described by Brubaker (1992) just before the recent changes in the legal systems of both countries.

In the last ten years, the number of naturalizations has tripled (not taking into account the naturalizations of ethnic Germans), and it has at the end of the 1990s reached the same level as in France (Hagedorn 1988: 44).

Ius soli has been widely discussed in public, and there has been a numerical majority in favour of it in both houses of parliament. Due to differences inside the ruling coalition, however, no decision has been taken. Thus the number of foreigners has risen to 7.3 million in 1996. As a consequence, there remains uncertainty over the legal status of the immigrants. The Turkish government is trying to establish an 'ethnic lobby' and supports the idea of giving dual nationality to Turkish immigrants in Germany. The aim is to facilitate chain migration.

Today's state of affairs can be characterized as the paradox of a huge control apparatus implementing an ambiguous policy. Another example of this was given when in January 1997 Germany introduced visa regulations for children under 16 of Turkish, Moroccan, Tunisian and ex-Yugoslavian nationality (*Bundesgesetzblatt* 14 January 1997; SZ 9–14 January 1997). The reason given was that arrivals of unaccompanied children had risen from 554 in 1990 to 2,068 in 1996, and that 400 of these had applied for asylum. As Germany has not introduced any elements of *ius soli*, this new regulation also included children born in Germany, and 400,000 Turkish and 200,000 other children therefore had to be registered during the year 1997.

In the future immigration control will increasingly be a problem of high politics. It will imply many detailed regulations, because of the involved relationships with countries like Turkey, Poland, Russia, and Yugoslavia, immigration for demographic reasons, and problems related to economic needs and the welfare system. Most shortcomings were self-inflicted, dependent on many historical factors, and they do not tell us that control will always be impossible. What is needed is a clear concept of an immigration policy for the future to be implemented with European and international co-ordination.

Breakdown of Control and Successful Externalization

Twice in recent years we have witnessed a breakdown of the German control system, and an overflow effect because of a discrepancy between the German openness and the successful implementation of control in the neighbouring countries. The first crisis was about asylum in 1991–93, the second about the construction industry's labour market in 1994–97. In both cases, deep ideological divisions blocked the German decision making process, laid huge burdens on the public households, and led to a political crisis. The immigration of Aussiedler from the CIS could easily be controlled, scaled down and adapted to the integration facilities, as soon as the government decided to do so. Moreover, a new controlled and assisted inflow – the CIS Jews – was created and smoothly managed. Lastly, the family reunification went on without problems, controlled by the conditions of sufficient income and housing, and by a market-oriented system, bound to visa requirements.

Going back to our central question of the effectiveness of control in a liberal society, the German experience shows that externalization has made the management of the size and composition of the inflows effective. This external control has a technocratic character and largely remains outside the public discussion. It can be administered explicitly, without restraint, but on top of that there are implicit ways to pursue it, like slowing down the processing and not providing sufficient personnel.

Once people have been allowed into the country, however, control becomes more difficult because of several reasons. There are economic interests, as in the construction industry and in the traditional areas of the informal economy, strengthened by the international trend towards a less formalized economy and the explicit demand for cheap labour in certain sectors. In the case of asylum, the opposition to control is humanitarian, driven by moral forces in society, and by people who develop a relationship with refugees or other migrants. In Germany, this can obviously also be explained by policies of the past and as a critical approach to any oppressive state activities. These normative aspects are suitable and well placed in a highly legalistic political process and in a system in which the division of state powers constrain the actions of the federal as well as the Länder governments. Thus explicit internal control can only be carried out at great costs. Implicitly, the largely universalistic welfare state and the growing pockets of the informal economy provide opportunities, which weaken the state control. The main implicit restriction on control is that (given a low level of naturalization) more and more denizens enjoy a stable economic and social existence in the country without obtaining citizenship.

References

Bommes, M. and Rotthoff, U. (1994), 'Europäische Migrationsbewegungen im kommunalen Kontext', in *Kommunen vor neuen sozialen Herausforderungen*, 93–114. St Augustin: Konrad-Adenauer-Stiftung.

Brubaker, R. (1992), *Citizenship and Nationhood in France and Germany*, Cambridge: MA., Harvard University Press.

Dieckmann, C. (1996), 'Als Fremdlinge im eigenen Haus. Sind wir Ostdeutschen Immigranten? Quatsch, wir waren schon immer hier!', *Die Zeit*, 24 May 1996.

Delfs, S. (1993), 'Heimatvertriebene, Aussiedler, Spätaussiedler. Rechtliche und politische Aspekte der Aufnahme von Deutschstämmigen aus Osteuropa in der BRD', *Aus Politik und Zeitgeschichte,* 1993: 48.

Groenendijk, K. and Hampsink, R. (1995), *Temporary Employment of Migrants in Europe*, Nijmegen: Katholieke Univ.

Gümrükcü, H. (1996), *Rechts(un)sicherheit in Europa? EG-Türkei-Assoziationsrecht als Grundlage zukünftiger Ausländerpolitik*, Vol. 1, Hamburg: ITES.

Hagedorn, H. (1998), Wer darf Mitglied werden? Einbürgerungen in Deutschland und Frankreich, in: *Thränhardt, D. (ed.), Einwanderung und Einbürgerung in Deutschland*, Yearbook Migration 1997/98, 9–16, Münster: Lit.

Harris, P. (1998), Jewish Migration to the New Germany. The Policy Making Process Leading to the Adoption of the 1991 Quota Refugee Law, in: *Thränhardt, D. (ed.), Einwanderung und Einbürgerung in Deutschland.* Yearbook Migration 1997/98, 105–147, Münster: Lit.

Hirsch, B. (1996), 'Die Fackel der Freiheit ist erloschen. Das Asylrecht bleibt demontiert. Karlsruhe hat sich der Kraft des Faktischen gebeugt', *Die Zeit*, 24 May 1996.

Hönekopp, E. (1997), *Labour Migration to Germany from Central and Eastern Europe. Old and New Trends*, Nürnberg: IAB Labour Market Research Topics No 23.

Hof, B. (1995), 'Zuwanderungsbedarf der Bundesrepublik Deutschland', in: *Einwanderungskonzeption für die Bundesrepublik Deutschland*, 50:17 f. Bonn: Friedrich-Ebert-Stiftung (Gesprächkreis Arbeit-Soziales).

Kosaka-Isleif, F. (1991), *Integration südostasiatischer Flüchtlinge in der Bundesrepublik Deutschland und in Japan*, Saarbrücken/Fort Lauderdale: Breitenbach.

'Ohne Papiere, ohne Lobby, ohne Schutz . . .' (1997), in: *Neue Heraus-forderungen für die Kirchenasylbewegung. 4. Treffen der Kirchenasy-linitiativen aus der Bundesrepublik und den Nachbarländern.* Mülheim an der Ruhr: Evangelische Akademie, Dokumentation.

Radtke, F.-O. (1996), 'Fremde und Allzufremde. Der Prozeß der Ethnis-ierung gesellschaftlicher Konflikte', in: *Ethnisierung gesellschaftlicher Konflikte*, 62:3 f., Bonn: Friedrich-Ebert-Stiftung (Gesprächskreis Arbeit -Soziales).

Schnoor, H. (1996), 'Deutschland ist ein Einwanderungsland ohne Einwanderungspolitik. Plädoyer für eine Politik, die die Fakten zur Kenntnis nimmt und die Probleme löst', *Frankfurter Rundschau*, 21 May 1996.

Silbermann, A. et al. (1998), *Die Synagogen-Gemeinde Köln: Partizipa-tion und Integration*, Köln: Synagogen-Gemeinde.

Thränhardt, D. (ed.) (1996), *Geschichte der Bundesrepublik Deutschland*, Frankfurt: Suhrkamp.

—— (1995), 'The Political Uses of Xenophobia in England, France and Germany', *Party Politics* 1: 323–45.

—— (1995), 'Die Reform der Einbürgerung in Deutschland', in: *Einwanderungskonzeption für die Bundesrepublik Deutschland* 50: 63–116, Bonn: Friedrich-Ebert-Stiftung, (Gesprächkreis Arbeit -Soziales).

Thränhardt, D. et al. (1994), *Ausländerinnen und Ausländer in Nordrhein-Westfalen. Die Lebenslage der Menschen aus den ehemaligen Anwerberländern und die Handlungsmöglichkeiten der Politik*, Düsseldorf : Ministerium für Arbeit, Gesundheit und Soziales des Landes Nordrhein-Westfalen.

Wolken, S. (1988), *Das Grundrecht auf Asyl als Gegenstand der Innen-und Rechtspolitik in der Bundesrepublik Deutschland*, Frankfurt am Main: Lang.

Zentralkomitee der deutschen Katholiken, (1996), *Zuwanderung gestalten. Politische und gesellschaftliche Aspekte der Migration*, Bonn.

3

Ideas, Institutions, and Civil Society: On the Limits of Immigration Control in France

James F. Hollifield

Introduction: Immigration and the Republican Tradition

Unlike other European states, France has a long history of immigration, dating back at least to the middle of the nineteenth century when industrialization began in earnest. Yet France was not the only European state compelled to import labour to feed the fires of industrialization. What distinguishes France from many other European states is the early willingness to accept foreigners as settlers, immigrants, and even as citizens. The acceptance of foreigners as potential citizens is part and parcel of what can be called a republican tradition, which stems from the French Revolution at the end of the eighteenth century. Republicanism is strongly egalitarian, anti-clerical (*laïque*) and opposed to monarchy. It stresses popular sovereignty, citizenship, and the rights of man. It can be nationalist and imperialist, while at the same time stressing universal political values, such as equal protection of all individuals before the law. Republicanism, as an ideology and a form of government, was bitterly contested in France throughout the nineteenth century and into the twentieth century (Hoffmann, 1963).

Even though France has a long tradition of immigration and was the first European state to grant citizenship to Jews, at the time of the Revolution, it was not until the culmination of the Dreyfus affair early in the twentieth century, under the Third Republic, that the main tenets of republicanism – *laïcité* or separation of church and state, equal protection of all before the law, a universalist conception of human rights, and popular sovereignty – were finally accepted by a majority of the French people. It was also during this period around the turn of the century that the French state began to lay the legal foundations for citizenship and naturalization, which would be based on the birthright principle of soil (*jus soli*) rather than exclusively on blood (*jus sanguinis*) as in Germany (Brubaker, 1992; Weil, 1991; Noiriel, 1988) Thus the republican tradition found its expression in a more open and expansive notion of citizenship, similar (but not identical) to the birthright principle enunciated in the Fourteenth Amendment of the US Constitution ('All persons born or naturalized in the United States, and subject to the jurisdiction thereof, are citizens of the United States') and in stark contrast to the more narrow, ethnocultural vision of citizenship evolving in Germany of the Second Reich. While Germany was struggling with the issues of national and territorial unification and would continue to do so – one could argue – until 1989–90, France was becoming more comfortable with its revolutionary and republican heritage, as reflected in an increasingly expansive policy of immigration and naturalization.

In contrast with the United States – the other great republic also founded at the end of the eighteenth century – France was not a *nation of immigrants*. The first period of intensive immigration in France did not begin until the 1850s, long after the Revolution of 1789. Hence immigration in France was never part of any type of founding myth, as it was (and still is) in the United States. Even though immigration and integration are closely associated with the French republican tradition, they are not crucial to French national identity, except for French Jews for whom the Revolution represents political and legal emancipation (Birnbaum, 1995). Sustaining an open and legal immigration policy is more difficult to do in France than in the United States, but easier than in Germany, which also has a republican tradition, albeit a young one dating from the founding of the *Bundesrepublik* in 1949 (Hollifield, 1997).

For much of the post-World War II period, French governments of the Fourth and Fifth Republics pursued expansive immigration policies, essentially for three reasons. The first justification – as can be seen in the various five-year plans – was primarily economic. During the period of reconstruction of the 1950s and 1960s (sometimes referred to as the *trente glorieuses*, or thirty glorious years of economic growth and low unemployment), France, like Germany, was in desperate need of labour. The second rationale for an open and legal immigration policy was the longstanding desire to boost the French population. Having gone through its demographic transition much earlier than other industrial societies, France was believed to have a huge demographic deficit and immigration was seen as one way to overcome this weakness. Finally, as I have argued elsewhere (Hollifield, 1994: 143–76), policy makers and politicians had great confidence in the ability of French society to absorb and integrate the newcomers, because of the strength of the republican tradition. Therefore, an expansive, legal immigration policy was coupled with the most liberal naturalization policy in Europe, quite similar in many ways to that of the United States.

Stopping Immigration

The consensus for an open immigration regime held until the early 1970s, when the *trente glorieuses* abruptly ended in 1973–74 with the first big recessions of the post-war period. Moreover, decolonization and the granting of independence to Algeria in 1962 radically altered the ethnic composition of immigrant flows, as North African Muslims rapidly replaced the largely Catholic flows from Italy, Spain, and (eventually) Portugal. Many in France began to question the strength of the republican model and its ability to assimilate the new Islamic populations coming from the Maghreb. Stopping immigration (*l'arrêt de l'immigration*) would prove difficult, however, because the mechanisms and instruments of control had not yet been developed by the French state, and cutting ties with former African colonies would not be easy.

Throughout the 1960s and into the 1970s, the recruitment of foreign workers was carried out largely by the private sector, as had been the case during the 1920s (Hollifield, 1992a: 45ff). Businesses recruited directly in the sending countries, bringing their workers to France, training them, then filing a request with the Office National d'Immigration for an adjustment of status (*régularisation*). This mode of immigration, which bypassed both external (border) and internal (labour market) controls, came to be known as immigration from within (*immigration interne*). The rate of adjustments of status (*taux de régularisation*), basically a ratio of immigration processed by ONI in France to that processed abroad, became a standard measure of immigration control, or lack thereof, during the 1960s and 1970s. The rate (or ratio) reached 90 per cent by the late 1960s, indicating the extent to which authorities had lost control of immigration. Re-establishing control over the flows of worker immigration (*travailleurs permanents*) would take many years (ibid: 74ff). Simply decreeing an end to immigration proved insufficient to master all the different flows (workers, family members, seasonals, and eventually refugees).

Apart from worker immigration, French authorities, like their German counterparts, also struggled to deter family immigration, which remained at fairly high levels (over 50,000 per year from 1974–80), even after the immigration stop imposed in 1974 (see Table 3.1). The justification for stopping worker immigration was clear in both countries: with the decline in economic growth and the rise of unemployment – especially in France – employers should no longer be allowed to recruit foreign labour, and the denial of visas (external control) and work permits (internal control) was seen as a necessary policy response to worsening economic conditions and as a way to head off a rising tide of xenophobia, which was increasingly evident in France, but also in neighbouring countries like Switzerland and Great Britain (Withol de Wenden, 1988; Betz, 1994; Thränhardt, 1997). This shift in policy reflected a widespread Malthusian impulse in Europe: if only the receiving states can stop immigration, it will solve the problem of unemployment, because there is a limited number of jobs in each national economy; and it will arrest xenophobic tendencies among the electorate.

Table 3.1 Immigration into France 1946-95 (Thousands)

Period	1946–55	1956–67	1968–73	1974–80	1981–87	1988–92	1993–95
1. Workers	325.2	1,205.9	801.3	192.9	195.1	118.6	55.8
Rate/year	32.5	109.6	133.6	27.6	27.9	23.7	18.6
% of immigration	49%	44%	39%	14%	17%	20%	21%
2. Seasonal workers	247.6	1,126.9	821.9	857.3	664.2	258.5*	31.0*
Rate/year	24.8	102.4	137.0	122.5	94.9	51.7	10.3
Per cent	37%	41%	40%	61%	59%	43%	12%
3. Family members	91.7	404.2	423.2	351.0	260.6	169.9	68.8
Rate/year	9.2	36.7	70.5	50.1	37.2	34.0	23.0
Per cent	14%	15%	21%	25%	23%	28%	26%
Total Immigration	664.4	2,737.1	2,046.5	1,401.2	1,120.0	601.1**	269.0**
Rate/year	66.4	248.8	341.1	200.2	160.0	120.2	89.7
Per cent	100%	100%	100%	100%	100%	100%	100%

* As of 1992, the Spanish and Portuguese are no longer counted among seasonal workers.
** Note that, beginning in 1988, total immigration includes other groups, such as refugees, not listed here. The annual rate for the years 1988–95 is inflated by the inclusion of flows not counted in previous years.
Source: SOPEMI reports on France by *André Lebon, Immigration et Présence Etrangère en France (Paris: La Documentation Française, various years).*

Notwithstanding this political and Malthusian impulse in France, one of the principal sending countries, Algeria, took steps in 1973 to prevent the free emigration of its nationals to the former *métropole*, because of the growing hostility towards Algerians in France. Yet immigration continued throughout the 1970s, in large part due to increases in family reunification, which was much more difficult to control. The economic rationale for stopping worker immigration did not apply to family immigration, which was deemed to be more humanitarian and social than economic. Still, French and German authorities tried to impose internal (labour market) controls to slow the influx of family members, by denying them work permits. In both instances, however, the courts ruled these policies to be illegal and/or unconstitutional (ibid: 83–9). The French also had to cope with the continued inflow of so-called seasonal workers (*saisonniers*), employed primarily in agriculture. From 1974–87, the number of seasonal workers entering each year hovered around 60,000 (see Table 3.1). Some of these workers came from Spain and Portugal, and the enlargement of the European Community and the extension of the freedom of movement clause of the Rome Treaty to cover Spanish and Portuguese nationals partially resolved the issue of seasonal migration (Tapinos, 1975 and 1982). In the late 1970s and early 1980s, Moroccans made up the bulk of seasonal flows, whereas in the 1990s North Africans were replaced by East Europeans, especially Poles.

What was happening during the presidency of Valérie Giscard d'Estaing (1974–81) was a radical shift away from the open immigration regime of the earlier Gaullist years towards a more closed regime. The methods used to achieve this objective (*l'arrêt de l'immigration*) were heavy-handed and statist – consistent with the centralized Jacobin state – and they produced many unintended consequences (Hollifield: 1992b). The most important consequence, which was certainly not unique to France, was to freeze the foreign population in place. By simply decreeing an end to immigration, France, like other West European states, inadvertently accelerated the processes of settlement and family reunification.

Switzerland offers an interesting point of comparison in this regard. Swiss authorities, unlike the French and Germans, kept in place their guestworker policies of rotation, even though they took steps to limit employers' access to foreign labour. But barriers to settlement and naturalization of foreigners in the *Conféderation Hélvetique* remained high, whereas in France liberal naturalization polices were not changed and the legal status of Algerians was such that it prevented the state from excluding them. Until 1973, Algerians were guaranteed freedom of movement under the Evian Agreements, which ended the Algerian conflict in

1962. Moreover, second generation Franco-Algerians acquired citizenship according the principle of double *jus soli*: Algerian children were born in France of parents also born in France. It was therefore impossible for French authorities legally to exclude first or second generation Franco-Algerians; and having raised expectations among the French public that the Jacobin state could simply decree a halt to immigration, the government of Giscard d'Estaing found that its hands were tied both by the law and by the virtually uncontrollable effects of chain migration. This did not prevent both the Chirac (1974–76) and Barre (1976–81) governments form making *covert* efforts to stop family reunification by denying visas and deporting family members. The Barre government also tried *overt* policies to encourage return migration by paying foreigners to leave (Weil, 1991).

In Germany, the state was caught in a similar predicament, but with more profound repercussions for German politics and society. As in France, the German federal state discovered that it could not simply decree a halt to immigration, nor was it able to entice foreigners to return voluntarily, but unlike France, Germany had no tradition of immigration and its nationality law, dating from 1913, did not allow for quick naturalization of a permanent foreign population. The republican tradition in Germany has little to say about foreigners, with the important exception of refugees who were covered until 1993 by Article 16 of the Basic Law. German political culture has not been strong enough to incorporate *de facto* immigration, whereas in France the problem of integrating the foreign population has been solved *de jure* – at least for the moment – by liberal naturalization policies. As we shall see, however, attempts would be made by subsequent right-wing governments under Chirac (in 1986) and again under Balladur (in 1993) to change French nationality law in order to discourage the naturalization of immigrant children. Here again, however, right-wing governments would be frustrated by their inability to exclude Algerian children, who continued to benefit from the double *jus soli* rule (see above). This type of psychological warfare against immigrants would be used increasingly by a range of OECD states, including the United States in the 1990s, in an attempt to stop immigration. In France and elsewhere in Western Europe, however, the principal outcome of the statist efforts in the 1970s to halt immigration was to accelerate the permanent settlement and naturalization of foreigners in the 1980s. The immigrant population in France as a percentage of the total population has remained virtually unchanged from 1975 to 1990 (7.5%), and it has grown in absolute terms to well over 4 million, according to the 1990 census (see Table 3.2). The same thing has happened in the US in the 1990s.

France

Table 3.2 Foreign Resident Population in France by Nationality and Citizenship 1975–90

Citizenship	1975	1982	1990
Spain	609,605	485,764	412,785
Italy	714,650	606,972	523,080
Portugal	659,800	644,428	605,986
Algeria	571,925	617,993	571,997
Morocco	244,945	358,296	446,872
Tunisia	151,125	177,544	182,478
Turkey	59,515	108,708	158,907
Sub-Saharan Africa	...*	123,392	182,479
Indochina	...*	124,420	158,075
TOTAL	3,920,430	4,071,109	4,195,952
% of population	(7.5%)	(7.5%)	(7.4%)

* Formerly under French administration.
Source: Census data; Michèle Tribalat, 'Chronique de l'Immigration,' Population 1 (1997), p. 176.

While the issue of control (immigration policy) would continue to be hotly debated in France throughout the 1980s and into the 1990s, the issue of integration (immigrant policy) surged onto the national agenda (Hammar, 1990). The realization that millions of North Africans were settling permanently in France led governments and political parties to reconsider their approach to immigration and integration. Political parties, the party system, and the electorate were increasingly polarized on both issues. The election in 1981 of a socialist President, François Mitterrand, and the first truly left-wing government since the Popular Front of 1936, set the stage for some important policy shifts, which can be described as a kind of liberal tradeoff, or what some analysts have called a 'grand bargain' (Martin, 1997).

The socialists decided to maintain tight (external) control of borders and stepped up (internal) control of the labour market to inhibit the development of a black market for undocumented workers (*travail au noir*). Regulation of the labour market was easy enough to accomplish by the use of *inspecteurs du travail*, who could make snap visits to firms and impose sanctions on employers caught using undocumented workers (Valentin-Marie, 1992). But at the same time the socialist government, led by Prime Minister Pierre Mauroy, offered a conditional amnesty to undocumented immigrants and longer (ten-year) residency and work permits for all immigrants. Anyone who had entered France prior to 1 January 1981 was eligible for a temporary residency permit, valid for three months, which would give the individual time to complete an application for an adjustment of status (*régularisation exceptionnelle*). By the end of the amnesty period (in 1983), over 145,000 applications had been received (Weil, 1991).

The idea behind this 'liberal policy' has been accepted by many high-immigration countries as the best compromise in the battle to control immigration. The US also enacted an amnesty in 1986. In a liberal and republican polity, strict control of entries together with an amnesty for illegals came to be seen as a good way to integrate permanent resident aliens, or as Tomas Hammar calls them, *denizens* (Hammar, 1990). In addition to the amnesty, to make foreigners residing in France more secure, the first socialist government under Mauroy (1981–84) relaxed prohibitions against associational and political activities by foreigners. The civil liberties of foreigners were protected by prohibiting the police from making arbitrary identity checks of foreign-looking individuals, but no changes were made in the nationality law or in naturalization policy, leaving this key element of the republican tradition intact. Foreigners would be welcome within strict guidelines of labour market rules and regulations; they would be integrated on the (republican) basis of respect for the separation between church and state (*laïcité*); and they would quickly assimilate.

Having thus reaffirmed the previous right-wing governments' commitment to strict immigration control, while at the same time taking steps to speed the integration of foreigners in French society, the socialists, it seemed, were forging a new consensus on the contentious immigration issue. But the issue literally exploded in everyone's face (on the left as well as the right) in 1984 with the municipal elections in the city of Dreux, an industrial town just west of Paris. The Front National – a grouping of extreme right-wing movements under the charismatic and flamboyant leadership of Jean-Marie Le Pen – won control of this city, on a platform calling for a complete halt to immigration and for the deportation of African immigrants. The electoral breakthrough of a neo-fascist, xenophobic, and racist movement profoundly changed the politics of immigration, not only in France but throughout Western Europe. For the first time since the end of the Second World War, an extremist party of the right was making itself heard and finding a new legitimacy, garnering support from large segments of the French electorate across the political spectrum. Within a matter of years, it would become, in the words of the political analyst Pascal Perrineau, 'the largest working class party in France' (Perrineau, 1995). From the beginning, the Front National was a single-issue party, taking a stand against immigration, and its leader, Le

Pen, called for a physical separation of the races. His discourse mixes xenophobia, extreme nationalism ('La France aux français'), and anti-Semitism, with appeals to the economic insecurities of the French working class. How did the breakthrough of the Front National affect French immigration policy and the republican consensus?

Crises of Control and National Identity

The rise of the Front National contributed heavily to a sense of crisis in French politics and public policy, with immigrants at the centre of the maelström. Suddenly immigrants were seen as the cause of the economic and cultural decline of the French nation, provoking a loss of confidence in the republican model, especially on the right. Immigrants were accused of taking jobs away from French citizens, thereby contributing to high levels of unemployment, and Muslims were deemed to be inassimilable and hostile to republican values. The socialist left, under President Mitterrand, and the neo-Gaullist/liberal right (RPR-UDF), led by Jacques Chirac, had very different responses to the Front National's populist appeals to economic insecurity and xenophobia.

Mitterrand added to his mystique as a Machiavellian politician, as he cynically manoeuvered to exploit the rise of the Front National for political gain. From his perspective, not only did the Front National divide the right-wing electorate, but by getting many working class votes, it also weakened the Communist Party, another traditional adversary of the socialists. Yet on a liberal note, in 1984 following the elections in Dreux, Mitterrand called for granting voting rights to immigrants in local elections, thereby forcing the parties of the traditional right (RPR-UDF) to take a stand on immigration and immigrant policy. Then, on a more cynical and Machiavellian note, the socialist government led by President Mitterrand and Prime Minister Laurent Fabius, changed the electoral system from a majoritarian, single member district system to one based on proportional representation, just in time for the legislative elections of 1986. The immediate effect of this rule change was to reduce the magnitude of the inevitable victory of the right and to allow the Front National, with roughly 10 per cent of the vote, to gain 32 seats in the new Assembly. For the first time since Vichy, the extreme right had representation in parliament, and a new debate over French national identity was under way.

The first step of the right-wing coalition of neo-Gaullists (RPR) and liberals (UDF), led by Chirac, was to change the electoral system back to the traditional Fifth Republic dual ballot system with single member districts. Under the old system, it would be nearly impossible for the Front

National to win seats in future elections, but the damage to the right had already been done, and the task remained of recapturing Front National voters. To accomplish this, the government set about reforming immigration *and* naturalization policy, handing the entire *dossier* to the tough Corsican Minister of the Interior, Charles Pasqua, whose name would become synonymous with immigration reform over the next decade. Pasqua's approach to immigration control was quite different than any of his predecessors. As Minister of the Interior, he viewed control primarily as a police matter, so he moved quickly to reinforce border controls by giving sweeping new powers to the *Police de l'Air et des Frontières* (PAF) to detain and immediately deport anyone who did not have proper papers. He also reinforced the power of the (internal) police forces to conduct random (and arbitrary) identity checks of any foreign or suspicious-looking individual. It was also during this time (1986) that there was a wave of terrorist bombings in Paris, connected to the Middle East, specifically Iran. The violence helped further to legitimize the new get-tough policy with respect to foreigners. The immediate effect of these measures was to restrict the civil liberties of foreigners, specifically North Africans, thereby launching a psychological campaign against immigrants and immigration. The policies were explicitly designed to win back supporters of the Front National, and to prevent any further loss of votes to the extreme right on the issue of immigration, but they also heightened the sense of crisis and contributed to the growing debate over a loss of national identity.

If we look at the numbers (flows), which measure the outcome of French control policies, what we find is considerable continuity. Total immigration hovered between 200,000 and 100,000 persons annually, throughout the 1980s (see Table 3.1). The only noticeable increase in flows, as in other European states, was in the number of asylum seekers, which peaked at 61,372 in 1989. With the end of the Cold War and the gradual implementation of the Schengen Agreement in the 1990s, the rate of rejection of asylum applicants rose from 57 per cent in 1985 to 84 per cent in 1995 (see Table 3.3). So, if flows were not raging out of control, what was the purpose of the first Pasqua Law of 1986? The most important and controversial aspect of the reform was the attempt to weaken the birthright principle of *jus soli*, by putting an end to the practice of 'automatically' attributing citizenship at age eighteen to the children born in France of foreign parents. In effect, this reform, which was intended to placate right-wing nationalists and win back Front National voters, was more symbolic than real. Having said this, it is important to note that there were some very real effects of the reform. For example, any immigrant who had been sentenced to more than six months in prison was deemed excludable and would not be allowed to naturalize. West Africans were no longer allowed to naturalize under the streamlined procedure known as 'reintegration into the French nation'; and spouses of French nationals would have to wait two (rather than one) years before they could file for naturalization.

Nevertheless, the thrust of the proposal was to require young foreigners to affirm their commitments to the Republic by formally requesting French nationality and taking a loyalty oath. What effect such a change might have on immigration flows was unclear; but the message was quite clear: the acquisition of French citizenship is a privilege, not a right, and it should be withheld from those who have not made a clear commitment to the French nation and society. Regardless of the intention of the reform, the first government of cohabitation succeeded in provoking a political firestorm of protest, as various civil and immigrant rights organizations, such as the La Ligue des Droits de l'Homme, GISTI, SOS-racisme, MRAP, and others, mobilized against the reform, leading Pasqua and Chirac eventually to withdraw the Bill from consideration. As pointed out above, these changes did not affect the second generation Franco-Algerians, because they were born in France of parents who were born in Algeria prior to 1962 – the year of Algerian independence. Both the parents and the children were French by birth (double *jus soli*), and therefore eligible to naturalize (Weil, 1991; Feldblum, forthcoming).

Table 3.3 France: Asylum Seekers in thousands and Rate of Rejection (per cent) 1985–95

Year	1985	1986	1987	1988	1989	1990	1991	1992	1993	1994	1995
n	29	26	28	34	61	55	47	29	28	26	20
Rate %	56.8	61.2	67.5	65.6	71.9	84.3	80.3	70.9	72.1	76.4	83.7

* *Source: OFPRA*

The withdrawal of the Bill constituted a political failure for the Chirac government, which had unwittingly provided the increasingly active French civil rights movement with a new rallying cry: 'Ne touche pas à mon pote!' ('Don't touch my buddy!') Thousands marched in Paris under this banner. In addition to altering the political landscape, launching a new debate about French citizenship and national identity, and creating new political opportunities for the left (Feldblum, forthcoming; Ireland, 1994), the attempted reform brought the power and prestige of the Council of State to bear. In ruling on the legality and constitutionality of the Bill, the Council of State put the government on notice that the rights of individual foreigners and the republican tradition must be respected. This was a lesson in immigration politics and law that Minister Pasqua would not soon forget. In 1993, he would have a much stronger hand to deal with the judiciary (see below), but in this round of reform, the right-wing government was forced to compromise and the decision was made to appoint a special Commission (*Commission des Sages*) to hold hearings on the possibility of reform of immigration and naturalization policy. The Commission was composed of political and intellectual elites, and it was chaired by Marceau Long, who, as Vice President of the Council of State, was deemed to have the moral and legal authority to tackle this difficult policy issue.

After hearing the testimony of many experts on immigration, the Commission simply reaffirmed the importance of the republican tradition by defending the birthright principle of *jus soli*, while at the same time stressing the importance of integrating foreigners into public and civic life (Long, 1988). The whole episode of reform during the first government of cohabitation had little discernible impact on immigration flows, which remained well over 100,000 during the late 1980s and early 1990s (see Table 3.1). The number of naturalizations remained in the average 50,000 range during the same period (see Table 3.4). However, if we look at changes in the ratio of naturalizations by decree (*par décret*) to those by declaration (*par déclaration*) for the period 1984–95, what we find is an upsurge in 1985–86 and again in 1995. This indicates that a larger number of individuals were filing for naturalization during the key years of the Pasqua reforms, whereas the number of those qualifying for 'automatic' naturalization (by simple act of declaration) remained relatively constant. The exception is 1994, when, with the implementation of the Second Pasqua Law (see below), the number of those declaring themselves to be French shot up to 43,035, twice the average of 19,911 for the period 1973–92 (see Table 3.4). In effect, one of the principal unintended consequences of tougher control policies in France was the revaluation of citizenship, speeding up the process of naturalization and integration of the foreign population, and inadvertently reinforcing the republican tradition. The same thing happened again in the mid-1990s in France and in the United States, where anti-immigrant policies were pushed through the Republican-led Congress in 1996, contributing to a wave of insecurity among foreigners and a tremendous surge in naturalizations.

The liberal and republican right (UDF and RPR) lost its battle to eliminate the Front National and it also lost the elections of 1988. Jacques Chirac was defeated in his bid to unseat François Mitterrand, who won a second, seven-year presidential term; and the right also lost the legislative

Table 3.4 France: Naturalisations by Decree and Declaration 1984–95

Year	Decree (a)	Declaration (b)	Total (a + b)	Ratio (a/b)
1984	20,056	15,517	35,573	1.3
1985	41,588	19,089	60,677	2.2
1986	33,402	22,566	55,968	1.5
1987	25,702	16,052	41,754	1.6
1988	26,961	27,338	54,299	1.1
1989	33,040	26,468	59,508	1.2
1990	34,899	30,077	64,976	1.2
1991	39,445	32,768	72,213	1.2
1992	39,346	32,249	71,595	1.2
1993	40,739	32,425	73,164	1.3
1994	49,449	43,035	92,484	1.1
1995	40,867	18,121	58,988	2.3
1973–92 (average)	30,740	19,911	50,651	1.5

Source: André Lebon, Immigration et présence étrangère en France (Paris: La Document-ation Française, various years).

elections, as the socialists, led by Michel Rocard, regained control of the Assembly, albeit with the necessity of forming a minority government. With a score of 14.5 per cent of the vote on the first round of the presidential elections, Le Pen continued to cause problems for the right. Since his party again exceeded 10 per cent of the vote on the first round of the legislative elections, but gained no seats in the Assembly, Le Pen claimed that the voices of a substantial segment of the French electorate were not being heard, specifically on the issue of immigration. In response, Charles Pasqua, now the former Minister of the Interior, tried to reassure Front National supporters that the RPR shared many of their 'concerns and values' with respect to the impact of immigration on French national identity. Public opinion polls at the time (1988–89) showed that approx-imately one third of the electorate had sympathies for the Front National's position on immigration.

The new left-wing government, led by the two old socialist rivals, Mitterrand and Rocard, essentially returned to the policies of the early 1980s, increasing regulation of the labour market, campaigning against illegal immigration, and taking steps to help integrate immigrants. To this end, Rocard created the Haut Conseil à l'Intégration, to study ways of speeding the integration of the foreign population, which still constituted over 6 per cent of the total population. (Haut Conseil à l'Intégration, 1991) For the period (1988–93), socialist governments fell back on a 'grand bargain' strategy of strictly controlling inflows in order to integrate those foreigners already in the country. The hope was to depoliticize the whole issue and defuse the national identity crisis. But no sooner had the left returned to power than it found itself confronted with a highly symbolic controversy, which struck at the heart of the republican tradition and risked splitting the Socialist Party itself into competing factions.

The controversy arose when three school girls of Moroccan descent came to a public *lycée*, wearing Islamic scarves (*foulards*), in direct violation of the principles of separation of Church and state (*laïcité*), one of the core principles of the republican tradition. The event immediately became a *cause célebre* for the anti-immigrant right, as well as the republican left, with more liberal (or pluralist) elements of the political and intellectual elite, including Rocard, caught in the middle. Allowing the girls to wear the scarves was bound to offend both the left and the right; but forcing them to remove the scarfs could open a new Pandora's box, concerning the dividing line between the public and private sphere, including the wearing of other religious symbols in the classroom, such as the crucifix or the Star of David. The event also heightened the sense of crisis with respect to immigration control, because of the widespread fear that the new immigrants from North Africa, as well as the second generation, were increasingly prone to Islamic fundamentalism and there-fore inassimilable in a secular, republican society, where the individual should keep his or her private life and religious beliefs completely separate from the public sphere. One of the leaders of the Socialist Party who was most adamant in his opposition to such overt violations of the sacred republican principle of *laïcité* was Jean-Pierre Chevènement, who held ministerial posts in various socialist governments.

Prime Minister Rocard and then Minister of Education, Lionel Jospin, took the decision to allow the girls to wear their scarves, so long as they agreed not to proselytize or in any way disrupt classes. As happened frequently with the issue of immigration and integration, when the rights of individuals vis-à-vis the state were in question, the Conseil d'Etat was called upon to help resolve the controversy. In this case, the Conseil d'Etat simply ratified the compromise position taken by the Rocard government, but the compromise did little to allay the growing fears of Islamic fund-amentalism among the French public, and the *foulards* affair, as it came to be known, raised a new spectre of multiculturalism (*à l'américain*), seen as yet another threat to French unity and national identity, exemplified by the 'One and Indivisible Republic.' At the same time, *le droit à la différence* (the right to be different) became the new rallying cry of those defending the rights of immigrants (Roy, 1991).

Despite the almost continuous atmosphere of crisis in French politics over immigration, integration, and national identity, dating back at least to the early 1980s, very little had changed, either in terms of policy outputs (actual policies for controlling immigration) or in terms of policy outcomes (Hollifield, 1992a). In the end, the first experience of *cohabitation* (1986–88) did little to alter the republican model and the rules of the game, as spelled out in the *ordonnances* of 1945 (Weil, 1991: 53ff) France continued to be open to legal immigration, with no quotas or ethnic/racial preferences (in contrast to the American model), even though everything possible was done by the left and the right to discourage purely economic (or worker) immigration. Flows, which are the best measure of policy outcomes, continued at the level of 100,000 or more a year (see Table 3.2), and the liberal nationality code allowed for the relatively quick naturalization of the foreign population (see Table 3.4).

In terms of immigration control, perhaps the most important change came in the area of refugee policy, with the conclusion of the Dublin Agreement, negotiated by the EU, and the establishment in 1990 of the Schengen group. In both instances, France committed itself to refuse entry to any asylum seeker who had passed through a 'safe' third country, thereby clearing the way for the *refoulement* of many asylum seekers. The Schengen Agreement also engaged France in the construction of a common European territory – a Europe without internal borders – requiring the harmonization of visa and asylum policies within the Schengen group, as well as increased policing of external borders. These new European initiatives in some ways would come to represent a challenge to the republican tradition, because of the limits imposed on due process and the attempt (via the Maastricht Treaty) to create a semblance of European citizenship and grant voting rights in local elections for permanent resident aliens (denizens) (Hollifield. 1994: 165–8; Weil, 1991: 181–4).

From a 'Threshold of Tolerance' to 'Zero Immigration'

When asked about immigration policy in 1991, President Mitterrand suggested that every society, including France, has a 'threshold of tolerance' (*seuil de tolérance*), beyond which instances of xenophobia and racism are likely to increase, but he refused to specify what exactly that threshold might be in the case of France. On the other hand, Charles Pasqua, soon to be (for the second time in his career) Minister of the Interior, stated bluntly that 'France has been an immigration country, but she wants to be no longer'. Like any good nationalist and populist, Minister Pasqua claimed to be speaking in the name of the French people. However, as a powerful member of the second government of *cohabitation*, elected by a landslide (the coalition of Gaullists and liberals won over 80 per cent of the seats in the Assembly) in the Spring of 1993, Pasqua made clear what the immigration policy of the new government would be: 'the goal we set, given the seriousness of the economic situation is to tend towards *zero immigration*.' This explicit linkage of immigration to the severe economic recession – which began in 1991–92 and would push unemployment in France to post-war highs of well over 10 per cent – was again aimed to appeal to the 12.4 per cent of French voters who supported the Front National in the first round of the 1993 parliamentary elections. Immigration and integration policies were still very much at the centre of French politics, and would remain so throughout the 1990s.

Faced with a badly weakened, divided, and demoralized socialist opposition, and having won an overwhelming majority in Parliament, the new right-wing government, headed by Edouard Balladur, had a virtually free hand to pursue draconian policies for (1) stopping all immigration, (2) reducing the number of asylum seekers to an absolute minimum, and (3) reforming the nationality code to block naturalization of as many of the resident foreigners as possible. These new policies represented a clear break from the old socialist 'grand bargain.' Even though Mitterrand was still President (and would be until 1995), he was clearly a lame duck and quite ill with prostate cancer. Hence, he was in no position to oppose what looked to be a truly dramatic shift in immigration policy. Only the courts could block the change, therefore the Balladur government wasted no time in launching a sweeping reform of immigration and refugee policy, designed to move France as close as possible to zero immigration. To discourage further settlement of foreigners, the nationality law would also be changed.

What distinguishes this round of reform (in 1993) from earlier attempts to limit immigration (in 1974 or 1986, for example) is the clear focus on rolling back the rights of foreigners across the board. The second Pasqua law presented a direct challenge to the republican model, as defined by the *Ordonnances* of 1945. Equal protection and due process (civil rights) were denied to foreigners by cutting off possibilities of appeal for asylum seekers and by giving the police much greater powers than ever before to detain and deport foreigners. Social rights also would be severely restricted by denying foreigners access to the benefits of the social security system, especially health care. On this point, however, a rift developed within the government between the Minister of the Interior, Pasqua, and the Social Affairs Minister, Simone Weil, who argued for maintaining emergency health care for foreigners.

The debate in France over social rights for immigrants parallels a similar debate that was gathering force in the United States, especially in California, where voters approved a measure (Proposition 187) in November 1994 to cut public and social services for illegal immigrants. Barely two years later (in 1996), the US Congress, under Republican control, would adopt similar laws to cut social services for legal as well as illegal immigrants, and the rights of appeal for illegals and asylum seekers would be sharply curtailed. Also in the US, proposals were made by prominent right-wing politicians, such as Governor Pete Wilson of California, to limit birthright citizenship, so that the children born of foreign parents would no longer be automatically entitled to American citizenship. Similarly in France, the second Pasqua law (like the first) sought to change naturalization procedures by requiring children born in France of foreign parents to make a formal request for naturalization, between the ages of 16 and 21.

Limiting Rights: Negative versus Positive Freedom

What we can see in these two old republics in the 1990s is a not-so-subtle shift in strategies and tactics for restricting immigration, away from a reliance on the classic instruments of (external) control of borders and (internal) regulation of labour markets to a new strategy of attacking and limiting the rights of foreigners. In liberal societies, external control of borders – with an emphasis on territorial sovereignty and the sanctity of law – is preferable to internal control of society, which may entail infringements of individual, civil liberties. All things being equal, liberal states will opt for external strategies of control, placing the most stress on border control, or control of territory. The reason for this is simple: territorial closure and sovereignty are essential to the maintenance of the social contract and the rule of law, and this cannot be questioned without questioning the authority and legitimacy of the state itself.

In the 1990s, neither the French (led by Gaullists and right-wing liberals) nor the American governments (led by a Republican Congress and a Democratic President) have abandoned the classic instruments of border control. On the contrary, they have reinforced them, especially in the American case in recent years where the liberal concept of *negative freedom* (implying a minimalist state and freedom to do whatever one wants within the broad confines of the law) has had a much more powerful influence on politics and public policy. The Clinton administration has placed great emphasis on (external) control of borders, as well as (internal) regulation of labour markets. If control cannot be easily externalized, then a series of internal control policies will come into play and the question then becomes: how far can a liberal state go in imposing such controls on individuals in (civil) society? Should foreigners and immigrants be considered members of civil society? The limits on internal control are imposed by ideas, institutions, and culture, as well as certain segments of civil society, which may resist encroachments by the state on negative and/or positive freedoms.

The GISTI has had a much more difficult time blocking reform in France, than the ACLU, which has effectively stopped the adoption of national ID cards in the US. To constrain worker and family immigration in France, the second Pasqua law (1994) required workers and foreign students to wait two years (rather than one) before bringing any family members to join them. To inhibit permanent settlement of foreigners and to control illegal immigration, the Law prohibited adjustments of status (*régularisation*) for any undocumented individual who marries a French citizen. Mayors were given the authority to annul any suspected marriage of convenience (*mariage blanc*). In this case the state inserted itself directly into the private lives of French, as well as foreign, citizens. Finally, under the second Pasqua law, any foreigner expelled from France would be denied re-entry into French territory for one year.

The second Pasqua reforms, together with the examples from recent changes in American policy (the 1996 laws), indicate *the lengths to which liberal states are willing to go in rolling back the rights of foreigners* (and thereby abandoning some aspects of negative freedom and the minimalist state) in order to restrict immigration. A somewhat easier target – more so in the US than in France – is *positive freedom* revolving around the welfare state and flowing from laws designed to help the individual take advantage of the opportunities afforded by negative freedom in a liberal society. The whole range of welfare benefits, from education to health care and pensions, has become a target for those wishing to restrict the rights of foreigners as a way of controlling immigration. Such actions taken by liberal states against foreigners would seem to be less threatening to citizens, depending upon the extent to which citizens are attached to social rights and determined to protect them for *all* members of society, even for the most marginal, disenfranchised groups, like children, immigrants, and foreigners. The French are certainly more attached to social rights (*les acquis sociaux*) than are Americans, but less so than the Germans, Dutch, or Scandinavians. Thus it is somewhat easier for the Americans and the French to cut welfare benefits for foreigners than it would be for the Germans or the Swedes, for example.

Looking at TH Marshall's classic trilogy of rights (civil, social, and political) (Marshall 1950), we can see that France – like other liberal, republican, and social democracies – has acted to constrain the civil (equal protection and due process) and social (welfare) rights of immigrants and foreigners. If we follow this policy (of limiting the rights of non-citizens) to its logical conclusion, then the ultimate rights that can be denied to foreigners are political (or voting) rights, which are tied to naturalization. To roll back these rights in a liberal republic requires tampering with the nationality law, and we already have seen evidence of this in both the first and second Pasqua laws. Birthright citizenship, enshrined in the Fourteenth Amendment to the Constitution, also has been challenged in the US in the 1990s, but changing nationality laws in a republic in order to deal with immigration or integration is exceedingly difficult and fraught with many political dangers, as we have seen in each case (France, the US, and especially Germany). Reform in this area often means opening up difficult, moral debates about national identity, with many political, historical, and constitutional overtones. The relative ease with which the Thatcher government changed British nationality laws in 1981 stands in stark contrast with similar attempts at reform in France and the US.

In the case of France, amending the nationality code means changing the universalist and nationalist republican model, as it has evolved since 1945. In the case of the US, it would mean amending (or at least reinterpreting) the Fourteenth Amendment to the Constitution, adopted in the wake of the Civil War, and designed to overturn the Supreme Court's *Dred Scott* decision by granting automatic citizenship to former slaves. In Germany (the Bundesrepublik Deutschland), the problem of control is inextricably linked to the problem of integrating a large, permanent foreign population. To solve the problem of integration in Germany it will be necessary to change the 1913 nationality law, thus abandoning a key aspect of German national identity, that is a community based on the ethnocultural principle of descent (*jus sanguinis*) rather than on the more universalistic and territorial principles of birth and soil (*jus soli*). When this change in the German nationality law is made, it will bring Germany more fully into the club of liberal republics.

Infringing individual and group rights or tampering with the social contract, the constitution, and national identity as a means of controlling immigration are fraught with danger for liberal and republican states, because the state or government runs the risk of undermining its own legitimacy and alienating and/or endangering its own citizens. Moreover, otherwise liberal politicians may inadvertently (or unwittingly) provoke a nationalist, xenophobic, and even racist backlash, which could redound against these same politicians and undermine the state (and rule of law) itself (Thränhardt, 1997). Fortunately, in states like France and the US, which have long histories of liberal and republican governance, there are institutional and ideological checks that work to protect the state and politicians from themselves. In France, as in other liberal states such as the US and Germany, the courts play a crucial role in this regard. As it did with the first Pasqua law (in 1986), the Conseil d'Etat – which functions in part as an institutional watchdog for any infringements of the rights of the individual by the State – warned the Balladur government that certain aspects of the proposed reform were illegal and possibly unconstitutional. The Conseil d'Etat was especially concerned with the impact of the second Pasqua law on the (constitutional) right of families to live together, and with the provisions of the law limiting the right of appeal for asylum seekers, but the Conseil d'Etat has no real powers of judicial review. Its opinions are only advisory, even though it is one of the most powerful *grands corps* – second only to the Inspection des Finances. Still it has great moral, political, and legal authority, and governments ignore its views at their peril (Stirn, 1991). Moreover, decisions of the Conseil d'Etat may presage a ruling by the Conseil Constitutionel, which does have powers of judicial review and may stop the implementation of any law deemed unconstitutional.

This is precisely what happened in August 1993 when the Conseil Constitutionel ruled that certain provisions of the second Pasqua law were unconstitutional. The judges rejected the one-year ban on re-entry imposed on anyone deported from France. Also found to be unconstitutional were the provisions dealing with family immigration, namely (1) the longer waiting period imposed on foreign students and workers seeking to bring immediate family members to join them, and (2) the restrictions imposed on marriages between French citizens and foreigners. In rendering these decisions, the Conseil Constitutionel relied specifically on the Declaration of the Rights of Man and the Citizen, referring to the universalist and egalitarian principles of this republican document, especially equal protection. Moreover, citing the Preamble to the 1946 Constitution – which requires that due process be accorded to all asylum seekers – the Conseil Constitutionel ruled that restrictions on the right of appeal and provisions in the law for the automatic *refoulement* of refugees were unconstitutional. This ruling seemed to jeopardize France's participation in the Dublin Convention as well as the Schengen Agreement, both of which require European states that are parties to these agreements to refuse asylum to any individual who has passed through a safe third country.

The efforts of the Balladur government to move France to 'zero immigration' did little to calm the national identity crisis. If anything, the second Pasqua law heightened the sense of crisis, and fanned the flames of xenophobia, leading to a constitutional debate, but one objective of the reforms *appears* to have been met: immigration flows fell precipitously from a high of 135,000 (including asylum seekers) in 1992 to 68,000 in 1995. The average annual rate of immigration for the period 1993–95 plummeted to its lowest levels (89,700) since the late 1940s and early 1950s (66,400 – see Table 3.1), but, as we shall see – in the crisis over the Debré law in 1997 – many of the previously legal flows were simply pushed underground, raising the size of the undocumented population (*sans papiers*), and increasing the level of insecurity among the foreign population as a whole. The numbers of individuals caught trying to enter the country illegally (*reconduites à la frontière*) rose steadily from 1993 on, jumping from 8,700 in 1993 to 10,100 in 1995 and over 12,000 in 1996, providing (indirect) evidence of increased illegal immigration.

Nevertheless, to combat the judges and complete his reform, the Interior Minister, Pasqua turned one aspect of the republican tradition (popular sovereignty) against another (birthright citizenship). Claiming that the people, having spoken through their representatives, want immigration reduced, he called for a constitutional amendment that would prepare France for entry into a border-free Europe and give the state the power to turn back asylum seekers without hearings or appeals. As provided by the Constitution, the amendment was voted in an extraordinary congress of the Parliament (the Assembly and the Senate) at Versailles in January 1994. Pasqua proclaimed that there would be no 'government by judges' in France, as in the US where many anti-immigrant measures, such as Proposition 187 in California, have been blocked by the Federal judiciary. Ultimately the US Supreme Court can rule on the constitutionality of American immigration control policies, especially when they impinge upon basic civil rights and liberties. The question remains open, however: how far can a liberal-republican state go in rolling back rights of individuals in its effort to control immigration? At what point does the liberal-republican model begin to break down? What is the appropriate balance between internal and external controls? Between negative and positive freedom?

Civil Disobedience and the Limits of Control

Immigration continued to agitate French politics and society into the mid and late 1990s, during the presidential election of 1995 and especially during the legislative elections of 1997. The election of Jacques Chirac as President of the Republic by a narrower-than-expected margin over the left candidate, Lionel Jospin, did little to change French immigration policy, even though Le Pen received a record number of votes (15 per cent) on the first round of the presidential elections. The new government, led by Chirac's lieutenant, Alain Juppé, had the support of the same crushing right-wing majority in the Assembly. The UDF and RPR still controlled 80 per cent of the seats, but one big difference was the absence of Charles Pasqua from the Jospin government. Pasqua had supported Chirac's rival, the former Prime Minister Edouard Balladur, for the presidency. He was replaced as Minister of the Interior by Jean-Louis Debré, son of Michel Debré, the first Prime Minister of the Fifth Republic and author of the Constitution. Debré *fils* would quickly make a name for himself by proposing further, draconian steps to limit the rights of foreigners in France and crack down on illegal immigration. The Debré law of 1997 would test the limits of strategies for (internal) immigration control, leading to civil disobedience, more court rulings, new elections (thanks to the political blunders of Chirac and Juppé), and finally a resurgence of the republican left.

In the summer of 1996, the tough control policies (described in the preceding section) were challenged by a group of Africans, mostly from Mali, who were caught in the web of the second Pasqua law (unable to obtain a residency permit, even though many of them had resided in France for many years and could not be legally deported) or whose applications for political asylum had been rejected. The *sans papiers*, as they were called, occupied a church in Paris, demanding that they be given an adjustment of status (*régularisés*), and several of them launched a hunger strike. The highly public *épreuve de force* with the new government was indicative of the willingness of immigrants openly to resist the government's policy and of the sympathy they were able to generate among certain segments of French civil society. Over 10,000 people marched in Paris in solidarity with the *sans papiers*, and even more embarrassing for the government were appeals by the clergy not to remove the immigrants from the church by force. Nonetheless, the police were ordered to storm the church, arrest the protesters, and break up the hunger strike. The government also proudly published statistics indicating that deportations for the first six months of 1996 were up substantially (by about one third) over the similar period for 1995. Any sign of weakness or wavering by the government in the face of immigrant resistance and civil disobedience was immediately condemned by Le Pen and the Front National.

Apart from occasional acts of civil disobedience by the African *sans papiers*, which continued throughout 1995–97, whether in the form of occupying churches or, in one case, the offices of UNESCO, the civil war in Algeria also had an impact on French control policy. Since the abrupt cancellation of the Algerian elections in 1992 – which Islamic fundamentalists were poised to win – a civil war has raged in the former French colony. The conflict pitted the Islamic radicals against the long-ruling revolutionary party, the FLN, which controls the military. The elections were cancelled with the blessing of the French government, which made no attempt to hide its support for the Algerian military. French involvement in Algerian politics led to a number of terrorist attacks by Islamic militants against public targets in France. These attacks forced the government of Alain Juppé to increase security throughout the country. The security sweeps by the police and the military, known as operation *vigipirate*, focused public attention on the Muslim (and African) communities in France, bringing the full power of the French state to bear in an effort to catch the perpetrators. In October, 1995, the police shot and killed one of the bombers – a young second-generation Algerian man – in the outskirts of Lyon. In the press, his life story was covered in detail and held up as an example of the failure of French society to integrate some segments of the young, Maghrebi population. These dispossessed youths, with no loyalty to the land of their birth, had joined radical Islamic groups and turned against the French Republic.

As in the 1950s, French foreign policy and relations with former colonies, especially Algeria, have become a driving factor in immigration and refugee policy in the 1990s. The government has felt compelled to grant asylum (or at least temporary residence) to many members of the Algerian political and intellectual class, while at the same time stepping up pressure to keep other Algerians out, and carefully observing the established Algerian community in France. This atmosphere of crisis and public insecurity together with continuing pressure from the Front National led the Juppé government late in 1996 to propose a new law, which came to be known as the Debré law, designed to resolve the ambiguous status of some of the *sans papiers*, particularly the French-born children of illegal immigrants and the foreign spouses of French citizens. These groups could not be deported, but under the Pasqua law they were not eligible for an adjustment of status. Under the proposed new law, the 'foreign' children under 16 years of age would have to prove continuous residence in France for ten years, and 'foreign' spouses would have to have been married for two years in order to be eligible (like the children) for a one-year residence permit.

Even though the Debré law had some liberal intent, it got much more publicity and became the focal point of controversy and protest because of a provision added to the Bill by the conservative National Assembly. The provision required all private citizens to notify local authorities whenever they received in their homes any non-EU foreigner. Moreover, mayors would be given the authority to verify that a foreign visitor had left the private citizen's home once the visitor's visa had expired. What is most interesting about the Debré Law is not so much the effect (or lack thereof) that it had on immigration control, but the response it received both from French certain groups in civil society and institutions of the liberal-republican state. Minister Debré, paraphrasing his predecessor Pasqua, stated that 'I am for zero *illegal* immigration . . . The State must be given the means to deter foreigners who want to enter France without resources, papers or jobs.' The focus in this statement is on those clearly outside the law the illegal immigrants; but public attention was focused on the effect that the law would have on private French citizens, who would (by law) be compelled to inform on foreign visitors. Such an intrusion by the state into the private lives of individuals and families was deemed by many to have crossed the invisible line beyond which liberal states are not supposed to go. The Debré law was denounced as an infringement of (negative) freedom and a threat to the basic civil liberties of all French citizens. The European Parliament even went so far as to pass a resolution condemning the law and equating it with Vichy-era laws that required French citizens to inform on their Jewish compatriots, so that they could be deported by the Germans to death camps.

Over the objections of the Conseil d'Etat, which warned the government that requiring citizens to inform on foreigners might be unconstitutional, the Assembly approved the Debré law in February, 1997, but with some important modifications. Taking a step back from infringements on the liberty of French citizens, the amended version of the law required the foreigners themselves to report their movements and whereabouts to local authorities. This compromise illustrates quite well the limitations on the power of the liberal state to pursue strategies for (internal) control of immigration that cross the invisible line between infringement of the liberties of citizens and those of foreigners. It is important to note also that the law exempted Europeans and visitors from 30 other countries from the reporting requirements, targeting undesirable African immigrants who were more likely to overstay their visas.

Not only did judicial or institutional checks come into play, the reaction to the law from certain elite groups in civil society was swift and severe, causing the government considerable embarrassment. Fifty-nine film directors launched a campaign of civil disobedience by publishing an open letter in *Le Monde*, declaring that 'we are guilty, every one of us, of harbouring illegal foreign residents . . . we ask therefore to be investigated and put on trial.' A rally in Paris to protest the new law attracted 35,000 people, but the French public, according to polls published at the time, was heavily polarized, with a clear majority (59 per cent) supporting the government's position. Earlier in February, the Front National again scored an electoral victory in municipal elections, as Catherine Megret, wife of the number two in the party, Bruno Megret, won the mayoral race in Vitrolles, a small town north of Marseilles. The victory gave the FN control of four French cities: Marignane, Orange, and Toulouse, in addition to Vitrolles.

The Debré law also seemed to violate the liberal principle that an individual is innocent until proven guilty. In order to renew their 10-year residence permits, foreigners would be required to prove that they were not a threat to public order and that they had maintained a regular residence in France, thus shifting the burden of proof from the state to the individual. This provision of the law, along with another that would have given police access to the fingerprints of all asylum seekers, were subsequently struck down by the Conseil Constiututionel, which, unlike the Conseil d'Etat, has powers of judicial review. Here again the precarious relationship between the individual and the state, which is so important in a liberal polity and which is the subject of constitutional law and interpretation, was threatened, but in a republican political system, which stresses popular sovereignty, the will of the people *qua* citizens (desirous to stop immigration, if opinion polls are to be believed) must be respected. As we have seen in recent American experiences, one way to get around this dilemma, which opposes the *liberal* against the *republican* half of the polity, is to focus the regulatory and police power of the state on *illegal* immigrants, thus leaving some legitimacy for legal immigration and the right to seek asylum.

The final version of the Debré law was passed by the French Parliament (Senate) in March, 1996. Provisions concerning notification of the whereabouts of foreigners had been watered down or eliminated altogether. The law required African visitors to prove that they had adequate accommodation and funds necessary to live in France during their stay and to return home afterwards. Throughout this period of policy reform, a major concern of the French government was to devise a system for controlling entries by Africans (and other foreign visitors coming from developing countries), but without imposing American-style quotas on visas, entries, or immigrants. The resistance to quotas is born of (1) the republican desire to maintain an egalitarian approach to the issuing of visas (where all or most applicants, coming from developing countries, would be treated equally) and (2) a desire to construct a system that would not be overtly discriminatory towards individuals coming from former French colonies in West and North Africa, but regardless of intent, the effect of both the Pasqua (1993) and Debré (1997) laws has been to severely restrict legal immigration of Africans.

A New 'Republican Pact'

To the surprise of many, President Chirac decided to dissolve the Parliament and call early elections in May–June 1997. The move cut short the life of the Parliament by about one year, and it was provoked not so much by controversies over immigration policy but by the difficulties of meeting the criteria of Economic and Monetary Union (EMU), scheduled to begin in January 1999. The Juppé government struggled to meet the stringent deflationary policies forced on France by the Maastricht Treaty on European Union, especially the requirement that budget deficits be less than 3 per cent of GDP before a member state can join EMU. Having been elected on a promise to heal the *fracture sociale* and lower the record high levels of unemployment, running at 12–13 per cent in 1996–97, Chirac and Juppé found themselves caught in a political and economic bind, unable to stimulate the economy because of their commitments to EMU, but unwilling to abandon French workers to their fate in a more competitive European and international economy. As a result, Chirac decided to seek a new mandate for his government and his presidency – a huge political gamble that he lost. The French socialists and their allies (a mixture of communists, radicals, and greens) won control of the National Assembly, launching the third period of *cohabitation* in a little over a decade, only this time the right would control the presidency and the left would control the parliament.

The change of government had major implications, not only for EMU, but also for French immigration policy. As in past elections, the Front National received about 15 per cent of the vote in the first round, but thanks to the dual ballot electoral system, it won only one seat in the Assembly, held by Jean-Marie Le Chevallier, Mayor of Toulon. What was different about this election was the refusal of the FN to cooperate with other parties of the right (RPR and UDF) by withdrawing its candidates – who had received the constitutionally required 12.5 per cent of registered voters on the first round – from the second round of voting. This set up over seventy *triangulaires* (three-way contests) in which the FN candidate essentially split the right-wing vote on the second round, thus helping to elect a candidate of the left. In effect, the FN had a big hand in bringing down the Gaullist-liberal government, and putting the socialist-communist left back in power. If the FN persists in this strategy in the future, it will intensify pressure on right-liberal and Gaullist candidates to strike electoral deals with the FN, which could lead to a further polarization of the electorate and the party system on the specific issue of immigration.

Notwithstanding crises over EMU, unemployment, public finances, and a further polarization of the electorate, the new government, led by Lionel Jospin, took bold steps to return French immigration policy to its republican roots and to resolve the ambiguous status of the *sans papiers*. In his opening speech to the new Parliament on 19 June 1997, Prime Minister Jospin announced that he would establish a 'new republican pact' with the French people, returning to the 'roots of the Republic' while striving to 'modernize French democracy.' In outlining his government's programme, the first two policy items were (1) the *school*, which he called the 'cradle of the Republic' where values of citizenship are taught (the most important being *laïcité*), and (2) *immigration*. With respect to the latter issue, Jospin laid out quite a detailed republican vision of immigration policy, reminiscent of earlier periods in French immigration history, from the turn of the century, to the 1920s, to the *Ordonnances* of 1945, to the early Mitterrand years in the 1980s. To quote Jospin:

> France, with its old republican traditions, was built in layers that flowed together into a melting pot, thus creating an alloy that is strong because of the diversity of its component parts. For this reason, birthright citizenship *(le droit du sol)* is inseparable from the French Nation (*consubstantiel à la nation française*). We will reestablish this right. Nothing is more alien to France than xenophobia and racism . . . Immigration is an economic, social and human reality which must be organized and controlled. France must define a firm, dignified immigration policy without renouncing its values or compromising its social balance (*Libération*, 20 June 1997).

To accomplish this goal, Jospin called for (1) a new republican integration policy, which welcomes immigrants, respects their human rights, but combats illegal immigration and black labour markets, thus returning to the 'grand bargain' strategies of earlier socialist governments (see above); (2) a new policy of cooperation with the sending states to help control immigration at its source; (3) a comprehensive review of immigration and nationality law, to be carried out by an interministerial task force, chaired by the immigration scholar, Patrick Weil. During the campaign, Jospin promised to repeal the Pasqua-Debré laws, and this promise would come back to haunt him (see below). Finally, (4) steps will be taken to review, on a case-by-case basis, the situation of all undocumented foreigners (*sans papiers*) caught in the maze of regulations and contradictions surrounding the Pasqua-Debré laws. The government issued orders to the prefects immediately to begin reviewing as many as 40,000 cases, and foreigners who had waited for months or years for their dossiers to be reviewed, suddenly found a new willingness on the part of administrative authorities to help them by issuing temporary residence permits.

The Weil report, published 1 August 1997, contained 120 propositions for modifying immigration and nationality law. For the most part, the report (like the Bills that would be presented to Parliament later that year) tried to steer a middle course: re-establishing the centrality of the principle of *jus soli* in French nationality law, going back to the naturalization procedure that existed before the 1993 Pasqua law, with a few modifications; but not creating a blanket birthright citizenship, as exists in the United States; re-enforcing the rights of asylum seekers and the rights of family reunification, but cracking down on illegal immigration – a position similar to the old socialist grand bargain. Finally, the report appealed to the republican tradition, linking immigration with an open, welcoming, but secular tradition in French law and history. The report was designed to placate the right, while trying to meet the pro-immigrant left 'half way.' The danger, of course, is that the proposed reform would please neither the pro-immigrant left nor the anti-immigrant right, which was consistent with Weil's stated ambition to 'depoliticize the immigration issue' (Weil, 1997; *Libération*, 1 August 1997).

By giving such a high priority to reform of immigration and nationality law, the Jospin government signalled its desire to confront this issue head on; and by appealing to French republican values as a way of resolving the immigration crisis, the government clearly hoped to return to the earlier 'republican consensus,' diffuse the issue, and seize the political and moral high ground (Hollifield, 1994). Attempts by right-wing governments to 'steal the thunder' from Le Pen and the Front National by cracking down on immigrants and thereby appealing to insecurities and xenophobia of the electorate – what might be called the Pasqua-Debré approach to immigration policy – did little to reduce levels of support for the FN. If anything, this strategy led to an increase in support for the far right, which won its most votes ever in the first round of legislative elections in 1997. Whether the socialists and communists could reconstruct the republican consensus would depend in part on their ability to reach out to elements of the liberal and republican right. This was the strategy adopted in the Weil report and subsequently by the government itself.

Two Bills were drafted and presented to the National Assembly in the fall of 1997. The Guigou law (named for the Minister of Justice in the Jospin government) dealt with reform of the nationality code, whereas the Chevènement law (named after the well-known Minister of the Interior) dealt with reform of immigration law. Both laws openly appealed to the republican tradition in an attempt to gain support from a broad spectrum of politicians on the left and the right. But the parliamentary debates demonstrated clearly how polarized the electorate and the party system are with respect to these sensitive issues of politics and public policy. By opting to amend rather than repeal the Pasqua-Debré laws, the left-coalition government of Lionel Jospin – which includes socialists, communists, and greens – offended the pro-immigrant left and opened a breach in the ranks of the left. The right-wing opposition of liberals (UDF) and neo-gaullists (RPR) saw this as an opportunity to embarrass and weaken the government, so any chance of rebuilding the old republican consensus would seem to have been lost. The National Front (FN) saw this as an opportunity for free publicity.

The Guigou law was adopted in early December, 1997 by a narrow margin (267 deputies voting for it and 246 against, with many communists and greens abstaining). The pro-immigrant left wanted to send a message to the government expressing its displeasure with the strategy of amending rather than repealing the Pasqua-Debré laws. This pink-green coalition was dubbed the 'moral left' which took a strong stand in favour of birthright citizenship, meaning an end to all restrictions on the natural-ization of individuals born on French territory. The right-wing opposition denounced the reform as unnecessary and detrimental to the national interest. One UDF deputy, François Bayrou, following the lead of the former President, Valéry Giscard d'Estaing, called for a referendum on the issue. The lonely representative of the National Front, Jean Marie Le Chevalier, called for the elimination of *jus soli* in favour of *jus sanguinis* as the organizing principle for French nationality law.

The Guigou law in effect reinstated the principle of *jus soli*, so that anyone born in France of foreign parents can acquire French nationality at the age of majority (eighteen), so long as that individual can show continuous residence in France for at least five years after the age of eleven. Any minor born in France of foreign parents can request naturalization as early as age thirteen, if his/her parents give their consent and if s/he has resided in France for at least five years since age eight. To insure that naturalization is voluntary, the law states that any young foreigner can refuse French citizenship in the six months before s/he turns eighteen or in the twelve months after his/her eighteenth birthday. To avoid having individuals fall through the cracks of the law, as happened with the *sans papiers* under the Pasqua law, the Guigou law created a 'republican identity card' (note the symbolism of the name!) to be given to every minor born in France of foreign parents. Finally, the law rolls back the waiting period for foreign spouses to request naturalization, from two to one year after the date of the marriage. During the debate over the new nationality law, a number of deputies went to the podium to recount stories of their immigrant ancestors and how grateful they are for the French tradition of hospitality – a scene very reminiscent of similar debates in the American Congress, where representatives and senators have often waxed grandi- loquent about their families immigrant origins and the contributions that they made to building the American Republic (*Libération*, 1 December 1997).

The fate of the Chevènement Bill was long uncertain. It did not pass, as first scheduled in December 1997. Several amendments were proposed, and only in May 1998 a new immigration law was finally approved by the National Assembly. The adoption of this law meant that the *ordonnance* of 2 November 1945, governing the status of foreigners in France, had been amended no less that twenty-five times, including five times in the last eleven years.

The major provisions of the Chevènement Bill were as follows: the Bill would get rid of the 'legal entry requirement' imposed by the Pasqua law on any foreigner seeking to adjust his/her status. However, the Bill keeps the 'threat to public order' as grounds for exclusion. One-year residence permits would be issued to (1) all minors entering under the auspices of family reunification, (2) all foreigners who entered France before the age of ten and who reside in France, (3) any foreigners who can prove that they have resided in France for fifteen years, and (4) foreign spouses of French nationals as well as the foreign parents of French children. These changes were intended to emphasize the importance and the sanctity of the family under French law. The one- year permits also will be issued to foreigners who are infirm. Special consideration in the issuance of residence and work permits must also be given to (1) foreign scholars and professors, invited to work in France, and (2) any foreigner who has a special personal or family situation. Foreigners who are a threat to public order or who engage in polygamy are prohibited from receiving residence permits. A special residence permit for retired people, valid for ten years and renewable, was also proposed.

Apart from these broad changes in the issuing of residence permits, the Bill eliminates a number of conditions imposed on potential immigrants by the Pasqua law, including the requirement that parents meet certain income criteria before bringing their children to France, and they need wait only one year (instead of two) after establishing their residence in France to request reunification of their family. Another important modification of the Pasqua law would be the elimination of 'housing certification,' which had to be approved by the office of the mayor of the commune. These certificates were to be replaced by a statement that the foreigner has a place to stay (*attestation d'accueil*), but the government seemed prepared to compromise with the left and eliminate this condition altogether. In a nod to the right, however, the Bill would limit appeals by foreigners denied a residence permit, keeping a special *commission de séjour*, whose opinions in any given case would be only advisory. Likewise, the government would not be required to justify refusal of visas, except in the case of immigration of family members. Criminal aliens would continue to be excludable, but the Bill would require the government to take account of the personal and family situation of the individual, already required by the European Human Rights Convention.

Finally, the Chevènement Bill creates two new forms of asylum for individuals persecuted because of their activities on behalf of freedom. This would be called 'constitutional asylum'. The Bill also creates a French equivalent of the old American 'temporary protected status', which would give the French Minister of Justice (like the American Attorney General) the power to grant 'territorial asylum' to individuals in imminent, personal danger, if they are returned to their country of origin. In another nod to the right, the length of administrative detention for irregular migrants was increased from ten to twelve days, but foreigners would have additional time to appeal against a deportation order.

The debate over reform of immigration law in 1997 has been heated, with immigrants rights organizations like l'association Droits devant!! calling for demonstrations against the government and anti-racist groups like MRAP denouncing the atmosphere of crisis and calling for vigilance against further outbursts of racism and xenophobia. The leader of the RPR group in the Assembly and former Minister of the Interior, Jean-Louis Debré, accused the Jospin government of waving 'a red cloth in front of the National Front voters'. Citing polls that show a majority of French voters to be against increasing the rights of immigrants, the opposition (RPR-UDF) called for a referendum on the reforms. In the midst of the political maelström, the Interior Minister, Jean-Pierre Chevènement, continued to search for the centre in an effort to resurrect the grand bargain and the republican consensus. In a speech before the Assembly he stated: 'To talk of strangers is simply another way of talking about France. All of you, on both sides of the aisle, have *a certain idea* [of France] which often, and thankfully, transcends partisan politics. The real issue here is access to citizenship [and] the French people are far more united on this subject than one might think listening to our debates in this chamber.' The republican and Gaullist overtones are clear in the Minister's words (*Libération*, 5 December 1997).

What does this new 'republican' strategy mean for French control policy and what will its effect be on actual flows? The emphasis will shift from internal controls – designed to limit and roll back the (civil and social) rights of resident aliens or denizens – back to a 'grand bargain' strategy of relatively tough, external control of borders, careful, internal regulation of labour markets, combined with a liberal policy for integrating and naturalizing immigrants. The effect on flows is likely to be modest. They should return to the annual averages of the 1980s and early 1990s (around 100,000, see Table 3.1).

Moreover, France under the socialists is likely to become a more cooperative partner in building a border-free Europe, in the context of the Schengen Agreement. If a liberal state has the capacity for extra-territorial control – as many member states of the EU clearly do – it will opt for further externalization of control, extending its authority to the high seas, to the territory of neighbouring states, or to the territory of the sending states themselves. The Schengen Agreement, to which France is a party, is a classic example of extraterritorial control, which creates buffer states, and shifts many of the burdens and dilemmas of control outside the jurisdiction of the liberal state, but in the context of the Westphalian system, which is based on principles of sovereignty and non-interference, there are few limits on the capacity of states, liberal or otherwise, for pursuing strategies of external control. With respect to internal control, liberal and republican states, like France, are constrained institutionally, ideologically, culturally, and ultimately by their civil societies. Strategies for internal control bend to these constraints. Otherwise, the legitimacy of the state itself is threatened.

Conclusion

Historically immigration has had greater legitimacy in France than in the other major receiving countries of Western Europe. The reasons for this, as pointed out in the first sections of this essay, are political, economic, and demographic. As is the case in countries that have a long history of immigration – such as the United States or Canada – the first waves of immigration in France in the nineteenth and early twentieth century were the result of industrialization and a strong demand for foreign labour. New sources of labour (initially Belgian, German, Swiss, Italian, and Polish) were needed because of the early demographic transition in France (compared with other European states) and the absence of a rural exodus. French peasants, unlike their English or German counterparts, refused to leave their farms for the factories, as the industrial revolution picked up steam in the nineteenth century. It is important to note that they (the peasant farmers) had the political clout to resist the economic pressures to force them out of the countryside. (Berger, 1972; Noiriel, 1986; Le Bras, 1986: 187ff). Well into the twentieth century, France remained a very rural society; and, even though their numbers declined precipitously in the 1950s and 1960s, French farmers, like their Japanese counterparts, continue to have political clout that is disproportionate to their actual numbers.

Even though France became a country of immigration because of these fundamental social, economic, and demographic pressures, what is most important from the standpoint of the politics and policies of control is to understand how these early waves of immigration were legitimized. In this respect, France looks less like her European neighbours, and more like the US. In both cases, immigration was legitimized through an appeal to republican ideas and ideologies. From the very earliest days of the Republic – when French Jews were granted citizenship by the revolutionary governments at the end of the eighteenth century – to the various post-war governments of the Fourth and Fifth Republics, politicians have appealed to republican ideals of universalism, egalitarianism, nationalism, and *laïcité*, as a way of legitimizing immigration and integrating foreigners. Thus it is not surprising to hear the Prime Minister, Lionel Jospin, calling in 1997 for a new 'republican pact' as a way of solving the latest social and economic crises, including and especially immigration. *The republican model is alive and well and living in Paris.*

Yet immigration, like republicanism, remains contested in France, more so than in the United States. Again to paraphrase Prime Minister Jospin, immigration is *not* consubstantial with the Republic. Immigration is not a 'founding myth' of the French Republic, therefore we cannot say that France is, like the US, Canada, or Australia, a *nation of immigrants* (Freeman and Jupp, 1992). Yet the Prime Minister is correct in asserting that immigration and birthright citizenship (*le droit du sol*) are inextricably linked with the evolution of republicanism in France, from the Third through the Fifth Republics (Noiriel, 1988). Attacking immigrants and their rights is to some extent tantamount to attacking the Republic.

Conversely, one of the best ways for a government to defend immigrants is to cloak itself in the values and symbols of the Republic.

Immigrants and immigration did come under attack in the 1970s, in large part because of the shift in the composition and ethnic mix of the flows, from predominantly Christian and European, to Muslim and African. This shift was the result of two developments. First of all, decolonization in the 1960s contributed to an exodus of North and West Africans to France. Secondly, European integration gradually eliminated immigration from neighbouring states, such as Italy, Spain, and eventually Portugal. In the early 1970s, the justification for stopping immigration was primarily economic: France had and still has high levels of unemployment. Consistent with a strong strand of Malthusian thinking, the reasoning went: if we can stop immigration, this will solve the problems of unemployment. This Malthusian and economic reason for stopping immigration – although still present today – quickly gave way in the 1980s to the arguments advanced by Jean-Marie Le Pen and others, that France was being transformed and destroyed by an influx of inassimilable African immigrants. According to this view, Muslims could never be good Frenchmen or citizens of the Republic, because of their inability to separate Church and state, and to keep their private, religious views separate from their public life. Their growing numbers were ostensibly causing a crisis of social cohesion and national identity (Kepel, 1991). Politicians began to play on these fears as a way of changing immigration control policies and as a way of getting votes (Thränhardt, 1997; Viard, 1996). Throughout the 1980s and 1990s, the tactic of appealing to xenophobic fears and instincts led to further polarization of the electorate on the issue of immigration and contributed to the rise of the Front National. Whether these fears (on the part of the French electorate) are rational or irrational is obviously open to debate, but there is no doubt that they were exploited by politicians for political gain (Weiner, 1995).

By the late 1990s, the strategies for immigration control in France (and in the United States) began to change dramatically. Instead of relying exclusively on the mechanism of external, border controls (which were nonetheless being reinforced and further *externalized* and Europeanized through the Schengen system) or on the more classic mechanisms of internal regulation of labour markets, the first right-wing government of the 1990s, led by Edouard Balladur, began to roll back and limit the rights of immigrants, first by attacking civil rights and liberties (due process, equal protection, and the like), then by going after certain social rights, specifically healthcare. Finally, political rights, naturalization, and citizenship were challenged, through a reform of the nationality code and the erosion of the principle of birthright citizenship. From a social science standpoint, this is where the story becomes interesting; because it is not clear how far a liberal republic can go towards limiting rights of immigrants and foreigners as a way of controlling immigration. We may not yet have a complete and satisfactory answer to this question.

In France, we can see quite clearly the progression of control strategies: the imposition of external controls (in the form of new visa regimes) in the early 1970s; the restriction on hiring foreign workers (in 1974); attempts to roll back the 'right' to family reunification in the late 1970s; increased labour market regulation during the socialist years of the 1980s; a return to external strategies of control with ratification of the Schengen Agreement (in 1990); limits on social and civil rights (the first and second Pasqua laws, as well as the Debré law); and finally attempts to limit citizenship by changing the nationality law (the first and second Pasqua laws). When the state crossed the invisible line between immigration control (on the one hand), to the point of becoming a threat to civil society and being at odds with the founding (republican) principles of the regime (on the other hand), institutional/judicial, ideological, and social checks came into play. As in other liberal republics, immigration control in France is not purely a function of markets, economic interests, or national security. It is heavily dependent on the interplay of ideas, institutions, and civil society.

References

Berger, S. (1972), *Peasants Against Politics,* Cambridge MA.: Harvard University Press.

Betz, H.-G. (1994), *Radical Right-Wing Populism in Western Europe*, New York: St. Martin's Press.

Birnbaum, P. (1995), *Destins Juifs: De la Révolution française à Carpentra,* Paris: Calmann-Lévy.

Bras, H. Le (1986), *Les trois France,* Paris: Seuil.

Brubaker, R. (1992), *Citizenship and Nationhood in France and Germany,* Cambridge MA.: Harvard University Press.

Feldblum, M. (forthcoming), *Reconstructing Citizenship: The Politics of Immigration in Contemporary France,* New York: State University of New York Press.

Freeman, G.P. (1995), 'Modes of Immigration Politics in Liberal Democratic States' in: *International Migration Review*, 1995: 881–902.

Freeman, G. and Jupp, J. (1992), *Nations of Immigrants: Australia, the United States, and International Migration,* Melbourne: Oxford University Press.

Hammar, T. (1990), *Democracy and the Nation-State: Aliens, Denizens, and Citizens in a World of International Migration,* Aldershot: Avebury.

Haut Conseil à l'Intégration (1991), *La connaissance de l'immigration et de l'intégratio,.* Paris: La Documentation Française.

Herbert, U. (1986), *Geschicte der Ausländer – beschäftigung in Deutschland 1880 bis 1980,* Bonn: Dietz.

Hoffmann, S. (ed.) (1963), *In Search of France,* Cambridge, Mass.: Harvard University Press.

Hollifield, J. (1992a), *Immigrants, Markets, and States*, Cambridge MA.: Harvard University Press.

—— (1992b), 'L'Etat français et l'immigration' in: *Revue Française de Science Politique* 1992: 943–63.

—— (1994), "Immigration and Republicanism in France: the Hidden Consensus' in: Wayne Cornelius, Philip L. Martin, P. and Hollifield, J. eds, (1994), *Controlling Immigration: A Global Perspective,* Stanford: Stanford University Press.

—— (1997), 'Immigration and Integration in Western Europe a comparative analysis', in Emec Uçarer and Donald Puchala (eds), *Immigration into Western Societies: Problems and Policies*, London: Pinter.

Ireland, P. (1994), *The Policy Challenge of Ethnic Diversity,* Cambridge MA.: Harvard University Press.

Kepel, G. (1991), *La Revanche de Dieu,* Paris: Seuil.

Layton-Henry Z. (1992), *The Politics of Immigration*, Oxford: Blackwell.

Lebon, A. (1974–1997), SOPEMI for France. Paris: OECD, La Documentation Française.

Long, M. (1988), *Etre français aujourd'hui et demain*, Paris: La Documentation Française.

Marshall, T.H. (1950), *Citizenship and Social Class and Other Essays,* Cambridge: Cambridge University Press.

Martin, P. (1997), 'The Impacts of Immigration on Receiving Countries', in Emec Uçarer and Donald Puchala (eds), *Immigration into Western Societies: Problems and Policies*, London: Pinter.

Noiriel, G. (1986), *Les ouvriers dans la société française,* Paris: Seuil.

—— (1988), *Le creuset français,* Paris: Seuil.

Perrineau, P. (1995), *Le Vote de crise,* Paris: Presses de la FNSP.

Roy, O. (1991), 'Ethnicité, bandes et communautarisme' in: *Esprit*, February 1991.

Stirn, B. (1991), *Le Conseil d'Etat,* Paris: Hachette.

Tapinos, G. (1975), *L'Immigration étrangère en France,* Paris: Presses Université de France.

—— (1982), 'European Migration Patterns; Economic Linkages and Policy Experiences', *Studi Emigrazione* 1982: 339–57.

Thränhardt, D. (1997), 'The political uses of xenophobia in England, France, and Germany' in: Emek Uçarer and Donald Puchala (eds), *Immigration into Western Societies: Problems and Policies*, London: Pinter.

Tribalat, M. (1997), 'Chronique de l'Immigration', *Population 1997: 1*.

Uçarer E. and Puchala, D. eds (1997), *Immigration into Western Societies: Problems and Policies*, London: Pinter,

Valentin-Marie, C. (1992), 'Le travail clandestin', *Infostat Justice* 1992: 29.

Viard, J. (ed.) (1996), *Aux sources du populisme nationaliste,* Paris: Editions de l'Aube.

Weil, P. (1991), *La France et ses étrangers,* Paris: Calmann-Lévy.

—— (1997), *Mission d'étude des législations de la nationalité et de l'immigration* Paris: La documentation Française.

Weiner, M. (1995), *The Global Migration Crisis: Challenge to States and to Human Rights,* New York: HarperCollins.

Wihtol de Wenden, C. (1988), *Les immigrés et la politique,* Paris: Presses de la F.N.S.P.

−4−

Immigration Control Without Integration Policy: An Austrian Dilemma
Rainer Bauböck

Introduction

On 23 January 1993 more than 300,000 people gathered in Vienna's Heldenplatz in Austria's largest demonstration since the enthusiastic welcome given to Hitler at the same 'Square of Heroes' on 15 March 1938. This time the demonstration was against xenophobia and racism and came as a response to an anti-immigrant petition launched by the right-wing Freedom Party and to the parallel *Lichterketten* (candle light marches) in Germany triggered by violence against asylum seekers. This event created expectations that Austria's coalition government might be ready to soften its harsh policy of legal discrimination against regular immigrants who were subjected to an internal control regime designed for short-term guest-workers. It took more than four years until parliament passed, on 11 June 1997, a long-announced comprehensive reform of the asylum and immigration and laws under the motto 'integration before new immigration'. However, the content of the legislation puts much more emphasis on stopping new immigration than on the legal and economic integration of those who have settled in Austria. The following account of the Austrian immigration control regime tries to explain the extraordinary difficulty Austrian society and its political system have had in coming to terms with the fact of permanent immigration.

Although, during the period covered by our project, Austria had one of the largest per capita immigration rates in Western Europe, it has rarely been included in comparative analyses of immigration policy. When it is mentioned, Austria is usually grouped together with Switzerland and Germany as an example of an immigration regime which started from recruitment of guest-workers, resulted in unintended permanent settlement but continues to restrict access to citizenship for most immigrants and their offspring. While this characterization is basically correct, there are also important differences between the three countries. I will argue in this report that the long-term policy targets of immigration control are generally determined by perceptions of national interests and national identities. National interests include targets of economic development or a certain demographic balance. National identities, on the other hand, refer to historical traditions of common culture or imagined common descent. Aristide Zolberg's characterization of migrant labour as wanted but not welcome (1987, 1996) illustrates the tension between the impact of interests and identities and gives an accurate description of the Austrian immigration regime until the early 1990s.

Immigration control pursues a positive target of selecting wanted and welcome groups and a negative task of keeping out or forcing to return the unwanted and unwelcome ones. However, control policies are often contradictory. Contradictions arise first from difficulties in aggregating conflicting interests in society (such as those of employers' associations and trade unions) into a single set of national interests, and second from the conflict between national interests and identities just outlined. I will try to show that Austria faces a specific problem on the identity dimension, which heavily impacted on the determination of welcome, admissible and excluded immigrants. There are some historical continuities of migration and control patterns stretching back to the late Habsburg monarchy, but these have been mostly buried by what one might call collective amnesias. As Ernest Renan understood well: 'L'oubli, et je dirai meme l'erreur historique, sont un facteur essential de la création d'une nation . . .' ('Forgetting and, I would even say, historical error, are essential factors in the creation of a nation', author's translation, Renan, 1882: 284–5).

The political process of choosing policy instruments to achieve these targets is strongly shaped by particular legal traditions, by a country's internal political regime and by its international position and orientation. In this regard, the available policy options have been shaped by Austria's constitution, by its permanent neutrality, by its system of 'social partnership' and, more recently, by its integration into the European Union. The actual choices among available options resulted from changing balances of forces among the political actors and their perceptions of changing public attitudes. During the period investigated the overall pattern can be described as a politicization of immigration policy, which represents an almost complete change compared with the pattern of decision making on immigration in the previous period (from 1962 to 1985). One factor that explains this change was the emergence of new political actors in the party system that challenged the traditional hegemony of the social democratic and conservative parties. A second aspect was an escalating spiral of mainstream politicians chasing the anti-immigrant vote by fuelling widespread but unrealistic fears about uncontrolled mass immigration from Eastern Europe.

In Austria this has led to strengthening the external aspects of control while maintaining the internal control framework established during the 1970s. The safe third country rule for asylum seekers was introduced earlier than elsewhere and interpreted very restrictively. For labour immigration and family reunification a system of annual contingents was introduced that requires application from abroad. Immigration control has also become more explicit with much more detailed legislation and less discretion for the various branches of public administration in interpreting the laws.

At the level of implementation and outcomes the instruments chosen for certain targets often turn out to be ineffective or inefficient. They may be either inadequate for reaching a policy goal or just too costly in relation to their results. Furthermore, constraints on control are also imposed by the rule of law and by constitutional rights of citizens and aliens. Often the courts take an active role in challenging control instruments that had been adopted by legislation or developed in administrative practices. In democratic states immigration control is therefore generally incomplete and leaves many loopholes. Austria is no exception in this regard.

Labour Migration Before 1985

The general development of immigration policies in Austria, as in other European states, started from the internal end-points of migration and has gradually extended control towards the external starting points. Of the five stages of immigration control identified in chapter 1, enforcement of return of economically unproductive migrants was historically the earliest one to be introduced.

Until World War I the emphasis of control over international migration was on exit rather than entry. The late Habsburg monarchy was a major source of emigration to the United States. Immigration into the territory of today's Austrian republic came almost exclusively from the other parts of the empire and profoundly changed the ethnic composition of its capital, Vienna, around the turn of the century. As in seventeenth-century Amsterdam or Paris in the second half of the nineteenth century, the extraordinary flourishing of cultural and intellectual life in Vienna at the turn of the century was accompanied, and partly caused, by a great immigration. Internal migration within the Austro-Hungarian monarchy was controlled by laws that tied poverty relief to residence in one's municipality of birth (*Heimatrecht*). Migrants living in other municipalities were liable to be deported when they lacked regular income (*Schubgesetz*). The underlying principle has been basically maintained until today and has been applied more vigorously in Austria than in most other Western and Northern European countries of immigration: keeping migrants in a non-permanent status of legal residence allows to enforce deportation when they threaten to become a public charge. Since World War I, after which the major sources of immigration became international, national citizenship operated as a functional equivalent for the older *Heimatrecht* in this regard.

The fourth stage, control over admission of migrants to employment, was added in 1925 during a period of rising unemployment in order to severe traditional migration chains with Czechoslovakia and Germany. The so-called Law for the Protection of Native Workers (*Inlandarbeiter-schutzgesetz*) established a system of work permits for foreign citizens that has existed in various forms ever since (Pelz, 1994). Compared with the strong emphasis on these forms of internal control, the instruments of control over admission to the territory and initial settlement were much less developed until very recently. After World War II the NS-system of work permits introduced by the *Anschluß* of 1938 continued to operate until 1975. This was a system of matching permits for the Austrian employer and the immigrant worker with the requirement that the employer had to prove that no native labour supply was available for the specific job.

During the late 1950s employers began to demand a more flexible policy that would allow them to recruit labour from abroad. In 1961 trade unions reluctantly agreed to a system of yearly guest-worker contingents in exchange for a strengthening of their involvement in national economic policy on wages and price control (Matuschek, 1985: 163–7; Wimmer, 1986a: 7). As long as a contingent was not exhausted there was no individual investigation of whether a native worker would have been available for a job. The two trade union conditions attached to this were, first, that guest-workers could only be employed at the same wage and working conditions as Austrian workers and, second, that foreign labourers should generally be rotated after a year and would have to be dismissed before Austrians lost their jobs.

During the following period, Austria developed a system of active recruitment of labour, which, in our understanding, is a form of proactive external immigration control that regulates and selects a wanted inflow by direct activity in the country of origin. Recruitment contracts were signed with Spain (1962), Turkey (1964) and Yugoslavia (1965) of which only the latter two became effective. This started a process of chain migration that has shaped the overall composition of today's immigrant population. In March 1997, 59 per cent of all non EU foreign workers were from former Yugoslavia and 20 per cent (the second largest group) came from Turkey. The division of tasks between organized labour and employers' associations was that the former would be represented in agencies ensuring internal control over admission to, and conditions of, employment, whereas the Federal Chamber of Commerce organized the external operation and set up recruitment offices in the countries of origin.

Control over admission to the territory was no real concern during the period of guest-worker recruitment. Migrants would be carefully selected before they came and would be exchanged for new ones after a short period of employment. The system was meant to be very different from the admission of immigrants. Control of entry at borders and of legal residence status was not considered as an independent policy instrument but rather as a corollary of employment policy. However, when demand for foreign labour increased strongly in the late 1960s, two key control elements failed: recruitment switched from formal to informal channels and temporary employment became permanent (Parnreiter, 1994: 124). Employers asked their migrant workers to bring in family members and friends. These new migrants came as tourists. During the economic boom years employment permits were issued generously and enabled them to regularize their residence status. Employers were also not willing to replace their migrant workers with new ones who would need new training for the job. Migrants themselves mostly failed in achieving short-term savings targets and prolonged their stay abroad. Several factors converged thus to stimulate family reunification: relatively stable employment, delayed plans for return, additional demand for foreign labour with an increasing share of jobs for women (in the textile industry and services), and informal recruitment. Family reunification and the birth of a second generation in Austria reinforced *de facto* permanent settlement (although the myth of return was still kept alive among the vast majority of migrants). The micro-rationality of employers and migrants had thus effectively overtaken the macro-regulation of the guest-worker system. Within a few years Austria had gone from almost no immigration over the organized import of foreign workers to virtually uncontrolled chain migration and permanent settlement. Much the same sequences of events can be found in several European countries, yet the pace of acceleration is somewhat quicker in Austria. Foreign employment rose from 16,200 foreign workers or 0.7 per cent of total employment in 1961 to 111,700 (4.7 per cent) in 1970 and 226,800 (8.7 per cent) in 1973 (Biffl, 1996: Table 4.2). The new control system that emerged from the economic crisis of 1973/74 also had its peculiarities. As elsewhere, formal recruitment was stopped and measures were taken to prevent further spontaneous inflows. Austria went, however, further than other Western receiving states in even reversing previous immigration. In 1974–76 the number of foreign workers employed was reduced by 23 per cent while the foreign population shrank by 12 per cent. In a second wave 1982–84 the equivalent figures were 19 per cent and 10 per cent.

The second surprising aspect is the belated and apparently inadequate adaptation of the legal control instruments. A new law on the employment of foreigners (*Ausländerbeschäftigungsgesetz*, AuslBG) came into force only on 1 January 1976 and basically reinforced the control elements of the system that had been developed during the period of guest-worker recruitment. The core provision of the law is that foreign workers can only be employed if the situation and development of the labour market and important public and national economic interests permit this. Within industrial branch contingents agreed upon by the social partners (namely workers' and employers' organizations) labour exchange offices did not have to apply this requirement to individual cases. Austrian employers had to acquire an employment permit for a specified job offered to a foreign worker. This permit was normally valid for one year and could be renewed. Only after eight years of nearly uninterrupted employment could foreigners themselves obtain an exemption permit that entitled them to change their employment.

Even more surprising is the fact that the regulation of legal residence and deportation (the Law on Policing Aliens, *Fremdenpolizeigesetz*) was never amended between 1954 and 1987. Neither the recruitment of guest-workers, nor the subsequent chain migration and permanent settlement were explicitly reflected in the legal regulations of entry and residence of foreigners. Over this whole period the locus of immigration control was the Austrian labour market and foreigners were merely seen as the most flexible element of supply in this market. Territorial admission and residence followed from admission to employment rather than the other way round. A status of permanent residence could be obtained only under very difficult and largely discretionary criteria and did not exempt from the requirement of yearly renewable employment permits, tying the foreign workers to a particular job which they could hardly risk to give up or change. A control policy that had been tailored for recruited and rotating guest-workers was thus kept in place and applied to permanently settled migrants. With this policy it was easier to reduce the numbers of foreign workers in times of economic downturn, which was the major goal of trade unions. However, there were also unintended side-effects. Blocked mobility and insecure legal status of migrants increased the general labour market segmentation between jobs for natives and immigrants and trade unions were unable to maintain wage levels and working conditions in the immigrant segment. The trade unions were caught in a dilemma. Their strong control power over supply of foreign labour was an important bargaining chip in negotiations between the social partners. As there was, at the time, no effective overall control system for immigration, unions could only regulate labour supply by restrictive internal controls (the system of employment permits) which turned immigrants into a highly vulnerable and dependent work force. This counteracted the general goal of the unions of preventing a downgrading of labour conditions and wages in sectors with high shares of immigrants (Bauböck/Wimmer, 1988). The overall effect of this control regime has been characterized by August Gächter as 'forced complementarity' between native and immigrant workers (Gächter 1995a). In order to prevent the much-dreaded substitution of foreign for native labour, legal mechanisms were used to confine immigrants permanently to a secondary labour market segment. A new control regime with a much stronger emphasis on external restrictions and regulation of admission was only established in 1993 and even then it did not replace the guest-worker control of the *AuslBG* but was added to it as a first gate to be passed before admission to the labour market.

Constructing an Austrian Nation

Among Western European countries Austria probably has been the most obvious case of a country being exposed to large refugee flows rather than taking them in actively or opening itself for free entry of co-ethnic groups. As in labour immigration this has pushed control strongly towards the internal side. With regard to refugees the situation is, however, more paradoxical. Although they were generally unwelcome as immigrants, defining itself as a country of first asylum became an important feature of Austria's national identity after 1955.

During the inter-war republic, Austrian politics had not succeeded in developing a widely shared and stable national identity. According to a well-known quote, 'Austria was the rest', the territory that had remained after the break-up of the Habsburg empire. In contrast with other empires, there was no national identity of the dominant core that a republican successor state could have adopted (as in Germany) or developed (as in Turkey). Whatever had been specifically Austrian had been linked to a supranational monarchy, and nationalism among the dominant core had always been German rather than of an independent Austrian kind. The

First Republic was generally seen as having been imposed by the victorious allies and unification with Germany was the goal not only of the German nationalist camp but also of Social Democrats and, to a somewhat lesser degree, of Catholic Conservatives. The dominant view was that Austria would not be viable as an independent state because it was too small and economically weak, but also because the national identity of its population naturally linked it to Germany. This birth trauma had severe impacts on citizenship, immigration, refugee and minority policies. Austria's multi-ethnic past never became a positive element of its national identity. Groups whose ethnic origins lay in the peripheries of the Empire could not be seen as welcome immigrants. Those who formed ethnic minorities in the territory of the republic were exposed to assimilation pressure or to suspicions of disloyalty.

In the negotiations of the St Germain Peace Treaty the Austrian delegation pressed successfully for a clause that subjects of the Monarchy, whose *Heimatrecht* (generally their municipality of birth) lay outside the territory of the new republic would be entitled to opt for Austrian citizenship only 'if they were different in race and language from the majority of the population there' and 'if according to their race and language they belonged to the German majority of the population in Austria' (Grandner, 1995). This rule ensured, on the one hand, that German speaking civil servants or entrepreneurs who had moved to the periphery of the monarchy were able to gain admission and citizenship in Austria. On the other hand, it made ineligible a huge number of pre-war immigrants and wartime refugees who had arrived in the Austrian territories during the late years of the monarchy. The language condition was specifically targeted against the largest linguistic minority, Czechs and Slovaks living in Vienna; the racial criteria intended to keep out Jewish refugees who spoke German or Yiddish. Whereas the Czech and Slovak minority was also welcome in their new republic and quickly decreased under the combined effects of push and pull, the Jewish population had no place to go. Virulent anti-Semitism, which had a long tradition in Austria anyway, was reinforced by this policy of declaring a large group of Jews to be racially different and undesirable aliens.

An Austrian nation – in the sense of widely shared collective identity associated with a given state – only emerged from the experience with Nazism, but its birth in 1945 was marked by another ambiguity. On the one hand, the two major political camps (Christian Democrats and Social Democrats) finally committed themselves to break with their past ambivalent attitudes towards Austrian nationhood and with the politics of confrontation that had escalated into civil war in 1934. On the other hand, the new identity was projected into the recent past in order to exculpate Austria as a nation from involvement in the crimes of the Nazi regime. According to the official formula, Austria was Hitler's first victim. One consequence of these circumstances of birth for Austrian nationhood was a strong emphasis on reconstructing continuity with the First Republic. In contrast with Germany, the new republic did not give itself a new constitution but reinstated the one of 1929 (which had already included some authoritarian elements). With political aspirations for unification discredited, the ethnic content of nationhood could no longer be defined explicitly as German, but it also did not embrace the ethnic diversity of Austria's past and continued to exclude non-German groups. There are no Czech-Austrians or other hyphenated identities among the large parts of the population who are descendants of immigrants from before the war. Whereas German national identity after 1948 had been characterized by the uneasy combination of ethnic and a republican elements (both enshrined in the Basic Law), Austria had to cope with a deficit on both dimensions. Positive elements of self-identification were only added in 1955 when permanent neutrality was established in conjunction with full sovereignty granted by the Vienna State Treaty. During the 1970s an expanding welfare state became the final confirmation of Austrian nationhood. Only then did opinion polls begin to show strong increases in approval rates for an Austrian national identity. The long-term trends of refugee admittance are related to these three features of Austrian nationhood. As a rather crude summary of the following analysis one could say that what I have called the double deficit explains a continuation of ethnic exclusion; neutrality in the Cold War explains the initially welcoming attitude towards refugees from Communism; and the neo-corporatist welfare state explains why admission and control policies were so strongly shaped by labour market conditions.

Refugee Admission Before 1985

In the immediate post-war era there were two large groups of refugees: DPs (displaced persons, including prisoners of war, workers brought in by the NS-regime from Eastern Europe to perform forced labour and Jewish survivors of the Holocaust) and ethnic Germans from Central and Eastern Europe expelled from their ancient settlements after the war. A third group were Jews who fled from new pogroms in Eastern Europe like the one in the Polish town Kielce in 1947. The Allied Powers were in charge of accommodating these refugees with the Austrian government bearing the costs for maintaining the camps. Initially both groups were seen as a burden for the collapsed economy and the Austrian government did not want to accept responsibility for their plight. Ethnic Germans remained stuck in Austria when camps in Germany could no longer take in more. However, from the very beginning, the Austrian government pressed the Allied authorities to remove specifically the non-German DPs from the territory of the republic (Stieber, 1995). The ethnic Germans were eventually accepted as permanent settlers and provided a welcome workforce for reconstructing the economy during the early 1950s. After 1954 they could opt for Austrian citizenship by declaration. Of more than 1 million who had been temporarily admitted into Austria about 530,000 stayed and were eventually naturalized and fully assimilated (Faßmann and Münz, 1995: 34).

Table 4.1 Austria: Foreign Resident Population by Citizenship 1981–1997

Citizenship	1981	%	1991	%	1995	%	1997	%
Germany	40,987	14.1	57,310	11.1	60,886	8.0	62,639	8.4
Other European Union citizens	15,577	5.3	20,220	3.9	30,500	4.0	31,090	4.2
EFTA citizens	5,521	1.9	7,599	1.5	–		–	
Turkey	59,900	20.6	118,579	22.9	143,533	18.9	140,841	19.3
Former Yugoslavia	125.890	43.2	197,886	38.2	337,180	44.5	331,536	44.6
All other former communist countries	12,773	4.4	65,281	12.6	–		–	
thereof								
Romania	*1,253*	*0.4*	*18,536*	*3.5*	–		–	
Poland	*5,911*	*2.0*	*18,321*	*3.5*	–		–	
Former CSFR	*2,032*	*0.7*	*11,318*	*2.2*	–		–	
Hungary	*2,526*	*0.9*	*10,556*	*2.0*	–		–	
Other countries	30,800	10.5	50,815	9.8	–		–	
Total	291,448	100	517,690	100	758,498	100	743,712	100

Source: Perchinig 1996, p. 11, calculated from diverse statistical sources, Central Statistical Office.

For the next waves of refugees, admission policies were determined by Austria's post-war position as a front state between the two military blocks. Permanent neutrality, which was originally a price to be paid for the restoration of full national sovereignty during the Cold War, became one of the cherished symbols of national identity. Yet neutrality never meant a policy of equidistance. While the Soviet Union had to be reassured that Austria would stay neutral in case of military conflict, the Western camp had to be shown that Austria's ideological alignment and domestic political and economic systems were unambiguously Western. Successive flows of refugees from Central Eastern European countries were occasions to demonstrate how well Austrian politics could perform this tightrope act. Austria was the first country of the Free West where they received shelter and protection. At the same time the traditional understanding of the right to asylum in international law ensured that the Soviet Union could not interpret the admission of refugees from its zone of influence as a hostile act. Refugees from the East thus visibly confirmed Austria's new role in international politics. During the Cold War, refugees from communism were welcome in most Western states because they seemed to share the same basic values of democracy and liberty. There was at this time an additional awareness that Austria itself might have only narrowly escaped the fate of Soviet occupation. Although being clearly non-nationals in ethnic terms, these refugees were thus perceived as something like close relatives who deserved to be admitted for reasons of national identity (Walzer, 1983: 41, 49).

These factors made for strong popular sympathies which showed in an extraordinary way after the smashing of the Hungarian revolution when hundreds of thousands came running over the border. Following a recommendation by the UN general assembly the Austrian minister of the interior decided to grant every Hungarian emigrant refugee status according to the newly adopted Geneva Refugee Convention (GRC) of 1955. There was thus virtually no control or individual screening. The law regulating the determination of refugee status was adopted much later in 1968 and had to pass its first test in the Czechoslovak crisis. In this case instructions were that refugees would have to apply individually for asylum but should be granted Convention refugee status without individual examination of their motives. Only a few of them used this opportunity. On the one hand, the border remained open until October 1969 and many wanted to wait for further developments before deciding to emigrate for good. On the other hand, during a time of guest-worker recruitment, Czechs and Slovaks who were often well qualified had good prospects to find employment and secure residence in Austria without refugee status. This was different for Poles who came in 1981/1982 during the second wave of reduction of employment of foreigners. They were already scrutinized individually for their reasons of emigration although the criteria for recognition were then interpreted quite generously compared with contemporary standards.

In popular perception the gradual tightening of refugee admission was primarily in response to a change in the motives of refugees. The Hungarians were perceived as heroes of resistance against Stalinism, Czechoslovaks (especially the later refugees of Charta 1977) as victims of political persecution; Poles were already frequently seen as economic rather than political refugees and Romanians in 1990 were finally stereotyped as phoney asylum seekers. However, each of these interpretations ignores some important facts. First, all groups of refugees from communist countries, including the Hungarian ones had mixed political and economic motives. Second, the motives of Austrian admission policy were similarly mixed; refugees became less welcome when there was less economic need for additional labour and when the Cold War confrontation attenuated. Third, and most importantly, Austria's willingness to admit refugees correlated strongly with the probability that they would eventually leave the country and settle at other destinations. This is the hidden truth in the frequently repeated assertion that 'Austria is a country of asylum but not a country of immigration'. Refugee transit made for a highly visible demonstration effect of Austria's asylum policy at a relatively low price, but the rates of transit varied strongly between groups. The highest rate (close to 100 per cent) was achieved among some 250,000 Jewish emigrants from the Soviet Union between 1973 and 1989, who were put up in Austrian camps before they went on to the United States or Israel. For the other Eastern European refugees the percentages of transit to overseas destinations became gradually lower from one crisis to the next. During the Polish events there were first indications that the USA and Canada wanted to limit the numbers admitted to their countries for settlement. Refugees from Eastern Europe were generally only welcome in Austria if they could be seen as non-immigrants. Below the surface the exclusionary effects of Austria's national identity continued even during the period of rather open admission when it built up its reputation as a country of asylum.

The New Alignment of Political Forces After 1986

During the period investigated in this book immigration patterns and immigration policy have changed dramatically in Austria. From 1987 until 1995 the number of foreign residents in Austria has more than doubled (from 326,000 to 723,500). The share of foreign citizens in the total population is now 9 per cent but the stock of immigrants, residents born abroad, is estimated at 16 per cent (Faßmann and Münz, 1995: 9). For the period from 1990 to 1993 the Central Statistical Office calculated an average net immigration of 80,500 per year. This represents a yearly per capita immigration of more than 1 per cent. Policies have changed alongside. Austria was one of the first countries in Europe to adopt a tough new asylum law and (simultaneously with Italy) a quota system for immigration. Both kinds of changes are normally explained by the fall of the Iron Curtain and the spectre of East–West mass migration. However, as I will try to show, this is a quite superficial explanation. It is at several points at odds with the sequence of events. First, foundations of the new policy were already laid before 1989. Second, the composition of the new immigrants does not reflect the expected sudden shift towards Eastern European origins.

The most important changes were caused by domestic politics. For forty years the Second Republic had a tripartite system with Social Democrats (SPÖ) and the conservative Peoples' Party (ÖVP) as the two big parties forming governments. The only stable parliamentary opposition was formed by the Freedom Party (FPÖ), which had emerged from the old German nationalist camp. Until 1966 government was held by grand coalitions, from 1966 to 1970 there was a brief intermezzo with a single party government by the ÖVP. From 1970 to 1983 the Social Democrats ruled alone. When they lost their absolute majority they took the FPÖ as a junior partner into their government. All three parties had integrated some of the broad Nazi following in Austria but the FPÖ most explicitly spoke for this group. At the same time, the FPÖ also claimed liberal credentials dating back to 1848. In 1970 Bruno Kreisky's first SP minority government survived only thanks to toleration by the FPÖ. Since this incident Kreisky pursued a strategy of strengthening the FPÖ in order to weaken the ÖVP as the SP's major rival, to split the 'bourgeois camp' and to increase the SP options of potential coalition partners. This latter strategy depended on the liberal current gaining the upper hand within the FPÖ leadership. In 1984 when the SP lost its absolute majority, the SP–FP coalition materialized. This led to a rapid decline of the FPÖ whose leadership was seen to abandon its traditional anti-socialist and German nationalist stance. At the 1986 FP party congress, the young and charismatic Jörg Haider staged a rebellion and took over the party on a right populist platform. As a consequence the SPÖ terminated the coalition agreement with the FPÖ and initiated general elections from which a new grand coalition under SP leadership emerged, which has ruled ever since.

One of the major traditional complaints of the FPÖ had been that they were not represented in the Austrian system of social partnership, which effectively secured peaceful co-operation between unions and employers but also worked as a machine for the distribution of political spoils to party functionaries and ordinary members. In 1986 Haider turned this exclusion into a trump by campaigning against the 'old parties' and their 'corrupt system'. As argued above, the social partners were clearly the dominant political actors in control over labour immigration, both by setting numerical targets and in administrative control over implementation. The closed forums of social partnership ensured that labour migration could never become a hot political issue. Furthermore, the two dominant parties had to some extent conflicting interests. The Social Democrats found themselves torn between a strongly restrictive position pushed by trade unions and traditional concerns about workers' solidarity across lines of nationality. The People's Party was even more obviously split between industrialists in favour of reducing state control over labour import and conservative themes of preserving Austrian culture and nationhood against the inflow of foreign citizens. No major organization affiliated to one of the big parties could therefore risk mobilizing publicly for its specific stance without alienating others in its own camp. This explains the remarkable stability of the legal and policy framework for labour migration control from 1961 to 1986. After Haider's take over, the FPÖ had no similar internal divisions or constraints and could openly play the anti-foreigner card in the political game.

At the same time, the party landscape also changed on the left side of the spectrum. Born from two successful campaigns against a nuclear and a hydroelectric power plant (in 1978 and 1984 respectively) the Green Alternative List managed to achieve eight seats in the national elections of November 1986, ending the traditional three-party composition of the Austrian parliament. As a new-born party the Green Alternatives had obviously also not been integrated into the system of social partnership. Moreover, the two successful campaigns were won against virtually unanimous resistance among the social partners who at that time saw ecological reform as diametrically opposed to the interests of workers and industrialists alike.

Given these starting points it is prima facie astonishing to see that both the FPÖ and the Greens were initially cautious in raising the issue of migration. The explanation is probably that the Green Party was then still struggling to win over the more conservative wing of the ecological movement and issues like immigration were seen as divisive in this regard. At the other end of the party spectrum, the FPÖ wanted to avoid being stigmatized as the rallying ground of old Nazis and young racists and used mainly coded messages – which were, however, well understood –

to shore up its profile as the major anti-immigrant force. Nonetheless, this change in domestic politics set a stage where immigration issues would become highly visible. They were increasingly played out in the open forums of electoral and media campaigns and served as a vehicle for symbolic politics.

While this potential of 'non-aligned parties' was emerging, the first impulse for reform of the Austrian immigration control framework did not come from politics, but from the judiciary. In 1985 the Constitutional Supreme Court annulled provisions in the *Fremdenpolizeigesetz* concerning the 'prohibition of residence' which made a foreign citizen not only liable to deportation but also denied her or him re-entry for a long or indefinite time. The Court found the law in violation of Article 8 of the European Convention on Human Rights (protecting private and family life) because the provisions were not sufficiently specific and gave administrative authorities wide discretion. After failed attempts to amend the law without changing the substance of the Article, a 1987 amendment finally required that public interests in a residence prohibition had to outweigh private interests of the foreigner (not to be separated from his or her family for example). The Constitutional and Administrative Supreme Courts have been quite active ever since, because lawyers and NGOs representing refugees and immigrants increasingly realized that carrying appeals to the highest level was one of the more effective (although slow) means of challenging government policies in this area. Judicial review has thus become an important part of the overall system of legislation on immigration control. The position taken by the Supreme Courts has, however, by no means always followed human rights concerns and the amendments caused by its decisions have rarely affected the substance of a law. One important limitation for judicial activism with regard to laws concerning immigrants is due to the fact that the Austrian constitution does not grant equality before the law to foreigners and citizens alike. This has prevented Court intervention in the many areas of legal discrimination against alien residents with regard to civil liberties and social welfare provisions. A second limitation emerged with the new legislation of 1991–93. The immigration and asylum laws caused an unprecedented flood of complaints, which almost paralysed the Supreme Courts. Although the percentage of eventually successful complaints was high, the limited capacities of the Courts created a backlog so that decisions took so long that they were often no longer relevant for the individual cases.

The Initial Reform Impetus

The challenge to the *Fremdenpolizeigesetz* triggered indirectly a quite important shift of responsibility within the government. Before 1987 the division of tasks was that the Ministry of the Interior dealt with refugee policy while the Ministry of Social Affairs was in charge of controlling labour immigration, with the Ministry of the Interior playing a subsidiary role in this area. The issuing of residence permits had been strongly tied to employment permits. It had not been used as a means to control new immigration but rather to enforce return of established foreigners in case of loss of employment or income. The incumbent Minister of the Interior Karl Blecha saw the challenge raised by the Court as an opportunity to strengthen his hand and to redraw the balance between the branches of administration. In 1987 he announced a 'total reform of laws on foreigners' (including the Employment of Foreigners Act) and convened several expert meetings on the matter. Although this attempt foundered it paved the way for a more decisive initiative by his successor Franz Löschnak and it contributed to opening the debate for the intervention of expert opinion outside the closed forums of social partnership.

This window of opportunity widened in 1988 when the government became seriously concerned about the long-term consequences of population development and organized an expert meeting on this topic. Declining fertility rates and an ageing population with a low retirement age would increase the burdens of intergenerational redistribution in the social insurance system dramatically. Problems were especially acute in Vienna, which, in addition to an ageing population, had also suffered an absolute decline of inhabitants. Some demographers propagated a 'compensatory immigration policy' with the goal of stabilizing population numbers and bringing in young and economically active groups (Faßmann and Münz, 1995). In this logic, what was needed was immigrants rather than guest-workers and their numbers were to be determined not only by short-term business cycles but by the aim of long-term continuity. All this led quite naturally to the proposal of introducing relatively stable immigration targets by setting yearly contingents for gross immigration. Such reform proposals were not primarily driven by humanitarian concerns about the rights of foreigners, but redefined the national interest to include immigrants rather than merely temporary workers. However, within this framework it appeared possible to reconcile interests of the receiving country with those of immigrants for more legal security and equal rights.

Such a reform was especially unwelcome to trade unionists who feared a loss of control. Nevertheless, under the new conditions even the rigid control system of the *AuslBG* had to be adapted by a series of amendments. The pattern of development was one of parallel rather than integrated reform in the areas of territorial admission and of control over employment with the latter system retaining its basic features. When the immigration contingent system was introduced in 1993 it left a previously established employment quota in place as a second level of control. Cautious liberalization in the *AuslBG* involved easier access to an 'exemption permit'. In 1988 foreign youth who had grown up in Austria were granted exemption permits. A 1990 amendment brought a reduction of the required period of previous employment to five years and a prolongation of the validity of the permit to five years. Simultaneously a new category of 'work permits' was introduced as an intermediary stage between employment permit and exemption permit. Work permits can be obtained after one year of continuous employment and they entitle foreigners to change their jobs within a province or economic branch. Yet prolongation of both work permits and exemption permits remains conditional upon continued employment. Before naturalization, immigrants are thus never finally released from labour market control. Long-term unemployment implies that they will lose their rights of mobility and fall again back to the initial stage of employment permits for new entrants. Because of a limitation on their entitlements to unemployment benefits the further consequence may be that even immigrants who have lived and worked in the country for years face the threat of losing their residence permit for economic reasons.

The 1990 amendment also introduced a new instrument of control: federal and provincial quotas that limited the share of foreigners in the total workforce. The federal limit was initially set at 10 per cent and later lowered to 9 per cent and finally 8 per cent with exceptions for foreign managers, youths and Bosnian war refugees. This regulatory instrument emphasizes once more the basic idea of the control system: it does not limit the new inflow of immigrant workers but the stock of workers with foreign citizenship. This whole group is still seen as a flexible supply in the labour market subject to a system of permits issued by the state. In times of crisis a lowering of their numbers is meant to reduce the supply pressure in the labour market. This is a flawed logic because the stock of foreign workers depends not only on immigration but also on birth rates and naturalization rates. When the quota is reduced to the actual share of foreign workers the labour exchange offices are not allowed to issue new employment permits. This means not only that there will be no more new labour migration but that legal residents are excluded from legal employment. As better status in the permit system depends on previous employment rather than on residence, new entrants into the labour market or persons with an interrupted work career will then be excluded. The groups hardest hit by this policy are women and youths who have not spent sufficient time in Austrian schools.

Integration Into a European Framework for Immigration Control

Not only the domestic line-up of forces but also the international conditions for immigration control had already changed in significant ways before 1989. Austria's westward integration into the European Union framework began to take shape before the opening of its Eastern borders. Since 1987 the Austrian Ministry of the Interior co-operated with the Schengen group in the framework of the group's consultation mechanism (Juen et al. 1996). The Ministry had already participated as an observer at the meetings of the TREVI groups. The intergovernmental co-operation in immigration and asylum matters in the framework of the Third Pillar of the Maastricht Treaty meant that Austria could participate in relevant policy forums even before it became a member of the European Union.

In the 1990s, when its new system of immigration was in place, the Austrian government saw itself as a precursor of a European immigration control system rather than as a latecomer that had to adapt to Western European standards. In 1991 Austria implemented in its new legislation on asylum core principles of the 1990 Dublin Convention. In 1993 a special commissioner of the government for refugee and migration affairs, Willibald Pahr, openly stated that Austria had set an example for Europe: 'I think we are the first country in Europe which has embedded a comprehensive migration policy in its legal order' (quoted in Davy and Gächter, 1993: 155, author's translation). In the same year the Minister of the Interior drafted a European Migration Convention that generalized the principles of the new Austrian legislation as a guideline for other states while also suggesting a system of burden sharing for the admission of war refugees (see Löschnak 1993: 125–44). This initiative did not get off the ground. The other partners in the European Union wanted to focus harmonization on asylum procedures and on border controls. With regard to the latter task Austria has long been seen as being rather inefficient in controlling its eastern border. In April 1995 Austria formally joined the Schengen Accord but full membership was delayed until 1 December 1997 and Austria was not obliged to abolish land border controls with Schengen neighbours until 1 April 1998. For Austria this implies the dilemma that it has to strengthen its border controls in the east and north in the short run while in the long run this may become a futile investment when Central Eastern European countries join the Union.

With eastern enlargement of the Union all of Austria's borders would become internal ones within the EU. However, when new members join the Union long transition periods will probably be negotiated for each individual country before abolishing borders. The EU would then again have an inner core with free movement (and a common currency) and an eastern periphery in charge of controlling external borders but still subject to control by other member states at the internal borders.

Austria has mixed interests in this regard. Profiting from free movement in the whole territory of the Union without being exposed to external migration pressure at land borders would obviously be a desirable position for Austria. This is one reason why relations with the 'Višegrad group' of states have ranked high on the Austrian immigration policy agenda. Austria was actively involved in building a multilateral framework for co-operation with the European Union in matters of asylum and immigration policy. The target is to transform these states into a 'buffer zone' (Wallace, et al. 1995) where migration flows heading westwards can be controlled and stopped. One major control instrument needed to achieve this purpose is readmission agreements for irregular immigrants and rejected asylum seekers that Austria has negotiated with all neighbouring countries. What these states expect to get in exchange from Austria is not so much economic assistance but a reliable promoter of their interests in the European Union. Recently, Austria has turned into a more reluctant neighbour. There are clear indications that the Austrian government will propose a rather long transition period before new members are granted freedom of movement and settlement for their citizens within the Union. Although, as long as the Eastern borders do not fall, Austria will have to carry the burden of controlling them for the other states in the Union; the interest in controlling access to its own territory and labour market from the East will prevail in the short run.

Joining first the European Economic Area (EEA) and then, on 1 January 1995, the European Union thus had important indirect consequences for the regulation of immigration from Eastern Europe. The direct impact of European Union membership on domestic regulation of immigration was a relatively minor one. A number of laws had to be amended to exempt European Union citizens from the far-reaching restrictions to which foreigner citizens are subjected with regard to entry, residence, employment, social welfare entitlements, access to the civil service and local voting rights. As in other European states, this was not used as an opportunity to revise some of the existing legal discriminations against foreigners, but led to constructing a three-tier structure of citizenship with native citizens enjoying all rights, EU citizens excluded from a few of them (like the franchise in parliamentary elections but also an unconditional right to residence), and third country nationals remaining subjected to a bundle of discriminatory rules whose content and severity varies greatly between the member states of the Union.

The strongest internal impact so far has been that of the Turkish association treaty with the European Union. After Austria's full membership there had been controversy about whether this Treaty was automatically and immediately applicable (see Juen et al., 1996). Some provisions of the Treaty would exempt Turkish citizens from restrictions on their employment and residence. In 1996 two decisions by the Administrative Supreme Court affirmed the immediate applicability of the Treaty, which contradicted the interpretation of the Ministry of Labour and Social Affairs that Austria's parliament must first formally ratify the Treaty. After some initial resistance and tinkering with ad hoc provisions the legal provisions on residence and employment permits have been finally adapted in 1997. Turkish citizens have now gained special rights concerning the prolongation of employment and work permits, and receive exemption permits and permanent residence permits earlier than other groups of immigrants. The three-tier structure has thus been further broken down into four categories of legal status attached to nationality. As Turkish citizens form the second-largest group of immigrants it might seem difficult to continue to apply the current restrictions to immigrants from former Yugoslavia or Eastern European states. However, norms of equal treatment between various groups of third country nationals, play a minor role compared to the overriding political determination to maintain established restrictions in all respects that are not plainly incompatible with legal norms of the European Union.

This same target of preserving the maximum scope for national policy-making with regard to internal control compatible with supranational and international legal obligations also explains why Austria has not signed or ratified the major European and international conventions concerning the legal protection of migrant workers and their families (ILO 1975 convention 143 and Council of Europe 1977 Convention on the Legal Status of Migrant Workers).

The 'Immigration Crisis'

The substantial increase in Austria's foreign population in the early 1990s was not the result of the widely expected great migration from Eastern

Europe after the fall of the Iron Curtain. It had two major sources both of which were linked to the fall of communist regimes but did not generate a big inflow of economic opportunity seekers from these countries. One source was the pull factor of a sustained economic conjuncture with a real economic growth of 4.5 per cent in 1990 and a boom in export-oriented industry and in construction (which traditionally employs many immigrants). To a substantial degree this conjuncture was a windfall benefit of German unification. Under these conditions employers activated the established migration chains rather than looking for new recruitment from Eastern Europe – or from European Union member states, which at that time still were not exempted from admission control. When the conjuncture petered out in 1993 there were simply less opportunities for new employment. This explains why the share of workers from the Czech Republic, Slovakia, Hungary and Poland has risen only very slowly to 10 per cent in 1995 and has remained stable at this level since then (BMAS, 1997). There are some indications that a major part of the big increase in foreign employment in 1990 and 1991 may actually not have resulted from new immigration but from access to the labour market for immigrants and their families who had already been in the country but could not find legal employment before the boom (Gächter, 1998). The second major flow was push related, but not driven by economic motives. These were war refugees from former Yugoslavia for whom Austria became a primary destination for three reasons: first, as a neighbouring state; second, as a former recruiting country whose largest contingent of immigrants came from the same area; and third, as a state whose foreign policy had raised expectations by favouring an early recognition of Slovenia's, Croatia's and Bosnia's independence and whose media and NGOs had been very active in organizing humanitarian aid.

There is a strange discrepancy between the substantial changes in Austria's immigrant and refugee population and the simultaneous change in the control policy that evolved from a public discourse focusing on largely imaginary threats coming from the east. The first visible effect of the opening of the eastern border was, however, not at all experienced as a threat. During the summer of 1989 about 45,000 GDR emigrants came over the Hungarian border and went into the Federal Republic of Germany. In 1989 these people symbolized a new era when communist regimes would no longer be willing or able to impede their citizen's free movement. Seen in retrospect they were really the last group of refugees or emigrants who were welcome because they contributed perfectly to the role Austria had assumed during the Cold War. The opening of the border with Hungary and later with Czechoslovakia produced a

Table 4.2 Foreign Labour in Austria by Citizenship 1994–97

Citizenship	1994	%	1995	%	1996	%	1997	%
EEA	19,009	6.6	21,476	7.2	23,492	7.9	25,063	8.4
ex-Yugoslavia	141,952	49.5	147,703	49.7	147,888	49.6	147,228	49.5
Turkey	53,866	18.8	54,733	18.4	53,570	18.0	52,803	17.7
Poland	11,168	3.8	11,186	3.8	10,986	3.7	10,893	3.7
Hungary	9,316	3.2	9,423	3.2	9,264	3.1	9,171	3.1
Rumania	9,576	3.3	9,575	3.2	9,309	3.1	9,142	3.1
Former CSFR	10,640	3.7	10,455	3.5	10,056	3.4	9,661	3.2
Switzerland	852	0.3	872	0.3	931	0.3	954	0.3
other states	30,464	10.6	31,959	10.7	32,512	10.9	32,724	11.0
Total	286,843	100.0	297,382	100.0	298,008	100.0	297,639	100.0
*all foreign citizens**	290,288		300,328		300,271		298,797	

Source: Hauptverband der Sozialversicherungsträger.
* The last row includes recipients of maternity or paternity leaf payments not counted by citizenship.

similar short-lived euphoria when people walked over what used to be the Iron Curtain.

This mood changed dramatically after the Romanian uprising when a growing number of refugees, many of whom were Romanies, came via Hungary to ask for asylum in Austria. Although the instability of the situation in Romania in 1990 and the numerous incidents of ethnic conflict would certainly have justified a thorough individual examination of asylum claims the Romanians were quickly stigmatized collectively as the proto-typical example of bogus asylum seekers. The public perception of the 'immigration crisis' was that economic opportunity seekers from Eastern Europe would use the asylum door to get into the country and benefit from the special privileges of refugees. In fact, the number of asylum seekers in Austria had risen continuously since the improvement of exit opportunities from 1986 onwards. In 1991 it reached 27,306, which was still much lower than the figures during the Hungarian and Polish crises. However, in accordance with wider trends in Western Europe the Austrian government was determined to close this alternative immigration route preventively. In spite of a much more dramatic increase of foreign employment at the same time the asylum problem was therefore given high visibility. Government activity quite deliberately created the impression of a severe crisis that would require a reform of the whole refugee admission system. In March 1990 Kaisersteinbruch, a small village of 260 inhabitants in the Eastern province of Burgenland, became the symbol of the new crisis when 800 male Romanian asylum seekers were assigned accommodation in deserted army barracks. This decision was reversed after the local population and outside supporters staged demonstrations and street blockades. A large percentage of the local population are workers commuting to Vienna and they argued that their wives and their property would not be safe while they had to be away from their homes.

The second sign of an emergency was the decision by the council of ministers on 4 September 1990 to mobilize the army for assisting the border and customs police 'in order to prevent the increase of numbers of economic refugees and in order to noticeably reduce the problems . . . occurring in connection with illegal border crossings' (quoted in Ecker et al. 1992: 23, my translation). Since then regular draftees (rather than only professional soldiers) have patrolled along the green border. They are, however, not allowed to use force and to formally arrest undocumented immigrants. When they detect persons trying to cross they may stop them and call in the border police who then carry on the investigation. This army assistance was meant as a temporary measure but has recently been prolonged. In the European context mobilizing the army is still an extraordinary means of border control. There was a pragmatic reason for this policy in the Austrian case. The eastern border had been effectively controlled from the other side and in 1990 there were thus not enough regular personnel to accomplish the new control tasks. Furthermore, using the army was a much cheaper solution than recruiting a new branch of the police. The administrative logic of this step is therefore not hard to understand. However, the political impact is clearly different. Using soldiers against illegal immigrants has highly symbolic connotations. The army's two tasks are to fight against foreign forces trying to occupy Austrian territory and to assist in cases of disasters and emergencies. The image of a threatening invasion by illegal immigrants combines these two ideas in a fateful way.

The New Asylum Policy

In 1991 the 'asylum crisis' was dealt with in two laws: one on federal assistance for refugees (*Bundesbetreuungsgesetz*) and a new law on determining asylum (*Asylgesetz* 1991). The former regulates access of asylum seekers and recognized refugees to accommodation and financial assistance provided by public authorities. The essential idea is to reduce material incentives for economic immigrants to choose the asylum door by restricting access to these benefits (Rohrböck, 1992: 86). Since then the numbers of assisted asylum seekers have dwindled. The burdens of accommodating refugees have quite explicitly been shifted to religious welfare associations like the Catholic Caritas and to parishes of various denominations. The asylum law introduced as a new core principle the 'third country clause', which enables authorities to deny asylum to those who could have found protection in another country, which they crossed on their way to Austria. In the strict interpretation that was subsequently applied this could include anybody who had come to Austria via land borders as well as persons who had only entered the transit areas of an international airport on a flight to Austria. One of the most controversial provisions of the law was that it did not grant asylum applicants a right of temporary residence until a final decision had been reached. This led to a practice of issuing deportation orders simultaneously with the rejection of a claim in the first instance. Appeals would then have to be pursued from abroad. A substantial number of asylum seekers are, however, not deportable because of the *non-refoulement* clause, because they are undocumented and their citizenship cannot be determined, or because a country of transit will not take them back. In such cases, they are regularly put into detention for deportation from where they have to be released after six months only to be immediately detained again. Of 26,443 asylum seekers and other detainees registered in detention centres between January 1996 and October 1997, 1,682 went on hunger strike, knowing they would be released when their health conditions became critical.

The law also included a clause on undocumented asylum seekers and those from safe countries of origin whose asylum claims could be rejected as manifestly unfounded without further examination. These provisions did not work as intended because many rejected asylum seekers filed appeals and authorities became cautious about issuing decisions without any reference to the merits of the case. Complaints that in the previous system all asylum decisions had been made by authorities within the Ministry of the Interior led to the creation of a new federal office for asylum (*Bundesasylamt*), which dealt with decisions in the first instance while the Ministry remained the authority to decide on appeals. As the new office was staffed with personnel from the Ministry this did not really create the kind of independent administrative or court authority that critics of the system had demanded. Since the law went into force on 1 June 1992, the numbers of asylum seekers have been drastically reduced without a substantial increase in the rate of recognition among the few who could still file an application. There are also few reports that those who had been successfully deterred by the new asylum law have tried subsequently to come in by illegal routes. So this seems to illustrate that concerted state action (in this case a simultaneous strengthening of border controls and restriction of asylum in combination with parallel action by other potential receiving states) can actually stop certain flows, at least for some time.

Still, the new asylum policy was not only criticized as immoral by the Christian, liberal and humanitarian organizations but was also perceived to be partly inefficient in by the authorities implementing it. One reason why the law was unsatisfactory in spite of the declining numbers from the latter point of view was the flood of complaints addressed to the Administrative Supreme Court, which questioned the lawfulness of administrative decisions and practices in this area. A second reason was the fact that nearly all asylum claims were filed from inside Austria rather than at the border. When the asylum office decided, as it generally did, to reject such claims, the aliens police had the task of enforcing deportations. However, deporting applicants is more costly and subject to more legal constraints than rejecting them before they have entered the country. There are two explanations why asylum seekers generally prefer to enter illegally rather than filing their claims at the border. If they think they have a good case to be considered as refugees they may fear that the border police will turn them back as soon as they say the word 'asylum'. If they know that they have no chance of obtaining refugee status they may hope to be tolerated eventually if they cannot be deported. So entering illegally is the only way to avoid a Catch 22 situation. These concerns led to a new asylum law adopted in June 1997. One core intention is to shift the control back towards the borders by establishing new guidelines for first examinations of claims there. A second major change concerns the interpretation of the third country clause, which now permits rejection of asylum applicants if they *can* find protection in another country, rather than if they are presumed to *have already* enjoyed such protection. The past-oriented interpretation under the old law had allowed Austria to push back asylum seekers even if it was well known that the country through which they had come would deport them to their state of origin. The new policy intends to keep the numbers of both asylum seekers and those granted refugee status as low as before while eliminating some of the administrative problems of enforcement and conflicts with general legal principles. Whether these two targets can really be pursued simultaneously is rather doubtful.

The Bosnian Refugees

The main contingent of refugees after 1989 did not come from the countries of the former Soviet Bloc (and would not have come from there even if there had not been the restriction on access to asylum), but from the Croatian and Bosnian war zones. These were refugees to whom reasons listed in the Geneva Refugee Convention (GRC) apparently applied. Most refugees were not just the unfortunate victims of a civil war between rival factions, but had been exposed to persecution that targeted them as members of ethnic or religious groups. It is difficult to think of more obvious instances of well-founded fear of persecution than those created by 'ethnic cleansing', collective rape, forcing soldiers to fight their own ethnic groups, detention of prisoners in concentration camps or deliberate destruction of churches and mosques (see Davy, 1995). Yet, like the German and some other European governments, the Austrian government sought a solution beyond the asylum framework. There were a number of reasons for this.

First, processing such a great number of refugees through the regular procedure for asylum determination would have overburdened a system that had just been reshaped to deal with smaller numbers. The alternative option to adopt the same policy as during the Hungarian or Czech crisis and to grant asylum on *prima facie* grounds for people coming directly from war-stricken areas was ruled out for political reasons as it would have meant abandoning the newly tightened asylum procedure. Second, asylum would have given these refugees a legal status with unlimited residence and free access to the labour market – better than that of regular immigrants. This was seen as undesirable during a period when the government was already trying to restrict labour immigration. Although the GRC does allow for a termination of residence when the situation in refugees' home countries no longer justifies their fear of persecution, the Austrian government was afraid that refugees from former Yugoslavia would settle as immigrants and not go back after the end of hostilities. Third, the UNHCR's main target was to convince European governments to respond quickly to the crisis by admitting large numbers of those already stranded outside their home areas within the former Yugoslavia. To assist a greater number of refugees more effectively was clearly more important than to insist that they had to be treated as refugees according to the Convention. The prospects for a solution of burden-sharing seemed more promising if governments could be seen to act on humanitarian grounds rather under the stronger obligations of international law.

All these reasons favoured granting these refugees temporary protection rather than regular asylum. It can hardly be denied that, given the current policy framework, this allowed for a more flexible and generous admission. However, all the reasons mentioned demonstrate that what drives the policy changes is not the shift in refugees' motives from legitimate fear of persecution to economic opportunity seeking but rather a shift in receiving governments' interests. Austria did have foreign policy reasons to admit war refugees from former Yugoslavia and was an obvious destination because of geographical proximity and established migration chains, but in contrast with people fleeing from communist regimes, these refugees could neither be used symbolically to demonstrate Austria's ideological alignment nor could they be passed on to other states. Temporary protection allowed not only for a maximum flexibility with regard to the duration of residence – it also made it possible to pass on these refugees *internally* from state care to civil society. Admission was premised upon the expectation that Churches, voluntary agencies and private individuals and families would take a large share of the responsibility for assisting and accommodating these refugees.

Refugees from former Yugoslavia came in two waves. From 1 September 1991 to 29 February 1992 about 13,000 refugees from Croatia were admitted temporarily. Many of them were accommodated in private homes. Established immigrants and the Croatian minority in Burgenland were among the most hospitable groups. The concept of temporary protection worked for this group and most of them went back after the end of hostilities. The following and much larger inflow of Bosnians took a very different course. From April 1992 about 80,000 to 90,000 of them were officially registered as war refugees and received some federal assistance; an unknown additional number was accommodated by relatives or friends. The highest number registered in the official programme of assistance at any point in time was 47,500 in June 1993. With the war dragging on and the amount of destruction and forced population transfers increasing, their return became unlikely. Maintaining them in camps on state assistance for years would not only have burdened the federal budget. It would have also increased hostile attitudes among the Austrian population against people living on taxpayers' money instead of becoming self-supportive and would have demotivated refugees to take care of their own future. In contrast with the unwelcome Romanian refugees the government took a much more positive attitude towards Bosnians. The Ministries of the Interior and of Social Affairs agreed to open the labour market for this group. The numbers receiving federal assistance could be reduced to 11,000 in January 1997. The majority has thus transformed its status from war refugees to regular labour immigrants. In March 1997 the current Minister of the Interior started a policy of repatriation that was somewhat less harsh than Germany's policy of forced return. About half of the refugees remaining on assistance were expected to leave. Refugees from the Republica Srpska would be allowed to stay. As a return incentive Bosnians were initially offered some financial aid, which decreased over time so that late departures received no assistance. When the difficulties of organizing repatriation became obvious the initial deadline for the final expiry of temporary permissions was postponed from August 1997 to June 1998.

Contrary to intentions, temporary protection has led to a substantial increase in permanent immigration. Seen in retrospect the whole concept was thus flawed both in its presumption of flight motives different from those laid down in the GRC and in its intention of providing for only short-term admission. Nonetheless, from the perspective of the government's aim of developing a system of immigration controls, the instrument itself cannot be seen as a failure. Defining the Croatian and Bosnian refugees as an exceptional and temporary inflow allowed for a flexible approach while preserving the rigid legal framework for other kinds of immigration from outside the EEA. The two principal channels of admission for labour and family immigration and for asylum could only be restricted by creating ever more complicated and detailed legal regulations. This is partly due to the fact that in constitutional democracies the rule of law exposes immigration control to judicial scrutiny and constraints of human rights. In the process of restricting access, democratic governments therefore generally also reduce their own scope of discretion in decision-making. Introducing a new instrument such as temporary protection widens again the flexibility of control for those groups not intended to be covered by the general restrictions.

The New Control Regime: Reducing Immigration and Postponing Integration

After the initial reform of the asylum policy in 1990/1991 the second step was the adoption of two new laws in 1992 regulating territorial admission, deportation and residence: the *Fremdengesetz* (Aliens Act replacing the *Fremdenpolizeigesetz* of 1954) and the *Aufenthaltsgesetz* (Residence of Aliens Act). The former regulates the issuing of visa, the loss of visa and residence permits, the enforcement of rejections at the border, residence prohibition, detention for deportation, fines for trafficking of immigrants, the collection of data on foreigners, and the special residence status of citizens of the EEA. The first sketches of the *Aufenthaltsgesetz* were still called the Immigration Act, the draft version had the title *Niederlassungsgesetz* (Settlement Act). This terminological shift is indicative of a significant change in the political agenda. It signalled a growing impact of the electoral successes of Haider's FPÖ on the immigration policies of the two government parties. Mainstream politicians became anxious to avoid the word 'immigration' and no longer wanted to challenge the FPÖ, which had by then already fully centred its campaigns around the idea that 'Austria is no country of immigration'. Secondly, it also documented the failure of attempts to oust the social partners from control over immigration. The first draft had still contained a paragraph that would have ended with a single stroke most of the discriminatory regulations in employment and social welfare. Immigrants holding a settlement permit would have obtained the same legal status as Geneva Convention refugees (§11 in draft version of 13 November 1991). In the final version the law added a system of control over admission and residence to the existing one centred on employment. The interlinkage between both is, however, far from perfect. In June 1997 the two laws regulating immigration and termination of residence were merged into a single new law.

The most basic change brought by the law was an annual contingent – a fixed, absolute number of new residence permits. By adopting this device of regulating immigration in traditional countries of immigration Austria has in a way implicitly recognized the fact that it has become such a country, too. The annual contingent is established in a procedure that guarantees the predominance of employment policy considerations and involves all the main actors of social partnership as well as the federal provinces. Apart from EEA citizens and Swiss citizens, any foreigner who wants to take up his or her main residence in Austria and intends to stay for more than six months has to obtain a residence permit. One of the main aims of the 1993 laws was to require that applications for new permits had to be filed from abroad at an Austrian embassy. This strict provision prevented a 'regularization' of visa overstayers or abusers. However, it also meant that those immigrants already settled in Austria who had missed a deadline for renewing their permits would have to leave the country and apply to be readmitted as if they were newcomers. The new Aliens Act of 1997 eliminates many of these mindless rigidities but retains the essential constraints: a residence permit can only be obtained if a foreigner can prove sufficient income and accommodation conforming to local housing standards. For immigrants to be newly admitted for employment a permit additionally requires that the total employment quota has not been exhausted.

A major intention of the 1993 law was to limit family reunification by including it in the contingent. Until an amendment of April 1995, the contingent included not only new admissions from abroad but also children of immigrants born in Austria with foreign citizenship. Moreover, once the contingent is exhausted, applications are transferred to the following year. The 1997 reform has further strongly reduced the chances for family reunification for already established immigrants, mainly by cutting back the separate contingent for this purpose from 10,320 in 1997 to only 5,150 in 1998 and thus increasing the already long queue of pending applications. For future immigrants a new rule asks them to state the number of family members who could join them in their first application. If immigration is granted, reunification will have to be applied for within the first year of residence or else the right to bring in the family is lost. A single immigrant will thus fill several slots in the following year's contingent, which should further reduce the chances for first admissions.

The contingents for new resident permits were set at 17,000 in 1995, 16,140 in 1996 and 18,400 in 1997. Of the 1997 contingent 10,320 were reserved for family reunion, 2,340 for foreign students and 1,610 for workers with special skills. An additional contingent of 5,000 was reserved for seasonal workers. The contingent planned for 1998 cuts legal immigration down to 50 per cent of the previous level. Total new admissions will be 8,660, of which only 4,600 are family members entitled to reunification plus another 550 minor children at the age between 14 and 19. Foreign students are no longer counted in the contingent and 2,760 slots go to key personel with special skills and their immediate family. The extra contingent for seasonal jobs remains at 5,000.

After five years a permanent residence permit may be obtained. The 1997 reform has for the first time explicitly introduced a principle of consolidation of residence, which protects long-term residents to a certain degree against a loss of their settlement permits. Before that – apart from not being counted in the contingent – the conditions for renewals were basically the same as for first admissions. However, even the new law has extraordinary long waiting periods before residence becomes reasonably secure. Estimates are that only 41 per cent of all legal foreign residents hold a permanent residence permit (see Gächter, 1998). A 'prohibition of residence' cannot be issued if a foreigner could be granted citizenship (which requires 10 years of residence) or has been raised and resident in Austria since early childhood. Foreigners who have been continuously unemployed for more than a year within eight years after entry will lose their current permit even if they have sufficient income or support by their family. The most severe handicap is that immigrants who have been admitted as family members before 1998 and would like to take up employment will not be allowed to do so unless they have been legally resident for at least eight years. New access of the immigrant population to the labour market is thus heavily controlled by two requirements: first, long periods of previous residence and, second, the overall cap of the employment quota. At present, there is an estimated labour potential of 60,000 legal foreign residents, most of whom have come under family reunification in 1991–93 and who are effectively denied legal employment.

As with the asylum law of the previous year the immigration control system (which came into full effect only in July 1993) was quite effective in reducing the numbers of new immigrants. The major problem was the severe consequences it had for the already established immigrant population. With the expiry of the mostly temporary old permits a huge number of applications for transition into the new system had to be processed within a few months. Many immigrants who missed a deadline lost their residence permits. Families who changed their accommodation or who had a new baby born suddenly no longer met the required housing standards (which in Vienna were defined as 10 m² per head). The 1997 immigration reform has a similar goal to the parallel one of the asylum procedure: increasing compatibility with general legal norms and increasing flexibility in individual cases without opening any new channels for inflows. Probably the most significant policy change between the initial reform plans announced in September 1995 and the final laws concerns the access of family members to employment. Neither employers, who want larger new contingents of skilled and seasonal workers, nor trade unions were interested in removing the present obstacles for this group. The outcome shows, once again, that social partners have the final say over any aspect of immigration policy that is seen to affect labour markets.

Rejections at the border of persons trying to enter Austria have remained relatively stable over the last years with 142,396, 134,735 and 133,978 in 1994, 1995 and 1996 respectively; 1997 has seen a significant drop to 80,706. More than 90 per cent of these concern persons without a valid passport or visa. Expulsion orders increased from 5,472 (1994) to 7,195 (1995) and remained at this level in the following years with 7,243 in 1996 and 6,872 in 1997. The main reason for the increase is the introduction of illegal employment as a new ground for expulsion. The strongest sanction against foreign residents is the so-called prohibition of residence, which denies them re-entry for a long or indefinite time. In 1994, 11,153 orders of this kind were issued, in 1995 the number had increased to 12,904 and 13,264 in 1997. In the same time period actual deportations rose from 9,951 in 1994 to 14,718 in 1996 and dropped again to 12,037 in 1997. (Source: Federal Ministry of the Interior and Biffl 1997.)

Asylum and immigration control has been at the centre of a strongly polarized public debate ever since 1991. A coalition of religious, liberal, green and left-wing forces opposed the laws. The FPÖ boasted that only its pressure had caused the government to act while at the same time rejecting the laws because they did not impose a complete halt to immigration. The strategy of the SPÖ had been quite explicitly to stop FPÖ inroads into its electoral core potential of industrial workers by being tough on immigration. The FPÖ tried to regain control of this agenda in autumn 1992 by launching a campaign for an anti-immigrant petition to parliament. The text proposed, among other points, a constitutional article that Austria is not an immigration country, a complete immigration stop and a limitation and segregation of foreign children in Austrian schools. An organization SOS-Mitmensch (SOS fellow humans) formed against this initiative. Mobilizations culminated in the *Lichtermeer* on 23 January, mentioned in the introduction. The number of signatures for Haider's petition remained far below his expectations. Moreover, these events triggered a split in his party leading to the creation of the new Liberal Forum, which has succeeded in maintaining its parliamentary represent-ation in recent elections and has consistently adopted a liberal stance on immigration.

In the final stages of mobilization before the *Lichtermeer* the SPÖ had given some token support but it refused to modify the new legislation after the event. Only when Haider's vote increased again in the national election of October 1994 did the Social Democrats change their strategies. The new Minister of the Interior, appointed in April 1995, enjoyed the support of liberal and left-wing forces inside the party and among the wider public. His reform package presented in September of the same year was, however, blocked within the government coalition both by the Conservative Peoples' Party and by strong resistance from the trade union camp. Budgetary reform laws (*Strukturanpassungsgesetz* 1996), which became necessary in order to bring Austria closer to the Maastricht criteria for monetary union, brought further restrictions in immigrants' access to social welfare benefits. Among these measures was also the unilateral cancellation of bilateral agreements on social security which Austria had concluded with the major sending states of guest-workers in the 1970s. For immigrants from former Yugoslavia and Turkey this implies that they no longer receive family allowances for their children living abroad (which had before been set at roughly half of the amount for children living in Austria). A predictable effect of this decision is that more immigrants will try to bring their children into Austria, which will further contribute to the backlog in legal family reunification. In October 1996 the campaigns for, and results of, elections to the European Parliament and the Vienna provincial parliament buried any short-term prospect for liberalization. With Haider's FPÖ gaining almost 28 per cent of the vote in both elections there was little political leeway left for liberalizing Austria's laws blocking the legal and social integration of immigrants. Immigration figures now less prominently on the political agenda than in 1990–93, and the new law will probably have the effect of further de-escalation. However, the legal heritage of the guest-worker policy has survived substantial changes in Austria's external environment. Neither the diminished immigration pressure since the end of hostilities in Croatia and Bosnia nor the impact of EU membership have so far eroded this peculiar national framework.

The elements of control left untouched by the new laws are probably as significant as the changes they introduced. Both in 1993 and 1997 the Employment of Foreigners Act was minimally adapted, but the Citizenship Act was explicitly excluded from the reform of immigration and has remained unchanged until the end of 1997. As Austria has one of the purest systems of *ius sanguinis* citizenship in the Western world this means that there is an ongoing reproduction of a population of native-born foreign citizens who will be subjected to a system intended for immigration control. In other major countries of immigration covered in our book such as the Netherlands, France and Germany the debate about conditions for naturalisation, dual citizenship and *ius soli* has occupied a centre stage during recent years. The official target of cutting back on new immigration in order to facilitate the integration of those already there would have required considering easier admission to citizenship. However, the sequence of the reform has now produced the exactly opposite result.

In July 1998 parliament adopted a reform of the law on nationality which retains all the core features of the present regulation (10 years regular waiting period, 30 years for a right to naturalization, *ius sanguinis* transmission and strict prohibition of retaining a previous citizenship in naturalizations). What is new is that the burden of proof is shifted to the individual immigrants who will have to show that they are sufficiently integrated to be worthy of Austrian citizenship. After restricting legal employment, asylum and family reunification, naturalization come to be seen as the remaining gate where control ought to be tightened.

There are two explanations for this shift of the reform impetus. One is that the laws already adopted have operated as a push factor by making naturalization increasingly attractive as an escape route from legal discrimination for long-term residents. Provincial authorities have already responded to this by removing discretionary grounds for naturalization before 10 years of residence and by introducing language and cultural assimilation tests that are not required by the law. The second explanation is the continuing competition within the party system for the anti-immigrant vote. The very success of the immigration stop campaign creates the temptation to shift the agenda towards the boundary that separates foreigners from citizens. Two factors facilitate this closing of the citizenship gate. One is external: as long as the European Union leaves the determination of its own citizenship entirely to the nationality laws of its member states, the impact from the liberalization of naturalizations elsewhere will remain negligible on the Austrian policy. The other one is domestic: in contrast with Germany, France or the Netherlands, there has not been any broader public debate which links naturalization conditions to rival conceptions of national identity.

Conclusions

In the period from 1985 to 1997 the Austrian system of immigration control has undergone significant modifications. There has been a marked shift of emphasis from internal control focused on access to employment to control of territorial admission. Immigration of 'third country nationals' is now regulated via a yearly contingent of new residence permits and admission of asylum seekers has been drastically limited by the 'safe third country' rule and by terminating their right of residence during the determination procedure. At the same time the available policy instruments for positive selection have been extended by introducing temporary protection for war refugees.

The monopoly of the social partners in developing the policy of labour immigration and monitoring its implementation has been challenged by new political actors such as the Freedom Party on the right and the Green and Liberal parties on the left, Catholic and Protestant organizations, NGOs and citizens' initiatives. Nevertheless, until today the organizations of the social partners have succeeded in maintaining their instruments with the effect that a dual system of control over residence and employment has emerged. This system is, on the one hand, inefficient because of administrative over-regulation but, on the other hand, highly effective in restricting access for new immigrants and keeping settled immigrants exposed to ongoing control.

The issue of immigration has been on the top of the domestic political agenda since 1990. Immigration control has thus moved out of the closed forums of policy making by the social partners and parties in government to more public and open arenas. As Ted Perlmutter has recently argued, this development is linked to the loss of control over the political agenda by the national leadership of mass parties in government (Perlmutter, 1996; Freeman, 1995). In the Austrian case, this has slowed down the transition from a guest-worker to an immigration policy with regard to internal controls while speeding up the introduction of external controls. The reform of 1997 intends to reduce some of the irritation over the fact that aspects of the control policy are incompatible with the rule of law or basic humanitarian principles. It will probably succeed in reducing public attention somewhat, at least until eastern enlargement of the European Union is sure to revive the debate.

There are some more general lessons about the instruments and mechanisms of immigration control to be drawn from the Austrian experience.

One is about the merits and flaws of the instrument of numerical limitation by quotas and contingents. This is a dual-edged sword. It can, on the one hand, signal a recognition that immigration has become a permanent feature of a country's domestic policy. On the other hand, the same instruments can also be used to sever existing migratory chains by putting numerical caps on admissions of family members or refugees, which had previously been formally unlimited. When such contingents also affect immigrants already settled in the country and when they are combined with an additional quota for employment, naturalization or other forms of status improvement, the effect will be to raise the hurdles for internal admissions of immigrants to full membership. In Germany a contingent system is today discussed as a reform that would signal a more rational attitude, which no longer denies that the receiving state has become a country of immigration. Just the same kind of mood prevailed in Austria at the time when this mechanism was suggested for the first time. Yet within a few crucial years the policy goal to be pursued by this instrument has been completely changed. It was used in the end to cut back spontaneous flows that had been driven by economic pull factors and chain migration without being coupled with the expected opening of internal gates for permanent settlement, access to employment and citizenship. The lesson is that a policy change of the latter kind would have required a broad political consensus about how immigration has permanently changed Austrian society and cannot be simply reversed. The core political actors in the field were never prepared to fully adopt this position.

A second lesson is about the effects of neo-corporatist arrangements and their erosion. The depoliticization of immigration control during the period of dominant control by the social partners was seen by many as a rational way of dealing with the issue without arousing xenophobia. However, on balance this has clearly delayed a necessary debate about a profound change in the composition of the receiving society. By reducing immigration control to the task of optimizing the allocation of labour while securing social welfare standards, this policy has detracted attention from conflicts between the construction of national identity and the ongoing pluralization of society through immigrant settlement. Moreover, the instruments of control geared to reconciling the conflicting interests of trade unions and employers have served to increase the social immobility of immigrants and to highlight the status of aliens as not belonging to this society. When the transformation of the party system created opportunities for politicizing the immigration issue, the two traditional mainstream parties had not been sufficiently immunized against temptations of playing the anti-immigrant card.

The third lesson is about the impact of national identity constructions. In some countries traditions of both emigration and immigration have created a national consensus about the value of relative openness for immigration. This does not prevent periodic cycles of restrictive policies or anti-immigrant sentiments, but it still seems to explain some of the long-term trends and the different ways in which various countries have reacted to quite similar changes in migration patterns. In the Austrian case these historic experiences of migration have become relevant by way of negation or amnesia. A strong nativist construction of identity that can be easily appealed to in politics seems to have compensated for the lack of a firm sense of a republican – or even a specific ethnic core of Austrian nationhood.

References

Basch, L., Glick-Schiller, N. and Szanton Blanc, C. (1994), *Nations Unbound. Transnational Projects, Postcolonial Predicaments and Deterritorialized Nation-States*, Amsterdam: Gordon and Breach, Overseas Publishers Association.

Bauböck, R. and Wimmer, H. (1988), 'Social Partnership and 'Foreigners' Policy', *European Journal of Political Research* 1988: 659–81.

Biffl, G. (1997), *SOPEMI, Report to the OECD on Labour Migration. Austria 1996/97*, Wien: WIFO.

BMAS, (1997), *Bewilligungspflichtig beschäftigte Ausländer und Ausländerinnen 1996*, Wien: Bundesministerium für Arbeit und Soziales, Arbeitsmarktservice.

Çinar, D., Hofinger, C. and Waldrauch, H. (1995), *Integrationsindex. Zur rechtlichen Integration von Ausländerinnen in ausgewählten europäischen Ländern*, Wien: Institut für Höhere Studien, Reihe Politikwissenschaft 25.

Davy, U. (1995), 'Refugees from Bosnia and Herzegovina: Are They Geniune?' *Suffolk Transnational Law Review*, 1995: 53–131.

Davy, U. and Gächter, A. (1993), Zuwanderungsrecht und Zuwanderungspolitik in Österreich, *Journal für Rechtspolitik*, 1993: 153–74, 257–81.

Ecker G., Kemmerling, M. and Parnreiter C. (1992), *Achtung Staatsgrenze! Zeitbombe Migration? Europas Krieg gegen die Armen*, Wien.

Faßmann, H. and Münz, R. (1995), *Einwanderungsland Österreich,* Wien: *Jugend und Volk.*

Freeman, G. (1995), 'Modes of Immigration Politics in Liberal Democratic States', *International Migration Review,* 1995: 881–902.

Gächter, A. (1995a), 'Forced complementarity: the attempt to protect native Austrian workers from immigrants', *New Community* 1995: 379–98.

—— (1995b), Integration und Migration, *SWS-Rundschau*, 1995: 435–8.

—— (1998), *Die Integration der niedergelassenen ausländischen Wohnbevölkerung in den Arbeitsmarkt*, Report for the Austrian Federal Chancellery, Wien: Institute for Advanced Studies.

Grandner, M. (1995), 'Staatsbürger und Ausländer. Zum Umgang Österreichs mit den jüdischen Flüchtlingen nach 1918', in: Heiss, G. and Rathkolb, O. (eds) *Asylland wider Willen. Flüchtlinge im europäischen Kontext seit 1914*, 60–85, Wien: Jugend und Volk.

Hauptverband der österreichischen Sozialversicherungsträger, (1997), *Statistische Daten aus der Sozialversicherung.* Beschäftigte Ausländer in Österreich, Jahresdurchschnitt 1996, Wien.

Juen, G., Perchinig, B. and Volf, P.-P. (1996), 'Migrationspolitik – zur Europäisierung eines Gastarbeitermodells', in: Tálos, E. and Falkner, G. (eds.) *EU-Mitglied Österreich. Gegenwart und Perspektiven: Eine Zwischenbilanz*, 201–220, Wien: Manz-Verlag.

Löschnak, F. (1993), *Menschen aus der Fremde. Flüchtlinge, Vertriebene, Gastarbeiter*, Wien.

Matuschek, H. (1985), 'Ausländerpolitik in Österreich 1962–1985. Der Kampf um und gegen die ausländische Arbeitskraft', *Journal für Sozialforschung*, 25: 159–98.

Parnreiter, C. (1994), *Migration und Arbeitsteilung. Ausländerinnen-beschäftigung in der Weltwirtschaftskrise*, Wien: Promedia.

Pelz, S. (1994), *Ausländerbeschränkungen Österreichs in der Zwischen-kriegszeit*, Salzburg: Universität Salzburg, Institut für Geschichte, Diplomarbeit.

Perchinig, B. (1996), *Österreich 1995. Migrationspolitik und Förderung der Freizügigkeit der Arbeitnehmer*, report for RIMET, Commission of the European Union, Wien: DGV.

Perlmutter, T. (1996), 'Bringing Parties Back In: Comments on "Modes of Immigration Politics in Liberal Democratic Societies"', *International Migration Review* 1996: 375–88.

Renan, E. (1882), 'Qu'est-ce qu'une nation?, Speech given at the Academie Française', in: *Discours et Conférences par Ernest Renan*, Paris: Caylman-Lévy.

Rohrböck, J. (1992), 'Asylpolitik und Asylgesetz in Österreich', in: Althaler, K.und Hohenwarter, A. (eds) Torschluß, *Wanderungsbewe-gungen und Politik in Europa*, 84–99, Wien.

SOPEMI (1995), *Trends in International Migration*, Annual Report 1994, Paris: OECD.

Stieber, G. (1995), 'Volksdeutsche und Displaced Persons', in: Heiss, G. und Rathkolb, O. (eds) *Asylland wider Willen. Flüchtlinge im europäischen Kontext seit 1914*, 140–156, Wien: Jugend und Volk,

Wallace, C. Chmuliar, O. and Sidorenko, E. (1995), 'Die östliche Grenze Westeuropas. Mobilität in der Pufferzone', *SWS-Rundschau*, 1995: 41–69.

Walzer, M. (1983), *Spheres of Justice. A Defence of Pluralism and Equality*, New York: Basic Books.

Wimmer, H. (1986), 'Zur Ausländerbeschäftigungspolitik in Österreich', in: Wimmer, H. (ed.) *Ausländische Arbeitskräfte in Österreich*, 5–32, Frankfurt/Main: Campus-Verlag.

Zolberg, A. (1987), 'Wanted but not Welcome: Alien Labor in Western Development.' in: Alonso, W. ed. (1987), *Population in an Interacting World*, Cambridge, Ma.: Harvard University Press.

—— (1991), 'Bounded States in a Global Market: The Uses of Inter-national Labor Migrations', in Bourdieu, P. and Coleman, J. S. (eds) *Social Theory for a Changing Society*, 301–35, Boulder: Westview.

—— (1996), 'Models of Incorporation: Toward a Comparative Frame-work', paper presented at the Conference: Citizenship and Exclusion, University of Amsterdam, April 1996.

Migration Control and Minority Policy:
The Case of the Netherlands

Hans van Amersfoort

Introduction

The history of migration control in the Netherlands shows interesting similarities and dissimilarities with other West European countries. Like other West European countries, with the notable exception of France, the Netherlands has not considered itself to be an immigration country and has only reluctantly accepted the reality of being one. Historians have repeatedly pointed out that immigration is not a new experience for the Netherlands. From the Middle Ages until well into the nineteenth century there was a constant migration especially from what is now Germany into the relatively well developed and prosperous Netherlands, but this has little political relevance because in the twentieth century the Netherlands has experienced more emigration than immigration. Especially since World War II the country has had a negative migration balance. The population density and the relatively rapid natural population growth were considered to pose a serious problem for future development. The government was actively stimulated emigration. It was therefore very difficult for the government and the general public to see the country as an immigration country. Interestingly enough the word 'immigrant', which exists in Dutch, was not used in most of the post-war period for people immigrating into the Netherlands. They were called repatriates, overseas citizens, refugees or foreign workers, but not immigrants. The obsession of the Dutch with population density is quite remarkable. It is repeatedly stated that 'we are the most densely populated country in the world'. This statement is not correct as there are even more densely populated countries. Moreover it is obvious that there are several areas of the size of the Netherlands that have an even greater population density, but the image of being a crowded country plays a role in the general discussion. As elsewhere, discussions about migration and migration policy in the Netherlands tend often to be symbolic rather than logical and factual in content. Since 1960 the country has had a consistent migration surplus, but this reality entered only slowly in the political definition of the situation. The immigrants were stubbornly classified as temporary residents who 'one day' would return home.

In 1983 the government published an important 'White Paper' (Ministerie Binnenlandse Zaken) wherein it was officially recognized that the Netherlands was *de facto* an immigration country and the myth that the Surinamese and Mediterranean immigrants would return home was given up. This brought a different discussion to the fore: a concern for the social position of the immigrants and their offspring in Dutch society. Dutch society is a highly developed welfare state that guarantees every inhabitant a certain level of income, a certain standard of housing, access to health care and has a system of compulsory education for all inhabitants between five and sixteen years of age. The working of this welfare state depends on a functioning consociational democracy, which can be described as a system of 'pluralistic integration' (Lijphart, 1977). The integration of the immigrant populations in this welfare state, became an important aspect of the wider discussion around immigration and immigration control. A policy aimed at integrating the immigrants already there implies a restrictive control over the prospective immigrants at the gate (Hammar, 1985: 273). This aspect became particularly salient when, in the period after 1980, the immigration increased and seemed to run out of control. New regulations were issued to show the public that the government was capable of successfully managing migration flows.

However, this discussion must not give the impression that the attitude of the Dutch government and the Dutch public in general towards migration and immigrants is absolutely negative. That would be too simple. The Netherlands has a very open economy. The country has always been dependent on trade and traffic. Rotterdam harbour and Schiphol airport are enormous hinges in the international flows of persons and goods. International companies have headquarters in the Netherlands and big Dutch firms have all kinds of linkages with other countries. The circulation of staff members of these companies is part of the globalization of the world economy. We can summarize the Dutch attitude towards migration as positive with regard to migration within the developed world and at least reserved if not outright negative for migration from the less-developed world.

How these general background attitudes work out in the formulation and implementation of migration control policies is the subject of this chapter. We will show that Dutch policy with regard to immigration has developed mainly ad hoc, as a direct response to particular situations.

The limited success of the classical external control mechanisms has stimulated the quest for internal control mechanisms. The implementation of migration laws has in practice been limited by considerations of a humanitarian nature, by contradicting principles in the total fabric of laws (including international laws and agreements), or simply because of its high financial and/or social costs.

In the next section we will define and describe the migrants in the Netherlands. We will analyse the most important migration flows of the recent past with regard to the implementation of control, and we will look at the sources of tension and the pressure for more control. Finally we will summarise our findings with regard to the Dutch case.

Definitions and Descriptions

The framework for control

In the introduction to this volume we defined migration as population movements across national boundaries. Implied in this definition is the acceptance of the way states look at migration and define immigrants. In the past local rulers have often interfered in population movements, sometimes inducing people with certain characteristics to settle in their territories, sometimes driving unwanted people out, but the systematic interference by governments in migration processes is a relatively new phenomenon connected with the rise of the modern state in the nineteenth century. It is related to the growing importance of the state as the institution regulating the general welfare of society. It is also related to the process of democratization. Only in the beginning of the twentieth century did general elections in which all adults could vote become the norm for democratic states. In the course of those historical processes definitions of citizenship became articulated and the distinction between citizens and 'non citizens' was systematically applied.

In theory the concept of citizenship is based either on the notion of common descent, an almost mythical property with deep historical roots (*ius sanguinis*) or on the notion of a territorial community (*ius soli*). In the first line of reasoning the nation is a given historical entity and the state is the political expression of this entity. In the second line of reasoning the state is created by the consent of citizens coming together out of their free will to pursuit their common interests. German nationalism has been dominated by the tradition of the *ius sanguinis*, whereas in the United States the *ius soli* notion dominates the national ideology. Modern historians see both notions as 'idea's' as 'ideal type constructs' not as descriptions of how states actually came into being, but although the descriptive value of these concepts of citizenship may be limited, we can not disregard them because they have an important impact on how citizenship is perceived and given form in the law.

In the Netherlands the first laws expressing an idea of citizenship were extreme examples of the *ius soli* notion. Citizenship was approached as a matter of birthplace and residence. The first 'modern law' on citizenship of 1892 brought a clear element of descent into the definition of citizenship. Since then Dutch laws have contained elements of both notions, but have remained on the *ius soli* side of the ideology, certainly if we compare the Dutch laws with the tradition in Germany on this point. Basically the Dutch look at citizenship as a legal property that can be acquired and consequently can also be lost. A consequence of this vision is for example the right to vote in local elections that all permanent residents in a particular area have, regardless of their nationality.

Another consequence of this vision is that naturalization for permanent residents is relatively easy. Persons born in the Netherlands have a right to Dutch citizenship when they apply for it. There is however one serious complication in the Dutch law on naturalization that has caused great confusion since 1991. The law as it is, does not recognise double citizenship. Dutch people who acquire citizenship of another country automatically lose Dutch citizenship. Foreigners applying for Dutch citizenship are demanded to give up their original nationality. However in practice this has been interpreted quite differently. Exceptions have always been made in those cases where it was considered to be unreasonable to demand the renunciation of the original nationality, for instance in those cases where the laws of the home countries excluded the possibility of a change in nationality. This is particularly relevant for Moroccans. In October 1991 a Member of Parliament, Apostolou (himself a Greek immigrant), succeeded in having a motion accepted wherein was asked for a new law that accepted the possibility of double citizenship. His arguments were twofold. In the first place the existing law left too much room for arbitrary decisions. When was a demand unreasonable? In the second place it was important to integrate settled immigrants as much as possible into society, and the demand of renunciation formed a needless emotional barrier to accept Dutch citizenship. The responsible ministers accepted these arguments, and, backed by a majority of the Tweede Kamer, ('Second Chamber', in fact roughly comparable to the British House of Commons) started to prepare a new law on naturalization, but at the same time, they sent instructions to the municipalities, announcing the coming law and ordering them to give the present law a liberal and generous interpretation. This resulted in the situation that from 1 January 1992, double citizenship was no longer seen as problematic and a cause for refusing naturalization. The number of naturalizations increased after 1992. In 1994 almost 50,000 persons acquired Dutch citizenship; in 1995 71,000 persons became Dutch citizens. Most of them were first and second generation immigrants from Turkey and Morocco and citizens from the Republic of Surinam (Heijs, 1995).

In the mean time the new law, permitting double nationality was debated in Parliament. It was finally accepted on 1 March 1995 by the Tweede Kamer. However conservative politicians mobilized so much resistance against the new law that they succeeded in blocking the procedural process in the Eerste Kamer ('First Chamber', a much less important chamber in the Dutch parliamentary system). It is not completely clear what will happen next. The government favours a law that will be more open with regard to double nationality, but at the same time more restrictive than the one accepted in 1995. As 1998 is an election year and this is one of those relatively unimportant but sensitive issues that may become important in electoral campaigns, it is impossible to predict what the outcome of the political decision making will be.

The relative open approach to citizenship and naturalization does not mean that citizenship is not important as an instrument for the regulation of migration. On the contrary, the first and foremost distinction the Netherlands make in classifying immigrants is between nationals and non-nationals. The Netherlands has, in the period under consideration, never tampered with the right of nationals to enter and reside in the Netherlands, even when this immigration was deplored. (See below about migration from Surinam.)

The immigration of foreigners is regulated by law. This has three aspects: the right of entry, residence and work – aspects that may, but do not necessarily coincide. Although in Dutch migration regulation the distinction between nationals and foreigners is basic, this is not to say that foreigners are treated as a homogeneous category. They have no automatic right of abode but a 'negotiated right'. These rights can be acquired on a personal title, such as a residence permit or a recognition as refugee, but it is important to note that these rights are often the consequence of bilateral or multilateral agreements about the rights of the respective citizens on entrance and abode. In our case the most obvious example is that of the European Union regulations about the free movement of European citizens within the countries of the union. In accordance with

Box 5.1 Immigrant Categories

A. Citizens of the Netherlands

B.1. Citizens of EU countries (other than the Netherlands)
Their status is regulated by the EU regulations with regard to traffic and residence. This category of immigrants is not further discussed in this chapter.

B.2. Citizens of all other countries.
Various sub-categories can be distinguished from a legal point of view, although the distinctions are sometimes difficult to apply in daily routine. The following are important for a discussion of Dutch immigration policy:

a. Visitors
They are not considered to be or to become residents, but only to stay for a limited period of time. Visitors are obliged to have valid papers (passports, or in some cases a visa) and sufficient resources, but are otherwise welcome. As visitors do not enter the migration statistics it would be possible to disregard them in a discussion of migration control. However, not all visitors behave as visitors and overstaying is a source of illegal residency. The regulation for visiting the country has been modified in the past decades in an attempt to prevent 'prospective immigrants' from entering the country as 'visitors'. Here we are right on the border of migration policies.

b. Foreigners with a temporary residence permit
This permit is valid for one year and has to be renewed every year. This temporary status cannot be lengthened indefinitely. After five years either further residence has to be refused or a permanent resident status granted.

c. Permanent residence permit holders

d. Refugees
Persons who are recognized as falling under the Geneva Refugee Convention (GRC) immediately receive permanent residence status.

e. Asylum seekers
People who have managed in one way or the other to enter the country and claim to fall under the GRC, but whose claim is still under consideration. As long as their status is not decided they do not figure in the migration statistics, but their number can be assessed from other sources.

f. Tolerated residents
Foreigners who have no residence title, but whose residence has nevertheless to be accepted. For instance asylum seekers whose claim has been refused, but who can not be deported because of international complications or personal circumstances. This 'in between' status is even recently institution-alised as a form of temporary residence (the VVTV-status, see page 153).

g. 'Illegal residents', who run the risk of being deported, if detected.

these regulations a number of immigrant categories can be found in the Netherlands (see Box 5.1).

The definitions of the categories reflect the legal framework regulating entry, residence and work of foreign citizens. It is, however, clear that the practical application of these definitions is not always easy, as is demonstrated by the existence of the category of 'tolerated persons'. The way the legal instruments are put into practice is influenced by the evaluations and perceptions of the general public, journalists, scholars and, finally, of the government of certain migration flows or certain migrants. Migrants from Morocco and Japan, should, according to the law be subjected to the same regulations, but that is not to say that they cause the same concern to the government, the general public or the police. The actual implementation of laws and regulations depends on a general evaluation of the following consequences of immigration:

- numerical consequences (does the country need more people?);
- economic consequences (is immigration contributing to our economy, or at least to sectors of it?);
- social consequences (what are the consequences for social housing programmes, the educational system?);
- cultural consequences (what are the consequences for our basic values and norms?).

The last three consequences are often summed up in the question of whether an immigrant will be integrated into Dutch society in the course of time. To put it more bluntly we can say that a framework of control is used that assumes that there is a 'Dutch interest' that should guide the letting in or shutting out of prospective immigrants.

The problem of illegal residency is politically very sensitive and has even led to a new and, for the Netherlands far ranging law, that will be discussed below. It is important to notice that these 'illegals' do not form a single category. In relation to the law we must at least distinguish between:

- *illegal residents* – people who have either entered the country illegally or who have overstayed a visitors term or temporary residence permit;
- *illegal workers* – people who have entered legally – but have no work permit (for instance tourists or students) but nevertheless enter the labour market.

From the point of control these are very different categories. Overstaying and illegal working are not affected by border control, however rigorously applied. Illegal working by immigrants is in many instances connected with the existence of a 'black labour' market, which is certainly not exclusively the domain of immigrant labour.

The efficiency of the laws affecting entry, residence and work as instruments for migration control should not be overestimated. Immigrants are usually only subjected to this control mechanism, for a limited period of time. As long as they only have a temporary residence status their rights are indeed limited. However, temporary residence status cannot be prolonged indefinitely. As we have described already immigrants acquire a permanent residence status after five years. This permanent residence status gives nearly the same rights as citizenship status; for instance it is not linked to a work permit and it gives the right to bring over dependants and marriage partners. This status, for which Hammar (1990) has coined the term 'denizen status' means de facto that the immigrant is no longer subjected to immigration control. The only relevant difference between a citizen and a permanent resident with regard to migration control is that the status of permanent resident is lost in the case of return migration.

There is one final point to be noted with regard to definitions and their applications. Dutch laws with regard to migration are defined in personal, individualistic terms, but in the case of migration regulation the object of the regulation is only rarely an individual. Leaving aside the exceptional cases of criminals or political spies, who seem to be able to enter the country anyway, the Dutch government is concerned about migration flows, not so much about immigrating individuals. There is so far no discussion about introducing quota systems or contingents in the Netherlands. (A quota is agreed upon only with the UNHCR.) In reality however the aim of the Dutch state is to manage migration flows. This can lead to ambivalent policies as can be clearly seen in the case of the asylum seekers.

The Netherlands as an immigration country

Migration to and from the Netherlands has been recorded for a long time, although unfortunately not always in the same way and with the same definitions. There is a substantial amount of information available in the publications of the Central Office of Statistics, especially in its monthly publications (Centraal Bureau van de Statistiek (CBS) *Maandstatistiek van de bevolking*). Summarizing overviews can be found in the yearly SOPEMI reports (Muus, 1994, 1995, 1996).

Although the Netherlands has had a positive migration balance since the early 1960s the processes of in- and out-migration do not show a regular pattern. There are many fluctuations both in the migration from and into the Netherlands, and overall figures for the last few years give only a rough idea of the impact of immigration on the population growth. To achieve a more profound understanding we must analyse how various migration flows contribute to the overall figures. In the previous sections we have outlined the classifications that form the framework for migration control. We will use this approach in our description.

Migration of Dutch nationals

After World War II the Netherlands described itself as an emigration country. The government encouraged Dutch citizens to emigrate especially to Canada, Australia and New Zealand. This type of emigration has practically come to an end. Nevertheless there is a constant flow of Dutch people settling abroad, in recent years between 37,000 and 39,000 persons annually. Much more interesting from a point of migration control has been the immigration side during the post-war period.

Contrary to expectations, the immigration of Dutch nationals into the Netherlands has been substantial, in some years even overwhelming. The main reason is the definition of citizenship, applied first with regard to the Eurasian population in Indonesia and later with regard to the population of Surinam and the Dutch Antilles. After 1954, Dutch law recognized only one form of Dutch citizenship. This implied that after that date Surinamese and Antillians were free to migrate to the Netherlands and the Surinamese, in particular did so in increasing numbers. The growing influx of 'Dutch nationals born in Surinam' became a matter of great concern to the government. It became the main reason to induce Surinam (with a lot of development aid) to become an independent Republic in 1975. In the mean time, out of fear of losing citizenship and the right to settle, the Surinamese started to migrate massively to the Netherlands. The Surinamese population doubled to about 120,000 people in a few years. The settled Surinamese population, could as citizens exert a strong influence on the further migration into the Netherlands, a development that only seems to have past its peak in the late 1990s. This explains why the migration balance for Dutch nationals has been positive in the 1970s and for most of the 1980s. There are now hardly any persons with Dutch nationality left in Surinam. The migration from the Antilles has always been numerically far less important. The immigration of Dutch nationals has therefore not only become much lower in numbers, but has also changed in character. It is a flow to date mainly consisting of people returning home after a shorter or longer stay abroad. Even the change in regime in South Africa, a country where a relatively large number of Dutch passport holders still reside, has not induced a substantial influx.

Although mainly a migration of the (recent) past, Surinamese migration to the Netherlands still merits attention in a study of migration control, in the first place because it has resulted in a specific and perhaps even unique form of migration control: the creation of an independent state, and in the second place the Surinamese, although Dutch citizens, are at the same time a distinctive subpopulation. It is not easy to come to a satisfying definition of this rather heterogeneous population now that the birthplace criterion is rapidly becoming inadequate, but, however defined, they form part of the Dutch immigration experience and are a category included in the Dutch 'Minorities Policy'.

In recent years, migration of Dutch nationals has shown a small but regular negative migration balance. This migration pattern fits well into the general idea of increasing but more-or-less reciprocal population mobility inside the developed world.

Population mobility within the developed world

The negative migration surplus of Dutch nationals is balanced by a positive migration surplus with the other EU countries and with other developed countries, mainly the US. If we do not look only at the net migration figures but on the whole of the migration movements within the developed world we see a strong increase in population mobility. However there is no (significant) numerical impact of this mobility pattern on the Netherlands. In the context of Dutch policy making this is an important conclusion. Moreover there seem to be no special problems concerning the social participation or integration of immigrants from the developed world. There is, of course, a certain effect visible in the composition of the population of the Netherlands according to nationality, but this does not cause any concern. This circulation seems to reflect the development of the business cycle quite closely; the favourable developments in the Dutch economy of the last years is directly reflected in an increase in the immigration from other EU countries in 1994 and 1995.

As far as migration control is relevant for this type of migration it is control on the individual level. People with negative characteristics such as criminals or drug addicts can be refused residence and even be expelled, because they are, after all, not Dutch nationals. This happens in a number of cases, in which migration regulation is in fact used as an instrument for social control.

Immigration from 'peripheral' countries

The real worry for the Dutch is immigration from the non-industrialized countries. It contributes substantially to population growth and creates immigrant populations that do not participate adequately in society. When the Dutch realized that this immigration was not a temporary phenomenon but a structural aspect of the modern world, it became politically salient. There has been a constant search for ways to control these migration flows, especially after the oil crisis of the early 1970s. We will look in more detail at this process with regard to the Mediterranean labour migration and the recent asylum crisis in the next section.

The flows that were most important in the recent past (Turks and Moroccans) seem to have past their peak. Although these flows may fluctuate somewhat with the rise and fall of the business cycle, it is unlikely that the figures for the period 1988–92 will ever be reached again. In the mean time new migration flows arise, for instance via asylum seekers, but also undocumented migrants from African countries – in particular Ghana and Asian countries such as Pakistan and Sri Lanka.

The statistics of the foreign population in the Netherlands seem to indicate at first sight that the political concern about immigration is a bit overdone (Table 5.1). The percentage of foreign nationals is only 5 per

Table 5.1 Foreign Resident Population in the Netherlands by Citizenship 1980–95

Citizenship	1980	1990	1995
Belgium	23,000	23,300	24,100
Germany	42,700	41,800	53,900
Italy	20,900	16,700	17,400
ex-Yugoslavia	13,700	12,800	33,500
Spain	23,500	17,400	16,700
UK	35,400	37,500	41,100
Morocco	71,800	148,00	149,800
Turkey	199,600	191,500	154,300
Other countries	42,800	152,900	234,600
TOTAL	473,400	641,900	725,400
Foreign population in per cent of total	*3.4%*	*4.3%*	*4.7%*

Source: CBS, Standstatistiek, table 5; Statistisch Bulletin 1984: 30; Muus 1996: 62.

cent. However a few points should be noted. In the first place 'foreign nationality population' and 'immigrant population' are not identical categories; especially as the Surinamese and Antillian immigrants are invisible in these statistics. It is also important that the number of naturalized immigrants has grown so much that according to the nationality statistics the number of foreigners has diminished during the last years. In this respect the statistics do not therefore adequately reflect social reality. Applying an 'ethnic' criterion instead of the nationality criterion, the immigrant population can be estimated at least at 9 per cent of the population of the Netherlands. This ethnic population, having a younger age structure and a higher fertility rate, is already constituting a growing percentage of the population even when there would be no further immigration. Finally it is important to be aware that the recent years of immigration experience, particularly in the big cities, have contributed to the fear for a continuously growing influx of 'alien' people. The reaction of Dutch politicians may (at least partly) be understood as based on the necessity to keep these developments under control, if the welfare state is to survive.

Control in Practice

So far we have described the framework for the regulation of migration only in general terms. In this section we shall try to come closer to the reality of migration regulation by describing how the Dutch government has reacted to two important migration flows. It is not our pretension to give a full description of these cases; our description will be concentrated on the operation of control mechanisms.

Mediterranean labour migration

When the Dutch economy recovered from World War II, classical industries such as textiles, coal mining and shipbuilding found it difficult to attract enough labour. This situation had occurred earlier in Germany, France and Belgium. Labour migration from the Mediterranean area into Western Europe developed in these circumstances more or less spontaneously. As there were already Turks working in Germany and Moroccans in France and Belgium, soon Turkish and somewhat later Moroccan men came to the Netherlands looking for a job. When they found a job they registered with the magistrates and received the necessary documents, including a work permit. Finding a job proved to be easy at that time, and the first pioneer migrants were immediately followed by fellow country-men. Everybody involved, employers, magistrates and the migrants themselves, considered this a temporary situation.

Nevertheless, this migration soon led to various difficulties. The trade unions became concerned about wage levels and the maintenance of other labour prescriptions such as working hours and safety regulations. Housing conditions were often below the standards of a modern welfare state with regard to sanitation and fire regulations. These circumstances forced the Dutch state to intervene and to try to regulate the migration process. These interventions took the form of Recruitment Agreements between the Netherlands and several Mediterranean countries, for instance with Turkey in 1964 and Morocco in 1969. These agreements gave the Dutch govern-ment and the governments of the sending societies some hold on the labour migration (van Amersfoort and Penninx, 1994). Recruitment could only take place at certain places, agreed upon by the governments. There were checks on the age and health conditions of the prospective migrants. The work permit had to be acquired in the home country and became a pre-requisite for a residence permit. The work permit, originally not intended as an instrument for migration regulation, became the most important tool for migration control. On the other hand the employers had to specify their need in numbers and kind of work and were obliged to provide minimum standards of housing.

However, not all (prospective) immigrants lived by the rules, neither did all employers. For the first time the Dutch government was confronted with the problem of 'illegality'. It led to numerous court proceedings and intricate legal discussions. Because Dutch administrative systems were not interlinked, it was in many cases not clear how 'illegal' certain persons were and if their 'illegality' had consequences for their right of abode. The courts generally decided in favour of the migrants. In 1975 the government decided to put an end to this legal confusion and issued a general regularization measure for illegal immigrants residing and working for a longer period in the Netherlands (Groenendael, 1986). Since that time the situation has become clearer but not completely clear. There is a continuous trickle of claimants who demand a recognition of their residence and/or work status. The interesting point for a discussion about migration control is that the Dutch courts have tended so far to consider a prolonged residence in itself as an important ground for a residence title, even when the previous residence was in one way or another not according to the law. This means that acquiring a 'denizen status' in the Netherlands is not dependent (or not only dependent) on legal residency as it is defined by the government for the purpose of migration control.

A second important policy development, took place after the oil crisis of 1973. In a time of rising unemployment the government not only stopped issuing new work permits, but also introduced sanctions against employers to discourage the employment of illegals. The law, introduced in 1979, had hardly any effect; partly because the sanctions were minimal, partly because the law was not applied rigorously and partly because the demand for manual labour had become negligible, but this does not diminish the fact that the principle of sanctions against employers for using illegal labour had been given a legal base.

With the oil crisis, labour migration as such came to a sudden halt but the numbers of immigrants especially from Turkey and Morocco did not decrease. The migration only changed in character. The Turkish and Moroccan migrants did not go home, but brought their wives and children. In a relatively short period the immigrant population not only increased in numbers, but also changed in age and sex distribution. This change confronted Dutch society with new problems such as a growing immigrant participation on the regular housing market and an influx into the Dutch schools of non Dutch-speaking children with a wide variety of educational backgrounds. As in other countries, notably Germany, the Dutch government tried to discourage the process of family reunification by making the rules more restrictive (Muus and Penninx, 1991). The age up to which children can join their parents has been cut from 21 to 18 years, but this had hardly any effect. After 1985 we see again a change of character in the migration process: the immigration of marriage partners. The coming of age of children brought over by their parents in their teens, has caused a strong immigration of young husbands and wives. Again the government tried to limit this migration by introducing the requirement that persons wanting to bring over their marriage partner should have a minimum income. The measure proved difficult to implement and was soon withdrawn. Like the right to family reunification the immigration of a husband or wife is a right connected to denizenship status and in a growing number of cases with citizenship status.

A different approach to the control of migration, very much in line with the ideology of not being an immigration country, was taken to stimulate return migration. Two sets of measures were taken. The first set comprised financial incentives to return such as the possibility of transferring certain benefits like unemployment money and departure premiums. There were also programmes for training and (re) schooling prospective return migrants. The second set was much more ambitious. The intention was eventually to eradicate emigration by stimulating development in the regions of origin, wherever possible by making use of the migrants and their funds. This concept resulted in the Dutch Minister for Overseas Development commissioning the REMPLOD project (1974–77), which gave rise to a number of bilateral co-operative projects between the Netherlands and several recruitment areas many of them short lived (van Dijk et al., 1978). West Germany launched a similar development programme with Turkey, in which workers' partnerships, set up and financed by labour migrants, were intended to stimulate regional economic development in Turkey, and at the same time to induce return migration.

Evaluation of these various attempts to influence migration movements are not positive about the effects (Lebon, 1984; Muus et al., 1983). Success appears to have been relative at best: the measures based on financial inducements for return migrants did indeed appear to influence the moment of departure for those who had already decided to return, but in the long term the effects were limited or even non-existent.

Nevertheless the return ideology died out very slowly in the Netherlands and even now has not completely vanished. From time to time the idea that a return to the home countries would be the ideal solution for all problems around immigration is brought forward again, both by Dutch politicians and in the Dutch media as well by certain circuits inside the immigrant communities. The interesting aspect of the Remplod project is that it is in fact an early form of the 'root-cause' approach, that has become fashionable in political discussion in recent years again (van Amersfoort 1996). In this sense the Remplod project is an early example of an attempt of indirect migration control.

The interventions of the Dutch government to regulate the migration and to prevent the coming into being of settled immigrant communities have not been successful, but it is relevant to note that the interventions have led to a specification and further application of already-existing legal instruments. The last step in this direction has been the introduction of visa regulations for persons from countries considered to be 'risk countries' such as Turkey and Morocco, who want to visit the Netherlands as a tourist. Slowly a set of regulations has been created that makes (legal) migration from Turkey and Morocco practically impossible for people who are not classified as a family member or marriage partner. This has given the settled immigrants a powerful position as gatekeepers for prospective immigrants. The settled immigrant population has become the most important factor in the further development of legal Turkish and Moroccan immigration into the Netherlands (van Amersfoort 1995). Moreover communities of settled immigrants offer a stepping stone for 'overstaying visitors' and other forms of illegal immigration.

For prospective immigrants who do not have relatives or friends among the immigrant communities the only gateway left open is to apply for refugee status, which indeed a number of especially Turkish immigrants have done, but that is a different chapter of migration control to be discussed in the next section.

Refugees and asylum seekers

As many other countries, the Netherlands has ratified the Geneva Refugee Convention of 1951 and the elaboration thereof in the New York Protocol of 1967. This implies that the focus is, in the first place, on the needs of the individual refugee and not on the interests of Dutch society. When the number of asylum seekers increased, the admission and reception policy was repeatedly revised but without (formally) giving up the right of asylum.

In Dutch practice an important distinction is made between 'invited refugees' and 'asylum seekers'. Invited refugees are persons whose refugee status is already established by the UNHCR. They are admitted to the country as such. The Netherlands, with its preoccupation with being an 'overpopulated' country did not want to accept too many and agreed with the UNHCR to accept 500 refugees a year. After 1984 a number of Vietnamese boat people who had been picked up by Dutch ships were allowed to settle as refugees in the country. The number of spontaneous asylum seekers started to grow and it became obvious that the immigration of refugees would be followed by a certain amount of family reunification migration after some time. These three developments made the government decide to bring the contingent of invited refugees down to 250, but under pressure from the UNHCR this was soon brought back to the original 500. In reality between 500 and 700 persons a year have entered the Netherlands as invited refugees (see Table 5.2). For the reception of refugees there is an elaborate programme of housing and schooling with the aim of integrating them as soon as possible into society.

The event that served as a catalyst for Dutch policy with regard to asylum seekers was the sudden arrival in 1985 of substantial numbers of Tamils, claiming refugee status. Until that time there had not been much of a special asylum policy. Asylum seekers had been temporarily lodged and given access to the general welfare security system (Algemene Bijstandswet) to meet the costs of living. After the arrival of the Tamils a formal regulation was introduced. Asylum seekers were lodged and given a small amount of money but given no access to general social security; neither were they allowed to enter the labour market.

From this time on there has been a constant modification of the rules in response to the sharp increase in the number of asylum seekers from various countries (Muus 1995, especially Chapter 5; Doomernik et al., 1997). Summarizing these developments from a control point of view we notice two basic elements. The first is that the reception should be 'human but austere', often popularized as the provision of bed, bread and bath facilities. The second element is that as long as people are not recognized as refugees, they should not integrate into society. The most important aspect of this exclusion is the denial of access to the labour market. These regulations rest on the assumptions that a more generous reception would induce more people to immigrate and claim refugee status and that it is more difficult to remove people whose claim is rejected when they have found already employment and have started to integrate in society. Both assumptions are difficult to prove or disprove, but they are considered politically to be statements of fact. Important considerations in the regulation of the influx of asylum seekers were the costs for reception and integration measures. It is obvious that the amount of money involved played an important role for the ministries that had to find this money and so did the general political climate around the issue of immigration. We shall come back to that in the next section.

The Achilles heel of the Dutch asylum policy is the time gap between arrival and the decision to grant or reject a request for refugee status. In 1992 a new scheme was launched to streamline the procedures. From then on applications have had to be made in a Investigation Centre (Onderzoeks Centrum), where it is immediately decided whether the request stands a chance or not. People making unfounded claims should not be allowed to enter the country and have to await their deportation in these centres. The 'normal' asylum seekers are housed in Reception Centres (Asiel Zoekers Centrum) and can await the decision with regard to their status there. The idea was (and still is) that asylum seekers would have to stay for a maximum period of six months in these centres. After that time they were either accepted and admitted to the refugee programme for integration or rejected and sent back. Time and time again this period of six months has proved to be too short to solve all legal puzzles. The influx of asylum seekers from (former) Yugoslavia and the complications around the legal process of granting refugee status have led to a further differentiation in residence status. A special temporary status of 'Displaced Persons' (Ontheemden) has been created. The idea behind this status was that in a period of open civil war people could not be send back, although they were strictly speaking not personally persecuted. They should however return to their home country as soon as the situation was

Table 5.2 Netherlands: Asylum Seekers and Invited Refugees 1977–97

Year	1977–79	1980–82	1983–85	1986–88	1989–91	1992–94	1995
Invited refugees	3,073	3,317	1,327	1,885	1,886	1,785	…
Asylum seekers	2,232	2,648	8,226	24,596	56,631	108,321	…
TOTAL	5,305	5,695	9,553	26,481	58,517	110,116	86,500
Main country of origin	Turkey	Ethiopia	Sri Lanka	Ghana	Somalia	Bosnia	Bosnia

Source: Gooszen 1988: 7; Brink and Pasariboe 1993: 20–1; CBS, Maandstatistiek van de bevolking 1996–98.

considered to be sufficiently normalized. In January 1994 this was formalized in a new official status, VVTV (Voorlopige Vergunning Tijdelijk
Verblijf; 'conditional temporary residence status'), which does not give
access to the labour market. This status is conditional in the sense that it
is tied to specific conditions such as civil war in the home country. This
intermediate status can, according to interpretations given by courts in
legal disputes, not last more than three years. It must than be transformed
into a normal temporary residence status that leads to a 'denizen status'
in five years.

The implementation of these regulations has caused a constant stream
of complaints and court proceedings. The main difficulty is, as mentioned
already, the time-consuming process that keeps people waiting and builds
up frustration and tensions in the centres where people in dire straits, often
with very different cultural and personal backgrounds, have nothing to
do but to await a decision. While decisions to grant or to refuse refugee
status are formulated on an individual basis, the real aim of the government
is not so much to regulate individual migration but to control migration
flows. This ambivalent approach to the problem has given birth to an
evasive rhetoric and the introduction of ambiguous concepts such as 'safe
countries' and the passage through 'safe countries', which already may
exclude claimants from making a valid request. In fact this has not made
the implementation of the legal procedures any easier.

The implementation of stricter regulations and the rising number of
people entering the country on a temporary base or as asylum seeker,
have resulted in an increased number of expulsions decrees (see Table
5.3). Two remarks must made with regard to this rising number of
expulsion decrees. In the first place it is totally unclear how many of these
decrees are indeed effectuated. Convicted criminals are mostly escorted
out of the country by the police. In many other cases the decree is
announced, but nobody seems to care how it is to be carried out. People
prove to have 'vanished', when the police finally try to detect them. Often
there is open resistance against expulsion from people in the same
neighbourhood, certain Church members or even local authorities. Several
municipalities have openly refused to implement expulsion decrees
because they think it is not their duty to expel people; they find it inhumane
and ineffective. In January 1997 alone, there were two widely published
instances of these reactions. In Amsterdam, a Turkish family, Gümüs, for
years operating a tailor shop, was found to be illegally residing in the
Netherlands. Neighbours and teachers of the local school organized
protests. Even Amsterdam Lord Mayor Patijn stepped in to plead for these
quiet and well-behaved people. The municipalities of Apeldoorn and

Leiden openly declared that they were not going to exclude people whose refugee claims were rejected from social housing and/or other social benefits.

Table 5.3 Netherlands: Expulsion Decrees 1989–95

Year	Total number of expulsion decrees	thereof asylum seekers	
		number	*per cent*
1989	8,975	1,605	18
1990	10,692	2,662	25
1991	14,333	4,006	28
1992	21,189	7,534	36
1993	20,229	7,186	36
1994	31,185	13,293	43
1995	40,024	14,509	36

Source: Ministry of Justice; Muus 1996: 15.

Serious sources estimate that not more than 30 per cent of all expulsion decrees result in departure from the country. It should also be noticed that those refused asylum seekers who remain in the Netherlands form only a part, and not the biggest part, of the illegal residents in the country. In recent years, the number of asylum seekers has come down, as in other EU countries. However, it is difficult to assess how far this decline is the consequence of migration regulation. The rise and decline in the number of migrants is also directly related to the countries involved at the sending end of the flows. The Netherlands had an influx from Latin American countries in the 1970s, whereas during the last period countries like Bosnia, Iraq, Iran, Somalia and Afghanistan have been important sources of asylum seekers. Nowadays events in all parts of the world seem to influence the number of asylum claimants in the Netherlands.

Fear of an increasing number of asylum seekers has also contributed to the sharpening of another migration control instrument: visa regulations. As we have seen already, visa regulations were used as an instrument of migration control in relation to countries such as Turkey, Morocco and Surinam in the early 1980s. This has later been extended to more and more countries. Furthermore people travelling without the required travel documents are already refused at the border, where the carrier is obliged to transport them back home. This gives transport companies the 'official' task of controlling passengers documents. The embassies and consulates in 'risk countries' have acquired specialized staff, to prevent people who are suspected to be prospective immigrants to enter the country on a tourist visa. There is no exact information about the handling of these visa requests. We only have some information about the requests that are send to the Ministry of Justice in The Hague for consultation, in cases that are complicated or unclear. Of these cases we know that 12.5 per cent was rejected in 1986 and 40 per cent in 1993.

In theory the control over immigration has become more sophisticated during the past decade. One may even wonder how people from countries such as Iraq still manage to enter the country to make an asylum request, but, as always, legal regulations have also a shady side. Every regulation produces its own evasions, sometimes even people who specialize in finding ways to elude the regulations. The lengthier and more complicated the procedures are, the more people are prone to find loopholes, especially when the trespassers have little or nothing to lose. The dark side of the more strict regulation of entry, residence and work for migrants is the production of 'illegals'. As nobody can tell how many and what kind of illegals there are, this is a continuous theme in the political discourse round the regulation of migration.

The Background of Migration Control Policies

The Dutch Minorities Policy

When the Dutch government finally accepted, in 1983, the fact that the Netherlands was an immigration country, the question of the integration of immigrants was automatically on the political agenda. Of course there had been ad hoc responses to the presence of immigrants before 1983, but there had not been a policy aimed at systematic integration of immigrant populations into Dutch society. It is important to note that the 'Minorities Policy' is not a policy directed at immigrants generally. As we noticed already in the introduction there is a sharp division in the Dutch reaction to immigration from developed and less-developed countries. The minorities policy is aimed at immigrant groups, who do not participate on an equal base in Dutch society and whose low participation tends to be continued over the generations. The general aim of this policy is to enhance the participation in society of these immigrant groups.

Participation in society is operationalized as participation on the labour market, the housing market and, for the younger generation, enrolment in the school system, as these are considered to be the central and decisive fields of societal interaction. Other fields of societal participation such as welfare work and health care also profit from funds available under this policy because they are thought to be helpful for the participation on the central fields of a modern society.

The moral foundation of this policy lies in the ideology of the welfare state. It is contrary to this idea for certain immigrant groups to develop into a 'minority' or as it is sometimes phrased into an 'ethnic underclass'. It is regarded not only as morally unacceptable but even as dangerous for the functioning of the welfare state. Because permanently marginalised groups are likely to form sources of tensions and conflicts. The horror image of the American ghettos is frequently mentioned in Dutch debates around the 'minorities Policy'.

Although the general aims of the minorities policy are clear, it is far less clear how these aims can be achieved. In accordance with Dutch tradition it was assumed that the immigrants themselves, by way of their organizations, would play an important role in the emancipation process. However the immigrants were hardly organized; in so far as some leaders had a following they were often not oriented to Dutch society but to the traditions of the home land. In the foundation of Islamic and Hindu schools the model of pluralistic integration is slowly being realized, but in general the role of immigrant organisations and their leadership in the emancipation process has been rather trivial. Their importance had been greatly over-estimated in the first years of the minorities policy.

The results of the minorities policy are not easy to assess. Indicators used to measure levels of social participation such as levels of unemployment, housing situation and school success show a mixed result and certainly not a unilateral improvement (Tesser et al., 1993; 1995; 1996). Ongoing immigration at a time of constantly high unemployment and a great number of immigrant children entering the Dutch school system at a relatively advanced age resulted in a high level of unemployment among young immigrants and a low level of school attainment among immigrant pupils. As usual, more positive developments received less attention in the media and the political debate. The rapid improvement in the housing situation of the immigrant families was for instance more-or-less taken for granted (van Amersfoort and Cortie 1996). The most recent evaluation report (Tesser et al., 1996) shows a modest improvement in nearly all fields, especially in the sector of education where a second generation is starting to participate.

The minorities policy had both direct and indirect consequences for migration control. The direct effects carried weight both with regard to external control and internal control. When several aims of the minorities policy, particularly lowering the high level of unemployment and improving the educational attainments of the young immigrant population, were found to be difficult to achieve, persons and agencies involved in the implementation of this policy became convinced that a strict control at the gate of the welfare state was a prerequisite for a successful integration policy. The reformulation of the rights on family reunification mentioned above was guided by this assumption. It was a paradoxical consequence of the minorities policy that those most committed to it (generally speaking the political left and the Christian groups) also became the advocates of a more strictly applied control policy. The same motivations have also influenced the quest for internal control.

For an analysis of the indirect effects on migration control policy it is important to note that the introduction of the minorities policy contributed to the opinion that migration was leading to social problems. This opinion has been particularly common in big cities and some old industrial centres with high unemployment figures and downgraded neighbourhoods. The paradox of substantial immigration in a period of high unemployment and social insecurity is striking in these areas and a source of social tensions. Moreover the presence of immigrant groups is to a large extent a big city phenomenon. This adds further to the political saliency of the problem because big cities always succeed better than other communities in exposing their problems in the media and on the political agenda. An indirect and certainly not unintended consequence of the minorities policy was that it soon formed a target for racist political propaganda and contributed to make racism a political factor in society generally and with regard to control policy in particular.

Racism as a political factor

As elsewhere in Europe 'racist parties' have made immigration and the presence of immigrants the core of their political propaganda. This strategy has been successful to a certain extent and has contributed to the attempts to control migration more rigorously. Racist groups have been able to exploit the opinion that immigrants create social problems that the parties of the democratic centre can not control. The asylum crisis not only in the Netherlands but in Western Europe in general was pointed at as a clear illustration of the menace of flows of uncountable 'economic refugees'.

In the Netherlands the racist propaganda concentrated its attacks on four problems. In the first place the racist parties have constantly tried to step up the discussion about the 'illegals' ('het illegalendebat'). It is a field where myth and reality are difficult to separate from each other. The number of people residing illegally in the Netherlands is hotly debated (Rath and Schuster 1995, in particular the contribution by Groenendijk and Böcker). The number game around 'illegality' is by definition unsolvable; moreover there are different kinds and shades of illegality.

The problem of the (supposed) connection between crime rates (criminals) and immigration is another sensitive issue, used repeatedly in the propaganda of racist groups. In the global economy crime has also become globalized. The trafficking of drugs, stolen cars and undocumented immigrants is not any longer the business of local, more-or-less amateurish, criminals. Professionally organized crime is connected with international migration because it is, just like legal business, dependent on international flows of products, information, capital and persons. Articles in the newspapers on subjects as the trafficking of drugs by immigrants, the forging of documents and the arranging of paper marriages provide racist groups with ammunition. However this is not the only and perhaps not the politically most sensitive aspect of the connection between immigration and criminal activities. Much more troublesome is the fact that among some sectors of the immigrant population the crime rates are very high indeed. Within some groups, young males seem to be prone to commit crimes and serious and violent crimes at that. The causes of this phenomenon are of course manifold and include the lack of opportunity in the regular labour market, interrupted socialization both in the home culture and in the new society and traditional images of 'manhood' acted out in a post-industrial urban setting (Tesser et al., 1996). The scientific researchers have long avoided this sensitive topic, afraid to contribute to negative stereotyping, but avoiding a difficult topic is rarely the way to combat popular image building and has not prevented a negative impact on the popular discourse about immigrants in criminal activities.

The third issue the racist propaganda has taken on are the conflicts and even violent clashes between certain immigrant communities such as Kurds and Turks and Sunni and Alawi Muslims. This is of course an awkward subject for a government trying to give immigrants an opportunity to participate in society on an equal base.

Last but not least, the racist propaganda has targeted the minorities policy as a waste of money and a burden placed on decent simple citizens by a spendthrift government. The propaganda around these points has grossly exaggerated the existing problems and has often been appalling but it has also shown some shades of respectability, which is difficult for the democratic parties to handle. However the electoral success of the racist parties in the Netherlands has been limited and irregular so far.

They have been most successful at some municipal elections, in particular in the big cities (Buijs en van Donselaar, 1994; Husbands, 1991).

The extremely exact proportional representation system, used in the Dutch electoral system is in itself favourable for small political parties such as the racist ones, but has until now not helped them to get a real impact in municipal councils or the parliament. The main reason for the lack of success, as compared for instance to the French Front National, may be the fact that the extreme right in the Netherlands has failed to produce a leader of any standing. The extremists are splintered into many groups and several parties, bitterly contesting each other. Nevertheless they have shown that racist agitation has made inroads into the electorate of the traditional democratic parties, especially in the areas of immigrant concentration. It was therefore almost inevitable that politicians gave in to it to some extent, making some of the arguments their own. They felt a need to assure the electorate that migration is or will be under full control. The tightening up of the control policies has to some extent been a consequence of the need of the democratic parties to assure the electorate that they were able to control immigration. This is also true for the search for a stricter internal control, to be discussed below.

On the other hand the democratic parties have fought back by associating the racist parties with the rise in discrimination and violence against immigrants and buildings such as mosques associated with immigrants. In 1980 there were only 22 cases reported of harassment of and violence against immigrants, in 1994 there were more than 1,000 of such incidents (Van Donselaar, 1996: 7–10). Many of these incidents have been more-or-less organized by 'vigilante groups', with contacts with and even members of extreme rightist parties. Officially however these parties refrain from this kind of actions to avoid legal action. Involvement in such actions would also harm their appeal to the general electorate. The leaders of these parties know that they must retain an air of respectability if they ever want to stand a chance of an electoral breakthrough. For the same reason it is important for the democratic parties to uncover the links between criminal acts and the extreme political right.

In this discussion of migration control we finally have to consider briefly how the immigrant communities have reacted to the increase of ethnic violence and harassment and the electoral success of racist parties at some of the council elections. Emotionally the impact can, of course, hardly be overestimated. It has also given rise to a certain counter-mobilization, although this has so far been limited in the Netherlands. From the point of migration control the effects have been non-existent or very slight indeed. It is, of course, impossible to know if some prospective immigrants have changed their mind or if some immigrants in the Netherlands have discouraged others from coming because of the unfavourable climate of opinion, but assumptions about the effect of racist agitation on the numbers of the immigrants returning home or applying for Dutch citizenship can be shown to be incorrect. In this respect the actions against immigrants or objects associated with immigrants can be classified not only as immoral and even criminal but also as totally pointless. They may have a negative effect on the integration process, but they have no (important) effect on the number of immigrants.

The Quest for Internal Control

The present-day flows of tourists and businessmen make effective border control virtually impossible. A stricter control would hamper these flows immediately. Not all European countries are, of course, equally affected by the growth in trade and traffic. The Dutch are, by their geographical position, probably particularly aware of the enormous volume of present-day passengers flows and the limited possibilities to supervise them by classical border control procedures. The inadequacy of external control mechanisms combined with the sensitivity of the migration issue adds up to a search for internal controls (Owers 1994). However this is not the only factor behind the quest for more internal control. In the Netherlands this quest cannot be separated from the general problem of social control.

The Dutch welfare state is going through a difficult period. It is over-burdened for various reasons such as the tremendous rise in the techniques for medical treatment, the ageing of the population and, not least, the high and lasting unemployment rates. Against this background is the world of welfare benefit fraud, undocumented labour and tax evasion. A government forced to cut down on welfare expenses is automatically confronted with the demand to put an end to these forms of fraud, undocumented labour and tax evasion. No Dutch Cabinet has failed to put these issues high on its priority list. Pressure for better control on the distribution of welfare benefits, the regularity of employment and the due payment of taxes is not directly related to migration control. By far the greatest number of offenders against these regulations are Dutch citizens, for instance Dutch students working in a 'black job' during the weekend in the tourist business. However, indirectly there is an important link between the quest for more control of the labour market, the tax and welfare systems and the quest for more immigration control. People without a residence title must earn their living in one way or another while remaining outside the searching eye of the bureaucratic machine. The tightening up of control affects their living conditions directly. We have seen already that excluding unwanted migrants from the labour market has been put into practice as a form of migration control. In this line of reasoning it is also logical to prevent illegal immigrants from using the benefits of the welfare state such as unemployment money, free schooling and medical care.

Until recently more rigorous internal control in the Netherlands was impossible because there was no standard central identification document nor were people in normal circumstances obliged to identify themselves. (The only standard exception was when driving a car.) There is great public resistance against a system of compulsory identification, a relic of the German occupation when everyone was obliged to carry an identification card, but by a new law that came into force in July 1994 (Wet Identificatieplicht) the number of occasions where identification can be demanded has been increased, and a limited set of permitted identification documents has been defined. The most important provision of this law makes it the duty of an employer, when contracting a new employee, to identify the person and to keep a copy of the identification document. In the case of a foreigner a copy of the residence document and the work permit (when necessary) should also be kept. Before the introduction of this identification law there was no systematic linking possible between the various administrative systems. This made it possible for illegal residents to live for years in the Netherlands, to rent a house in the social sector, to work and even to pay taxes. A long residence under these illegal conditions was regularly presented in court appeals as sufficient ground to be given a permanent residence title and such appeals were in many cases successful. The new tightened administrative system has already become an instrument for controlling illegal residency, although that is certainly not its only function. However this is the sole purpose of the 'Koppelingswet' (linkage law).

This new law was read in the most important chamber of the Dutch Parliament on 5 November 1996. Since that date there has been much speculation about the consequences of this law. In the mean time further necessary procedures have been almost completed. The law has the explicit purpose of linking the residence status of foreigners to their entitlements such as housing, education, and unemployment benefits. The law has skipped the word 'illegality' with its range of diffuse meanings. In a commentary on the law, Ms van Craaikamp, the head of the Directorate for Foreigners of the Ministry of Justice has declared that the 'law for the first time has explicitly spelled out the connection between the residence titles and the entitlements to the collective benefits of the welfare state. This explicitness is very important for the implementation of the law. The administrative institutions and the municipalities that have to implement the regulations were in need of a law that is absolutely clear about who is entitled to a certain benefit and who is not' (*Voortgang*, 10 December 1996, interview, my translation). There can be no doubt that this new law is also thought to be an instrument for indirect migration control. In the same interview Ms van Craaikamp states that the Ministry of Justice expects that the 'Koppelingswet' will send a strong message out to people considering (illegal) migration to the Netherlands.

The big question with regard to this law is, of course, how it will be implemented. Already during the preparation of the law this question has been hotly debated (Minderhout, 1994; Wentholt, 1995). It was pointed out that excluding children from the educational system is in contradiction to the international Treaty of Children's Rights. Persons under 18 years of age are therefore excluded from the controls in the law as it was finally proposed. This means that children, whatever the residence title of their parents have to be included in the Dutch school system.

Although the law had not yet come into force when this chapter was written, it still merits consideration in a discussion of immigration control because it illustrates very clearly the drive towards increasing control. The pressure on governments to show that they can manage migration processes leads to a search for internal control instruments when the traditional external control instruments are obviously not achieving satisfying results. It also merits discussion because it brings in the open the dilemma welfare states have to face when they are forced to choose between integration of immigrant populations and migration control. An important implicit aim of the law is to discourage people from coming to the Netherlands without a clear residence title. If people enter the Netherlands 'undocumented', they should have less chance to earn a living and remain unnoticed. The idea behind this is, of course, that illegal residency, detected in an earlier stage, leads to an easier procedure to expel people.

The serious problem is that if the new law fails to discourage the settlement of undocumented immigrants and does not lead to a more effective policy of detention of illegal residents the outcome will be the marginalization of part of the immigrant population. A full and strict implementation of the law could make the realization of the aims of the minorities policy as started with the White Paper of 1983 much more difficult. It is likely to induce stricter surveillance of immigrant communities in general as social and ethnic networks form the main port of entry of legal and not so legal immigrants. It is therefore to be expected that agencies and institutions committed to the emancipation of the immigrant populations will not be enthusiastic about the implementation of the new regulations, but it is at present impossible to foresee in how far the law will be enacted and what the results will be. It is, however, not far fetched to assume that the implementation of the 'Koppelingswet' will meet with the same barriers all forms of internal control have met so far: other interests and definitions of the situation by the various branches of the state apparatus (such as welfare offices, educational boards, medical agencies), other priorities in the police apparatus and generally the costs and personnel involved in a really drastic implementation of the law.

Conclusions

In the period under description, migration control in the Netherlands has developed as a reaction to migration in the previous decades. Some indirect control measures have been specific for the Netherlands, such as the change in citizenship status of the Surinamese population and the Remplod-project, but in general the development of Dutch migration control policy fits into the broader West European pattern. The search for more effective control instruments is a response to developments since the period of economic restructuring that was triggered of by the oil crisis of 1973/74. The industries dependent on a high input of low-skilled manual labour have either moved to low-wage countries or have been technologically rejuvenated and they need now much less (and more highly skilled) labour. This development has resulted in a level of unemployment that had been unknown in the post war period. This rise in unemployment has been especially marked among immigrant populations dependent on the classical 'blue collar jobs'. Nevertheless the number of immigrants increased, contrary to the conventional wisdom that regarded migration primarily as a response to labour market developments. The search for (more) immigration control has aimed at overcoming this paradoxical situation. This explains why migration flows that are not part of this paradox (flows within the European Union or the developed world in general) do not play a role in the migration control discourse. This discourse and the policy measures based on it are in fact aimed at getting the immigration from 'peripheral countries' under control.

The classical control of passports and visas at the border and other points of entry such as harbours and airports has been tightened up in an endeavour to stem the rising tide of immigration. At the same time the tremendous increase in the number of border crossings (tourists, business people, visitors) make this control increasingly difficult to execute effectively. This has lead to two developments. In the first place, *external-*

ization: the classical border control has been shifted (as much as possible) from the border to the country of departure. Documents have to be acquired at the embassies and consulates in the homelands. Even 'unofficial' agencies such as transport agencies have been made responsible for the execution of control. In the second place, *implicit control:* instruments that were originally not intended to be instruments for migration control have been used as such. The work permit, that was originally a mechanism to protect the indigenous worker on the labour market, was made an instrument for migration control in the early 1970s.

External control mechanisms are aimed at preventing unwanted immigrants from entering the country. Nevertheless, many immigrants succeed in entering and try to regulate their status afterwards. This is especially the case with the people claiming refugee status. For them, however, a different control mechanism is used. Although these people are already inside the country they are excluded from society, especially from the labour market, during the (often lengthy) examination procedures. What happens to those applicants who are refused is less clear. Some of them leave the country voluntarily, whereas others are made to leave by force. However, many (perhaps as much as 70 per cent) 'vanish' and augment the number of illegal residents.

The strategy to exclude unwanted immigrants has become increasingly important. This strategy is not only implemented by what are officially called migration management instruments. Sanctions against employers, identification obligations and a more tight control of the recipients of welfare benefits, are in the first place intended to fight fraud and tax evasion. At the same time they are clearly also used to make illegal residency more difficult. The internal control mechanisms can be described as explicit migration control in so far as they indeed lead to the detection of illegal residents and to their (forced) return. However the scale on which voluntary and not-so-voluntary return migration takes place is so low that the success of these mechanisms as explicit migration control instruments can be seriously called into question. It is of course hard to prove or disprove whether they have any direct or implicit effects. It is however likely that the indirect effects exist more in the minds of politicians than in reality.

So far we have only looked at the official, governmental policies. However there are also 'unofficial' reactions in society that could lead to the deterrence of prospective migrants and/or an inducement to return migration. The increase in xenophobic feelings, in violence and other forms of harassment and the electoral success of racist parties could be described as a form of 'spontaneous' implicit migration control. These practices are deplorable but they do not seem to have a notable effect on the processes of immigration or return migration.

Internal control confronts the welfare state with a deep and practically unsolvable dilemma. Ineffective control mechanisms, unsuccessful in reducing the number of illegal residents, could bring about a different and totally unwanted result: the creation of marginalized subpopulations, or in the terms of Dutch policy makers, of ethnic minorities. In this way the quest for more control over migration is in direct contradiction to the aim of the 'minorities policy, to include the immigrant populations as soon as possible in the social fabric of society.

References

Amersfoort, H. van (1995), 'From Workers to Immigrants: Turks and Moroccans in the Netherlands, 1965–1992' in: Cohen, R.(ed.), *The Cambridge Survey of World Migration,* 308–12. Cambridge: Cambridge University Press.

—— (1996), 'Migration: the limits of governmental control', *New Community,* 22: 243–57.

Amersfoort, H. van and Penninx, R. (1994), 'Regulating Migration in Western Europe: The Dutch Experience 1960–92', *The Annals of the American Academy of Political and Social Science,* 534: 133–46.

Amersfoort, H. van and Cortie, C. (1996), 'Social Polarization in a Welfare State? Immigrants in the Amsterdam region', *New Community,* 22: 671–87.

Brink, M. and Pasariboe, M. (eds) (1993), *Asylum seekers in the Netherlands,* Amsterdam: University of Amsterdam, ISG.

Buijs, F.J. and van Donselaar,J. (1994), *Extreem-rechts,* Leiden: Liswo.

Dijk, P.C.J.van, Koelstra, R.W., De Mas, P., Penninx, R., van Renselaar H.C. and van Velzen, L. (1978), *REMPLOD-project; slotconclusies en aanbevelingen.* Den Haag: IMWOO/NUFFIC.

Donselaar, J. van (1996), *Reacties op racistisch geweld,* Tijdelijke Wetenschappelijke Commissie Minderhedenbeleid, Amsterdam: Het Spinhuis.

Doomernik, J, Penninx, R. and van Amersfoort, H. (1997), *Migratiebeleid voor de toekomst: mogelijkheden en beperkingen.* Tijdelijke Wetenschappelijke Commissie Minderhedenbeleid, Amsterdam: Het Spinhuis.

Gooszen, H. (1988), *Vluchtelingen en asielzoekers; demografische en sociaal-economische positie,* Den Haag: NIDI.

Groenendael, T. van (1986), *Dilemma's van regelgeving. De regularisatie van illegale buitenlandse werknemers 1975–1985,* Alphen a/d Rijn: Samsom/H.D. Tjeenk Willink.

Hammar, T. (ed.) (1985), *European immigration policy. A comparative study*, Cambridge: Cambridge University Press.

—— (1990), *Democracy and the Nation State, Aliens, Denizens and Citizens in a World of International Migration.* Aldershot: Avebury.

Heijs, E. (1995), *Van vreemdeling tot Nederlander. De verlening van het Nederlanderschap aan vreemdelingen 1813–1992*, Amsterdam: Het Spinhuis.

Husbands, C.T. (1991), 'Phoenixes from the ashes? The recovery of the Centrumpartij '86 and the Centrumdemocraten, 1989–1991', in: *Jaarboek,* 84–102, Groningen: Rijksuniversiteit Groningen, *Documentatiecentrum Nederlandse Politieke Partijen.*

Lebon, A. (1984), 'Return migration from France: policies and data' in: D. Kubat (ed.), *The Politics of Return Migration:* 153–69. New York: Center for Migration Studies..

Lijphart, A. (1977), *Democracy in Plural Societies: A Comparative exploration.* New Haven: Yale University Press,.

Minderhout, P.E. (1994), 'De koppeling van voorzieningen aan het verblijfsrecht van vreemdelingen', *Migrantenrecht* 179–86.

Ministerie van Binnenlandse Zaken (1983), *Minderhedennota* Den Haag.

Muus, P. (1994, 1995 and 1996), SOPEMI-reports to the OECD on the Netherlands., Amsterdam: University of Amsterdam, Human Geography.

Muus, P, Penninx, R, van Amersfoort, J.M.M, Bovenkerk, F. and Verschoor, W. (1983), *Retourmigratie van Mediterranen, Surinamers en Antillianen in Nederland.* Den Haag: Ministerie van Sociale Zaken en Werkgelegenheid, 's Gravenhage.

Muus, P. and Penninx R. (1991), *Immigratie van Turken en Marokkanen in Nederland.* Den Haag: Ministerie van Binnenlandse Zaken.

Owers, A. (1994), 'The age of internal controls?' in Spencer, S. (ed.), *Strangers and Citizens. A positive approach to migrants and refugees:* 264–81. London: IPPR/ Rivers Oram Press.

Rath, J. and Schuster J. (ed.) (1995), 'Illegalen', *Themanummer Migrantenstudies,* 101–64.

Tesser, P.T.M. (1993), *Rapportage Minderheden 1993.* Rijswijk: Sociaal en Cultureel Planbureau.

Tesser, P.T.M., van Praag, C.S., van Dugteren, F.A., Herweijer, L.J. and van der Wouden, H.C. (1995), *Rapportage Minderheden 1995. Concentratie en Segregatie.* Rijswijk: Sociaal en Cultureel Planbureau.

Tesser, P.T.M., van Dugteren F.A. and Merens, A. 1996, *Rapportage*

Minderheden 1996. Bevolking, arbeid, onderwijs, huisvesting. Rijswijk: Sociaal en Cultureel Planbureau.

Voortgang (1996/1997) Uitgave no.10 en11 van het Centraal Orgaan opvang asielzoekers en de Immigratie- en naturalisatiedienst.

Wentholt, K. (1995), 'Het sociale-zekerheidsrecht en de verblijfsstatus van vreemdelingen', *Sociaal Maandblad Arbeid*, 1995: 562–77.

– 6 –

Closing the Doors to the Swedish Welfare State
Tomas Hammar

Introduction

In the 1980s the context of Swedish immigration control changed in three respects. Firstly, the end of the Cold War made Sweden's geographical location in the very north of Europe, far from the most frequented routes of international migration, less advantageous than before. When furthermore, the Soviet system's efficient emigration control disappeared, Sweden suddenly feared large and irregular migration flows from the East. Secondly, as a small country with highly developed technology, Sweden had always been dependent on international trade and capital. In the 1990s this dependence increased heavily with consequences for Swedish immigration control and not least for refugee policy. New policy programmes were formulated including new forms of international coordination and an intensified cooperation within the European Union and the Schengen agreement. Thirdly, a trend towards deregulation of the labour market encouraged the growth of an informal sector, weakening the social control that until recently had prevented most illegal immigration.

During this period Sweden has closed its doors to numbers of new immigrants, especially from less fortunate countries in the South and in the East, in the same way as other countries in the industrialized world have done. Although some of the conditions have changed, Sweden's ability to control immigration has remained high thanks to know-how and trained people as well as well-established aliens legislation. Both external and internal control methods have long been used. Sweden has until recently combined control and integration into one immigration policy under one immigration administration. However, in 1998 two Ministries became involved, the Ministry for Foreign Affairs and the Ministry of Interior. In June 1998 a new central integration authority was established alongside the Immigration Board, which as before remains in charge of immigration control.

Sweden is not a traditional immigration country, but it has employed a policy of permanent immigration. In the early 1980s with a foreign-born population of 630,000, the less than eight million people born in Sweden did not worry much about their nation's identity. Maybe the low-key national self-confidence of the Swedes was based on the country's long history of independence and peace, and on the fact that for many years, ethnic or religious divisions have not been of major political significance. Both the Same-nation (about 10,000) and the Finns in the Torne Valley along the border to Finland and in the North (about 30,000) are native people, which at long last have been recognized as minorities.

In this chapter I shall present an overview of the control system before and after the breaking point in the end of the 1980s. Without going into too much detail, I shall describe internal and external control methods and discuss their interrelations. I shall also discuss how a long tradition of keeping immigration policy outside party politics came to a sudden end, as well as some of the consequences thereof. At the end of the chapter, I shall discuss the control's efficiency, the costs and consequences of control, its externalization and international co-ordination, and finally the implications for the legal and personal status of aliens in Sweden as well as the mechanisms binding control policy and public opinion together.

An Historical Overview

During the last fifty years, a relatively high number of foreign-born persons have settled in Sweden. There is no single explanation for the flows and the policies. Rather, there have been several mechanisms, domestic, international and transnational. The relevant international economic and technological developments are, of course, the same for Sweden as for other industrialized countries, and the business cycles have often led to simultaneous changes in the national immigration regulations, towards either more or less strict control. Historic, economic, cultural and linguistic ties have formed the bilateral relations between specific emigration and immigration countries (Hammar, 1985).

One example is Finnish emigration to Sweden. A Nordic labour market, with several forerunners, had been formally agreed upon in 1954 (Fischer and Straubhaar, 1996). Citizens of Nordic countries have been exempted from immigration control in the Nordic countries, free to travel without a passport and free to work and take residence without a special permit since then. In other words, the Nordic labour market has established a zone of free circulation for all citizens of the Nordic countries, but not for third country citizens – a Nordic zone comparable to the labour market of the European Union in the 1990s. It is important to note, that Nordic citizens still enjoy this exemption from immigration and alien control, and that the following discussion therefore does not apply to them. Furthermore, since the beginning of 1994 when Finland and Sweden became members of the EU (while Norway remained outside), immigration control does not apply to citizens of the member states of the EU or the EEA-agreement either. At the end of this century, Swedish control is therefore directed solely to citizens of countries outside these regions.

Box 6.1 Periods of Swedish Immigration Control in the Twentieth Century

1. Before 1914 free international migration (but control of immigration from tsarist Russia)
2. 1914–45 successive creation of immigration legislation and of specialized alien and immigration authorities
3. 1945–72 a market system of labour import, monitored with trade union consent
4. 1972–89 a control system, first liberal, then gradually more restrictive
5. 1989– a strict control, but nevertheless an increase of illegal residence and work

---

Up to the 1970s, the major flows of immigration came from Finland to Sweden for economic and historic reasons, and because of the Nordic labour market. The demands of the Swedish labour market were for a long period matched by a surplus supply in the Finnish labour market. Early on, Italian and Hungarian migrants had come to work, but it was only at the end of the 1960s that large-scale labour migration started from Yugoslavia, Greece and Turkey (Lundh and Ohlsson, 1994).

A distinction between general and individual control is useful. The former aims at steering the flows of migration, whereas the objective of the latter is to check individual aliens, for example, to exclude persons with personal characteristics like criminality, terrorism, poverty, illness or some special disease (HIV), or perhaps some religious faith or cultural behaviour, or even ethnicity (Roma blood). In many European countries the original purpose of immigration control was to supervise individual foreigners, and when general control later emerged, it was shaped in the same form, as that already used in the control of individual persons. Maybe this is why the present international refugee system is still in theory based on an examination of individual claims for refugee status, although in practice more and more exceptions are made, such as temporary permits for categories of people.

In 1917 Sweden introduced a control system, which was intended to be general but which in practice came to be an individual one. It made direct use of both external instruments such as passports and visa requirements and also of internal control methods such as work and residence permits. In 1927, the first Aliens Act was approved by the Riksdag as a summation of all the previous innovations, but this Act was valid only for five years, as it was still considered to be an emergency Act. In 1954, the Riksdag enacted the first permanent legislation, a symbol of the fact that immigration control was also considered necessary under normal conditions.

Box 6.2 Periods of Swedish Integration Policy in the Twentieth Century

1. – 1945 no policy of integration. From the 1920s social and economic rights for denizens. In 1939 the first Riksdag decision to grant refugee assistance (0.5 Million SEK).
2. 1945–64 assimilation was considered to be an automatic social process, and immigrants were expected to adapt to Swedish norms and patterns of behaviour without any integration policy.
3. 1964–75 a policy making period. The policy aims were shifted via mutual adaptation to freedom of choice: language training, home language instruction for children, local immigrant councils etc.
4. 1975–85 towards a multicultural Sweden: implementation of the principles of 1975: voting rights for aliens, subsidies to immigrant associations, churches and press, a new refugee resettlement programme and, in 1989, the integration of refugees.
5. 1985– Emphasis on Swedish language and culture, more than on ethnic pluralism. Halt in the further development of support for immigrant minorities and cuts in home language instruction. Crisis in refugee resettlement because of high unemployment among Swedes and aliens.

The first special alien and immigration control authority for the whole of Sweden was a section of the Stockholm police, which was provisionally made responsible for the implementation of the national policy. In 1937 when a lot of public attention was paid to an 'invasion' of a few hundred

Jewish refugees from Hitler's Germany, a special aliens' bureau was established within the National Board of Social Affairs (Socialstyrelsen). This temporary arrangement lasted until 1944, when it was disclosed that the head of this bureau's confidential archive of personal acts had been giving the German embassy in Stockholm secret information about refugees in Sweden. The bureau was replaced by an independent, but still temporary, authority called the Aliens Board. Its main task was to control individual alien, to decide about permits and deportations. In 1969, twenty-five years later, after heavy public criticism, the temporary Aliens Board was replaced by the first permanent state agency, the Immigration Authority (SIV). The name indicated that this agency was given responsibility not only for control but also for integration of immigrants. This was also a remarkable innovation from an international perspective, as one and the same ministry or state agency usually does not handle both sides of a country's immigration policy (Hammar, 1985).

An end to the recruitment of labour

In 1965, because of a sudden and unorganized flow of temporary workers from Yugoslavia, the Swedish government issued a decree of fundamental importance for the control of immigration of labour, and did so without asking for the formal consent of the Riksdag. Foreign citizens were from this time obliged to apply for work permits before they arrived, and this gave the immigration and labour market authorities increased power to plan, select and organize the immigration of foreign labour (Lundh and Ohlsson, 1994: 77 ff).

Fifteen years later, in 1981, the same system (application before arrival) was also used for residence permits. Sweden had in the meantime also experienced the need for external control of immigrants other than migrant workers. A few thousand refugees from Eastern Turkey, called the Assyrians, had caused some economic and political unrest, and they had finally been allowed to settle (Björklund, 1981). External control before arrival was introduced in the hope that this would prevent future unwanted attempts by other religious or ethnic communities. The Minister of Immigration wrote in a Bill to the Riksdag (RD prop. 1979/80:96:32), that control before arrival would also reduce the time used for examination of the asylum applications. It would thus decrease the cost to the state, and at the same time also reduce the psychological pressure on the applicants who were waiting for a decision that was of great importance for them – an argument that foreshadowed a theme of many future debates.

Table 6.1 Sweden: Foreign Residents by Continents 1980–97

| Continents | Foreign resident population in per cent | | | n |
	1980	1990	1997	1997
Europe	84%	64%	66%	343,331
thereof				
Nordic citizens	57%	40%	31%	162,221
Other EU-citizens	13%	10%	10%	50,095
Other European citizens	14%	14%	25%	131,015
Africa	2%	4%	5%	27,839
Asia	9%	21%	20%	103,186
North America	2%	3%	3%	13,386
South America	3%	5%	3%	18,436
Other countries	1%	3%	3%	15,871
TOTAL	100%	100%	100%	522,049

Source: Statistics Sweden.

The peak of labour migration to Sweden occurred in 1969–70, and the recruitment of foreign labour was terminated two years later, during a short recession in February 1972 (Table 6.1). Again, a radical policy change was made without the approval of either the Riksdag, or the Government. It was instead proclaimed by the national organization of trade unions, the Landsorganisation (LO), which used its veto against the import of labour, and made this known only in a circular letter to local unions (Hammar, 1988).

Similar decisions were taken shortly thereafter in many other West European countries, such as Germany, France and Norway, but in these countries they were made explicit in declarations, clearly signalling that labour immigration was to be stopped from now on (Hammar 1985: 284ff.). It was different in Sweden, where the political system was not directly involved, and the general public was not informed. Even if probably the same decision would have also been taken by the political parties, had they been asked for an opinion, the impact of this corporativistic and tacit political behaviour might have been significant during the following years, not only on policy formulation but paradoxically indirectly also on public opinion, which in the absence of any political debate was not informed about facts and arguments. We shall return to this lack of politicization of immigration, the apolitical tradition.

A Policy of Permanent Residence

Until 1972, the trade unions accepted the recruitment of foreign labour on the condition that foreigners were given the same working and wage conditions as any other worker. They should be members of the union and, if fired, they should not be deported but enjoy the same unemployment benefits as all other union members. They should be entitled to social rights and benefits and also to some political rights. In sum, they were accepted as denizens in the sense of future citizens of the country. In contrast to many other European countries, Sweden embarked on a policy of permanent immigration, not on a guest-worker policy, and this had great implications for the regulation of immigration flows.

With the union's consent, the companies had been allowed to recruit foreign workers, and those recruited had, after one or two years, been given denizen status – a permanent permit to stay and take up any work in the country (in Swedish called a PUT or Permanent Residence Permit). Only those who had committed serious crimes, or voluntarily left the country for a long period, could lose this permit. The principle that foreign-born workers should enjoy the same conditions and opportunities as native born workers without delay, made applications for renewal of permits a formality. Immigrant workers were, in other words, quickly exempted from most immigration or alien control. As a consequence Sweden could not reduce the number of foreign-born residents, neither by the promotion of return in individual cases, nor by mass deportation. The only way to limit the numbers was to stop new immigration. It is true that the policy of permanent residence (in itself a control measure) was first of all aimed at the integration of migrant workers into the welfare system. However, in order to create conditions favourable for integration, Sweden had to regulate the immigration flows, using a combination of external control before arrival and control at the border.

This interdependence of integration and control is manifested also in other ways. A permanent residence policy and a well-developed social welfare system made the country attractive for immigrants. Sweden acquired an image of being benevolent and relatively open to immigration, although, after 1972, only two categories were wanted or tolerated (refugees and family members). When the demand for labour decreased sharply, the generous image became a problem: Sweden, more than several other countries, had to show its will and power to strictly limit the numbers. Restrictions were also needed to protect welfare resources, for available social goods were more scarce, and in the late 1980s asylum seekers were soon claimed to be a heavy burden. Accordingly, the permanent policy of integration into Sweden required an effective immigration control.

During this period, thanks to the policy of permanent immigration, the well-organized trade union movement was able to exercise institutionalized social control, not in all trades, but especially in the big industries with many employees per enterprise. Employers could not hire illegals without repercussions, and foreign citizens could not get a job without a work permit. One example was the construction industry, which in Sweden traditionally, and also at the time of labour recruitment, was closed to most foreign citizens. As a result, there were until recently few illegal immigrant workers in the labour market – much fewer than in most European countries. It is only during the 1990s that the union control has been weakened and several foreigners without work permits have found jobs in a growing informal labour market.

Why a Policy Change in About 1985?

From the mid-1980s, both integration and control policies have successively changed for international as well as for domestic reasons. In the autumn of 1984, an unexpected growth in immigration to Western Europe was also noticed in Sweden. While around 5,000 asylum seekers per year had been received previously, the numbers more than tripled in 1985–88 up to 15–20,000 per year, and then continued to increase up to about 30,000 per year in 1988–91. The peak came in 1992 when a record number of 84,000 asylum seekers arrived, mainly from former Yugoslavia.

Nordic immigration, previously two-thirds of the total, fell to one-third and less, while immigration from countries outside Europe grew above 50 per cent of the annual net immigration. Asylum seekers came from the Kurdish struggle for independence, the war between Iraq and Iran, the civil war in Lebanon, and several other political conflicts. This increase in the number of asylum seekers was part and parcel of the general increase in Western Europe at this time, caused by warfare and repression in Africa, Asia and finally in the former Yugoslavia. Compared with other countries, Sweden had received many asylum seekers, and co-ordination and burden sharing was called for in Europe, especially as the general increase was often seen as a beginning and a foreboding of future much larger flows, both from the poverty-stricken south and from the chaotic political situations in the new states in the east, the successors of the former Soviet Union. In this perspective, discussions began in Sweden about a new and comprehensive immigration policy, which would integrate control policy

Table 6.2 Sweden: Asylum Seekers by Continents and Regions 1984–97

Continents	1984–88	1989–93	1994–97	1984–97 n	Per cent
Europe	7,800	128,900	18,100	154,800	47%
Thereof f. Yugoslavia	*1,900*	*115,900*	*17,000*	*134,900*	*41%*
Africa	4,500	14,400	2,900	21,800	7%
Middle East	40,600	43,000	12,200	95,800	29%
Latin America	11,600	3,200	2,400	17,200	5%
Other countries	10,200	19,200	7,500	36,900	12%
TOTAL	74,700	208,700	43,100	326,500	100%

Source: SIV and Police statistics, Sweden Statistics, Meddelanden Be 1995–96.

with foreign and security policy and with Swedish development assistance (Ministry of Labour, 1990).

Behind this new policy development were also two domestic factors, a record high rate of unemployment, and a new programme for refugee resettlement. Since the 1930s, Sweden had successfully implemented a Keynesian full-employment policy. In 1992, later than in other European countries, and after the growth in non-European immigration and after the end of the Cold War, the proportion of unemployed on the labour market rose from around 3–4 per cent and up to 8–10 per cent, and the rate for unemployed foreign workers climbed to above 20 per cent. The number of foreigners outside the labour market thereafter remained at extremely high levels, with striking implications for the welfare system in general, and especially grim consequences for the newly arrived immigrants and refugees. As most of them have not found employment, they have been segregated and marginalized, at high public cost. At the end this has also brought about more outspoken negative opinions towards immigrants and immigration, as well as heavy demands for more effective control (Statistics Sweden, 1997).

In addition to unemployment, in 1984 there was a second factor, a reform of the national system for integration of refugees. Local neighbourhoods with good supplies of housing, job, schooling and language training, counselling and so forth were asked to provide a rapid integration. The programme was planned for about 6,000 refugees per year, which would have been more than enough during the previous ten years, but it was immediately overloaded and had to be quickly expanded because of new refugee immigration.

The original idea was largely maintained and implemented, but the refugees had to be spread to many more municipalities all over the country. The 'burden' of receiving them had to be carried in solidarity. This programme soon provoked demands for a more strict control, which could reduce the state's costs for refugees. The Immigration Authority (SIV) had to use some pressure to make local politicians ready to accept new refugees in their municipalities. Around 1990, outbursts of openly visible xenophobic trends occurred in or around refugee centres or against asylum seekers living there.

The Apolitical Tradition

Summing up this historic sketch, we may call the integration policy developed from 1968 to 1975 a piece of social engineering. Sweden tried to adapt its welfare policy to the needs of new, immigrant groups. When general social welfare ideology was combined with an already old policy of permanent immigration, this meant that the principle of equality was recognized as valid for all legal residents, citizens and denizens alike. Social and political participation became central objectives, and to this was added vague ideas about ethnic minority rights in a future multicultural Sweden. The whole was summarized in 1974 by a Parliamentary Commission on Immigration in the following, often quoted three words: equality, freedom of choice and partnership.

In general, this policy was well received by the public, the political parties and the policy makers. It was seen as successful and even quoted as a model for other countries. The trade unions had accepted the recruitment of foreign labour. Most immigrants had been Finnish, and the number of asylum seekers had been small. The political parties seemed to agree that immigration should not be brought into the electoral campaigns. A broad tacit consensus, or what we might call an apolitical and corporativistic tradition, characterized this period (Hammar, 1997).

In line with this apolitical tradition some very important political reforms were made without decisions of the Riksdag: we have mentioned the end to spontaneous labour immigration in 1966–67 and the end to recruitment in 1972 (Lundh and Ohlsson 1994: 77f). All parties were also united in 1995 when the Riksdag sanctioned the principles of Swedish immigration policy. The debate was short and the decisions unanimous. Even in the late 1980s, many complained that the local efforts to integrate immigrants were not publicly appreciated, that politicians did not bother, and that media only published sensational events. Although there were more than one million people of 'immigrant background', either of the first or second generation, in a population of less than nine million people, and although a lot of criticism was often heard in private conversations, there was no public political debate.

The radical change occurred in the end of the 1980s, when the taboo against xenophobic arguments in political debate was lifted. Several events anticipated this change. In 1987, one of the most spectacular among them took place in a minor municipality, Sjöbo, in southern Sweden. The local council refused to participate in the national refugee resettlement pro-gramme, and this refusal was made into a major national issue when a local referendum was arranged at the time of the general election in September 1988. This referendum gave a clear result: 65 per cent voted against the admission of refugees. For the first time, it was demonstrated that there were strong negative opinions in the electorate, opinions that none of the traditional political parties had given voice to. These opinions, negative towards immigrants or immigration or against the immigration policy of the country, were more common in some parties than in others, but they were now voiced in all the parties. Three years later, in the election of 1991, a rapidly founded populist party, New Democracy, exploited the discontent with Sweden's immigration and refugee policy, directly gaining 8 per cent of the national vote. To counter this political situation, the traditional parties changed their strategies, changed the political debate and broke the apolitical tradition. It was in this political context, that a new, more restrictive control policy was introduced in December of 1989 (Fryklund and Peterson, 1989; Alsmark and Uddman, 1990).

Control Policy in the 1990s

Year by year since 1985, both internal and external control have been strengthened. Initially little seemed to change. Sweden's refugee policy remained generous and family reunion went on as usual, but after almost a decade the change was visible in law and in practice. It is a matter of debate, however, how much more restrictive the system has become and what the consequences are. It is also debated how much of this change has been Swedish policy and how much the impact of intensified European cooperation. Efforts to make control more efficient have been made everywhere in Western Europe, and they have been increasingly co-ordinated in various fora and several different forms. From the Maastricht summit in 1991, and especially after the Amsterdam meeting in 1997, most of this co-ordination takes place within the EU, and even if Sweden has few problems adapting to EU-policy, regard is always paid to this policy both in legislation and implementation.

External control

Scandinavian territorial borders are favourable for control of immigration, even in comparison with those of the United Kingdom. The peninsula, surrounded by the Atlantic Ocean and the Baltic, has a land border only in the very north. Small boats have on many occasions, and some of great historic significance, crossed these waters illegally and secretly, but surveillance has become more and more effective, as modern technology is used to discover smuggling not only of goods and drugs but also of refugees. During the Cold War, the Eastern shore of the Baltic had been closed by the USSR for military reasons but also to prevent emigration, and Finland had given protection to Sweden by strict surveillance of its Eastern borders. In the post-Cold War era, illegal passages across the Baltic are again seen as a major problem.

According to the Nordic Passport Union of 1957, Nordic borders are completely open for citizens of Denmark, Finland, Iceland, Norway and Sweden. Control at the Swedish borders with Norway, Denmark and Finland has therefore long been rather casual and easy to escape. Until recently, the last thorough border control for travellers from the south on motor ways or railways to Sweden has been at the Danish border with Germany and in the ferry ports of Sweden. From 1999 these checkpoints will also be weakened, as the freedom to travel without a visa or even a passport is extended to all EU-citizens, and thanks to a special agreement also to Norwegians, although Norway is not a member of the EU (see Chapter 2). Control at the inner borders between the EU countries will be replaced by control at the outer borders, at the periphery of the EU. To the east of Sweden and Finland, this periphery is close, as long as Russia, the Baltic states, and Poland remain outside the union, and the outer border is in the waters of the Baltic Sea (RD prop. 1996/97:25:78 f).

There are still passport checkpoints at the Swedish borders, harbours and airports, but the control there is hardly good enough to stop all illegal entries. The police check all those who go through the doors for non-EU citizens, and then also – in a discriminating manner – those who pass through the Nordic (European) doors but look as if they should not go there. Often a sort of simple language test is used. The traveller is asked to say a few words, for instance in Swedish, and is allowed to pass without showing a passport, if the 'sound' is all right. EU citizens are exempted from the alien control and enjoy the status of legal residents and workers without special permits. As a result, the task of the alien control is reduced, although probably not facilitated. In 1999 less than half of Sweden's foreign residents remain under alien control, and among them only a small number are illegal residents or workers (SOU 1997: 128:112).

There are regular transportation routes by air and sea to Sweden from Poland and the Baltic states. During some years the German Democratic Republic allowed asylum seekers from the Middle East transit even if they did not have a visa to enter Sweden. After several discussions with the GDR government, parallel to talks initiated by the Danish and West-German governments, this transit came to a halt in the end of 1985. It was soon followed by a similar agreement also with Poland. The trafficking of refugees continued via Russia and the Baltic states, however, both on regular lines and in small private vessels, and despite intensified Swedish surveillance, the confiscation of several vessels, and the imprisonment in Sweden of captains and even members of the crews, this smuggling of human beings has not been completely stopped (RD SfU 1985/86:21: 8 ff.).

The visa system

As mentioned, Sweden early developed a system of external control, requiring permits before arrival, first for work and later also for residency. Visa requirements had first been applied to most countries in the world, but over time more and more countries were exempted. From the middle of the 1980s, more emphasis was again placed on visas and transit visas and at the end of the millennium, Sweden required a visa from citizens of several European and most non-European countries, and especially from citizens of those countries from which unwanted immigration might be expected. As a member of the EU and a supporter of the Schengen agreement, Sweden has adapted and extended the list of visa countries. If other European countries required a visa, while Sweden did not, potential flows would come immediately, just as, to mention one example, many more Cuban refugees asked for asylum in 1994, when visa requirements were upheld in other countries, but not in Sweden (RD prop. 1996/ 97:25:121 ff.).

In the early 1980s, few would have foreseen that the visa system would soon be re-activated as one of the most important instruments to reduce or stop unwanted immigration. In retrospect, this sudden reversal of the visa policy gives an indication of the fundamental change that has taken place both in control policy and in public opinion. In 1983, a government Bill had asked for a liberalization of (what was then seen as) a much too restrictive visa practice. At that time, there were no doubts in the mind of the Minister that SIV too often refused visa to relatives of aliens residing in Sweden, and that SIV often exaggerated the risk that these relatives would change their mind and against their own declarations try to settle in Sweden (Wikrén and Sandesjö, 1990: 50f.). These statements about a liberalization of visa practice from 1983 were completely forgotten in the restrictive mood of the 1990s.

In June 1993, the Government made two significant decisions. Firstly, refugees from Bosnia-Herzegovina, already in Sweden, were granted permanent resident permits. Secondly, visas were introduced for other citizens of the same country, who from that day wished to visit Sweden. These decisions almost completely stopped the flows. In practice, refugees in need of international protection were prevented from travelling to Sweden. Humanitarian organizations and refugee groups criticized the decisions as serious mistakes and violations of the principle that refugees should be given an opportunity to escape to another country and ask for asylum there. The government answered that visa requirements usually did not prevent people from seeking international protection, but could prevent them from doing so in Sweden (RD prop. 1996/97:25:123). If this involved a too heavy burden for some other countries, this should be solved in international co-operation and by burden-sharing. The Swedish refugee quota, the annual transfer of internationally recognized refugees, was useful for this purpose.

Anti-trafficking policy

A single country alone can seldom stop the smuggling of illegal immigrants. To achieve this takes international co-operation. Sweden is, as mentioned, active in the EU and Schengen, in the Council of Europe, and in several relevant UN organizations (the UNHCR, ILO, IOM, and others). In several policy areas, and within the general framework of Swedish foreign policy, high priority is given to a broad co-operation with the Baltic states. In 1996 Sweden promised to assist these countries in the development of an efficient Western-style migration control. As part of this co-operation the Swedish visa requirements have been or will be lifted, as soon as the Baltic states have become signatories to the Geneva Refugee Convention, being obliged as first asylum countries to readmit asylum seekers who have passed their territory. Sweden has also given strong support to these countries' applications for membership of an extended EU (RD prop. 1996/97:25).

Since the 1930s, smuggling of people has been a criminal offence in Sweden, and from the 1980s this has applied also to attempts and preparations. This has not stopped the traffic, however. The smuggling went on and for a time even increased. In October 1992, an Estonian ship stranded on the Swedish coast. It was not seaworthy and carried 20 Iranian Kurds, who asked for asylum, saying that they had been transported via Turkey and Russia. During the following months, four more ships of the same type arrived. The captains were imprisoned, but not the crews, as they might not have been aware of what kind of transport they worked for. From 1994 assistance in trafficking was also made punishable. When human lives were endangered in a reckless exploitation of people who are vulnerable in need, the legal consequences had to be severe enough to deter the organisers and their assistants from continued trafficking (RD prop. 1993/94:52; Ministry of Culture Ds 1993:25).

These legal steps could not halt all illegal entries, and they were therefore combined with other methods. Refugee attachés, alien police officers and specialists from SIV were placed in some embassies. Information campaigns about Swedish restrictive immigration policy were organized in potential emigration countries. Regular transport companies, both in the air and on the sea, had since the 1950s been obliged to pay for the return of passengers if they were refused entrance to Sweden because they did not possess required passports or permits. This regulation was made more strict in order to counteract new abuse, namely the destruction of identification and travel documents (RD prop. 1988/89:86:233). To avoid extra costs, the companies must check the travel documents upon embarkation, and as no exception is made for asylum seekers, this may also stop some of them.

Sweden has directly returned many to the embarkation countries. In 1994, for example, a large group from the Middle East was sent back to Lithuania, where they were detained in a prison for more than two years. Russia did not allow them to enter or transit, and in Lithuania as in the other Baltic states, alien legislation was not yet developed. Lithuania did not possess adequate resources, and at one time Sweden sent furniture to the prison. In 1996, some of the families were allowed to enter Sweden, on condition that the remaining groups were allowed to settle in other countries. Recently, Sweden and some other countries funded IOM to return about 250 of these stranded migrants to their countries of origin. It is expected that what happened to this group of people as well as to many other groups might have had a deterrent effect on others who might have considered using illegal routes.

Internal Control

The internal alien control is most intense during the first months and years after arrival in Sweden. After a short period of legal residence, some socio-economic and even political rights are granted, but it is only when full citizenship is obtained, for example by naturalization, that the internal control comes to an end, at least as seen from the perspective of the state.

Police officers may ask foreign citizens for their passports in the streets or for example in a railway station. After several incidents, directives were given that this kind of identity control was to be used only when there were grounds for a suspicion that the foreigners worked or stayed illegally in the country, and the policemen should always politely explain their reasons (Wikrén and Sandesjö 1990: 176f). In combating crimes, drugs and terrorism, police officers may sometimes suspect that some aliens (or those who look as if they might be foreign citizens) are involved. Foreign citizens are actually overrepresented in Swedish prisons, something that may be explained by the fact that they are more intensively supervised and more often suspected by the police.

The examination of applications for permits, permanent and temporary

We have mentioned the problem that many asylum seekers throw away their passports and tickets before they meet the border police. They may have wanted to conceal that they have already stayed in another country, which for them would be the first asylum country. As a result, the examination of their application is rendered more difficult. The asylum seekers lose credibility, and they may lose even more by telling the police a story that many others have told before. If they later tell the full and correct story, the original version will speak against them. They will often not be believed. The reasons given for negative decisions are therefore often missing documents, a dubious and inconsistent narrative and the generalization that this indicates a lack of credibility. Furthermore, because of their uncertain identity the applicants may be taken into custody.

These negative assumptions may sometimes be erroneous, however. Some asylum seekers may have experienced police-harassment in other countries and tend to project this on the police in Sweden. This may be the reason why they hesitate to give the full story in the first interrogation. Some arrive without documents because they have escaped under conditions that made it impossible for them to get passports or wait for a visa. Others could perhaps leave their country and travel to Sweden only with the assistance of agents whom they had to pay. These agents may have arranged falsified documents and told them what to tell the police. The immigration authorities may have strong reasons for their disbelief and suspicion, and the opportunities for them to check facts and evidence are often minimal. Their judgement must often be based just on assumptions about applicants and their credibility. However, many asylum seekers may also have good motives, and their behaviour may be both rational and natural. Many have placed a great hope in the flight to Sweden, and some even see the decision that they are waiting for as a matter of life and death. According to a principle, repeatedly acknowledged by Swedish governments (Wikrén and Sandesjö, 1990: 95), asylum seekers shall be given the benefit of the doubt, but in cases where so much is at stake for the individual and where often so little evidence can be given to prove the asylum claims, the problem is how much or how little doubt.

Many efforts have been made to shorten the period for examination of asylum applications, often referred to as the 'waiting time'. When the number of asylum seekers increased from 1985, the police and the national immigration authority (SIV) employed more staff, and trained them in the alien legislation and in the rules of thumb used in the evaluation of applications. Nevertheless, the asylum seekers had to wait for months for the final decision, and as the state budget had to cover the costs, all political parties declared that they had an interest in a shortened examination period, although not at the expense of legal security and a due process (SOU 1982:49:211ff).

During the waiting time, most asylum seekers were accommodated in refugee centres, organized by the SIV. When these centres were filled up, they were supplemented with numerous temporary quarters, small hotels or inns, out-of-season cabins for summer or winter vacation, even old ships in some harbours. They were not allowed to take jobs and they were supported by the state in the form of social benefits or asylum allowances. Before 1994 only a few asylum seekers were allowed to stay with relatives in Sweden, while most had to live in the refugee centres. Once granted asylum or a residence permit, the refugees were dispersed to the municipalities through a national distribution system agreed upon between SIV and the local governments. In this model for temporary integration, there was an element of control, as asylum seekers were closely followed and supervised (or, as it was called, 'taken care of') by SIV and then also by the local authorities. After 1994 asylum seekers are free to opt for private accommodation, and more than half of them have chosen this alternative.

As mentioned in the Sjöbo case, public opinion was also affected, and in two opposite directions. In several places, like in Sjöbo, there were demonstrations against refugees, asylum seekers and the immigration policy in general (Fryklund and Peterson, 1989; Alsmark and Uddman, 1990). In other municipalities where good neighbourly relations had already been established during the waiting period, friends and school-mates protested against decisions to deport a family they had learned to know (the Sinkari case in the municipality of Åsele is the most well known). The long waiting periods and the local accommodation thus had an impact both on the social control during the first period in Sweden, and on public opinion.

The new Aliens Act of 1989 was a better-formulated version of the previous Act, re-edited in order to make it easier to understand and interpret the Act. In 1989, SIV was reorganized and decentralized with regional offices in nine cities. Both these two reforms were meant to shorten the waiting time. Furthermore, the government reduced the great number of undecided applications by granting residence permits to some categories of asylum seekers (such as families with small children and those who had arrived before a certain date). Only a few 'amnesties' of this sort have been granted, because of a fear that if they were more often used, they might induce a belief in other forthcoming amnesties and thus result in numbers of new applications. Amnesties may also create an image that the examination process is unpredictable and even a 'lottery' in which some by chance are the winners while others – with equally valid reasons – are the losers.

In 1997 the Riksdag again adopted a number of amendments, this time with the intention to make the Aliens Act 'clear, distinct and consistent' and thereby speed up the examination. This new Act also included changes in the criteria for refugee protection. Two categories in the previous Aliens Act were abolished, namely the de facto refugees and the war refusers. Asylum seekers in these categories are given protection only if they have exceptionally strong reasons. Also abolished was the widely used practice of giving residence permits on humanitarian grounds. This meant a much more restrictive position, but several other amendments went in the opposite direction. The Geneva Refugee Convention should be given a more liberal interpretation, in line with recommendations from the UNHCR. Important, too, is a new provision in the Act that grants asylum to those whose 'well founded fear of persecution' is caused not by actions of the state authorities but instead by the state's inability to give effective protection. Furthermore, asylum is extended to those who risk capital or corporal punishment, or torture, and also to those who need protection because of war or civil war, or environmental catastrophes, and finally also to those who fear persecution because of their sex or homosexuality. Temporary residence permits will, as mentioned, be given for two, or a maximum of four years, in mass refugee situations. Immigration of relatives shall be restricted to the nuclear family. Attempts were made to estimate in advance the possible outcome of these at the same time both restrictive and liberalizing changes in the Aliens Act. Something like an 8 per cent increase in rejections was expected.

Oral interrogations are used more frequently to secure justice in asylum cases. The national immigration authority, SIV, has taken over the border control and the first interrogations from the police. Both negative and positive grounds for decisions about permits or deportations shall be disclosed by SIV. Until 1992, appeals against negative decisions were adjudicated by the government. From that year a new administrative court, the Aliens Board, took over, but this will not last long, for after a lot of criticism in the media and also from the political parties, the Aliens Board will probably be replaced in 1999 by some twenty already existing, regional administrative courts.

Internal control and illegal immigrants

Illegal or undocumented workers have traditionally been few on the Swedish labour market. In the late 1970s, when several immigration countries reported hundreds of thousands of illegal workers, Sweden was not aware of any similar problems. When a UN-organization, the IOM, at that time organized a conference on the topic, Sweden took part reluctantly and only to give evidence about a country where illegal immigration had little significance. What were the reasons for this absence of illegal immigration? Was the answer that the internal control system was effective, or that the labour market was thoroughly organized?

A tentative answer may be that both had an impact. Two factors support the informal internal control system. Firstly, the general system of personal identification, and secondly, the corporativistic organization of the Swedish society, and especially its thoroughly organized labour market. In contrast to many other European countries, the Nordic states use personal identification numbers (of similar but not identical type). Data about the year, month and day of a person's birth are combined with a personal code. This ID number is more-or-less used in all walks of life, and it is directly tied to the population register and to the tax system. You need it to open a bank account, to seek legal employment, and to be treated by a doctor or at a hospital. To obtain an ID number, foreign citizens must enter the population register, and in principle this can be done only if they are going to stay for at least one year. Although general in its application, the ID number has consequences for the internal control of aliens. It does not directly distinguish native-born persons from others, nor aliens from citizens, but it makes it more difficult to stay and work illegally in the country.

Secondly, trade unions have achieved a very high level of unionization and formed several strong central federations. The employers are also well organized, and several important decisions on immigration policy have been made in negotiations between these two parties in the labour market. The trade unions have enjoyed a right to veto work permits to new immigrants since 1919, and they have also successfully required that immigrant workers join the local unions. This corporativistic system and the well-organized, 'formal' labour market have given little room for illegal workers, but exceptions are trades with a low rate of union membership, and a growing informal labour market.

Sanctions against employers have been applied since the 1920s, but they have been fully effective only in big workplaces with a high rate of union membership. The alien police have made sporadic investigations at random and on complaints in specific cases and in some trades. The informal labour market, traditionally small and specialized, has started to grow and spread, however, and this is a general phenomenon, characteristic for the whole of the Swedish labour market, even if it is more pronounced in some branches and trades. As both income taxes (around 30 per cent) and employment fees (above 40 per cent) must be paid on the formal market, both employees and employers can 'save' a lot of money by keeping a job informal. On top of this, in shops and small firms unemployed persons and family members may give a hand against payment with no receipt. Not least, in private households, domestic service is often informal, a practice that many seem willing to accept.

The size of the informal labour is difficult to specify. In an international comparison in 1997, the rate in Sweden was estimated to approach 4–5 per cent of the GNP, but this is a most uncertain evaluation. The informal labour market is growing, however, and it includes a large number of foreign citizens. Many Poles, for example, have worked during the three months they are allowed to visit Sweden without a visa, and they can return several times for another three months. Arrangements of this kind are even semi-officially accepted in some branches, like in the harvest of fruit and strawberries, but they have also spread to trades where union membership is rare or difficult to check, small shops and restaurants, for example. Illegal workers have even been employed in the cleaning of some offices and schools in Stockholm, where employers were more concerned about cutting costs than checking the legality of sub-contracted firms.

Employers get less expensive labour, and those working get a temporary job and a tax-free income. Workers do not receive the social benefits, which go with regular jobs, but they may make some extra money by importing/selling and buying/exporting. The outcome may be reasonable from their point of view, especially if their reference income is much lower. Nevertheless, the result of these illegal activities is a weakened internal alien control and an increase in the number of illegal immigrants.

Deportations

Many rejected asylum seekers leave the country while many others do not, but stay despite of the negative decisions they have received. Sweden has a long tradition, and even some kind of a reputation, as a country in which deportation orders are fully implemented – where those who are rejected are also forced to leave. There have always been many difficult cases, however, and they have become more numerous in the 1990s. As we have seen, many asylum seekers arrive without passports or other identification documents. Their formal citizenship is therefore often very hard to establish. Various attempts are made to find at least their origin, and one of these is a language test. The voice of, for instance, an African asylum seeker is recorded on tape, and native speakers from relevant countries then listen to identify, if possible, the dialect in the English or French, spoken by the asylum seeker. In 1998 these tests were heavily criticized by linguistic scholars. They were misleading and useless. But the testing method was defended by the SIV as a much needed instrument in the difficult task to arrange and implement deportations.

From the 1990s, the number of asylum seekers from non-European countries has increased. Return often involves a long flight, and the distance itself has made it more difficult to deport directly to the country of citizenship. A transportation system that is usually used by the criminal authorities is also responsible for the coercive deportations of aliens, and in 1997 this service organized the transport from Sweden of almost 3,500 persons, of whom about 1,500 were escorted by police or other staff. The numbers had been more than twice as high in 1993 and 1994. According to the national police, about 6 per cent of the deportations were among the most complicated or 'recalcitrant' cases, and in many other cases the police had also had to use coercion. There has been criticism in the media about the methods applied in forceful deportations, and especially against the so-called 'Japanese Barrow' on which a person to be deported lies bound during the whole flight to a far away country. The government, in a Bill before the Riksdag in May 1998, proposed changes in the implementation of deportations, but without mentioning this extreme method. Nevertheless, it is explicitly said in this Bill that deportations shall be carried out in a humane and dignified manner. In other words, the political intentions seem to be good, but the difficulties involved in these cases are not fully faced. A proposal is made, however, to encourage deported aliens to return without coercion, using some monetary support for the journey, but mainly a psychological support to help them to understand and accept the Swedish decisions not to let them stay (Riksdag 1997/98:173:15:41; Stoop 1996:232 f; Aftonbladet, 20–27 April 1998).

Asylum seekers underground

The rate of rejections has increased during the 1990s, and so has the number going underground. Among them were families who, after a long waiting period and several negative decisions, had received a final rejection, and then decided to avoid deportation and stayed illegally. How many there were is not known, but a qualified guess would be that there were some 6,000 to 10,000 persons in the middle of the 1990s, but according to police statistics only 3,580 were posted as wanted by the police at the end of 1997 (SOU 1997:128:111f).

To hide illegal aliens is no offence against the law, nor is it an offence to tip the police about where illegals could be found. But the risks of hiding are high, and the stress of living underground for weeks or months may be extremely hard. Many do not feel that they have much choice. Some have no realistic idea about the future, only a vague hope to get an amnesty. Their daily life underground is often miserable and drastically restricted, even in cases when children may continue to go to school. Hospital treatment may be available only in emergency situations, even if some private doctors arrange medical services for illegal patients. Until recently the police maintained that waiting is better than active searching. According to the Aliens Act, some key authorities should inform the police and the SIV when illegal aliens ask for their services, but this legal instrument has not been enforced. In the more restrictive climate of 1998, the government studied a proposal to make use of this information duty and even see to its effective implementation (SOU 1997:128:122 f).

Going underground is possible only with support of friends and neighbours, both native and foreign born, and of churches and voluntary organizations. A counter-control activity has been developed, which may be a nuisance to the police and the state and in some cases create great problems, but usually priority has not been given to the task of actively searching for illegals, and the police have seldom come into direct conflict with people who assist those who live underground. In other words, the formal control instruments (available to the police) are not actively used all the time (Segerstedt-Wiberg, 1997).

For several years, Sister Marianne, the head of a convent in Alsike close to Uppsala, has given sanctuary to groups of asylum seekers, threatened by deportation. Several times, the local police inspected the place and questioned the nuns, without searching the place thoroughly. When the police finally ransacked the convent and caught some hidden families, a storm broke out. The archbishop of the Swedish state Church joined a broad general public protesting against this 'intrusion'. The result was an informal agreement that the police should not trespass against the holy sanctuaries of the Church, and although the house of the convent was not a church, it was included in this agreement. Since then the police have stayed outside the churches and many asylum seekers in all parts of Sweden have therefore spent several weeks there as guests. Sometimes, refugees in despair have mounted hunger strikes, hoping to convince a responsible politician or at least an immigration officer to visit them.

The sanctuary movement has not only given assistance to Christian asylum seekers, but also to many others, and those who organize private hiding places are not all Church members. Several associations give active support, counsel and legal assistance, among them the Red Cross, the Swedish Amnesty International, the Save the Children of Sweden and some refugee councils. Representatives of these organizations often express critical views both of the Swedish control policy in general and of its implementation in individual cases.

In the early 1990s, the government temporarily reinforced the ordinary alien police, giving a special police force the job of following and searching for illegals who had gone underground, overstayers and aliens who had received a deportation decision. It is true, that in relation to the total number of missing people, the result was relatively meagre, but information was privately given to SIV and to the police by the public. A number of persons were taken into custody and some were forced to leave the country. Still, the majority was never found, and the temporary assignment was not prolonged.

Formal internal control and the detention of aliens

Internal feuds among immigrants in the country have resulted in negative publicity and extra police surveillance. In 1971, members of the Croatian

Ustasja killed the Yugoslavian Ambassador in Stockholm, and one of the assassins was afterwards helped to escape from a prison by friends who hijacked a domestic flight within Sweden (Larsson, 1972). Another most dramatic struggle has been fought between groupings among the Kurds in Sweden. After the assassination of Olof Palme in February 1986, the head of the police investigation for a time openly pointed to the Kurds as being the main suspects, and special police operations were conducted in their localities, with no results, however. The Kurdish PKK was supposed to be involved, and some Kurds were during a long period of time sentenced to something that was nicknamed municipality arrest. As they could not be deported to any other country at the time, the government decided that they were not allowed to travel within Sweden but instead were obliged to stay in the community where they were registered and to regularly report to the local police there (RD prop. 1988/89:86:102 f).

An obligation to report regularly to the police is, of course, much less far-reaching than being arrested or sent to prison. This so-called detention is not a punishment but a measure used to examine aliens with uncertain identity and especially to secure pending deportation orders. It has frequently been practised because of growing numbers both of asylum seekers without passports or other identification documents and of illegal aliens underground. Children (under 18 years of age) may be detained only under extraordinary circumstances, and adults may not be held in detention more than two weeks, unless there are extraordinary reasons for a short prolongation of another two weeks. However, the time in detention may last two months if a deportation decision has already been taken but cannot yet be effectuated. To mention one example, an African man, who was to be deported but who would not be admitted anywhere, was in 1996 repeatedly detained for several periods of two months, and this did not require a court decision, only administrative decisions by the immigration authority, SIV. From 1997, SIV is responsible both for detention decisions and for those special localities, only for detained aliens, which have replaced the previous police arrests (RD prop 1996/97:25: 42 f; SOU 1997:128).

Discussion and Evaluation

Four questions will be discussed here: firstly the relative weight of various control instruments, secondly the efficiency and the consequences of control, thirdly the risk that lack of respect for asylum seekers has a negative impact on all alien residents, and fourthly the politicization of control.

Externalization, internalization or both?

Has the relative weight of various control instruments changed over time? Has a more restrictive policy given more emphasis to external or internal, explicit or implicit, direct or indirect modes of control? Some new methods have been introduced, and they are mainly external and both direct and indirect. Among the direct external methods is the anti-trafficking legisl- ation, the use of fingerprints and bodily visitations at border stations, and the obligations of the transport companies. Among the indirect external instruments a whole battery of methods are used to prevent new flows of emigration from starting in the first place and then from growing into large waves of immigration.

Control policy was up to recently mostly reactive. Control measures followed upon the arrival of often-unexpected groups of immigrants. The new principle of an active migration policy 'in a global perspective' was first launched in the 1990s, in a government programme for a coherent and active refugee and immigration policy. It was emphasized that the totality of 'refugee, immigration, integration, and return policy' should be developed in close co-ordination with the country's 'foreign policy, security policy, trade policy and development policy' (RD prop.1996/ 97:25). This was a new and creative long-term perspective in the sense that before 1990 immigration policy had never been considered within such a coherent framework, but instead as a distinct and specific policy area, which had little to do with security policy, and hardly anything to do with Swedish development assistance. Even if no immediate results were gained, this changed the policy debate.

The intensified co-operation in immigration policy both in the Schengen group and in the European Union turned visa requirements into the main control instruments and extended them to several new countries. Sweden has promoted this visa policy and could, also thanks to its favourable geopolitical position, use it to block unwanted flows of immigrants. The decrease in the number of asylum seekers in the period from 1993 to 1997 was probably to a great extent the result of the revitalization of the visa and transit system, combined with transport controls and information campaigns in potential emigration countries, but there remain major holes in this external system, as long as control and asylum policies have not been fully developed in the Baltic states and in Russia. Sweden gives priority to intensified co-operation in the Baltic region in the hope that this will prevent uncontrolled immigration from the east. This is one example of the close relation between Swedish external immigration control and the country's security and development policy.

Internal control remains indispensable as a supplement to external control, but Sweden's internal-social control, traditionally strong, with ID cards and a well-organized labour market, has lost part of its power. The informal labour market has grown and so has illegal immigration. Furthermore, a Swedish sanctuary movement has developed and even found some acceptance as a system of counter-control. Whereas, earlier, almost all rejected asylum seekers were forced to leave the country, there were up to 10,000 hiding underground in the middle of the 1990s, but at the same time many more foreigners were directly rejected at the borders, many more asylum applications were dismissed, and many more were finally deported – even escorted by the police to the countries of origin in Asia, Africa and Latin America.

Control of foreign citizens is more intense during the first years of their stay in Sweden, and it is especially directed at those waiting for an asylum decision, yet without a job and a permanent residence permit. As soon as someone has received residence and work permits, individual control seems to be almost over. However, in the middle of the 1990s, control was again intensified even for immigrants with a long stay in Sweden. A programme started to revoke residence permits, even after many years of stay, in cases when they had been issued on false or incorrect information from the applicants. After political reaction against several deportations, new guidelines were given to guarantee that permits of aliens with very long residence would not be revoked (SOU 1997:67).

Efficiency, costs and consequences

Since the First World War, immigration control has been reactive and pragmatic. Whenever it was found to be ineffective in some way, either doing too much or too little, the practice was changed first, and the legislation only much later. This is a policy style apt for an area in which decisions must often be made on shaky forecasts and without full knowledge of all the facts. However, the policy formulated at the end of the 1990s aims to overcome these problems and to be long-term, active, preventive and European.

The long-term demographic consequences of immigration were previously seldom debated and no efforts were made to evaluate the country's capacity to integrate or absorb the immigration of new people over a long period of time. Major decisions about control were based on short-term considerations, such as the demand and supply of labour. In periods of low demand, and even high unemployment as in the 1990s, labour immigration was almost completely stopped. In the 1990s few family members and refugees have found regular jobs and many have therefore become an economic burden to society.

On some occasions, for example in 1976 and 1989, the government has issued general declarations that Sweden did not have sufficient capacity to integrate new immigrants and that therefore no more large flows of asylum seekers could be admitted for the time being. Too many had already arrived in a short period of time, and there were not enough resources to examine all the applications, to house those waiting for asylum in the refugee centres, and to provide them with a first integration service. Alternative solutions, such as allocation of more resources, or granting asylum collectively and after a less thorough examination, were not seriously debated. On some other occasions, however, the latter solution has been used, and temporary residence permits will in the future be given in mass-refugee situations (Dacyl, 1997: 121 f).

It is difficult to answer the elementary question of whether control has been effective and successful. If the aim is to keep 'everything under control', this has not been achieved, but this is an aim that can hardly be achieved at any time. The outcome depends far too much on what happens in other countries. New political regimes, wars and civil wars, poverty and ecological disasters may suddenly induce new movements. Refugees will arrive unexpectedly, and when the first arrive, it is hard to know whether this is the beginning of a major 'invasion'. If the aim is set more realistically, for example, that the government should not 'lose control', then Swedish policy could largely be called successful. It is true that new flows have arrived suddenly and may do so in the future, but there is a readiness to handle this and instruments are available. By intensified external control (in EU co-operation, directly using the visa system, and sending restrictive signals to potential asylum seekers), Sweden was like other EU-countries able to reduce the number of asylum seekers year by year from 1993 to 1996. At least this fact is often taken as evidence of that the control has been effective.

Control is expensive. The budgetary costs of the Swedish control system have for a period of time been extraordinary. In 1991, the cost for one asylum seeker was estimated as about US $30.000 per year (SOU 1991:1: 108). The state's total expenditure for the process of asylum examinations plus for the cost of living of all asylum seekers and refugees amounted, in the early 1990s, to around one billion US dollars, but the costs in 1998 had fallen to less than half that amount, mainly because of the declining number of asylum seekers. No wonder, however, that opponents of this policy – especially at the record peak in 1992 with 82,000 asylum seekers – asked questions about these expenditures and about the even larger, but unknown total social costs for all refugee immigration. Indeed, the high costs for the state budget, and the political demands to cut them, have put strong pressure on the government to be more restrictive.

The overall consequences for society at large were mixed at the start. On the one hand, some cities found that they could gain advantages by renting otherwise vacant apartments to asylum seekers and refugees, for whom the state paid during at least the first three years, but most of these cities suffered from economic stagnation and internal out-migration, and jobs were therefore seldom available. When many of the refugees were still unemployed after several years, the local government had to carry the costs. On the other hand, the big and most attractive cities of Sweden which were first relieved by a nationwide distribution of refugees, soon found that an increasing number of refugees returned to them. As many refugees remained outside the labour market, the local costs increased everywhere, and in a tough budgetary situation the state did not want to pay the bill. Negative political reactions, such as those that had started much earlier, for instance in Sjöbo, were then felt almost everywhere.

The risk of failing respect for aliens

Immigration control may foster a sort of disrespect for asylum seekers, and often also for other aliens. This trend may be stronger and more manifest, the more restrictive the control is, the less wanted and the more feared the flows of immigration are, and also the lower the esteem of a group of aliens, for example, because of their political ideals, or their ethnic or racial background. Partly, this failing respect for aliens may be a consequence of the control's impact on the public opinion. Partly, it may also be a direct consequence of some of the administrative routines that the authorities use to establish control.

Immigration officers are trained for a job where they need legal competence and good judgement. They shall unveil the true reasons for an application, and must be prepared to disclose that applicants conceal what is negative and present (or even invent) what is positive for them. Scepticism and suspicion are therefore essential parts of the professional routine, but with time, this creates an inclination not to trust anyone, not to believe in documents or narratives and not to give asylum seekers the benefit of the doubt. This is an imminent danger in periods of very strict control, as for example in Sweden in the 1990s, when the selection criteria are tight and only a few are admitted.

The rate of rejected asylum applications gives an indication of the rigidity of control implementation. In the middle of the 1980s from 10–

15 per cent were rejected, while this applied to about 80 per cent fifteen years later. Negative decisions were given a written motivation by both the SIV and the administrative court of appeal, called the Aliens Board, and these are published (Sandesjö and Björk, 1995; Alcala, 1996). They include a short evaluation of the situation in the country from which an applicant has escaped, and often a stipulation that the probability is low that an applicant, if deported, would be persecuted or punished. Some of these statements reflect a cool and even cynical attitude to the applicants. Even asylum seekers, who had undergone torture have been rejected with an assurance that this would probably not be repeated again. A woman, previously bodily punished in Iran for political activities, was deported to Iran with the explanation that such a long time had elapsed since that had happened to her (at the time when her husband was executed) and that she had little to fear if she returned and lived a quiet life. In May 1996, a United Nation commission declared that in another case Sweden had violated the convention against torture, and heavy criticism about Swedish asylum policy has also come from Amnesty International and from the Human Rights Watch (RD 1996, Debate Dec. 5).

Political consequences

The apolitical tradition in immigration policy has yielded to a more open and rather vivid public debate about the scope and methods of control. The political parties do not unanimously support one and the same policy any more. The attentive public is divided, demanding a more restrictive and on the other hand a more liberal and humane policy.

Quite contrary to this politicization of the immigration policy is the depoliticization of the appeal procedure. The minister of immigration was up to 1993 in the last instance responsible for appeals from aliens denied permits or about to be deported. The ultimate decisions were taken by the government in plenary sessions. As long as this procedure was followed, the political responsibility was obvious. The Minister was often heavily criticized for coldness and indifference, and political pressures were often mounted in media campaigns. By establishing an administrative court, called the Aliens Board (the Utlänningsnämnd or UN), a lot of energy and time was saved for the Minister, and this also set him free from political and personal attacks. It placed the Alien Act in the centre, and emphasized the legal aspects instead of the political. The UN is neither an ordinary court, nor a political body, but something in between. It has usually met allegations only with references to legal interpretations, although the appeal decisions also include political evaluations, among others, of the political situations in other countries. In sum, a deliberate depoliticization has taken place, constraining the government's ability to steer the practice of control.

The relationship between public opinion and political decision-making may be interpreted in two different ways. Some Swedes had probably long been of the opinion that the immigration and refugee policy was too liberal, even if they had not voiced this criticism openly. According to one interpretation these people had not felt free to speak. At the end of the 1980s, growing refugee immigration and the dispersal of refugees around the country caused negative reactions and even some acts of hostile aggression against refugee centres. Some local and regional campaign started the politicization, and the national break-through came in the Sjöbo referendum. The national political parties tried to adjust to this new situation, by more-or-less turning towards a more restrictive policy. The second interpretation starts with the change in control policy, which was manifested in the government decisions in 1989 and later. It says that the new restrictive policy induced negative attitudes towards foreigners or immigrants. The distinction between 'us and them' was made more clearly visible than before and also in a new way legitimate. These restrictive policy decisions implied that Sweden had already admitted too many, that the right of asylum had often been claimed without or with too little ground, and that the budgetary public costs were running too high.

The two interpretations differ in where the process started, but they may well be combined. The politicization of the immigration issue and the establishment of a more restrictive control may have reinforced each other. In the election campaign of 1991, New Democracy successfully exploited negative opinions. To regain what had been lost, the other political parties had to move in the same direction – towards more restrictions. Some traditional parties took over part of the populist programme. We must not forget, however, that this new protectionism is part of an international and European context. Sweden cannot remain liberal alone, in a period when all other European countries protect themselves. Furthermore, Swedish policy has not been developed in isolation but first in an informal and then in a gradually more formalized and very active European co-operation. In fact, Sweden initiated the attempt to formulate a comprehensive policy that was restrictive and at the same time also expressed a will to share the burdens and to tackle the root causes of international migration. This new formulation did not make the control policy less restrictive, nor practice less rigid, but it broadened the issue.

Two Principle Aims

I have discussed the period of ten to fifteen years, in which Sweden went from a liberal to a restrictive control policy. There were several reasons: growing refugee immigration from non-European countries, stricter control in most other European countries, intensified and institutionalized co-operation within the EU, and a long-lasting economic recession and record high unemployment, implying budget deficits and heavy cuts in the welfare system. To make Swedish control more restrictive, the alien legislation was revised, the control administration reorganized, and the terms of admittance increasingly more demanding. While the right of asylum was maintained, the definition of a refugee was restricted, and the rate of refusal and deportations rose. Precautions were taken to impede asylum seekers from coming to Sweden, through transit agreements with East Germany and Poland, visa requirements for Bosnians, and embarkation control at the airports and other ports of entry. The efficiency was improved both in internal and external control, but as long as many refugees arrived from the former Yugoslavia, this did not seem to be enough. Only from 1993, when the number of asylum seekers fell, did the new system seem to work.

The first main aim of this restrictive policy has been 'not-to-lose-control', but politicians and administrators could never be sure that they had done enough to stop or reduce immigration. In recent history, asylum seekers have often arrived unexpectedly, and they could do it again. Nobody knows how immigration might grow in the future, nor how much control would be needed to prevent some imagined potential flows. In this situation policy makers tend to play safe, to be sure that they do not lose control, and control agencies (like the SIV and the Aliens Board) tend to be more severe in their judgements, even when they are allowed discretion for more leniency. Furthermore, they must act quickly all the time as there is a risk that a first group of a few hundred from a new source country may be followed by many more, if the reactions of the control system are not fast and resolute. In order 'not-to-lose-control', they might make control excessive, with negative consequences for the aliens (such as asylum seekers, refugees, persons to be deported, those detained) and also for society and the political system.

Firstly, there is a risk that foreign citizens will not be treated as they deserve to be treated. Many have emigrated from desperate situations, and the authorities' decisions are of utmost significance for them. The outcome may be a matter of despair or hope, health or incurable illness, life or death. Even if the SIV and the Aliens Board may consider such humanitarian grounds, they are not obliged to do it, and in a restrictive policy climate they tend to do it only in rare cases. It is often only when the mass media have published individual life stories, that humanitarian grounds are fully heeded.

It may be forgotten that aliens in the country, illegals as well as legals, are entitled to respect and integrity. It is not a crime to be an alien asking for a residence permit, and even violations of the Aliens Act are mostly minor offences. Nevertheless, enforcement has long been entrusted to the police. Regular jails or prisons have been used for detention. The right of appeal has been respected, but not always the right to have a legal adviser. The Act of 1997 has brought about several improvements in these respects but the restrictive policy climate remains, and so does the restrictive implementation, which gives priority to the first principle aim, 'not-to-lose-control', and tends to forget the second, the respect for the human dignity of others.

When the Riksdag debated the Aliens Act in 1997, the Minister responsible for refugee policy, Pierre Schori, explicitly mentioned the dilemma of combining the two principle aims. Swedish control policy must function efficiently in the nation's interest, he said, but it must also be implemented in such a way that solidarity and full respect for the human dignity of the other is shown, even though this other person is a non-citizen. Our discussion has shown both that these two aims are of great significance, and that one of them, the control aspect, is often too strongly emphasized, while the other aspect, the human dignity of the alien, is easily forgotten and neglected. The task of combining the two aims also in a restrictive period like this requires not only conscious and active efforts and a coherent long-term policy, but also media exposure and an open political debate, and not least a lot of political will and courage.

References

Alcala, J. (1996), 'Fischerström måste bort', Dagens Nyheter, (DN) 19 November.

Alsmark, G. and Uddman, P. (1990), Att möta främlingar, vision och vardag, Lund: Lund University Press, Cesic, Studies in International Conflict 3.

Bergman, E. and Swedin, B. (1982), Vittnesmål, invandrares syn på diskriminering i Sverige, Stockholm: Publica.

Björklund, U. (1981), North to Another Country, The Formation of a Suryoyo Community in Sweden, Stockholm: Eifo.

Dacyl, J.W. (1997), Flyktingars Rättsställning i Sverige, Stockholm: Ceifo.

Fischer, P.A. and Straubhaar, T. (1996), Migration and Economic Integration in the Nordic Common Labour Market, Copenhagen: Nordic Series 2, Nordic Council of Ministers.

Fryklund, B. and Peterson, T. (1989), 'Vi mot dom' det dubbla främlingsskapet i Sjöbo, Lund: Lund University Press, Cesic, Studies in International Conflict 1.

Hammar, T. (ed.) (1985), European Immigration Policy, Cambridge: Cambridge University Press.

—— (1988), 'Invandringspolitikens ideologi och historia', Arbetarhistoria, 12:2.

—— (1997), 'Flyktingpolitiken i hetluften', in: Brobyggare, en vänbok till Nils Andrén, Göteborg: Nerenius and Santérus.

Larsson, J. (1972), Ustasj, Stockholm: Aldus.

Lundh, C. and Ohlsson, R. (1994), Från arbetskraftsimport till flykting invandring, Stockholm: SNS.

Ministry of Culture, (1993) Pm ang skärpta åtgärder mot människosmuggling, Stockholm: Regeringskansliet.

Ministry of Labour, (1990), A coherent Refugee and Immigration Policy, Working paper, Stockholm: Regeringskansliet.

Riksdagen (RD), Debates (reports of proceedings); prop. (Bill to the Parliament); and SfU (the stated opinion of the Standing Committee on Social Insurance), Stockholm.

Sandesjö, H. and Björk, K. (ed.) (1995), Utlänningsärenden – Praxis, Utlänningsnämndens och regeringens beslu, Göteborg: Publica.

Segerstedt-Wiberg, I. (1997), Gömmarna och andra. Göteborg

SOU, Statens Offentliga Utredningar (Command Papers published by Government Commissions), Stockholm: Regeringskansliet.

Statistical Central Bureau (SCB) (1992), Statistics Sweden, Stockholm.

Stoop, C.D. (1996), Haal de was maar binnen, Amsterdam: De Bezige Bij.

Wikrén G. and Sandesjö, H. (1990), Utlänningslagen med kommentarer, Uppsala: Publica.

Redrawing Lines of Control: The Norwegian Welfare State Dilemma[1]

Grete Brochmann

The year 1995 witnessed two events that made immigration control a front-page issue in the Norwegian media. Firstly, the European Schengen Accord disturbed the consolidated non-EU-membership of Norway due to the entry of Sweden and Finland into the Union, and the consequent quandary of the Nordic Passport Union. Secondly, the local elections in September were made into an opinion poll on immigration, dominated by the rightist liberal (and anti-immigration) Progress Party (FrP).

The intergovernmental Schengen Agreement, with its concern with border control and asylum policy, exposed the Norwegian public to the complexities of the immigration issue within the European Union. This was ironic as immigration was hardly an issue at all during the extended campaign over the EU membership question the year before. Nevertheless, by voting down EU membership, Norway retained (at least formally) the ability to define the country's immigration policy independent of the EU system in the years to come. By opening up for a Schengen association, a more developed (in terms of harmonization) immigration/border control policy might be introduced through the back door. The organization 'No to EU' consequently remobilized.

The Schengen issue was put on the agenda in Norway basically because it affects the Nordic Passport Union, which since 1959 has implied free movement between the Nordic countries and equal treatment of labour, among other arrangements. With Sweden and Finland entering the European Union, the long internal Nordic border between Sweden and Norway became an external EU border – with all the security issues involved. In Norway the Nordic issue is of high symbolic significance. Most Norwegians would strongly disapprove of having to carry a passport when travelling internally in the Nordic area. Besides, many of the no-

1. The author is thankful to Espen Thorud and Aud Korbøl for useful comments.

voters on the EU question saw the Nordic Union as an assurance against the isolation of Norway, economically and politically.

The other event in 1995 that turned immigration control into a top issue in Norway was of a more internal character. The local (and regional) elections made the relationship between immigration and the development of Norwegian society a focal point. Major criticism was raised against the authorities for not having control over the process related to integration and surveillance. The elections came out as a major protest against politicians who had not taken the immigration issue seriously, and the Progress Party – the only party flagging immigration – came out as the grand winner.

These two events have left the country at a crossroad when it comes to the control complex we are dealing with in this book.

Context for Control

We have decided to concentrate on the period after 1985. It is nevertheless evident that in order to provide the context for, and to explain Norway's current immigration policies, a much longer time span needs to be analysed.

As we will see, Norwegian immigration control followed the pattern of gradually stronger public regulation, and the development of the welfare state has accentuated this tendency. In this way, the study of current immigration regulation in Norway needs to take into account the generation of the very same regulation, when explaining why and how it has come about. In relatively stable political systems, continuity becomes an explanatory force in itself: new legislation is, to a large extent, continuously built on the existing order. Likewise, new institutions or bodies are often established through continuation, fusions or extensions of existing institutions. Politicians often use the 'existing principle' argument as a point of departure when amending laws (Thorud, 1989).

The period 1985–98 was marked by both continuity and change. Concerning the Norwegian external control policy – within which there are two main target areas, general immigration regulation and refugee/asylum policy – the first target area is predominately marked by continuity, whereas the latter is subject to more recent change. The explanations for the general regulation therefore must be sought further back in history – a fact that necessitates an historical detour. The analysis of refugee/asylum policy – which in some ways can be seen as a function of policy implementation (or unforeseen consequences of such) – can be concentrated in a more recent period. There are two 'events' or points of reference that epitomize these changes: the new policy of 1975, officially called the 'immigration stop', and the refugee inflow triggered by the war in former Yugoslavia.

It is the dynamic interplay between various forces – motivational factors and structural conditions nationally and internationally – that is our prime interest here, as we saw in the introduction. This dynamic interplay will have different expressions depending on the historical context. Yesterday's actions become today's context for decision-making and behaviour.

In this chapter a brief historical review will first be presented, to provide the basic economic, political and ideological background for the formation of the national control complex and the generation of today's legislation in Norway. The circumstances surrounding the introduction of the 'immigration stop' is given more attention as this intervention has formed the backbone of general immigration regulation thereafter. The current interaction between external and internal control mechanisms is presented and analysed. The tendencies in the field of refugee/asylum policies, contained in the Bosnian crisis will be given special attention as a marker of a new methodology in the sphere of external control. Lastly the international context is discussed in terms of the influence exerted by the European Union on the national scene.

Historical Overview

It was basically the First World War that introduced more comprehensive immigration regulation to Norway, as was the case in most European countries. International parameters influenced the formulation of control policies in different ways. On the one hand, other countries' law systems could serve as model for Norwegian legislation, and on the other hand, other states' policy could have a stronger pressure on Norwegian borders as a consequence, according to public documents. It was also argued that immigration control, generally speaking, was inevitable in the course of change: structural transformation in terms of industrial expansion and more mobile labour. National security was nevertheless a central concern. In the early years of our historical exploration, the question of 'social control' was important, and in particular so with a view to Jews and Gypsies, who remained subject to discriminatory measures straight until the Second World War, and in the case of Gypsies even longer (Skjønsberg, 1981; Hanisch, 1976).

The security issue remained a central feature of Norwegian immigration control in the years until the Second World War. The Norwegian state used different approaches: traditional border control; internal alien control in combination with expulsion measures; specific citizenship legislation and discriminatory rules for trade and business; as well as what has been termed a general policy of 'Norwegianization' ('fornorskning') (Eriksen and Niemi, 1981).

The Norwegianization policy has to be viewed in the light of the independence of Norway from the union with Sweden in 1905. The policy had a wide scope, covering both cultural and linguistic matters, and it was targeted not least at the Lappish minority in the northern part of the country. According to Eriksen and Niemi, this policy is a striking example of a conscious nation-building strategy related to the ethnically most heterogeneous regions of the country. This policy of external border control, and internal assimilation of minorities, became a marker of the new sovereignty of the nation state (ibidem: 322). The combined approach was based on the assumption that a nation state needed to be as homogeneous as possible to persist. In Norway there was broad popular support for this policy, including, with a few qualifications, the labour movement. Basically this is explained by the ambiguity attached to Norwegian nationalism: it was perceived more in terms of a 'progressive' mobilizing force against dependence of neighbouring states, than a reactionary weapon in the hands of the bourgeoisie (Østerud, 1984 and 1987). The novelty of the Norwegian nation state and the vulnerability as a small country recently being 'colonized' may explain the strength of the concern to protect 'the Norwegian culture'. This concern has, on and off, been a significant feature of Norwegian public discourse in this century, and it has recently again gained strength, as we will see.

The new legislation from the First World War represented a tightening up of immigration policies in terms of both entry control and alien control. The First World War legislation was introduced as a temporary ordinance, yet it was in operation for more than ten years, until 1927 when there was a major revision of the law.

The basic motivation behind immigration control was the same through-out the period from the First World War until the Second, although the emphasis changed in the direction of economic and labour market considerations. The control system as such (laws, regulations, institutions) was developed, co-ordinated and centralized in this period, and there was a broad consensus in the population and among the political parties behind the policy.

Post War Laissez-faire and the Nordic Dimension

The two first decades after the Second World War were marked by growth and reconstruction. The unemployment rate was low, and there were even shortages of labour in certain sectors. This latter fact made the authorities suggest a liberalization of immigration regulation from the pre-war period. The liberalization was related to foreign labour in demand, and it was perceived as highly rational from a national economic point of view.

During the first 20–25 years after the Second World War immigration to Norway was limited, in terms of both labour migrants and refugees. Norway had signed the United Nations Geneva Convention, and the refugee policy was not controversial. This consensus also applied to the revision of the Aliens Act in 1956. Some changes were made: protection of refugees was included whereas the so-called 'Gypsy paragraph' was taken out. Economic and security matters were used as arguments for a flexible enabling Act (fullmaktslov).

A clear characteristic of the immigration pattern in Norway until the end of 1960s is the domination of Nordic citizens. It is on the whole striking how little immigration there has been from non-Nordic countries up till the 1970s, apart from Norwegian–American returnees as well as some Germans. In fact Norway was a net emigration country throughout the first six decades of this century, with the exception of the 1930s.

After the Second World War border control between the Nordic countries was gradually eradicated. This process had started before the war. Sweden in particular was in favour of liberalization of labour regulations within the Nordic area, and from 1945 onwards there was in real terms free movement of labour across the borders. The process of formalizing this situation through a Convention went through different stages, yet in 1954 a common Nordic labour market was established, including Sweden, Denmark, Finland and Norway (Iceland joined in 1982). Through the same process, passports were no longer required among Nordic citizens. In 1959 these agreements were supplemented by a common passport-control area. Foreigners (third-country nationals) should be checked at an external Nordic border, and thereafter only be subject to spot checks within the territory. This rather drastic renunciation of national sovereignty in terms of immigration control was passed without any major controversy in Norway. The explanation for this is obviously the homogeneity that existed in the region, both economically and culturally (particularly between Sweden, Denmark and Norway), as well as the historical bonds that were established over the centuries. This Nordic

Union has, as we have seen, now become a stumbling block in the Schengen context.

If we look at the period after the Second World War, Norway is an extraordinary case in the sense that the country was only marginally affected by the immigration waves that reached Europe. It was not until the late 1960s that Norway was touched by the new migration climate in Europe, and even then the scale was modest compared to most West European receiving countries. When most immigration countries in Western Europe introduced heavy restrictions on immigration in the wake of the oil crisis in the beginning of the 1970s, Norway entered one of the most prosperous growth periods in its history, due to the discovery of oil on Norwegian territory in the North Sea. The dramatic price increase of oil, which caused the deepest world economic recession since the inter-war period, embodied high expectations for Norwegian economy, and made Norway become attractive for foreign labour. At the same time, Norwegian labour gained opportunities for mobility through economic expansion, and started leaving less attractive jobs in parts of the industry and in the service sector. Various factors, internationally and domestically, thus, placed Norway on the map for potential labour migrants from the late 1960s. The typical migrant at this stage was an unskilled male, aged between twenty and forty, increasingly coming from distant origins like Morocco, Yugoslavia, Turkey and in particular Pakistan. From 1973 onwards, new groups of refugees appeared: Chileans first, then later Vietnamese and Eritreans among others.

As already stated, there has been a remarkable continuity in Norwegian immigration legislation throughout the current century. The way in which these regulations were put into practice has, however, varied over the years, depending on economic and political factors. Nevertheless, when the labour migrants started coming in the late 1960s and the beginning of the 1970s, the state, and in particular the labour authorities, had a very low profile in terms of organization and recruitment, much less than was the case in some of the other West European countries. By and large immigrants to Norway came individually, and through networks (Thorud, 1985). It was basically labour market parameters that defined the migration order. This (temporary) laissez-faire approach is interesting considering the considerable state involvement, generally speaking, in economic management and polity in this period.

Popular Mobilization Against EEC and the Subsequent 'Immigration Stop'

The first major popular mobilization against Norwegian membership of the EEC coincided with the inception of immigration to Norway. This fact made a rather peculiar structure of opinion appear in relation to the immigration issue. The opposition–the left and the farmers' organizations–through their common anti-EEC stand appeared to be against immigration, although for different reasons. The most articulate opponents, from the (wide) left, argued that the European Community represented the most cynical exploitation of foreign labour, with detrimental effects for both the immigrants themselves, and the labour market/society into which they entered. The arguments from (parts of) the left were strikingly protection-istic, and at times even nationalistic (Thorud, 1985: 126). It is nevertheless right to say that immigration was not the major concern within the left. It was rather a question of exposing the cynicism of the capitalist system in the form of the EEC. The groups in favour of Norwegian membership, including (the majority of) the Labour Party, refused to see immigration as a problem in relation to the EEC. This was so both because immigration was not seen as a significant problem as such, and because it was argued that national control could be maintained within the Community.

The whole mobilization process against the European Community generated a series of radical arguments in favour of a restrictive immi-gration policy, which in many ways served to provide legitimacy for the 'immigration stop' two years later (Thorud, 1985: 126).

This 1972 panorama was quite different from the political configuration in the second mobilization, this time against the European Union in 1994, where the opposition against membership saw the EU countries' immi-gration policy as a threat to humanitarian values. Even though immigration was a marginal issue in the EU debate as such, the 'Fortress Europe' metaphor appeared occasionally to underscore general arguments. During the 1980s, the smaller parties to the left, which strongly defended restrict-ions in the early 1970s, changed their viewpoints. Both leftist parties, SV and AKP, now wanted to remove restrictive entry control.

Immigration into Norway began at a moment when traditional immi-gration countries in Europe had started constricting migration movements. Flows of information about conflict potential, social marginalization, and housing deficiencies reached Norway, making the conceptions of the anticipated problems grow out of proportion. Thus, when most countries on the European continent introduced more restrictive immigration regulation, Norway followed suit, before immigration was even close to becoming a significant phenomenon. The juxtaposition of this fact and the unprecedented boom witnessed in the Norwegian economy posed a dilemma for the Norwegian government: how to restrict immigration, at the same time letting in labour related to the rapidly expanding off-shore industry.

The 'premature' introduction of an 'immigration stop' is an interesting example of an implicit European harmonization of immigration policy in the absence of international institutions to this effect.

By and large Norway followed the predominant pattern in most European immigration countries in terms of stopping immigration and granting exemptions (Brochmann, 1996). Immigration was to be curbed to facilitate a better integration of established immigrants – to guarantee equal treatment/possibilities as compared to the nationals. Explicit exemptions were made for refugees, certain family members of legally residing immigrants, as well as specifically defined 'key personnel'. The latter category accommodated the needs in the important initial phase of oil production. 'Key personnel' in this respect basically meant short-term, skilled labour from OECD countries, in terms of seasonal, contract labour.

The so-called 'immigration stop' was implemented in Norway on 1 February 1975. It was initiated as a temporary ordinance, yet in 1981 it was relabelled 'immigration regulation' (White Paper 1979–80: 74). It was basically motivated by the aim of reducing immigration from developing countries. On the one hand, the restructuring of the economy made this kind of labour less attractive, on the other hand, the increasing concern over 'adaptation' problems and differences in living standards also applied to immigrants from the developing world.

As was the case in most receiving European countries, the 'stop' had a number of unforeseen consequences. The picture of immigration flows to Norway after the 'stop' follows, by and large, the pattern of other destination countries in Europe: immigration did not stop, it only changed character. The 'peripheral' status of the country in terms of geography and immigration tradition has nevertheless made the impact less substantial in terms of numbers. When the legal labour channel was closed, other entry channels were tried out. Figures from the last 15 years reveal that persons from countries in the Third World predominately arrive through family reunification, as refugees, students, and as asylum seekers who acquire residence on humanitarian grounds. The relative number of immigrants from the developing world has increased during this period (White Paper 1987–88: 39: 30). The unforeseen consequences, in terms of increase in immigration from Third World countries, have been tentatively accommodated through various adjustments/new restrictions in the period after the 'stop', contained in a new Aliens Act. The most important changes were the requirement that the immigrants should be able to support their families, and the definition of a minimum housing standard to be allowed in cases of family reunification. Visa requirements for Pakistani citizens were reintroduced in 1976 as was the case with citizens of Bangladesh and Turkey in 1978 and 1981 respectively. It was realized that the 'stop' did not function as such, and that certain forms of immigration had become a persistent phenomenon in modern Norway.

With the policies of the 1980s and the 1990s the external/internal control issue discussed in the introductory chapter has become relevant. Norway has joined the traditional European receiving countries and is experiencing the same dilemmas, quandaries and tensions in the realm of immigration.

Before entering into a discussion of the basic trends, analytical inter-connections and future prospects, we will briefly present the existing policy as it has been implemented in the 1990s.

Current Legislation – External Control

The Immigration Act

The Ministry of Local Government and Labour is responsible for the overall immigration policy with, since 1 January 1988, the Directorate of Immigration (UDI) as the implementing body. The Ministry of Justice is responsible for the Immigration Act. The current law that regulates immigration to Norway, the Immigration Act, commenced January 1 1991.

The purpose of the Act is to

> provide the basis for controlling the entry and exit of foreign nationals and their presence in the realm in accordance with Norwegian immigration policy. The Act shall secure protection under the law for foreign nationals who are entering or leaving the realm, who are resident here or who are applying for a permit pursuant to the Act. The Act shall provide the basis for protection against persecution for refugees or other foreign nationals who are being persecuted. (Chapter 1: 2)

As to the juridical status of foreign nationals, 'unless otherwise provided by legislation currently in force, foreign nationals have during their stay in Norway the same rights and obligations as Norwegian nationals' (Chapter 1: 3). It adds (Chapter 1: 4) that 'the Act shall be applied in

Table 7.1 Norway: Foreign Residents by Continents 1980–97

Continents	*Foreign resident population in per cent*			*n*
	1980	*1990*	*1997*	*1997*
Europe	64%	51%	61%	95,908
thereof				
Nordic citizens	*33%*	*24%*	*27%*	*42,516*
Other EU-citizens	*23%*	*16%*	*16%*	*24,449*
Other European citizens	*8%*	*11%*	*18%*	*28,943*
Africa	3%	7%	7%	9,989
Asia	16%	29%	22%	34,900
North America	14%	7%	6%	9,873
South America	2%	5%	3%	5,295
Other countries	1%	1%	1%	1,572
TOTAL	100%	100%	100%	157,537

Source: Statistics Norway.

accordance with international rules by which Norway is bound when these are intended to strengthen the position of a foreign national'.

Within the Immigration Act there is (1) *a system for permissions*; permission of entry (visa), residence permit, work permit and settlement permit; (2) *a control system* consisting of passport and visa control, control of specific border points, internal controls; (3) *a sanctions system* consisting of cancellation of permits, expulsion and deportation (Haagensen et al., 1990).

Concerning *visa regulation* – one of the major external control mechanisms – the main rule in Norway is that foreigners must have visas to be able to enter the country. Then there are numerous exceptions from this rule. In practical terms, a visa is today required for citizens from countries that have traditionally 'produced' labour migrants and refugee/asylum seekers. Thus, the visa requirement is used to accommodate security and foreign policy interests. Currently the visa policy is increasingly used as an instrument to regulate immigration.

All persons who want to work in Norway (except citizens of the EEA area) need a work permit. With the 'immigration stop' a largely new policy was introduced: a work permit was only to be granted to exempted categories (foreigners born as Norwegians, researchers and artists, 'key personnel' and certain seasonal labour as well as a few others). At the same time the requirements for work permit were made more restrictive:

(1) The first issue of a work permit is linked to a specific job and a specific employer. (2) Applications must be submitted from the country of origin (or another country where he/she has had legal residency for more than six months). (3) There must be a concrete job *offer*. (4) The contract must last at least one year. (5) Salary and work conditions must follow wage agreements. (6) Health certificate can be required. (7) The applicant must have access to satisfactory housing conditions.

Settlement permit was introduced with the Immigration Act of 1988. This permit implies a permanent residence and work permit, and it provides protection against expulsion. Three years' continuous residence in Norway are required before a settlement permit is granted, yet persons who have been residents for a specific purpose, such as education will normally not be granted settlement permit.

Rejection and expulsion. Expulsion is more serious than rejection. Expulsion implies that the foreigner can not re-enter at a later stage, unless the expulsion is made temporary. Among the most common reasons for rejection are: (1) The foreigner does not have valid travel documents. (2) He/she is not in possession of visa, work permit or residence permit. (3) He/she does not bring sufficient means for daily survival. (4) The foreigner has a criminal record and/or has been expelled earlier from Norway or one of the other Nordic countries.

Within all these areas of immigration control the tendency has been towards more restrictive practice. Three other central documents in relation to current immigration to Norway are the White Paper 1987–88: 39 *On Immigration Policy*; the White Paper 1994–95: 17 *On Refugee Policy* and the White Paper 1996–97: 17 *On Immigration and Multicultural Norway.*

White Paper 1987–88: 39

In this White Paper, Norwegian immigration control was for the first time to include *preventive* measures, or control mechanisms beyond its national borders. It was re-emphasized that 'Norway cannot solve the refugee and migration problems of the world by letting everyone who desires to settle in the country, do so' (p. 8 author's translation). However, as a kind of compensation for this reiteration of a restrictive entry regulation, international involvement was underscored as a means to stem and prevent migration flows. In this White Paper the quest for a 'holistic approach' to the immigration issue was introduced: development aid, foreign policy and peaceful conflict resolution through the United Nations were all given as ingredients related to a sound immigration policy.

It was furthermore reiterated that social and structural concerns made it necessary to continue the general restrictive line on labour immigration (the 'stop'-policy), with the same exceptions referred to earlier, and additionally with White Paper no. 39 and the Immigration Act the regulation of labour immigration was made permanent. An implicit demarcation was made in the White Paper between 'economic' and 'real' refugees, by stating as a central aim for the Government to accept 'the people in real need of protection' (p. 8). A number of measures were introduced or re-emphasized to limit the number of asylum seekers: active use of the option of refusing asylum seekers at the border, in 'obviously unfounded cases', for example with reference to the rule of the first country of asylum, a more restrictive assessment of visa applications for visitors from certain countries, and the introduction of visa requirement for a number of new countries. The rate of recognition of refugee status has also been declining.

Control with asylum seekers was institutionalized through a reception system. The reception procedure in relation to asylum seekers belongs in the intersection between internal and external control. The reception centres remain an external control mechanism until the examination process is carried through, yet at the same time, they serve as an internal control post on a daily basis. The responsibility for the reception of refugees and asylum seekers as well as settlement of persons granted asylum or residence based on humanitarian grounds, is divided between the state and the municipalities. Every asylum seeker received in Norway is in principle supposed to live in a reception centre until the application is processed within a period not exceeding six months. The ones who are accepted are then settled in local communities by the state. Quota refugees are normally settled directly in the municipalities. The existing reception system was initiated and established with White Paper 1988–89: 39, yet changes in terms of refugee composition and the size of flows have made continuous adjustments necessary. The reception process can be divided into three phases: the transit phase, the primary and the secondary phase. The transit phase lasts normally from one to three weeks, and consists of police examination and health checks. The primary phase denotes the period until a final decision is taken, and the third phase marks the period from a positive decision until settlement in a municipality is implemented.

Family reunification applies primarily to spouses and children under 18. Occasionally other family members are allowed – as parents, non-married partners and other close relatives. Persons receiving refugee status have the right of family reunification immediately. Persons with residence permits granted on humanitarian grounds may have their family join if economic support is secured. After three years of residence with a work permit family reunification is a right regardless of support capacity (the marriage must have lasted at least three years). The Bosnian refugees received family reunification independent of support capacity, and the categories qualifying for reunification were defined more liberally.

'Equal Treatment' – Explicit and Implicit Internal Control

The major explicit argument for the general restrictive immigration policies was the Norwegian principle of 'equal treatment' within its national borders. The basic motivation for this was the welfare state concern of not creating systemic differences based on ethnic lines, and since welfare benefits were limited goods, restrictions in terms of access was necessary. The Norwegian authorities wanted to lay the ground for, principally, the same opportunity structure for foreign residents and Norwegian citizens. Since 1981 interpretations of the public line on immigration had been diverse due to the vagueness of the guidelines. The major aim in 1988 was consequently to clarify the aims of the public policy, and to rank the different goals (Haagensen et al., 1990). From 1988 onwards the overriding concern has been to gain as much equality ('reell likestilling') between immigrants and Norwegians as possible. A concrete manifestation of these intentions was that the immigration policy was incorporated as a part of the general welfare policy of the country.

Since the question of equality has been stressed so distinctly in Norwegian immigration policy, the question of 'positive discrimination' or specifically targeted action ('særtiltak') has been somewhat intricate. Generally Norwegian and foreign citizens have the same rights according to the law, but there are exceptions to this. Foreign citizens cannot become Members of Parliament, they cannot vote in national elections (since 1983 they can vote in local elections after three years residence) and they may not undertake military service. There are certain jobs in the public administration which are not open to foreign citizens. From the middle of the 1970s, some arrangements have been made, mostly subsidies, specific- ally for immigrants, and in the 1980s some reception facilities have been developed for refugees, asylum seekers and persons who are given residency on humanitarian grounds. The rationale behind these specific arrangements is 'that the immigrants, practically speaking, shall have the same possibilities as the nationals to utilise all public services, and to influence their own living conditions through active participation in society'. As the institutions in society (including public services) are based on Norwegian, socio-cultural premises, however, and are also initially aimed at Norwegian citizens, there are immigrants who cannot utilize the services the same way and to the same degree as Norwegians. Consequently, equality must imply certain targeted action from the outset, such as action in the field of education, housing, health and labour market. In other words, these are not to be considered as advantages for immigrants but rather preconditions for the equal opportunity policy. (The latter point is stressed rather strongly.)

Box 7.1 Foreign population

The immigrant population in Norway – defined by Statistics Norway as persons having two foreign born parents – consisted of 225,000 persons in 1996. This accounts for 5.1 per cent of the Norwegian population, and includes immigrants who have gained citizenship; 157,537 of the immigrant population were foreign citizens in 1996. Half of the immigrant population has its origins in Europe, 1/3 from Asia, 8 per cent from Africa and 4 per cent from South and Central America (UDI 1997). Of the immigrants from non-OECD countries 45 per cent live in Oslo. The immigrant population of Oslo again accounts for more than 10 per cent of the total population in the capital (Valen and Aardal, 1995).

The 'equal opportunity approach' strikes a central cord in Norwegian mentality. For better or worse, Norwegians are raised to believe that a just society is a society with a high level of equality. Anthropologists have emphasized that Norwegians more than others tend to think in terms of a very literal equality, which in Norway has the label 'millimetre-justice'. Specifically targeted (favourable) arrangements are therefore easily conceived as unjust. The well-intended 'særtiltak' in Norwegian immigration policy are increasingly challenged in society. There are important norms concerning the limits to acceptable deviation from equality. Norwegians are also known to have limited tolerance for difference and, accordingly, fairly strong social control – particularly in smaller communities.

The various policy measures to promote equal opportunities may be seen as an explicit control instrument to avoid marginalization along ethnic lines. Labour unions are in this respect more occupied with the economic dimension of immigration, including political effects of the economic implications such as reduced bargaining power as a consequence of economic competition. Generally speaking, however, Norwegian labour unions have engaged in immigration policies only to a limited degree – a fact that, one could say, reflects the relatively minor role immigration has played in Norwegian history until recently. The National Labour Union (LO) has nevertheless been occupied with effective control throughout the period since its inception. The Union either supported entry control measures that were suggested by the government, or contributed to the internal control.

The ultimate internal (explicit) control is represented by the institution of citizenship. Norwegian citizenship legislation has traditionally been based on a *jus sanguinis* (ancestry-founded) principle. A person, born in Norway of two foreign citizens will have to wait until he or she is 18 to apply for citizenship. At the end of the 1980s, the Norwegian government made a draft to change the citizenship law and it was proposed that the required residency of seven years be amended to five, in line with the policy in Sweden for example. This proposal was, however, not realized, as it was met with widespread scepticism. There has nevertheless been a clear increase in the number of naturalized foreigners from 2,851 persons in 1985 and 4,757 in 1990 to 12,200 in 1996. The citizenship issue was again discussed in relation to the White Paper on Immigration 1996–97. The seven-year requirement was upheld with reference to the strict rules on expulsion of immigrant criminals, as well as the collective protection rule of four years (see later). It was also argued that the poor language skills of many immigrants pointed in the same direction (White Paper 1996–97: 17).

Possibly one important difference between Norway and most other European countries in this period is the insignificance of illegal immigration. This fact probably has partly to do with geographical location and partly structure of the labour market: the 'transparency' and structural control through the position of unions as well as the general state/municipal presence in the economy. Besides, Norway has for years employed ID number systems for internal control purposes. It is very difficult to operate in Norwegian society without being registered through the ID system. All residents have a personal identification number that is often required when, visiting a doctor or a hospital, when registering children in school and so forth. These mechanisms do not *obstruct* illegal sojourn, but they make life as an illegal resident in an advanced state more difficult.

There is yet another control: the *implicit* control that follows from attachment to and dependency on welfare provisions. The structural paternalism epitomized in the welfare state does have social control as a side effect (Culpitt, 1992). These mechanisms have probably been most discernible among asylum seekers and refugees who are dependent on special assistance upon arrival, through a system for reception and settlement. Often they remain in a client situation, because they are not capable of finding a job. This 'clientalization' or generation of dependence can also be seen more generally among legal foreign residents who for various reasons may have greater problems than the average national in finding appropriate work or adjusting to local conditions. This control mechanism could be viewed more as an unintended consequence of the welfare approach, and it is also relevant in relation to disadvantaged nationals. The 'clientalization' aspect has been strongly focused in Norway, especially after the 1995 elections, as an investigation among refugees in Oslo revealed that close to 50 per cent of the refugees (on average) received welfare benefits as their major source of income (Djuve and Hagen, 1995).

White Paper 1996–97: 17 *On Immigration and Multicultural Norway* kept the general perspective on equality of White Paper 1987–87: 39, although stronger emphasis was placed on participation by the immigrants, and their responsibility when it comes to integration. This White Paper stresses three major areas in Norwegian integration policy: targeted work against racism and discrimination; improved language training in Norwegian for children and adults, and targeted action to qualify immigrants for the Norwegian labour market. White Paper 1996–97: 17 must be seen in relation to two other Bills, namely White Papers 1994–95: 17 *On Refugee Policy*, and 1989–90: 61 *on Settlement and integration of refugees and persons with residence permit on humanitarian grounds, organization, resource allocation and finance.* As in most other European receiving countries, it is the refugee/asylum policy that has been most controversial, and which also has gone through the most marked changes over the last decade. It was the protracted crisis in former Yugoslavia and the consequent major refugee flows that speeded up policy changes, as was the case to a large extent elsewhere in Europe.

The Bosnia Crisis – A Marker in Norwegian Refugee Policy

The Yugoslavian crisis has injected urgency into the process of restructuring the Western European refugee strategy. The majority of Western European countries discarded their normal practice of considering each case individually, and introduced temporary protection on a collective basis. This reflects a realization that a strict definition of a refugee, as stated in the 1951 UN Convention relating to the Status of Refugees, is not a particularly suitable tool when it comes to mass migration. The refugee crisis has also put pressure on governments to tackle the refugee question on a more extensive basis, and a number of comments at national level have called for a more 'comprehensive approach' to migration in which the question of cause, in all its complexity, is given greater attention. Expressions such as 'the right to stay', 'early warning', 'flight prevention', 'the creation of safe areas', and so on, have emerged in the international debate.

Box 7.2 Facts and Tendencies

In the 1970s and the beginning of the 1980s there was a slight increase in immigration (from 11,000 to 13,000 annually). From the mid-1980s, however, there have been marked fluctuations in the picture. In 1987 and 1988 more than 23,000 immigrants entered Norway, followed by a steep decline in 1989 and 1990 to figures 30 per cent below the 1988 level. The decrease was most pregnant for immigrants from Nordic countries (minus 37.5 per cent in 1989) and from the rest of Europe. For citizens from Third World countries the decrease was 15 per cent in 1989 and more than 20 per cent in 1990. The changing tide in the middle of the 1980s was basically due to an increase in the number of asylum seekers, whereas the reverse in 1989 is explained by the highest unemployment rate in Norway since World War II, making the demand factor much weaker, not least for the neighbouring countries (Østby, 1990). In 1993, the number of immigrants to Norway was higher than ever before, reaching close to 32,000. The steep increase was mainly due to the peak inflow of refugees from former Yugoslavia (primarily Bosnians). When Sweden and Denmark introduced visa requirements for Bosnian refugees in June 1993, the number entering Norway reached 2–3,000 per month until the Norwegian government followed suit in October, reducing the number by 80–90 per cent (Brochmann, 1995). This ad hoc introduction of an extremely effective control mechanism, made 1994 the year with the lowest number of asylum seekers since 1985.

In Norway a change of direction in refugee policy has taken place during recent years, primarily for similar reasons to those of the rest of Western Europe. These changes have been sparked off by the situation in the former Yugoslavia, but should also be seen as reflecting something more than this. The authorities have wanted to extend the range of solutions available to them as far as types of protection are concerned, as well as pave the way for greater flexibility in enforcing policy. The prospect of a continuing influx of refugee groups and the corresponding strain on national budgets, has also created a backdrop for new thinking in Norway.

Through the Bosnian war refugee situation, Norway has opted for a new control model for large-scale refugee migration. This entails *temporary protection conditional on return to the country of origin when the need for protection ceases*. The model is said to 'encompass both voluntary repatriation and obligatory return when the reason for exile has ceased' (Landrapport, 1994: 6). There are three factors behind the new approach: (1) International developments with an increasing number of refugees; more large-scale migration situations due to war and other unacceptable conditions; positive experience with conflict solving, giving local assistance and with large-scale repatriation operations. (2) New signals from the UNHCR and from the Norwegian Refugee Council accepting temporary protection in large-scale migration situations. (3) An independent political process in Norway; the development of a 'comprehensive refugee policy'.

During recent years, Norway has also formulated a more comprehensive refugee policy in line with tendencies in Sweden, Denmark and the Netherlands with the same emphasis on efforts on an international scale, preventive work – focusing on root causes, concentration on local areas, temporary protection as a means of helping greater numbers, and so forth. The comprehensive approach will according to the White Paper 1994–95: 17 'increase appreciation of the priorities chosen in refugee policy'. More emphasis will be placed on preventive measures and greater effort concentrated on local areas. The aim of preventing migration entails, according to the report, giving higher priority to 'democratic measures, monitoring human rights, and conducting focused development aid'. As far as assistance to local areas is concerned, the report states that refugees should receive 'assistance and protection as close to their homes as possible'. In addition to the fact that return in the event of peace can be facilitated by following this 'principle of proximity', it is also pointed out that Norway can help far more people in their home regions than is possible in high-cost Norway.

This White Paper is both the result of experience with the Bosnian refugees, and also an attempt to consolidate a new general way of thinking within refugee policy. Emphasis on the temporary aspect represents a new element, even though there was no new legislation to bring it about until 1994. Through the White Paper, the authorities wish to create a new set of expectations – both among the Norwegian general public, and amongst the various refugee groups. Former Political Advisor at the Ministry of Local Government and Labour, Mr Roger Ingebrigtsen, pointed out that the greatest challenge facing Norway 'is to make repatriation an obvious and natural element in refugee policy; amongst refugees, the general public, in the mass media, etc.' (Nyhetsbrev, 1995).

The Norwegian authorities emphasize that the temporary aspect is already incorporated in the Immigration Act of 1988: a settlement permit cannot be granted until the applicant has been resident in Norway for three years, and the authorities can withdraw asylum or refuse to renew a residence permit. What is new, according to the authorities, is that the temporary element will now be activated: the authorities are now willing to put into practice something for which there is already scope in the legislation. In this respect, the Bosnian war refugees represented a 'test case' for an active repatriation policy. The authorities argue that the temporary aspect is important in principle in order to distinguish between refugees and other immigrants: it is the temporary dimension that makes refugees a special group among other immigrants, in as far as the need for protection is in focus rather than a general offer of a better life. Moreover, increased emphasis on the temporary aspect can be a signal to other potential asylum seekers without a need for protection: getting asylum does not necessarily result in permanent residence in Norway. A further argument is that repatriation is important in principle in order to be able to help more people.

'State of Emergency'?

Initially, a great deal of emphasis was placed on the Bosnian refugees being a special case. The Bosnians represented something different from the general influx of individual *ad hoc* refugees to Western Europe, particularly during the mid-1980s. The refugees from Bosnia-Herzegovina are a fairly homogenous group in terms of language and culture, and they arrived over a fairly concentrated period of time. The Bosnians were victims of disputes in an area geographically close to Western Europe, and 'ethnical cleansing' was involved. The conditions could clearly be classified as mass migration, and called for the use of measures other than those provided by the UN Convention relating to the Status of Refugees. A further factor was that the refugees had escaped from armed conflict that, from its outset, had received a great deal of attention from the media. Few other conflicts have been more in focus in the mass media than those in the former Yugoslavia. In Norway, this was further emphasized by its direct involvement at the negotiating table.

The unusual situation also explains why the UNHCR recognized 'state of emergency' measures and an explicit stress on the *temporary* factor. As far as the UNHCR's – and the European national governments' – view of temporary protection is concerned, there is a striking element of ambiguity present: it is argued that the temporary element has existed in the protection of refugees all along, through the so-called 'cessation clause' when the need for protection has ceased, and that it is the Bosnians' special situation as mass refugees that justifies their receiving special treatment. This ambiguity factor has been apparent in the Norwegian debate associated with the launching of the White Paper. Temporary protection is something new but at the same time, it is not new at all.

The least that can be said is that Norway has only, made use of its 'cessation clause' to a minimal degree. Protection has been synonymous with a permanent residence permit. Consequently, the introduction of temporary protection of refugees from Bosnia-Herzegovina may be seen as a flexible tool in a crisis – as the only realistic way to get governments to accept extraordinary reception of refugees. At the same time, there is plenty of evidence to suggest that the Yugoslavia crisis has activated a temporary perspective, which had been lying latent in existing general asylum policy. A number of questions emerge in the wake of activating temporary protection and with it the question of repatriation and return. Should the temporary state of the situation be interpreted as a general instrument, or should it only be applied to mass refugee situations? Who should define the duration of the temporary element, and what rights should refugees have during the protection period?

With the recent White Paper, Norway has come far in a European context in defining its terms: the government wishes to apply collective protection in situations involving mass migration, and to be able to delay processing asylum applications for up to three years from the time temporary residence was granted. The government will consult the UNHCR when it comes to categorizing a situation. Contrary to the expectations of many, the Norwegian government has not introduced temporary protection as a general instrument in refugee policy. Instead, it has opted to play on the ambiguity factor we mentioned earlier, which is already present in the general protection of refugees: the government regards the current regulations to be sufficiently flexible in that they already incorporate different forms of protection, and can therefore remain as they are. The consequence of this is that the political climate in Norway at any one time will determine the extent to which the temporary element is applied or not. This flexibility is nothing new in Norwegian immigration regulation, as indicated earlier.

This political vulnerability was clearly illustrated in the autumn of 1996 where all of a sudden the government cut short the new dual strategy by granting all the Bosnian refugees permanent residence permit – approximately one year ahead of the formal deadline. This was, interestingly enough, a popular tribute from the newly established Jagland government. The tough line on return had been heavily criticized in the media. The 'test-case' represented by the Bosnian refugees was consequently not taken to its end.

These drastic changes have been passed in a climate of rising concern about migration pressure and problems of exclusion/marginalization of already settled immigrants. This concern is as much about *projected problems* as existing ones. The role of public opinion, and the control of *social definitions* are central in this respect, to win support for anticipations.

The Role of Parties and Public Opinion

It should be pointed out that 'public opinion' is a difficult and unclear component, with internal disagreement and often important variations. What may be a small element in the total picture can receive a disproportionate amount of attention. Public opinion basically belongs to the realm of implicit internal control. On the one hand, the climate of opinion may influence the extent to which immigrants are 'let into society'. On the other hand, public opinion is a central force in policy formulation. There is here an intricate interplay between politicians and what is defined as public opinion at any point in time. Nevertheless, opinion polls may give indications as to tendencies and changes – and indeed, polls themselves may influence the very same tendencies.

In Norway there was, according to studies, a discernible increase in animosity towards immigrants from 1990–95 (Valen and Aardal, 1995: 170). By and large political parties have agreed substantially on immigration matters, although the Progress Party (FrP) has capitalized on anti-immigrant feelings in election campaigns in the last ten years. Whereas the other parties have shown avoidance symptoms as regards immigration matters in general, the FrP has used immigration as its flag issue. In 1989, 26 per cent of the FrP constituency thought immigration was the most important issue in the campaign. This figure rose to 42 per cent in the 1993 election but went down again to 22 per cent in the 1997 general election. In the 1995 local elections, immigration turned out to be the target for public interest, and the Party, which had received less than 4 per cent in 1985, increased its performance to 13 per cent in 1995 and more than 15 per cent in the 1997 parliamentary elections. In certain parts of Oslo (traditional Labour areas), as much as 30 per cent of the constituency voted FrP.

During the campaign all the other parties had to different degrees been reluctant to address problems related to immigration policy. The 1995 election result served as an overwhelming protest against this fact, although there are indications that 'hostility towards immigrants could be an "organizing principle" for the opposition against a whole range of other factors in society – a protest against the elite and the political establishment' (author's translation) (Skånvik, 1992: 127, cited in Valen and Aardal, 1995). After the election in 1995, the atmosphere changed significantly. The whole political spectrum has had to rethink immigration politics, and it became legitimate to reveal worry about the climate for integration of ethnic minorities – and 'lack of willingness' among immigrants to adapt to 'the Norwegian way of life'.

This process of questioning the traditional welfare approach to immigrants started even in Social Democratic circles in the early 1990s. During the summer 1991 the Labour leader of the City Council of Oslo took his party fellows (and numerous others) by surprise when he launched a new attitude towards immigrants in combination with 'other marginalized groups' in society. He accused his own party as well as the authorities at large of having been too kind ('kind to a fault') to these groups, the consequence being irresponsibility and dependence on public welfare. He particularly attacked education for immigrants in their mother tongue. According to the Labour leader this education had hindered the children in learning Norwegian, and postponed their integration in society.

This intervention upset large parts of the Labour Party in the country, basically because they felt it undermined the value system of social democracy; that the people in need, for one reason or another, should be taken care of and given the necessary means to survive. The Labour politician was accused of pandering to parts of the public and their sense of fairness in times of economic constraints. The debate that followed, called 'snillisme-debatten' ('niceism'-debate), was never really *salonfähig* within the Labour Party until the election in 1995 changed the climate for discussion.

The situation in Norway between the 1995 and 1997 elections has been peculiar in terms of public opinion. On the one hand the xenophobic or hostile sentiments came out in the open in an unprecedented way. On the other hand, the press – by and large – has been very critical towards the restrictive line of the government, particularly in relation to asylum seekers, and the Bosnians. This has put pressure on the government to move in a more liberal direction. Additionally, the overall sentiments in the population started to move in a slightly more positive direction in 1996. More people indicated that they were in favour of a more open attitude towards asylum seekers. This sheds light on the somewhat surprising move by the new Labour government in 1996, where the Bosnian refugees were granted permanent residence – undermining the newly established (by another Labour government) policy on temporary protection. Before the change of government in 1997 (from Labour to a Christian Democratic coalition), signals were given that the asylum policy was going to be liberalized. The Christian Democratic government seems to follow this line of moderate change. Thus Norway represents an interesting case in our European context: in the midst of a tight European control regime, there is in Norway, at least symbolically, some movement in a more humanitarian direction.

'Good Fences Make Good Neighbours'

It is often hypothesized that there is a connection between the economic performance of a country and the climate for tolerance among the population. Another hypothesis, which most receiving states have subscribed to, is that a restrictive entry control is necessary to facilitate the integration of settled immigrants.

Norway makes an interesting test case in both respects. Norway's current economy has hardly ever been stronger; entry regulations have barely been more restrictive; and – at the same time, despite the recent mild change – xenophobic reactions and discrimination are not negligible. These observations are, of course, not a final rejection of the hypotheses, yet they may stimulate a more developed analysis.

It is not possible, however, to go into this terrain in depth here. Such an analysis would demand a much broader tableau of variables in fields where data are hard to come by. Let us nevertheless briefly discuss a few central points that may indicate why the hypotheses are too simplistic and general to have explanatory power.

The Norwegian economy has been amazingly strong in the 1990s compared to other Western European countries. It is nonetheless also a fact that the Norwegian economy has been going through quite extensive structural changes over the last 10–15 years, in which the sustainability of the welfare state has been questioned. Shrinking budgets have implied pressure towards privatization even in the core areas of social security; health, pensions and education. When public budgets are restrained, legitimacy becomes an issue as to who should benefit and who should care for themselves. Then it becomes more explicit which implicit obligations society attach to the 'welfare contract'.

The problem of solidarity arises when new people arrive – people who have not invested over a lifetime (let alone over generations). The survey revealed the attitude that those who for a long time had lived and worked in the country, had the right to enjoy the goods first. There should be a correspondence between what one puts in and what one gets out. The concentration of the 'anti-immigrant votes' in socially disadvantaged groups in the 1995 and 1997 elections may suggest that there is an intermediate variable in the economy, which may explain the perception of immigration as a threat in parts of the population. Despite the healthy national economy, insecurity was growing, which probably makes hypotheses of 'relative deprivation' more relevant than macroeconomics.

The second hypothesis, the connection between entry control and tolerance, is highly disputed, although a number of scholars have adhered to the logic of the argument. Michael Walzer (1983) has claimed that societies can be open only if borders are at least potentially closed; whereas Stein Rokkan drew attention to the more formal 'interaction between external and internal boundary-building strategies' (Rokkan, 1974: 49). Even poetic expressions have been made to the same effect: 'Good fences make good neighbours' (Frost, 1967). In the Norwegian context something can be said for this hypothesis. The effective control policy of the 1980s and 1990s might have created a feeling of trust in the Norwegian population that the government is in command of the external control system. This might in turn have made larger, and maybe new groups indulge in a more generous attitude. Regardless, restrictive entry control cannot be a sufficient means to promote respect and acceptance of newcomers.

Arguments could also be followed to support an opposite view to the one presented so far. It is possible to turn the hypothesis upside down, claiming that the 'stop' policy contributes to a worsening climate rather than alleviating relations between immigrants and 'nationals'. The heavy emphasis on control in Norway has made it difficult to avoid the rising stigma attached to immigrants in society. After the immigration 'stop' was introduced, ethnically 'visible' immigrants were (in people's minds) not supposed to come in at all, apart from a very few traditional bona fide refugees. The word 'immigrant' has become synonymous with 'unwanted', which again may affect public attitudes towards ethnic minorities in general.

Anyhow, this is a highly complicated and complex landscape, where the historical context in all its complexities must be considered for a richer understanding.

Control at What Cost?

We introduced the question of costs in the first chapter, as all kinds of immigration control have consequences: there can be unforeseen consequences – and there can be foreseen consequences with unforeseen costs, which in the process appear as dilemmas or trade-offs. Some of these costs may not be conceived as such until some time has passed. 'Costs' here pertain to consequences beyond the financial costs. Certain types of control can fairly easily be estimated in terms of expenditure, through border police expenditure, asylum processing accounts and so forth. Yet other, more subtle effects on society like people's feeling of security, threat perceptions, the atmosphere in terms of respect and tolerance, are much harder to assess. The costs or the consequences of a specific policy in terms of changes in society would usually be impossible to quantify or even identify in the first place. It would not be feasible to isolate the causal factors in order to trace the connection to immigration.

There will also be political disagreement about the interpretations and social definitions. What is a cost for some, can be a benefit for others. The quest for a 'cost-benefit' analysis of control/immigration policies is in itself a normative venture. This was amply clear in a Norwegian parliamentary debate in 1995 when asylum/refugee issues were discussed. The Progress Party suggested calculating the price of immigration for the country and was supported by the majority of the parliament. After the decision was taken, a media discussion started that revealed some of the pitfalls of trying to estimate the monetary value of human agency. In the end there was hardly any research institute that wanted to take responsibility for the complete analysis. The Minister of Local Government and Labour announced that it was a 'mission impossible', and came up with a White Paper 1996–97: 17 'on the whole complexity' and, in addition, a more limited cost–benefit analysis of immigration within the public sphere. The irony was that this analysis showed that the whole group of immigrants seen together broke even – a fact that completely demobilized the FrP on the issue.

The European Union and Norwegian 'Outsidership'

As we saw in the introduction to this chapter, the Schengen Agreement has made control policies of the EU member countries enter the back door of Norwegian politics shortly after the national referendum that voted down membership in the Union. It has raised the question of the quality and degree of national self-determination in an area of strong international interdependence. Norwegian authorities managed to negotiate an attachment accord with Schengen together with Iceland in 1997. A vigorous parliamentary debate followed the signing in February, which ended with a majority in favour of endorsement – only few weeks ahead of the Amsterdam Summit in June 1997. The Schengen Accord was integrated into the EU structure at this summit, thus leaving Norway in a peculiar situation as a non-member country.

One can argue that as long as immigration pressure on Western Europe is significant – as long as *upgraded control* is the dominant concern within the Union, and as long as Norway places itself in the more restrictive wing of Europe in this respect, the difference between membership and 'outsidership' for the country is small.

The assessment of the Norwegian situation is based on the assumption that the 'pull-forces' – the relative attraction of the country – must be significantly stronger in Norway than in the major immigration countries within the Union to have immigrants *prefer* to try Norway. Of course, this is not a static situation. Norway's attraction will partly depend on the economic, political and social development of the Union, and partly Norway's development *compared* with that of the Union. A whole range of factors will together constitute the 'pull-package' of both.

Firstly, the labour market will play a central role. Information about possibilities in the formal and informal labour market received by potential migrants will be one important factor in decision making. Secondly, rights for legal foreign citizens, social benefits and welfare policy generally speaking, could also be considered. Thirdly, factors like language, climate, and 'culture' broadly speaking would play a part in combination with the network dimension, where former immigrants can serve as a communication and service channel. Weak external border control may even function as a 'pull-factor', if other attractions are present.

The importance of each and every factor will vary with the kind of immigration in question. For illegal immigrants, the labour market and the internal control systems will be most important. For asylum seekers, ease of access, and generosity in terms of social benefits, possibilities for family reunification and so forth will in the first place be central, yet labour market considerations might also be a part of the long-term judgement. For all migrants the third, rather vague domain of language, culture and climate will make a difference in one way or another. Border control is important as a precondition for access to other possible goods whereas the network factor can be both a precondition for access and a separate 'pull-factor'.

If we now consider all these factors together, Norway has until now been placed rather far down on the 'priority list' of attractive/possible destination countries in Western Europe. This is so, despite the impression internationally that Norway is a peaceful and democratic country with a highly developed welfare system, high salaries and relatively low unemployment as compared with the European average. The de facto low rate of immigration to Norway may partly be a result of effective external and internal control and/or convincing communication to the outside world that Norway is a highly regulated country with a strict immigration policy. It is very probably also a reflection of the rating on the 'language-culture-climate' cluster. More important, as a cumulative consequence, is the network factor. Since immigration to Norway historically has been limited, the network effect is so far also smaller. Norway's position relative to Sweden is central here. Sweden has in the first place very similar 'pull-factors' to Norway, yet as Sweden had a larger labour market and a more liberal immigration policy in certain respects at an earlier stage, the cumulative network effect has made Sweden a much stronger 'magnet'. Consequently, Norway has been in the shadow of Sweden throughout the period we have been dealing with.

This situation *might* change now, with Sweden being a part of the European Union, and with the parallel/consequent tightening of immigration policies. Regardless, even though Norway's relative attraction will increase, it is not necessarily the case that actual immigration will increase. Norway has so far retained its sovereignty in terms of immigration control, and it is likely that this situation will last in the foreseeable future. Possible Schengen affiliation will only partly affect the conditions. Norwegian authorities have already introduced visa requirements for certain 'refugee-producing' countries, a mechanism that is likely to be used every time a large-scale conflict is emerging. Illegal immigration has so far not been a significant problem in Norway, and this is not likely to change unless the border control situation and the general internal control systems are altered.

The Norwegian immigration authorities have improved substantially in terms of efficiency since the late 1980s. There are better technical facilities to increase control, and the execution of negative decisions has become more vigorous. The overall picture is, thus, that the rules and regulations have been quite stable, yet the *practice* turned more restrictive, at least until the Christian Democrats took power. This fact again serves to reinforce the signal to the external world: Norway is not easily accessible.

Final Reflection

Considering the fact that 'Norway appears to be on the periphery of most major migration flows' (White Paper 1994–95: 17: 3, English version), it seems somewhat puzzling that the Norwegian government has placed itself in the most restrictive flank of the West European countries when it come to most elements of control.

The basic consensus that has been prevalent in Norwegian politics on immigration concerning external control may be explained primarily by two structural features of postwar Norway: the general level of regulation in society and the welfare state. Having control with the influx – the first gate to the territory – is a precondition for keeping up the internal regulation. The universalistic welfare model, basically being an inclusive, yet limited asset, at the same time necessitates selection or delimitation.

Yet, as we have seen, there have been fluctuations throughout the period we have been dealing with. Economic considerations have been central components in forming these fluctuations in policy implementation. The emphasis of the economic argument has changed, however. From the turn of the last century until the end of the Second World War, protection from competition in the labour market was central. After the war, economic growth and labour demand turned the economic argument upside down. This liberal period in terms of immigration control lasted, as we have seen, until the early 1970s. Since the period around the introduction of the 'immigration stop', protection of the welfare state, and the established (principally) universalistic provisions for residents of Norway has been dominant. This focus was re-emphasized from the 1980s onwards, when refugee immigration started escalating.

As we have concluded earlier, it is not likely that the Norwegian authorities will ease external control mechanisms significantly in the future. The new more liberal signals related to the asylum field does not change this general picture. It is in fact probable that the the control mechanisms will be refined and diversified further in terms of stronger emphasis on 'long distance control'. The tendency is quite clear in this respect – steadily more focus on preventive measures outside Norwegian borders: 'early warning systems', 'flight prevention', 'right to stay', 'safe areas', and 'root causes' are all concepts that now provide premises for decision making. Norway is caught in a negative spiral that predominates throughout Western Europe. Each European government has to consider the other states' policy due to the international character of current migration flows. It is a question of mutual expectations that might become self-fulfilling prophecies: each receiving state is afraid of the 'magnet effect', which in practice means that the policy of the most restrictive state will set the tone.

Concerning *internal* control mechanisms, the Norwegian political consensus has cracked. Generally speaking, this represents a more complex scenario, which is much harder to come to grips with in terms of control and regulation. It is basically not a police issue (although certain aspects are), but a question of stability, social security and integration of a population as such. It has to do with the factors that make a society good to live in for its members – new or old. Norwegian polity, with a long tradition of thorough government way into what in many places is regarded as the private sphere, has faced limitations in this realm. It has proved insufficient to use general welfare state measures in addition to specifically targeted actions towards the newcomers to facilitate a sound development and eventually integration. The structure and the framework for integration have been regulated, yet the authorities have not managed to control *reactions* and *attitudes*.

It is too early, however, to write the story of the integration of ethnic minorities into Norwegian society. Significant numbers started coming only within the last twenty years. It is also too early to judge how the preconditions for control – external and internal – will develop. The 'dualism' of the Norwegian control complex – the tough front and the soft inside – might face adjustments, considering both the Schengen quandary and the changing climate after the 1995 elections. Norway is caught in the squeeze between humanitarian values and obligations on the one hand, and the need for *realpolitik* on the other. In the years to come we will witness a quest for a legitimate balance of this dilemma.

References

Brochmann, G. (1995), *Bosnian Refugees in the Nordic Countries. Three Routes to Protection*, Oslo: Ministry of Labour and Local Affairs.
—— (1996), *European Integration and Immigration from Third Countries*, Oslo: Scandinavian University Press.
Brox, O. (1991), *Jeg er ikke rasist, men . . . Hvordan får vi våre meninger om innvandrere og innvandring?* Oslo: Gyldendal.
Culpitt, I. (1992), *Welfare and citizenship. Beyond the crisis of the welfare state?* London: SAGE.
Djuve, A.B. and Hagen, K. (1995), *Skaff meg en jobb!. Levekår blant flyktninger i Oslo,* Oslo: FAFO.
Eriksen, K.E. and Niemi, E. (1981), *Den finske fare*, Oslo: Universitetsforlaget.

Frost, R, (1967), 'Mending Wall'. In Robert Frost. *Complete Poems,* London: Jonathan Cape.

Haagensen, E, Kvisler, L. and Birkeland T. (1990), *Innvandrere – gjester eller bofaste? En innføring i norsk innvandringspolitikk,* Oslo: Gyldendal.

Hanisch, T. (1976), *Om sigøynerspørsmålet.* Oslo: Institutt for samfunns-forskning.

Hernes, G. and Knudsen K., (1990), *Svart på hvitt. Norske reaksjoner på flyktninger, asylsøkere og innvandrere.* Oslo: FAFO.

Landrapport til Nordiskt Integrationsseminarium, (1994), Söderköping, 1–3. Juni.

Nyhetsbrev om norsk flyktning- og innvandringspolitikk, (1995), no. 2.

Rokkan, S. (1974), 'Entries, voices, exits: Towards a possible general-ization of the Hirschman model', *Social Science Information,* 13: 1.

Skjønsberg, H. (1981), *En flyktningepolitikk blir til* Oslo: Oslo University, Department of History.

Skånvik, A.-S. (1992), *Interessekonflikt eller samfunnsprotest?* Oslo: Oslo University, Department of History.

Thorud, E. (1985), *Norsk innvandringspolitikk of arbeiderbevegelsen. Fra åpne dører til innvandringsstopp,* Oslo: Oslo University, Statsvitenskap.

—— (1989), *Norsk innvandringspolitikk 1860–1960,* Oslo: Oslo University, Retts sosiologi.

UDI, (1997), *Fakta om innvandrere of flyktninger,* Oslo: UDI.

Valen, H. and Aardal, B, (1995), *Konflikt og opinion.* Oslo: NKF-forlaget.

Waever, O. et al. (eds.) (1993), *Identity, Migration and the new Security Agenda in Europe,* New York: St. Martin's Press.

Walzer, M. (1983), *Spheres of justice: Defence of pluralism and equality,* New York: Basic Books.

White Papers, (1979–95), Oslo: Ministry of Labour and Local Affairs.

Østby, L. (1990 and 1993), *International Migration to Norway,* 1990 and 1993. Reports for the SOPEMI of OECD, Oslo: Central Bureau of Statistics.

—— (1992), 'Trenger Norge innvandring?' in: Long Litt Woon (ed.), *Fellesskap til besvær,* Oslo: Universitetsforlaget.

Østerud, Ø. (1984), *Nasjonenes selvbestemmelsesrett.* Oslo: Universitets-forlaget

—— (1987), 'Nationalism och modernitet. Ett skandinaviskt perspektiv', in: G. Therborn et al. (eds.), *Lycksalighetens halvö.* Stockholm: Sekretariatet för framtidssudier.

–8–

Planning in the Dark: the Evolution of Italian Immigration Control[1]

Giuseppe Sciortino

A New Immigration country

Since the 1980s, the countries in Southern Europe (and Germany) have received most of the immigration into Western Europe (King and Rybaczuk 1993: 177). Former emigration countries have rapidly and unexpectedly been converted into receiving countries. These new immigration countries are characterized by high levels of official unemployment and by a significant shadow economy. Obviously their experience of immigration is sharply different from the traditional Western European targets of international migration (Freeman 1995). Can we say the same about their systems of immigration control?

In the analysis of scholars and decision-makers alike, it is commonly taken for granted that the border control of southern European countries is in a permanent state of crisis. Even Italians subscribe to the fact that the Italian system of external control is structurally weak and fragmentary (Bolaffi 1996) and that authorities show a widespread tolerance, if not even a benign attitude, toward irregular migrants (Calavita 1994; Zincone 1994). According to this vision – for which frequent amnesty programmes provide empirical evidence – Italy is a true heaven for clandestine immigrants and the main entry door for all those who want to settle in other European countries.

It may be argued, however, that this vision is more a product of stereo-typical reactions than of a sustained analysis. As a matter of fact, the most noticeable feature of the evolution of Italian migratory policy is the rapidity with which Italian authorities (and public opinion, generally) have adopted a stop-and-contain vision similar, and openly related, to the approach

1. The author wishes to acknowledge the financial and institutional support of the Fondazione Cariplo-Ismu for his research activities on immigration controls.

developed earlier by the north European countries. An analysis of Italian immigration policy in the last decade, moreover, reveals that, with some occasional tendencies to the contrary, Italian migration control shows a clear and fairly consistent restrictive trend both in relation to new inflows and to immigrants already present. This has resulted in an exclusionary definition of social membership and a comparatively quick tightening of the institutional apparatus dealing with migrants.[2] These changes are even more striking as they have taken place in an overall political context in which the Italian political system has faced its heaviest systemic crisis. A generalized policy crisis – with a traditionally rather ineffective public administration suddenly put under heavy budgetary restraints – has coincided with a general political crisis, in which a whole political class has disappeared in less than two years and stable moloch parties have turned out to be paper tigers (Mershon and Pasquino, 1993; Katz and Ignazi, 1994). We could even talk about a polity crisis, in which an electoral significant populist party has arisen, which is openly calling for the end of the unified Italian polity (Caciagli and Ketzner, 1995). Phenomena such as the repeated use of amnesties and the presence and reproduction of a population of undocumented immigrants deserve a better explanation than 'Mediterranean exceptionalism'. They have to be explained within the framework of the changing policy context and especially with the overall design of Italian immigration policy. Here the convergence with the 'European' approach has introduced a specific unwillingness to recognize the existence of a structural demand for immigrant labour and therefore to plan, regulate and select the channels of legal entry.

Historical Background

For a very long period of time, immigration was hardly a serious concern for the Italian state. Once established (in 1861), the Italian state was fairly liberal in its treatment of foreigners and refugees. After all, nearly all the heroes of Italian *Risorgimento* had lived in exile at certain times in their lives. Moreover, Italian national discourse had always been liberal in character, seeing the nation as a community of common culture and

2. This is not to deny that in the political debates there are voices openly in favour of immigrants, particularly inside the Catholic Church and in some sectors of the left. These opponents, however, have until now emphasized ethical principles rather than ethical consequences, thus giving a nice contribution to their own defeat. The main obstacles to a fully fledged restrictionist stance are administrative inefficiencies and the inert strength of the established state organization, rather than liberal movements.

lifestyle rather than as a ethnically or racially bounded population. Even when a formal distinction between Italians and foreigners was introduced in 1865, foreigners were granted exactly the same civil rights enjoyed by the Italians.

The kernel of a system of immigration control was developed only from 1919, and thereafter particularly during the fascist period, with the establishment of a centralized alien bureau (1929), the collection of statistics on resident foreigners (1930), the establishment of a visa policy targeted to avoid the entry of politically subversive or 'immoral' individuals (1930) and the introduction of a residence permit to be issued by the Home Office (1931). The entire design of the control system was concerned with political 'immigration': prefects and police forces were consequently the main actors. The birth of the Italian Republic had again been influenced by the political and moral views of people with a personal experience of the exile. According to the new Constitution of 1948 (provision 10), the conditions of aliens were to be considered a matter of law, thus protecting foreigners from any kind of administrative discretionary power. Moreover, the Constitution promised asylum on Italian soil to any foreigner who was in practice refused the democratic liberties granted to Italian citizens by the Constitution. For a long time, none of these constitutional norms were implemented, however. Italian authorities restricted asylum to refugees from the Soviet bloc (with a small exception for some Chileans in 1973) and the control system established in the 1930s was left intact, with a few changes introduced through administrative directives from the Home Office and the Ministry of Labour. The prevailing lack of interest in a comprehensive immigration policy may be easily understood in the country that was concerned mainly with the emigration of its own citizens. From 1945 to the mid 1970s, the very idea of immigration to Italy seemed to many utterly bizarre. The few legislative innovations dealing with immigration were, until the mid 1980s, basically the result of international treaties Italy had signed in order to protect its own emigrants. Internal control of labour migrants was introduced in Act 1961: 5, in which the residence permit was the keystone and a secondary labour permit (*autorizzazione al lavoro*) was required for access to the labour market. According to this law, an employer wishing to hire a non-EEC worker was requested to file an application to the local employment office.[3] The office was then expected to verify that no native workers

3. In order to understand Italian immigration policy, its is crucial to keep in mind that according to Italian law the brokerage of labour is reserved to state agencies. Employment centres are the only agencies, authorised to supply low and medium skilled workers.

were willing to fill the position. If native workers were not available, the office issued a labour permit and the prospective employer was then requested to obtain a *nihil obstat* (a 'green light') from the police. Only at this point, could the foreign worker apply for the visa. The granted residence permit was linked to the work contract, and the termination of the contract implied that the residence permit also came to an end, except in cases of a job-to-job transition.

The initial stock of immigrants in Italy was aggregated during the early 1980s through a variety of independent processes. In the Italian border areas some migratory networks had functioned for decades, related both to Yugoslavia and to North Africa. While some migrants viewed Italy as a temporary location (waiting to overcome northern European stop policies), some others – mainly women looking for domestic work – entered the country through the internationally ramified network of Catholic missions and aid agencies. Others arrived from the former Italian colonies, whereas still others came from other European countries, or followed Italian firms active abroad. Finally, some immigrants just scouted around. In no way may such immigration be imputed to an active policy of collective recruitment: it originated in a web of molecular contacts. The early waves of immigrants found employment in the small and medium-sized enterprises, which constitute the backbone of the Italian economy, and in Italian households.

Given such context, the established immigration procedure – designed for large firms actively recruiting large numbers of workers abroad – could hardly work (and in fact hardly worked). For years, the control was constantly bypassed, and the employment centres became accustomed to authorising labour contracts with foreigners already living in Italy. The system of immigration control was at the time basically a double circuit, on the one hand of police checks – mainly concerned with the 'morality' of immigrants (as well as of employers) and with issues of public order – and on the other hand of decentralized decisions by the employment centres. The problem of external control was still on the whole unrecognized, except by a few police officials. Administrative memorandums give an idea of the slow attention paid at the time to issues of external controls. In 1973 the Home Office reminded the Embassies of the necessity of applying strictly the existing procedures for issuing visas, mentioning that

---

Empirically, however, only a tiny percentage of Italian workers has ever found employment through the employment centres. In the last years, the labour market has been fairly liberalized, but it is still disputed whether this liberalization is to be extended to non-EU immigrants.

their lax implementation has created 'heavy drawbacks'; in 1975, legislative provisions restated that a foreigner without legal sources of income might be expelled and that a foreigner found guilty of drug dealing should be expelled; in 1979 the Home Office repeated and specified the procedures for granting sojourn permits mentioning 'the relevant dimension of the flow of foreigners, with worrying consequences for the public order and security'. Even when – in the early 1980s – immigration flows started to be noticed and recognized as a political topic, policy actions were still largely confined to the implementation of international conventions. At the end of 1981, the signing of the ILO convention No. 143 on irregular migrations triggered the first legislative action. The Ministry of Labour presented a legislative draft of an immigration law, designed to introduce a stricter control on new entries, modelled on those developed after 1972 by northern European states. At the same time the same Ministry adopted an administrative freeze of the work permits, paradoxically justifying this decision with the need to prevent immigrants from taking irregular employment. While this freeze was implemented, the frontiers were still substantially open to immigrants, who could get a tourist visa or who did not need a visa. The intention might have been to put pressure on the Houses for a quick approval of the draft legislation, but the freeze made a fateful beginning, as the highest intake of immigrants took place between 1984 and 1990 (Zincone 1994), making illegal immigration and illegal employment endemic.

The promised law came into force only four years later. On the whole, the Act 1986: 943) is focused on labour migration and adopted the kind of neo-corporatist framework common in those years. A specialized division was created inside the Ministry of Labour, as well as two committees entrusted with the duty of monitoring the implementation of immigrants' rights, the management of the migratory flows and the repression of illegal migration. The law listed a series of rights for immigrant workers ranging from the principle of equal pay for equal work to family reunification, and also some undefined right to 'cultural identity'. The law, moreover, reformed the system of internal control. First, the length of residence permits was separate from the length of the employment contract. Second, having thus created the possibility of being an 'unemployed immigrant worker', the law mandated the employment centres to create special lists, giving priority to unemployed foreign workers before relatives of resident immigrants and to these two categories before prospective immigrants still living abroad. Employers could hire from these lists once it had been verified that no Italian or EU citizen was interested in the job offered. Prospective immigrants were expected to register on special lists held by the embassies, creating a queue for their entry. The entry lists, however, were never implemented. The law introduced the first seed of an employment sanction programme and created a fund – to which immigrants have to contribute with 0.5 per cent of their salary – to cover the return of immigrants lacking the necessary means of living. Eventually, the law launched the first major regularization programme for all the immigrants irregularly employed (Table 8.1).

Table 8.1 Italy: Amnesties and Regularisation Programmes 1982–1996

Year	Decision about Programme	Number	Requirements
1982	administrative	12,000	(1) Employer willing to hire or documented past stable employment and (2) past irregular employment
1986–88	legislative	118,349	(1) Ongoing or (2) past irregular employment
1990	legislative	234,841	Presence on Italian soil before 31 December 1989
1995–96	legislative	248,501	(1) Employer willing to hire or irregular jobs in the last four months or (2) relatives of regular immigrant.

Source: Italian Home Office 1986–92 and Ministry of Labour 1982.

Act 1986:943 was hailed as a major step towards the construction of a rational Italian immigration policy, and it received fairly good coverage both in the parliamentary debates and in the public opinion. The edifice, however, began rapidly to crumble. The purpose of the law had been to reproduce the tools – from bilateral agreements to neocorporatist committees – which Italy had encountered in other immigration countries, when still itself a sending country. As the immigration flows were different both on the sending and the receiving side, the new framework was not able to provide a consistent instrument for control, but instead produced new segments of illegal immigrants. As the law allowed those registered as unemployed to keep their residence permit, it provided a convenient category for all the immigrants employed in the shadow economy. The measure, trying to improve the bargaining power of the immigrants versus their employers, rapidly became an incentive for evading, in a mutually beneficial way, the burden of taxes and social insurance. As many

Italy

immigrants chose to register as unemployed, their number justified a new freeze on new entries. Moreover, despite three decrees that extended the length of the programme up to the end of 1988, the very same amnesty was applied with a stop-and-contain attitude (Sciortino 1991). The section on employer sanctions had already been substantially weakened during the parliamentary discussion and was never a priority for the public officials. On the whole, Act 1986:943 had a strong and lasting impact on the public opinion mostly through its hidden consequences: the reproduction of a significant irregular immigrant population, composed by those newly arrived and by those who did not qualify for regularization, and a large number of immigrants registered as unemployed.

Since the end of the 1986–88 amnesty, the policy emphasis shifted from internal, labour market control, to external control and public order issues. In 1987, the Lower House approved the draft of a new Act concerning restrictive entry procedures, a revision of the rules for issuing residence permits, a programme of sanctions both against irregular immigrants and those giving them lodging, and a revision of the procedures concerning expulsion. The draft never became a law, however, owing to the premature end of the legislature, but three years later, several of its provision found their way into an executive decree, later converted into Act 1990: 39, better known as *legge Martelli*. This Act, which constitutes the second pillar of the current immigration law, was introduced in a fairly heated political climate, in which a rather unstable parliamentary alliance had to be kept together. The result was a patchwork of provisions with very different aims. Some provisions of the Act are fairly liberal. It has generalized the right to asylum, previously restricted only to East European citizens. Furthermore, it included a new – and quite liberal – regularization program, open this time to any immigrant living in Italy regardless of his/ her occupational status (Table 8.1). It should not be forgotten, however, that most of the Act deals with a restrictive reform of external controls. New entries are regulated strictly with a yearly contingent and a restrictive system of visa requirements. Immigration is moreover considered a potential source of disturbance for public order. The number of immigrants from a certain country sentenced for drug dealing in the last three years is to be used as a criterion for decisions about visa requirements in relation to that country. Moreover, a long section of the decree aimed at a reform of the deportation procedure, producing an enduring assumption that deportation decisions should be the cornerstone of the internal system of control: expulsions were made compulsory for a long list of offences.

In the literature – as well as in public discussion – both Act 1986: 943 and Act 1990: 39 are regarded as ineffective and weak, and they are usually identified only with the regularization programmes they started. Judging from available evidence, however, they have been fairly successful in establishing a first restrictive system of immigration control. Firstly, after less than a year, Act 39 showed its effectiveness in dealing with the waves of Albanians refugees. Italian authorities successfully managed the forced repatriation of several thousand Albanian citizens in a very short span of time. By virtue of the Act, visa requirements were quickly introduced for all the North African countries and the number of both border rejections and expulsions has significantly increased (Table 8.2). The restrictive implementation of the Acts has limited the numbers of new legal entries, particularly for asylum seekers and labour migrants (Table 1.3). The increased effectiveness of the Italian system of external control may also be assessed indirectly, as there is some evidence that fares for illegal entries have been skyrocketing during the 1990s.

Table 8.2 Expulsions and Rejections at the Border 1990–94

Year	Expulsions	Border rejections
1990	2,800	61,800
1991	4,100	62,300
1992	4,000	63,100
1993	5,600	61,300
1994	7,500	67,600

Source: Home Ministry.
Note: Expulsions in this table refer to implemented decisions. The total number of expulsion decrees amount to 7 to 8 times higher numbers. The number of border rejections is about twice as large as it was in the 1980s.

However, this enhanced effectiveness of Italian external control has not reduced the moral panic over immigration issues, which has spread during the 1990s. The social alarm began in the political conflict over the approval of Act 1990: 39, where immigration was described as an epochal event, and by the Albanian refugees crisis of 1991, which made the 'invasion' rhetoric common in public discourse (Sciortino 1997b). Not surprisingly, the rise of moral panic has triggered several further attempts to reform immigration legislation, making it more restrictive and closing the loopholes exploited by immigrants. In 1992, the parliament reformed the law on Italian citizenship, making it easier for descendants of Italian emigrants to regain citizenship but also much more difficult for immigrants to apply for naturalization.

The attempts to provide a comprehensive immigration reform – in the period from 1992 to 1996 – have, however, failed partly owing to the same moral panic. The ongoing deep restructuring of the Italian political system made it too risky to place immigration high on the political agenda. On one side, immigration was too 'hot' to be dealt with by the feeble and constantly changing political coalitions. On the other side, the crisis of the party system has given significance to groups such as the populist Northern League and the post-fascist National Alliance, with a position on immigration too extreme to allow successful parliamentary deals.

A case in point is the 1995 attempt to reform the immigration laws. The temporary 'technocratic government' ruling at the time, rushed to promulgate an executive decree (commonly known as the Dini decree) dealing mainly with expulsions and border rejections, as requested by the Northern League, but also introducing a new regularization programme, designed to please the Catholic and left parties. The Dini decree, not particularly well thought out and full of legal ambiguities, turned out to be a clear policy failure. It was not enacted within the constitutionally mandated sixty days. The decree was therefore re-issued several times, sometimes with an identical text, but more often altering or deleting whole sections. Several key provisions were deleted as plainly unconstitutional, some others because they had been successfully appealed against in the courts. Eventually the whole reform of expulsion procedures was in such a bad shape that even the police lobbied for a return to the original norms. Such series of policy failures have reinforced the moral panic, as they have been widely interpreted as a lack of concern for the 'victimized' citizen.

The appointment of the Prodi Cabinet in May 1996 may be a sign that the party system has started to stabilize. As far as immigration is concerned, it has implied a return to the immigration reform circle interrupted by the party system breakdown in 1992. The government has in fact managed to get an approval of the legislation needed to fully comply with the Schengen agreement, and it has obtained from the Houses the approval of a new comprehensive immigration reform Act (1998: 40). The new Act carefully balances some integration measures with a systemic review both of external and internal controls. It also closes the administrative loopholes that have weakened some of the control tools. The willingness of the Prodi Cabinet to adopt a consistent restrictive position has been also tested by the Albanian crisis in 1997. In order to deal with the influx of refugees, Italian authorities have externalized immigration control to international and Albanian waters, have allowed border authorities to select at discretion between bona fide refugees and 'irregular immigrants', have granted only short-term protection linked to the permanence of the refugees in specific places. Such measures have drastically contained an otherwise large flow (Table 8.3). Given the enactment of this legislation, Italy will in a decade have made a complete turnaround of its system of immigration control, assuming a position that is at least as restrictive as those of its European partners. This will become clear when we now move from a longitudinal description of the evolution of the system of control to a synchronic description of the set of mechanisms currently employed in external and internal control.

Table 8.3 Italy: Management of the 1977 Albanian Refugee Crisis

Survey date	27 April 1997		9 May 1997		30 June 1997		30 July 1997	
Total: Refugees arrived	13,450	100%	16,320	100%	16,798	100%	16,964	100%
Deported to Albania	1,302	9.7%	3,140	19.2%	4,398	26.2%	6,517	38.4%
Accomodation centres	5,200	38.7%	5,815	35.6%	3,853	22.9%	3,446	20.3%
Private accomodation	3,300	24.5%	3,922	24.0%	5,023	29.9%	3,935	23.2%
Gone Underground	3,648	27.1%	3,443	21.1%	3,524	21.0%	3,066	18.1%

Source: Home Offce.

The System of External Immigration Control: Visa and Legal Channels of Entry

Before 1990, visa policies were basically a patchwork of partial agreements and decentralised decisions. Still in 1985, the Hon. Scalfaro, heading the Home Office, felt the need to write a preface to a directive reforming the procedures to be used in external control. Here he stressed the enduring humanitarian traditions of Italy, the need to facilitate tourism and, the 'painful', even if necessary, nature of screening foreign visitors (Ministero dell'Interno, memo 19.08.1985). In that year, tourist visas were not required for citizens of 78 countries, among them Morocco, Algeria, Tunisia, Columbia, Senegal, Mauritius and several other sending countries. Italy's interest in tourism and the Italian low-key 'Mediterranean' foreign policy weakened any attempt to develop a strong control of temporary entries. Five years later, visas had become the key instruments of Italian immigration control, and the Minister of Foreign Affairs was required yearly to define the visa requirements, taking into consideration both the origin of the immigration flows and the nationalities of those sentenced for drug trafficking in the prior three years. In 1990, visas had been introduced for Senegal, Gambia, Algeria, Tunisia, Morocco, Mauritania and Turkey, at the time seen as the most immigration-risky countries. The visa requirements have been increasingly tightened in subsequent years. In 1995 Italy, after some resistance also complied with the introduction of visas for some Balkan countries that, although mentioned in Schengen's 'negative list', had been kept visa free for diplomatic reasons. Beside tourism, the most important visas are those issued to 'regular' long-term immigrants: foreign workers and relatives of resident immigrants.

As far as foreign workers are concerned, Italy has moved from the absence of any kind of planning to the adoption, with Act 1990:39, of a yearly ceiling decision, contingent upon the state of the labour market. According to the law, the Minister of Foreign Affairs shall each year issue a decree concerning the number of foreign workers who are allowed to enter the country the subsequent year. Until now, however, Italy has utterly failed to follow this procedure, owing both to the difficulties of estimating the future demand for immigrant labour and to a badly designed decision-making process.[4] As a result, the planning process is purely ritualistic: the ceiling was set to zero the first year and subsequent decrees have either basically authorized the entries of foreigners who had already entered (as workers, individually requested by employers, as family members or refugees) or have been issued too late for being of any use. The decree concerning the year of 1995 was, for example, issued at the end of September 1995; the decree concerning the year of 1996 on 27 December 1996. The 1994 decree was not even issued. In the absence of a functioning planning system, the legal entry of foreign workers is monitored mainly by requiring the request of an Italian employer for a permit for a specific foreign worker. A widespread use of this rather complex bureaucratic process, involving both the local employment centres and the police authorities, is not likely for two reasons. Small and medium entrepreneurs,

---

4. Judging from those few preparatory documents to which I have been able to gain access, the yearly suggestions are based on such unreliable indicators as the official rate of unemployment (not even broken down by skills), the number of immigrants registered as unemployed in the employment centres, and the gross figures on sojourn permits released by the Home Office. It is indicative of the low relevance given to planning new entries that even senior government officials find difficult to locate such documents in the archives.

as well as families looking for household staff are hardly interested in looking for their workers abroad and at long distances. Consequently, beside those who can rely on established migration networks, preference is de facto given to irregular migrants already in Italy rather than to prospective regular migrants. Secondly, bureaucratic complexity has created a double regulation circuit with a high degree of discretion: the Ministry of Labour has several times changed the procedures, in order to make the request of individual foreign workers either easier or more difficult.

Family reunification is managed through a parallel procedure. Relatives of resident foreigners may get a visa if the immigrant has an adequate income, stable work and a convenient lodging. The relatives are not allowed to work for a year. An application must also in this case be made to an employment centre, followed by a *nihil obstat* from the Home Office and a final approval by the Ministry of Foreign Affairs. For some years, family reunification has been marred by administrative inefficiencies, seemingly used in order to keep the number of immigrants low. In 1992, however, a joint memo from the Home Office and the Ministry of Foreign Affairs has set a 90-day time limit, bringing about a steady increase in the number of issued visas. In 1995, however, a ceiling was for the first time announced also for family visas. This decision was quickly set aside by the launch of the 1995 amnesty (open also to the relatives of resident immigrants reunited irregularly), but it may constitute a precedent that could significantly alter the flows of relatives in the future.

Visa requirements do not apply to asylum claimants, who may request their visas directly at the border. Since the removal of the geographical restriction in 1990, there has been some fears that asylum could become an out-of-control entry door for irregular immigrants. The examination of asylum application has therefore been made progressively quicker and tighter, and border authorities have been allowed a certain autonomy when checking the grounds for such applications. As a result, Italy has a very low number of asylum claimants, a high rate of refused applications (ranging in recent years from 83 to 92 per cent) and a low level of appeals. A second category of migrants who may apply for a visa directly at the border is the refugees accepted on 'humanitarian grounds'. This new way of entry was created in 1992 in order to deal with the refugees from Somalia and later on also from the former Yugoslavia (Act 1992: 390). It is a temporary discretionary protection measure. It allows accepted refugees to work but entitles them only to a limited amount of public assistance. Even more recently, during the 1997 Albanian crisis, Italian authorities have introduced an even weaker form of temporary admittance.

Albanian refugees have in fact not received a temporary residence permit but rather a 90-day non-renewable *nihil obstat* that does not allow the access to the labour market.

The System of External Control: Tightening the Border

Traditionally, Italy did not pay particular attention to the control of its borders, except for geopolitical reasons in some particularly sensitive areas. Moreover, as long as tourist visas were fairly easy to obtain, clandestine border crossing was a negligible phenomenon in comparison with overstaying. The introduction of visa requirements, together with restrictions on all forms of legal entry, has made the issue of border control more salient in recent years. Since 1986, every immigration Act has strengthened surveillance of the frontier areas and increased the penalty for smuggling of immigrants. In 1995, the government authorized the use of the Army for border control along the Apulian coast for a period. This increased emphasis on border surveillance does, of course, not mean that Italian frontiers are now secured, but the chances of crossing the border undetected have sensibly decreased.

Strengthened border control has reduced the immigration flows but has also brought about a new kind of illegal border crossing, exploiting remaining loopholes. Traditionally, attempted illegal entries involved small groups of immigrants looking for routes with low visibility. In the summer of 1996, however, a series of large-scale smuggling attempts from Tunisia was detected in the waters surrounding the tiny island of Lampedusa. Prospective immigrants, sank their worn-out boats or were moved to rotten sloops immediately after entering Italian waters. The maritime authorities were obliged to rescue them and bring them onto Italian soil. At this point, technically, their case fell under the expulsion procedure rather than under that of border rejection, but as expulsion orders granted a few days' grace period for leaving the country and did not allow detention, the immigrants could use these days to disappear underground. The Lampedusa crisis was met by increased patrolling and increased diplomatic pressure on the Tunisian authorities, which had seemingly turned a blind eye to the boats' departures. In the autumn of 1997 a similar strategy was used by groups of Kurdish immigrants in Apulia. The adoption of such elaborate plots may well be the best proof that the previously common secret paths have been closed. To deal with the new strategies, Italian authorities have further increased their patrol activities and have enhanced cooperation between the police forces and the navy. The new Act has subsequently introduced the provisions necessary to further close the loopholes, allowing the detention of all those caught in the process of illegal border crossings. The Lampedusa crisis has demonstrated, however, the need for co-operation with sending and transit countries. Here the policy of immigration control meets Italian foreign policy.

Between Immigration Control and Foreign Affairs

From the onset, Italian migration policy has never been a purely 'national' matter. It has, since the beginning, developed within an ongoing regional and international interaction. On one hand, Italy is both a receiving and a transit country. Its control system is thus a matter of interest for several other European states. On the other hand, the issue of immigration control is closely related to the traditional 'Mediterranean' focus of Italian foreign policy. It is an Italian foreign policy interest to establish a working co-ordination with the Mediterranean sending and transit countries in order to encourage them to control emigration and to repress illegal departures to Italy from their shores and land borders. In official Italian political rhetoric, such a strategy is characteristic for both 'realist' politicians – who love the idea of having a new bargaining chip to turn Italy into a Mediterranean regional power – and the left and Catholic movements, lobbying for more development aid and more solidarity with the oppressed. This strategy has been marred, however, by the heavy reductions in the Italian budget for international co-operation, as well as by a widespread worry that using aid as a bargaining chip in relation to the authorities of the sending countries could make mass emigration a powerful weapon in the hands of these countries. The strategy has therefore been reformulated. Italy has renewed its support for the doctrine of burden-sharing and has tried in several ways to keep the EU's southern front on the political agenda at least as much as the eastern front (Papademetriou and Hamilton 1996). The result has been fairly mixed, owing both to the political instability in Italy – which has weakened its foreign policy more than anything else – and to the condition of several sending countries. Since 1996, Italy has, however, succeeded in signing formal treaties with some transit countries, notably Albania and Turkey, aiming at an easier repatriation.

The externalization of control has been pursued with particular vigour in the case of one major sending country, post-communist Albania, a country with strong economic and diplomatic connections to Italy. Very early – during the refugee crisis of 1991 – the Italian authorities realized that irregular migration could be prevented only in close collaboration with the Albania authorities. A bilateral aid programme was launched (distributing around US$150 m in four years), and Italy lobbied success-fully in the EU to make Albania the recipient of the Union's highest per capita aid grant. Although a limited flow of illegal migration between Albania and Italy continued during all the 1990s, the Italian authorities have been fairly successful in preventing further massive emigration and the use of Albania as a launching pad to Italy. Geopolitical influence has also been instrumental in managing the 1997 refugee crisis. The Albanian authorities have authorized the Italian navy to enter well into the Albanian waters in order to 'dissuade' departing vessels.

Italy has faced great difficulties in its efforts to integrate its system of control into that of other European countries, and also, more subtly, in achieving recognition as a reliable and trustful partner in immigration policy. An explanation of these difficulties may be that the implications of the European project on immigration issues are still largely unclear, but the problem is more general, as Italian authorities also have problems in keeping up with the whole of the integration project. Migration is, however, one of the most critical points of Italian integration, something that is best exemplified by the case of Italy's participation in the Schengen Treaty. The initial core group who founded what would become the Schengen Agreement of 1985, was composed of five out of the six original EEC countries. The only one missing was Italy. Moreover, the Italian application to join Schengen, presented in 1987, was delayed for years, with a fairly open intention of defining in detail the content of the agreement before letting Italy (and other southern European countries) have a say on the matter. Italy signed the convention in 1990. Act 1990: 39 had paved the way toward this outcome. In the following years, how-ever, the Houses did not succeed in approving the legislation concerning the protection of personal data and the introduction of separate queues in the airports. This became the main stumbling block, as Italy did not match the formal Schengen criteria. Several deadlines were given and by-passed over the years. As a result Italy has been put in the peculiar position of paying for a control structure from which it was not allowed to benefit. Full integration into the Schengen system was achieved only in 1997 (to be completed in 1998), within a framework strictly defined by northern European countries. The failure to integrate quickly into the Schengen area has also played a role in domestic politics as a powerful political weapon in the hands of anti-immigration groups. They have been quite successful in explaining the failure of Italy to join Schengen with the supposedly liberal (and therefore 'un-European') Italian immigration policy.

Internal Immigration Control

The main thrust of immigration reform has been focused on external control. Italy has restricted legal entries and strengthened surveillance over illegal entries. The internal control mechanisms have not been reformed to the same extent as the external ones, thus paving the way for a constant reproduction, albeit at a lower pace, of a sizeable population of irregular immigrants. The failure to establish an adequate system of internal control may be explained by the political risks involved in an open confrontation with the Italian shadow economy.

The main pillars of the Italian system of internal control are the residence permit (*permesso di soggiorno*) and the labour permit (*autorizzazione al lavoro*). The first, issued by the Home Office, is a personal document that immigrants must always carry and show at any time in a police control or a kind of public service centre, or to any prospective employer and landlord. Within eight days on Italian soil an application for a residence permit must be filed at the local police office, in this way notifying the authorities about the foreigner's presence. Later on, any change of address must be communicated to them in writing. Residence permits differ in length, and in the access they give to the labour market. Some permits are renewable, others are not, and the renewal is contingent upon proof of a legitimate income at least equal to the social pension. This pension, granted to any needy elderly regardless of the contributions paid, is the closest official equivalent of a poverty line. In 1996, the *pensione sociale* amounted to 535,000 ITL a month. The *autorizzazione al lavoro*, issued by the Ministry of Labour, is in the same vein supposed to follow the immigrants, to codify the sector and kind of employment to which they are entitled, to register any change of employer, as well as to document any unemployment spell. It is illegal to employ immigrants without having checked their *autorizzazione al lavoro*, and there are heavy fines, and even jail penalties for illegal employment. Together, these two documents provide a complete, nearly panoptical, view of the life of any immigrant.

The trouble with this officially complete transparency and surveillance is that it differs widely from the mundane reality in Italian everyday life. Immigrants, as well as Italian citizens, may live for years without leaving any track of their activities, and where such tracks are made, they will most likely become lost in the quantity of paperwork resulting from separate and rather unconnected bureaucratic structures.

While this condition is widely acknowledged both by the public opinion and decision-makers, the immigration policy debate has hardly touched on the issue of internal control. It may be argued that the identification of clandestine entries as the main problem of immigration control combined with strong pressures to do something about this problem has indirectly produced a neglect of internal control. On a deeper level, however, the overemphasis of external control may be explained by the disinclination to open the Pandora's box of the relationship between state and society. To focus on internal control is in fact to take a political risk: it means dealing with the unpleasant facts of a burgeoning shadow economy, of a large shadow segment in the housing market, of the poor performance of the public administration and of the lack of state control in several areas of the country.

By not introducing adequate internal control, it has been possible to avoid placing these sensitive issues on the political agenda. Instead the emphasis has been placed on the police forces as the main agencies for internal control. On one hand, the police officers are among the few civil servants who enjoy a certain level of trust from the Italian public. As a matter of fact, the police forces are often the only state agency that immigrants get in touch with, and they are often the only one intervening in social conflicts between natives and immigrants. On the other hand, the dominant rhetorical vision of immigration as a phenomenon out of control has helped to shape a symbolic law and order approach. The more that prospective immigrants are portrayed as huddled masses trying to enter the country by any means and at any cost, the more difficult it is to see them, once entered, as rational and deserving people with whom to share willingly a common space.

This law-and-order approach has also gained broad acceptance because of the fact that a significant number of immigrants commit crimes. Even with all the precautions required in dealing with criminal statistics (Ismu, 1996; Barbagli, 1998), it is likely that the peculiar history of immigration into Italy has amplified the participation of foreigners in lowlife activities. Firstly, most immigrants have experienced a protracted phase of irregular sojourn. This implies that the initial phase of adjustment has been longer and more fateful for most individuals than it would have been otherwise. Long periods of irregularity have also weakened the social differentiation between immigrants and 'criminal' immigrants and brought irregular immigrants and native deviants closer together. This has in turn confirmed the ethnic stereotypes and delayed the growth of social control mechanisms internal to the migration networks. Secondly, the weak internal control structure and the lack of an effective administration have put most regulation into the hands of the police.

The result of the prevailing law-and-order approach may be clearly seen in the legislative evolution described above. Act 1986: 943 was basically concerned with labour migration and public order was not even an issue. Act 1990: 39 was mainly aimed at increasing the external control of the borders and at integrating the immigrants who had already arrived. Public order measure were fairly conspicuous, but were considered to be last-resort options. From 1992 onwards, however, the policy debate on migration issues has been focused largely on the issue of expulsion, now taken as the keystone of an effective system of internal control. In policy discussion, we can identify two distinct but interrelated attempts: (a) to increase the grounds for expulsion; and (b) to find effective ways to implement expulsion decisions. The former attempt has on the whole been quite successful; the latter has gained some partial victories but also some frustrating drawbacks.

When Italy, in the 1920s, introduced the institute of expulsion, it was mainly targeted against subversives, spies and beggars. Fascism used it, for example, mainly as a sanction against foreign journalists guilty of unfavourable reporting on the regime's achievements. Quite early in Italy's conversion to a receiving country, expulsion was also used as a sanction against criminal activities (in addition to imprisonment) and as a last administrative resort if foreigners remained in the country although their permits had expired or been revoked. Later on, expulsion was made an automatic consequence for all kinds of crimes involving a penal sentence of more than a decade. Expulsion was extended to drug-related crimes in 1975 and enlarged further in 1990 to cover such diverse crimes as the destruction of parts of the cultural heritage, illegal labour brokerage, use of false identities, and sexual crimes and pimping. From 1988 to 1995, the number of expulsions has increased sensibly, and there are also indications of a slight increase in the capacity to execute them (Table 8.2). The attempts to make expulsion a generalized control tool have been rather frustrating, however. To destroy documents has become a common practice, and the co-operation with the sending countries, Albania apart, has remained problematic. Furthermore, the law used to give the expellees a fourteen days' grace period, which they could use to disappear. Act 1998: 40 has however authorized authorities to detain expelled immigrants during the time of the appeal, thus making possible a more effective implementation of expulsion decision.

There are reasons to believe, however, that expulsions in the future will be inadequate instruments for internal control. Firstly, expulsions are controversial measures. There is already in Italy a small but influential opposition against the expulsion of those irregular immigrants who have not committed serious crimes. This opposition, which is particularly outspoken in the southern Catholic hierarchies, has already started the kernel of a sanctuary movement. Also some pro-immigration groups, which are not willing to explicitly advocate a policy of open borders, have found the defence of 'innocent' irregular migrants a workable strategy. The most frequent argument is that an unauthorized immigrant should not be considered a criminal and that deportation should not be used when the only ground is lack of a sojourn permit. Even less controversial expulsions, like those of immigrants who have committed a crime, involve, however, costs in terms of flight tickets, salaries and travel allowances to the police escorts (often required by the airlines) and a lot of administrative paper-work.

Controlling the Labour Markets: Amnesties and Inspectors

The Italian labour market is structurally characterized by the presence both of a highly rigid official sector – in which workers enjoy high levels of benefits and a job security equal and often superior to average European standards – and of a burgeoning shadow economy, which employs around 17 per cent of the labour force. The shadow economy is not necessarily utterly exploitative: even if appalling work conditions are common, in most cases there is a positive pay off between employment insecurity and higher salaries (made possible by the avoidance of taxes and social insurance contributions). Both labour markets include immigrant labour. There is a significant demand for immigrants in the formal economy, where some unskilled or low-skilled positions have been increasingly hard to fill otherwise and where immigrants are commonly employed as a buffer labour force in order to overcome the rigidity of current employment patterns (Ambrosini, Colasanto and Zanfrini 1991; Zanfrini 1996).

As the legal employment of foreign workers has long been regulated, a significant number of immigrants have gone into the underground economy. Migratory networks and employment chains have gradually amplified and reinforced the underground labour market. Retirement benefits and other kinds of long-term social insurance are, of course, not offered on this labour market, and it usually provides only unstable forms of employment. It offers, however, higher flexibility, quicker and less selective hiring procedures and sometimes a higher net monetary salary, owing to tax dodging. These features may be appealing to those newly arrived immigrants who are interested in maximizing short-term monetary gains but do not plan to stay long enough in the receiving country to reap retirement benefits. While being the only chance for irregular immigrants, the shadow economy is also interesting to those legal immigrants who may register as unemployed, keeping their residence permit and getting some health coverage, while receiving in cash part of what they would have paid in taxes had they been regularly employed. It is then hardly surprising that less than 50 per cent of the potentially employable immigrant labour force is regularly employed in salaried occupations, self-employed or agricultural workers. The Italian National Statistical Institute reckons (maybe with some overestimation) that undocumented immigrants provide 4.3 per cent of the labour supply but that they amount to nearly one third of the standard labour units employed by the shadow economy (Istat, 1995).

The existence of a dual labour market – and of a dual demand for immigrant labour – explains several puzzling features of Italian immigration policy, and not least the frequency of amnesties. Amnesties and regularization programmes have always been used in Italy to regulate the periodic transfer of immigrants from the shadow to the official labour market (Table 8.1). Many attempts have been made to find a middle way between the opposite imperatives of draining the waters in which shadow entrepreneurs swim but at the same time of preventing a sudden new influx of immigrants into the official labour market. Each of the four amnesties (1982, 1986–88, 1990 and 1995–96) was provoked by the fact that a large number of immigrants had settled definitely, although they were still undocumented, and by a growing fear that their presence could become an incentive for entrepreneurs to switch from the rigid official labour market to the shadow one. This helps us to explain why the trade unions – usually the quintessential restrictive actors – have given active support to all the amnesties, and more generally to any measure targeted to bring the immigrants out of the underground economy and into the official labour market. There are large differences between these four amnesties, however. In most cases their aim has been to regularize employment relations (the residence permit being contingent upon the regularization of past, current or prospective employment) and – in one case – to regularize individual workers (the residence permit being contingent upon presence in Italy, regardless of occupational status). Socially, the two strategies present quite different policy implications. In the first case, there is a high risk either of policy failures – if the employers are not willing to co-operate – or of a political failure – if the extension of the shadow economy suddenly comes into the open, and if tens of thousands of Italian employers would face fines and prosecutions. If, on the contrary, the purpose of the amnesty is to regularize anyone who lived in the country at a certain date, the most likely outcome is that a large number of immigrants would register as 'unemployed'. It is therefore hardly surprising, that Italian employers have been treated quite generously in the Italian amnesties. The motivation has been that this would make the amnesty for immigrants successful. The employers have enjoyed a kind of parallel amnesty, either cancelling all the benefits and social contributions previously unpaid by them, or reducing the amount they should pay to ludicrously low fractions of what was due.

Beside amnesties, the main Italian control mechanism on the labour market is the imposition of employer sanctions. Italy developed in 1986 an employer sanction scheme, in which the sanctions have been made progressively heavier in every following Immigration Act. Unfortunately, it is difficult to find data on labour inspections and they are often released only in formats that do not allow longitudinal comparisons. Moreover, as the inspections are not random but rather targeted to the most problematic situations, the results cannot be used as a survey of Italian firms and families. On the whole, however, available evidence indicates a growing vigilance on the irregular employment of migrants. In 1990, the labour inspectors visited 7,882 firms, finding that 2,345 immigrants, or 66 per cent, were irregularly employed. In 1992 the inspectors visited 53,347 firms, finding 4,860 immigrants irregularly employed. In 1994 and 1995, the labour inspectors visited a smaller number of workplaces, more targeted to the employment of immigrants. This is revealed by the steady increase in the number of immigrants checked There are, however, great regional differences in the intensity and frequency of control, which do not seem to be related to the number of firms operating in the regions, nor to the diffusion of the shadow economy. The islands (Sicily and Sardinia) where the shadow economy is hegemonic, have witnessed only 35 inspections in a year. In Lumbardy, one of Italy's economic engines, 850 firms were inspected, while three times as many inspections took place in the tiny Trentino. In other words, the level and intensity of inspections is still too low to be effective in the fighting of irregular employment, for natives and immigrants alike. Without a radical reform of the labour inspections, it is doubtful whether employer sanctions will effectively deter employers from hiring irregular immigrants.

Holding the Citizenship Line

The size of Italy's immigrant population is, relatively small and it could be argued that the label 'receiving country' is at least premature. Immigration, however, plays a symbolic role in Italy, far more relevant than any demographic analysis could reveal. Since the beginning, immigration has been a vicarious object in the discussions about Italian identity and

Italy's future, in the country's relation to Europe's imagined community, and also indirectly in the uneasy relationship with Italy's emigratory past. Immigration flows have become a matter of great public concern and the cultural construction of immigration has been framed accordingly. On one hand, it has been repeated over and over again that Italians are not 'used' to cultural diversity and that consequently Italy remains particularly open to a xenophobic backlash. On the other hand, the cultural diversity has – regardless of the real situation – been extremely overemphasised, in order to turn immigrants into a symbolic category easily differentiated from the natives, and functioning as a reserve 'other'.

The consequences of this cultural construction are particularly visible in the reform of the citizenship law that took place in 1992. While the newspapers and magazines were busy constructing immigration as an epochal phenomenon, and while politicians almost daily issued press statements about the urgent need for integration, the parliament, without any widespread opposition and without even provoking a significant public debate, approved a citizenship law in which the immigrant population in Italy was 'explicitly absent' and the good old proletarian nation of the past held the centre stage again. The enactment of the new citizenship law demonstrates that the Italian debate about immigration and multi-culturalism is often a mere bonfire of vanities. On a deeper level, it also shows the strength of the exclusionary dynamics in the current Italian polity.

Before 1992, Italian citizenship was defined by a law of 1912, enacted during one of the most intense periods of emigration from Italy and when patches of 'Italian' land and population were still unredeemed. Consequently, the 1912 citizenship law was basically a mix of a dominant *jus sanguinis* component, a limited *jus soli* provision, plus several grounds for naturalization through residence (*jus domicilis*). On one hand, the law, and all subsequent provisions, allowed emigrants living abroad to keep their Italian citizenship as long as possible, and to allow them and their close descendants to regain it once lost. On the other hand, it was emphasized that the nation was based on civilization rather than on ethnicity and that 'Italians' from the unredeemed lands should be taken into account. The law therefore also included naturalization after residence in Italy for a significant period of life.

According to the law of 1912, Italian citizenship could be acquired either at birth by a child of an Italian father, when coming of age, if born on Italian soil and after long residence, or through naturalization. In the former case, he would have automatically become an Italian citizen at the age of 22 or even earlier (if he had served in the armed forces). In the latter, the law stated four different grounds for applying for Italian citizenship: the foreigner should have

1. served the Italian state for at least three years;
2. been living in Italy for at least five years;
3. married an Italian spouse and lived in Italy for three years or, finally,
4. given 'exceptional services' to the nation.

The law of 1912 was partly modified in 1983 in order to remove the main elements of gender discrimination. At this time the Italian state achieved quite an international reputation as a country favouring liberal attitudes toward dual citizenship. Empirically, of course, the main tracks of naturalization were residence and marriage, with the latter enjoying a simpler and less arbitrary procedure. For several years, a comprehensive reform of the 1912 citizenship law had been advocated, in order to remove the entrenched inequalities between fathers and mothers and to manage the problems related to subsequent generations of Italians (and hyphenated Italians) around the world. During the 1980s, moreover, the European Union and its precursors increased the value of an Italian ancestry as it offered a chance to keep a foothold inside the union, through a dual citizenship or to an easy way to regain lost Italian citizenship. The new citizenship law of 1992, approved by a broad political consensus, however, had also other aims. It made an explicit and open, but low-key, attempt to introduce an ethnic principle in the definition of national citizenship. The most remote offspring of Italian emigrants were embraced, whereas naturalization of individuals void of any Italian ancestry was made more difficult. This meant a dramatic increase in emphasis on *jus sanguinis*. The right to citizenship was extended to any grandson and granddaughter of an Italian citizen (provided they had lived in Italy three years). In contrast, no consistent *jus soli* principle was introduced.

A two-tier system for naturalization has been established with a distinction between EU and non-EU foreigners. An EU national may apply for naturalization after four years. For non-EU foreigners who cannot claim Italian ancestry, the period of continuous legal residence required for naturalization has been made twice as long (it has been increased from five to ten years). Furthermore, this extension of the residence period to a decade has been applied retrospectively to immigrants who in 1992 had already spent more than five years in Italy, and even to immigrants who had filed an application already under the law of 1912.

In other words, it is likely that the aim has been to reduce the number of non-EU citizens entitled to apply for naturalization. The imposition of the requirement of a continuous residence was meant in the same spirit to keep this naturalization of non-EU immigrants low in the future. As a matter of fact, this strategy seems to have been fairly successful. The number of naturalized citizens, although increasing, has been kept at a very low level (Table 1.3). The predilection for an ethnic definition has not disappeared after the approval of the citizenship Act. From 1994 to 1996 the Houses hotly debated a legislative draft, proposed by MPs from several parties, according to which hyphenated Italians, who were citizens of other states, should be given the right to vote in Italian general elections. They even suggested that some kind of an 'overseas constituency' would be allowed to elect its own representatives to the Houses on an equal footing with Italian citizens. This proposal raised immediate diplomatic reactions from some settler states, worried about the weird idea that their citizens might also be unilaterally granted political rights in the Italian republic. Another often-debated example of the same phenomenon is the idea that the offspring of Italian emigrants, mainly from Latin America, should be recruited as a potential substitute for African and Asian immigrants. In this case, the problem is not internal opposition but the plain difficulty of filling available unskilled jobs by recruiting immigrant labour among middle-class, educated descendants of Italian emigrants.

Holding the Line: Which Line?

It has been argued in this paper that Italian immigration control is quickly converging toward that of other European immigration countries. Far from embedding a liberal and laissez-faire system of control, Italy has quickly developed a fairly restrictive policy. Border control is heavily emphasized, and a foreign policy has been developed, encouraging Mediterranean sending countries to drastically curtail their emigration. In the internal immigrant policy there are several indications of a growing emphasis on public order. In other words, Italy seems to be a perfect case for the more general argument that the current 'crisis' of control is much more in the eye of the beholder – a product of unrealistic expectations and perhaps of symbolic and vicarious fears than a structural feature of the real processes. As Rogers Brubaker (1994: 230) has recently observed in reference to the German case,

'systems of immigration controls are very effective indeed – when effectiveness is measured not against some utterly unrealistic ideal of zero immigration but rather against the extremely large and rapidly growing demand for admission. Seen from the inside – that is, from the point of view of the citizens of favoured countries – immigration controls may be strikingly imperfect; but seen from the outside – from the perspective of those turned down for tourist visas, or those willing to pay large sums of money and undertake risky voyages in order to circumvent barriers to entry – immigration controls appear all too effective'.

This chapter has also argued that the main problem of Italian immigration control does not lie in the state of border control, but rather in the weakness of internal control, particularly with regard to the employment of irregular immigrants. The existence of a significant population of undocumented immigrants and of many amnesty programmes may then be viewed as consequences not of a failing immigration control but rather of the special, well-entrenched mode of relationship between the Italian state and Italian society. The reproduction of large populations of undocumented immigrants is also connected to the lack of a supply, adequate to meet existing demands of immigrant labour. Here Italian immigration policy reveals its mythical foundations.

The wish to cast the Italian situation inside the European framework – assuming that immigration is currently mainly a 'push' phenomenon – has led to an enduring refusal to acknowledge the structural relevance of several 'pull' factors that operate in the Italian economy. Seen from this point of view, the real question in the analysis of Italian immigration control is not whether these systems are empirically able to hold the line, but rather whether the line held is really the best empirical option.

Finally, it has also been argued that Italian immigration policy has developed as a two-faced Janus, where a few rather liberal measures to integrate immigrants into the welfare system are matched by an exclusionary dynamic in the definition of the national membership. Previously, this ambivalence has mainly been a product of the configuration of the Italian political system, where the need to keep together unstable political coalitions, usually ended up in carefully mixed Acts. In the past few years, however, public opinion has consistently turned toward a negative view of immigrants (and of immigration as such), and an exclusionary and restrictive policy has been increasingly identified as a condition for membership of the European club. These developments have drastically curtailed the room for manoeuvering. Political rhetoric aside, it is therefore likely that immigration policy in the near future will expand further along the parallel tracks of external control and internal policing, while the need for an active policy of new immigration will remain in the dark.

References

Ambrosini, M., Colasanto M. and Zanfrini L. (1991), *Principali risultati di una indagine diretta su un campione di immigrati da paesi del terzo mondo e dell'Est europeo nell'area milanese,* Milano: Oetamm.

Ascoli, U. (1986), 'Migration of Workers and the Labour Market: Is Italy Becoming a Country of Immigration?' in R. Rogers (ed), *Guests Come to Stay,* Boulder: Westview.

Barbagli, M. (1998), *Immigrati e criminalità in Italia,* Bologna: Il Mulino.

Bolaffi, G. (1996), *Una politica per gli immigrati,* Bologna: Il Mulino.

Brubaker, W.R. (1994), 'Comment', in W.A. Cornelius et al. (eds), *Controlling Immigration,* Stanford: Standford University Press.

Bruni, M. (ed.) (1994), *Attratti, sospinti, respinti,* Milano: FrancoAngeli.

Caciagli, M. and Ketzner, D. (eds) (1995), *Italian Politics: The Stalled Transition,* Boulder: Westview.

Calavita, K. (1994), 'Italy and the New Immigration', in W.A. Cornelius et al. (eds), *Controlling Immigration,* Stanford: Standford University Press.

Freeman, G.P. (1995) 'Modes of Immigration Politics in Liberal Democratic States', *International Migration Review,* 29: 881–902.

Katz S. and Ignazi P. (eds) (1994), *Italian Politics: The Year of the Tycoon,* Boulder: Westview.

King, R. and Rybaczuk, K. (1993), 'Southern Europe and the International Division of Labour: From Emigration to Immigration' in R. King (ed.), *The New Geography of European Migrations,* London, Belhaven Press.

Ismu (1996), *Migrations in Italy. Secondo rapporto sulle migrazioni,* Milano: Franco Angeli.

Istat (1990), *Gli immigrati presenti in Italia: una stima per l'anno 1989,* Roma: Istat.

—— (1995), *Occupazione e redditi da lavoro dipendente 1980–1994,* Roma: Istat.

Mershon, C. and Pasquino, G. (eds) (1993), *Italian Politics: Ending the First Republic,* Boulder: Westview.

Ministerio dell'Interno (1985), *Memorandum,* 19 August 1985.

Montanari, A. and Cortese, A. (1993), 'Third World Immigrants in Italy', in: R. King, (ed), *Mass Migration in Europe,* London: Belhaven Press.

Nascimbene, B. (1988), *Lo straniero nel diritto italiano.* Milano: Giuffré.

OECD (1995), Sopemi Report 1994, Paris: OECD.

Papademetriou, D.G. and Hamilton, K.A. (1996), *Converging Paths to Restriction: French, Italian and British responses to Immigration,* Washington DC: Carnegie Migration Programme.

Sciortino, G. (1991), 'Immigration into Europe and Public Policy: Do Stops Really Work?', *New Community*, 18: 88–99.

—— 1997a, 'Troppo Buoni? La politica migratoria tra controlli alle frontiere e gestione del mercato del lavoro', *Sociologia del Lavoro*, 64: 50–84.

—— 1997b, *The flow and the Flood. Making Italy a 'New Immigration Country'*, Milano: Fondazione Cariplo-Ismu.

ter Wal, J. (1991), 'Il linguaggio del pregiudizio etnico', *Politica ed Economia*, 32: 33–47.

—— (1996), 'The Social Representation of Immigrants: the Pantanella issue in the pages of La Repubblica', *New Community*, 22: 39–66.

Zanfrini, L. (ed.) (1996), *Il lavoro degli 'Altri'*, Milano: Ismu.

Zincone, G. (1994), 'Immigration into Italy: Data and Policies', in Heckmann, F. and Bosswick, W. (eds), *Migration Policies: A Comparative Perspective*, Bamberg: EFMS.

–9–

The Emergence of Migration Control Politics in Hungary
Kristof Tamas

Introduction

Hungary has only recently moved through the transformation to a liberal democratic state, and is less industrialized and economically developed than the Western European states. Economically, the transition to a market economy has not yet been completed. Politically, democracy has been achieved, but the relics of the long period of state socialism will inevitably only fade gradually. The legacy of structural and systematic violations of individual rights, for example has, made Hungarian law inconsistent and lacking in transparency. This affects the area of refugees and migration, as Hungary is still at an early stage in the process of establishing a legal and institutional framework for migration control. As in most Central and Eastern European states, nationalism has historically been based more on ethnic identity than on liberal, civic values. The turbulent history of the region has also affected the ethnic map with trans-border, ethnic loyalties. Despite such a background, four decades of state socialism made refugees and immigrants into political novelties at the dawn of transformation in the late 1980s. Commitment towards refugees was greatly influenced by sentiments of ethnic solidarity, but is increasingly balanced against economic considerations, although most migration to Hungary still consists of ethnic Hungarians. Rapid political change has brought about new aspirations in Hungary, which now are centred on the aim of being counted internationally among the recognized liberal democracies and to acquire membership of the European Union. Both the historical and the future dimensions of Hungarian nation building are therefore essential elements in the framework within which policies in the field of migration control are chosen.

Hungary as a New Country of Immigration

Pre-1989 emigration and immigration

Migration has characterized the area inhabited by Hungarians or Magyars both before and since the establishment of the Hungarian Kingdom at the onset of the eleventh century. Hungary has never been ethnically homogenous as various ethnic groups have coexisted on the shared territory. As the actual territorial borders of Hungary have undergone many transformations, not all population movements have been considered as international migration. Migration flows within the vast Austro-Hungarian empire were considered as internal flows so most of these were not registered. The year of revolutions, 1848, had brought about many migratory movements as well as the later break-up of the empire with its overwhelming territorial changes. People moved quite frequently from and within the Austro-Hungarian Monarchy, established in 1867. Between 1899 and 1913, for example, more than 100,000 Hungarians migrated to Romania, about 36,000 to Germany and smaller numbers went to Italy, Russia and Serbia – about one fourth of these later returned. Around the turn of the century, some 270,000 Hungarians resided in Austria, while 200,000 Austrians were more-or-less temporarily living in Hungary. On the transcontinental level, the latter part of the nineteenth century and early twentieth century saw large-scale emigration flows to America – one and a half million emigrated in this period from Hungary. Only a third of these migrants were actually ethnic Hungarians and almost every fourth returned (Dövényi 1992, 1995; Juhász 1995: 202).

As a consequence of the World War One peace treaty at Trianon, two thirds of Hungary's territory and 60 per cent of its population were lost as 3.2 million Hungarians found themselves residing in the new neighbouring countries of Hungary. It is sometimes said that it was not they who left Hungary but the borders that left them; 350,000 ethnic Hungarians moved from these areas to the reduced Hungarian territory, many of them as a result of ethnic discrimination (the largest number fleeing from Transylvania, which had become Romanian) (Dövenyi 1992: 2). During the Second World War, the turbulence also caused large-scale movements to and from Hungary. More than 300,000 fled temporarily to Hungary, half of them Polish soldiers. Meanwhile, thousands of Jews fled or were deported, numerous prisoners of war were sent to the Soviet Union, 70,000 Slovakians left partly within a population exchange with Czechoslovakia, and 200,000 Germans left the country either voluntarily or through forced resettlement. With the war a large number of ethnic Hungarians were also resettled or moved on their own to Hungary (Dövenyi, 1995; Sik and Tóth, 1991: 119; Juhász, 1995: 204).

These historical experiences have influenced national identities in Hungary. There has emerged a feeling of being in the centre of Europe, at the crossroads between East and West, with a great past, but a victim, ill-treated by historical processes beyond its own control. There has also persisted a feeling of being ethnically and culturally isolated in *Mittel-europa*, with Slavic speaking people to the east and the south, and with the Germanic speaking neighbours to the west. As István Bibó has pointed out, the nations in Central and Eastern Europe have more been based on linguistic nationalism and identity than on historical, territorial developments. Thus, historically, the boundaries constituting the Hungarian identity have been more based on cultural, linguistic and ethnic markers than the historical shifts of the geographic and political borders of the Hungarian state (Bibó, 1991). The presence of Hungarian minorities outside mainland Hungary has therefore been an important precondition for subsequent migration flows to the country (Tóth, J., 1995: 57).

As Hungary was made part of the communist bloc during the Cold War, severe limitations were imposed on the mobility of people to and from the country for forty years. Emigration was seen by the regime as an act of disloyalty to the state and declared illegal. The Hungarian revolution in 1956 resulted in a temporary, large exodus of about 200,000 people. Between 1957 and 1987, annual legal emigration was estimated at 2,000–4,000. The number of those who left the country 'illegally' was around 4,000–5,000 per year (Rédei, 1994: 86). In late 1989 a new law finally lifted the limitations on free exit for Hungarians. The large-scale exodus that had been feared by Western European countries did not, however, take place (Juhász, 1995: 211).

The limited number of migrants who did come to Hungary during the Cold War period entered as refugees or students for ideological reasons, to support the worldwide struggle for communism. Notably there were groups of refugees from Greece and Chile, and from various countries in Africa, Asia, the Middle East and South America. A few thousand Cubans and Vietnamese were given work in the Hungarian textile industry. There were Chinese working in Hungary's major truck factory and Poles came to work in the mines (Szöke, 1992: 307). Until 1985, an average of 1,500 migrants per year had come to Hungary (Tóth, 1995: 75). Because of the very small number of immigrants, and the predominance of ethnic Hungarians, the country has been socially, politically and administratively unprepared for large scale migrant flows.

Post 1989 refugee migration

The decision of the Hungarian government to let tens of thousands of East German refugees transit through Hungary to the West in 1989 was a historical event that contributed to the fall of the Berlin Wall and the end of the communist system in Central and Eastern Europe (Szöke, 1992: 308; Loescher, 1993: 3). This move by the Hungarian government also signalled a form of official critique against the Soviet Union and the system in the communist bloc countries (Giorgi, et al., 1992: 27). The East Germans had been preceded by refugees from Romania, most of them ethnic Hungarians, who were fleeing from repressive treatment and discrimination by the Romanian government (Dövenyi, 1992: 6). In 1985, some 1,700 Romanians were registered in Hungary as asylum applicants, and these were followed by a growing number in subsequent years (around 3,300 in 1986, and 6,500 in 1987). Many of them came to Hungary with transit visas and stayed on or crossed the borders illegally (Szöke, 1992: 307). By 1988, Hungary had become an immigrant-receiving country, with a positive net immigration (Tóth, J. 1995: 57; Giorgi et al., 1992: 27). The government was faced with an increasingly problematic choice of how to act. Hungary was not prepared for this kind of refugee flow. There was no proper institutional framework to process asylum applications or to administer settlement. Moreover, as people were fleeing a neighbouring socialist country, the refugee flow constituted a politically sensitive issue. Eventually, in 1989, Hungary signed the Geneva Refugee Convention. This was done initially with a geographic limitation only accepting refugees from events taking place in Europe, which was lifted in December 1997 with the new Act on Asylum.

The major refugee flows to Hungary are depicted in Table 9.1. The first influx from Romania has been followed by a second large-scale refugee flow from the conflict in former Yugoslavia. Between October 1989 and the end of 1996, almost 4,300 refugees received Geneva Convention refugee status (about 3 per cent of the total number of registered refugees or displaced people in Hungary). Temporary protection, or asylum status, has been given to over 75,000 people from former Yugoslavia (almost 57 per cent of the total number of refugees) (Office of Refugee and Migration Affairs 1996). The peak in 1991 consisted mainly of refugees from Croatia, and most of these have already left the country. They have either gone back home or further on to other settlement countries in the West (Pataki, 1994: 36). By May 1996, the number of refugees from former Yugoslavia with temporary protection in Hungary

Hungary

Table 9.1 Hungary: Asylum Seekers 1988–97

Year	All countries	Romania	ex-USSR	ex-Yugoslavia	Other countries
		Registered Asylum Seekers			
			Thereof from:		
1988	13,173	13,173			
1989	17,448	17,365	50		33
1990	18,283	17,416	488		379
1991	53,359	3,728	738	48,485	408
1992	16,204	844	241	15,021	98
1993	5,366	548	168	4,593	57
1994	3,375	661	304	2,386	24
1995	5,912	523	315	5,046	28
1996	1,259	350	268	559	82
1997	2,109	131	90	329	1,559*

* In 1997, asylum seekers from non-European countries were for the first time registered. They were in all 1,411, and the number of asylum seekers from 'other countries' increased to 1,559.
Source: Hungarian Office of Refugee and Migration Affairs.

had dropped to around 6,000 (Office of Refugee and Migration Affairs 1996; Láczkó 1995: 172).

It should be noted that the figures in Table 9.1 only show flows and not stocks of asylum seekers. Moreover, available statistics are not very reliable as they do not include figures on return and the same migrant may appear several times in various registers and categories. It is estimated that about 20,000 refugees in Hungary from former Yugoslavia and Bosnia were not registered as refugees, never appearing or only showing as tourists in the statistics (interview with Nagy). Nevertheless, these figures are useful when analysing a country that had not previously been used to or prepared for large-scale immigration of refugees. The two refugee waves, and in particular the second one from former Yugoslavia, have had a large impact on the legislation and infrastructure for migration control. It was because of them that refugees and migration became a politicized issue area. It is important, however, to note that migration in Hungary is still a marginal issue and has not become equally politicized as in most Western European countries.

In the ageing and decreasing population of about 10.2 m, immigrants make up a very low share in Hungary. According to OECD figures for 1996, there were approximately 140,000 long term residence permit holders in Hungary; 80,000 of these were permanent residents (OECD/ SOPEMI, 1997: 113). Residence alone does not equal immigrant status. Three years of stay with a valid residence permit are required in order to be registered as an official immigrant. Immigrants have then an open-ended residence permit. Those who apply for family unification are excepted from the three- year rule (OECD/SOPEMI, 1995: 145). Most of the immigrants came from neighbouring countries, where Romania, former Yugoslavia and the former USSR dominate almost entirely (OECD/ SOPEMI, 1994:130). Moreover, migrants from the former USSR have to a large extent been ethnic Hungarians. Less numerous migrants have come from a wide range of ethnic and cultural backgrounds from over a hundred countries around the world. The largest and most significant non-European group of immigrants is the Chinese. According to the Ministry of Interior data, 27,330 Chinese entered Hungary in 1991. It is unclear how many of these stayed on a long-term basis, but in 1995 an estimated 10,000 Chinese were residing in Hungary. For the Chinese, Hungary is more and more becoming a destination country, rather than a transit country (Nyiri, 1995: 195, 228).

The requirement for naturalization and acquisition of Hungarian citizenship has been raised from three years to eight years of uninterrupted residence. This places Hungary among the most restrictive countries in Europe in this regard. People of Hungarian ethnicity, however, can be naturalized after only three years of residence (ECRE, 1994: 240). Ethnic Hungarians constituted 90 per cent of the almost 61,000 naturalized 1990–95 (OECD/SOPEMI 1997: 114).

Preconditions: Legislation and Institutions

Emerging legislation

Due to the fact that Hungary is a new country of immigration, adequate legislation or an institutional framework have not yet been fully developed. As I will attempt to show, this inadequacy is present both within the external and the internal control area. Two ideas seem to have guided Hungary's approach in migration legislation. One has been the fear of mass immigration and illegal migration, which might have repercussions on domestic security, public order and economic policy (although these aspects are often exaggerated). The other has been preference and concern for ethnic Hungarians living outside the borders of the country.

The first basic legal document in the area of migration was passed by the parliament in September 1989. Although the parliament was still dominated by the Communists, a round-Table including both the opposition and the government had agreed to the Act that established that:

> [n]o foreigner can be allowed to immigrate if his/her settling in Hungary is detrimental to the security of the state, to law and order, to public health, to public morals or to the rights and liberty of others or if the foreigner has committed a grave crime or lives the life of a criminal. The permission to immigrate can be denied to the foreigner whose living and housing in Hungary is not guaranteed, who was expelled from Hungary earlier or whose adaptation to Hungarian society cannot be expected. (Szöke, 1992: 309)

This quotation indicates both guiding ideas of Hungary's control policy towards immigration and control can accordingly be exercised both directly and indirectly. The conditions are directed at individuals and not collective groups, thereby enabling a measure of selectivity both in terms of volume and in terms of ethnic or cultural adaptability. A similar basic standpoint can be found in relation to short-term migrants and refugees. The requirements in terms of financial resources and ability to adapt to Hungarian culture and society are in practice quite harsh. Moreover, the implementing authorities have been given wide discretionary scope in order to check these conditions (Szöke, 1992: 309; Tóth, J. 1995: 64).

Migration policy has unfolded parallel to the broader societal changes in post-Cold War Hungary. In September 1990 a 'Board of the Prime Minister's Counsellors' suggested a general 'Programme for National Renewal'. The programme included, among other points, measures in the area of immigration control. It was suggested that the procedure for processing asylum applications and receiving refugees should be consolidated and that there should be a better co-ordination of measures to facilitate the integration and social adaptation of refugees into Hungarian society. The Board also suggested new legislation on citizenship and on asylum, which has formed the basis of the subsequent acts (Szöke, 1992: 310).

At this time the perception of the policy advisors was coloured by the problems of transition to a market economy and the fears that an influx of large numbers of refugees might place undue strains on a society with large unemployment and social transformation problems. The Board thus stressed that 'the establishment of material conditions for dealing with refugees should not endanger the treatment of the social problems of Hungary's population'. At the same time, the isolation during the Cold

War was to be replaced by recognition of the increasing globalization and openness in Hungarian economy and society. It was seen as unavoidable that borders should be kept fairly open, and the Board noted in its programme that 'state borders should not obstruct the free flow of persons, ideas and [. . .] information' (Szöke, 1992: 310). In this vein, visa regulations have also been made less severe for tourists. No citizens of European countries, except Albania and Turkey, need tourist visas for shorter visits (IOM 1994: 12). As indicated by the high number of annual border crossings, 40 m registered in 1993, border control cannot be watertight (Juhász, 1995: 206). Hungary is trying to be open for tourism and business, but at the same time maintain efficient external and internal control. This balance may be even harder for Hungary than for many Western European countries, given Hungarian history and given the general process of establishing openness.

Following the initiative of the Board, two major and more comprehensive Acts regulating immigration in Hungary were introduced in 1993. They have in general led to more restrictive measures compared to the previous, less regulated procedures. The Hungarian Citizenship Act was adopted by the Parliament on the 1st of June, 1993 (Tóth, J. 1995: 57, 64). It is based on *ius sanguinis*, descent by blood, which favours ethnic Hungarians applying for citizenship, and this principle goes back to the 1920s (Rédei, nd: 22; Tóth, P.P. 1995: 76):

> Ethnic Hungarians [. . .] enjoy legal preferences. They need bring less formal evidence to the process and/or they need to meet limited requirements in comparison with other applicants. This means that ethnic Hungarians' cases are considered, by law, as exceptions from the general rules. This is so despite the fact that they have created the majority of applicants, immigrants and new citizens. (Tóth, J. 1995: 60)

Although this preference for ethnic Hungarians is evident both in direct and indirect aspects of the emerging control policies, the economic requirements for immigration and naturalization can also affect ethnic Hungarians. There are, for example, cases of ethnic Hungarians from Vojvodina, who do not qualify for immigrant status as they can not afford 'guaranteed' housing and source of income (interview with Köszeg).

The second major legislation has been a new Aliens Act that was passed on September 14, 1993, and became effective on 1 May 1994. As in most other countries, the Aliens Act lists a number of minimum requirements for aliens to enter Hungarian territory. It also contains provisions for who should be eligible for limited term or long duration open-ended residence permits. There are also a number of procedures that govern the internal control of aliens and of illegal residence, for example, the scope of action and regulation of the alien police (Tóth, J. 1995: 58).

Both these Acts may have broader effects, which I will discuss later. I will particularly more in detail return to the legislation with respect to refugees and labour migrants. Legislation underwent a long birth process in the area of refugee policy. A draft outline for a new Refugee Act was produced by a specially assigned committee. In November 1996 this outline was, however, removed from the parliamentary agenda. It was said that a new Refugee Act would have to wait until the new Constitution was decided on. Some researchers and organizations have argued that the reasons may have been that the government had little interest in these issues, and that it wanted to wait lifting the geographic reservation to the Geneva Convention (interview with Tóth, J.). A Refugee Act was finally accepted by the Parliament in December 1997 and entered into force in March 1998.

Emerging institutions

Most of the institutions that were established to administer and implement the two Acts from 1993 (on Aliens and Citizenship), still function in an *ad hoc* and inconsistent way (Tóth, J. 1995: 59–60). Several ministries and authorities are in one way or another dealing with refugee and migration issues. The Border Guards and the National Police are responsible for control at borders and internally. The Aliens Control Department within the National Police is dealing with shorter and longer term residence permits. The customs authority is responsible for checking that people have sufficient money when crossing the borders, and this is ultimately the responsibility of the Ministry of Finance. The Ministry of Foreign Affairs is responsible for providing background information on the situation in the countries of origin of the asylum seekers, although this is done very sparingly. The Ministry of Labour is issuing work permits. The Ministry of Interior and various authorities are responsible for the remaining aspects of the migration issue area.

Formally, the Ministry of Interior (the Office of Refugee and Migration Affairs) is the central migration policy authority, responsible for co-ordination of action among the ministries. There has, however, been a lack of formalized co-ordination, and contacts between various authorities have emerged in an *ad hoc* fashion. There has been no central steering of migration issues, the policy area being characterized by fragmentation.

The authorities administering and implementing the Citizenship and Aliens Acts respectively, have 'broad discretionary powers' to decide on their own policies and procedures. Both Acts contain general formulations and terms in order to give the administration a certain flexibility of interpretation and to adapt to the volume and type of immigration in question (Tóth, J. 1995: 60; Nyiri, 1995: 210). The need for such flexibility is said to depend on public opinion and economic conditions (internal) and state, foreign policy interests (external) (Tóth, J. 1995: 60). The need for flexibility in Hungary is not much different from the Western European countries. What may be particularly interesting in the Hungarian case, though, is how a lack of transparency, in terms of which institution is accountable for what policies and which migrants, functions to avoid criticism from the public and media. Critique may be more difficult to express if the facts about the existing legislation are difficult to pinpoint and the government keeps a low profile (interview with Tóth). Public debate was, for example, very limited in the period leading up to the passing of the two acts in Hungary. This lack of public discussion may also be explained by the observation that none of the parties wanted to risk losing voters by being too generous on the issue of migration and refugees in Hungary (interview with Juhász).

Both legislation and the institutional structure in Hungary in the area of migration affairs are thus still only emerging and several representatives of the control authorities have indicated that control is not sufficient in relation to those few clear goals that have been established. The lack of efficiency may result in a larger degree of implicit policy making, such as erratic and sporadic decisions on the part of officials and border guards. I will try in the following sections to show that this has been the case in Hungary, both in terms of external and internal control. Migrants are affected by these shortcomings, and officials in the relevant ministries appear to recognize this as a problem and are trying to gradually improve the system.

Context for External Control

Geopolitical considerations are always present when a country is choosing control instruments and establishing external border control. To become a member state of the European Union and to be counted among the European liberal democracies are major foreign policy goals of Hungary. The concern for Hungarian ethnic minorities in the region is another dominant feature in foreign policy. These orientations have also functioned as external determinants of Hungary's immigration and refugee policy (Tóth, J. 1995: 58; Bonoli, 1993).

Back to Europe

Szöke has argued that 'Hungary's approach to migration [. . .] is now mainly shaped by the country's intention to be reintegrated into Europe and to have its migration practice harmonized with that of the Western democracies' (Szöke, 1992: 305). The Ministry of Foreign Affairs has declared that '[r]efugee policy has become a lasting strand of Hungarian foreign policy in multilateral and bilateral relations', just like in the Western European countries (Ministry of Foreign Affairs 1993).

Hungary's break with its socialist past and its deliberate orientation to the West may be symbolized by the accession to a number of international conventions and organizations (Bonoli, 1993). When Hungary joined the Council of Europe in November 1990, it also took on to act in accordance with the European Convention on Human Rights and Fundamental Freedoms, as well as the large number of international treaties, conventions and agreements within the framework of this organization. The framework of the OSCE (Organization for Security and Co-operation in Europe) has also contributed to Hungary's increasing adherence to international human rights principles (Nagy, 1995: 33–4).

It is true that the importance of a humanitarian image in terms of a generous, humanitarian policy towards refugees has been losing ground in Western Europe. The EU did not seem to put any overt pressure on Hungary in terms of lifting the geographic limit of the Geneva Convention, or for that matter on establishing an integration policy (interview with Láczkó and Tass). Thus, the West orientation in terms of principles of humanitarianism and equality for immigrants may be perceived as contradictory or piecemeal but it is a process that is also attuned to the increasing restrictiveness of migration policies in Western Europe.

This duality is indicated by some of the international activities of Hungary, such as participation in fora that focus on the issues of illegal and mass migration. High-level, intergovernmental *ad hoc* meetings have taken place within the so-called Vienna and Berlin Groups. Important conferences have been held in Vienna (24–25 January 1991), in Berlin (30–31 October 1991), and subsequently in Budapest (15–16 February 1993), where Hungary actively contributed with a plan for exchanging information on refugee and migration issues and suggested the establishment of an information agency based in Budapest. The Vienna Group has now dissolved and part of its activities has been taken over by the European Council, which regularly collects information about migration flows and policies (interview with Sándor).

Regional co-operation among the Central and Eastern European countries has also developed and an important ministerial meeting took place in Prague in March 1993. Interior ministers from Hungary, the Czech Republic, Slovakia, Poland and Slovenia at this event made a joint statement about migration regulation, declaring migration to be a serious security problem (Nagy, 1995: 39). Hungary was also active in establishing a working group on migration in the so called Pentagonale (later Hexagonale) group of Central and Eastern European countries (Szöke, 1992: 314; King, 1992: 18). This has now been replaced by the Central European Initiative (CEI), which also has an informal working group on migration for regional co-operation and information exchange on existing and potential migration flows. The fifteen-country group has been headed by a Hungarian representative (interview with Sándor).

While Hungary's orientation towards Western Europe is evident from some of these examples, there is an important difference between the interests of Hungary and other Central and Eastern European countries on the one hand and Western European states on the other. The former group of countries focus mainly on the flows and not on the stocks, as the number of permanently settled foreigners is still limited and the issue of integration is not yet as urgent as in Western Europe. Hungary seems to place much more emphasis on external borders and preventive control mechanisms than on internal, domestic control. This does not, however, mean that there is also an incentive to fund preventive policies and root cause interventions. Both the available resources and the migrant flows that reach Hungary are, after all, relatively limited (interview with Sándor). Moreover, most migrants see Hungary as only a transit country. As Hungary is less economically developed than the West, has a high unemployment rate and a relatively limited social welfare system, and the Hungarian language is often seen as difficult and isolated, the country is less attractive for migrants. Hungarian policy makers know that most clandestine migrants do not want to stay in Hungary and this reduces the incentive to stop such transit movements (interview with Láczkó and Tass). For this reason, Hungary is still not focusing as many resources on the quest for controlling illegal and clandestine migration as Western European countries.

With Hungary aiming to become a member state of the EU, attempts are being made to ensure that the country's external border controls are up to the EU standards of 'safety' – tight enough to prevent illegal border crossings (interview with Láczkó and Tass). One strategy to achieve this has been to sign readmission agreements with neighbouring countries, both to the east and west. The agreements establish an obligation for the signing countries to readmit or allow transportation of their own citizens or third country nationals who are not eligible for residence or asylum in the destination country. With these agreements, control policy has been externalised to a certain extent (Nagy, 1995: 37). Another attempt has been to adapt Hungary's migration policies to the mainstream in the EU countries. A special unit in the Ministry of Interior is dealing with relevant Schengen issues and some measures have already been taken in order to bring Hungary's migration policy into line with that of the Schengen countries, e.g. in terms of restrictiveness. This anticipatory harmonization has, for example, consisted of bringing Hungary's visa regulation more in harmony with the Schengen visa list (interview with Vég).

There have also been fears in Hungary, as well as in other Central and Eastern European countries, that they would turn into a 'buffer zone' of the European Union towards the East and South, thereby becoming main receivers of mass migration flows (Loescher, 1993: 165; Collinson, 1996). Government representatives have repeatedly made statements about the inability of Hungary to receive large-scale migrant flows. Sometimes such arguments have been used to persuade the EU states to include Hungary in their co-operation. The possibility of mass-migration flows into Hungary has been regarded as a threat to the political stability and economic development in the country (Szöke, 1992: 305). The likelihood of such mass-migration is, as elsewhere in Europe, often exaggerated. Should it materialize, then Hungary, and the Czech Republic, could be regarded as the most attractive among the Central and East European countries, given their geographic position and their relative affluence in the region.

Lászlo Szöke, at the time an official in the Ministry of Foreign Affairs, alleged in the early 1990s that:

All the partners of Hungary should be well aware of the fact that Hungary will not be able to withstand any significant migration pressure even if adequately aided financially. As announced in front of the Council of Europe as well, the society of Hungary does not possess the material and psychological resources to cope with large-scale immigration. . . . It is one of the main tasks of the country's foreign policy to convince its partners that this question can be addressed only in an all-European framework and that there must be a broad co-operation to deal with emergency cases. Thus, Hungary cannot accept the approach that it would be basically responsible for the countries bordering whatever is left of the former USSR and Yugoslavia to contain the possible waves of migration coming form these states. (Szöke, 1992: 321)

Some of these fears have emerged in response to the restrictive policies in the EU states, which do have the potential of increasing the number of would-be transit migrants who remain in Hungary (Láczkó, 1995: 177). That Hungary became one of the main recipients of the refugees from former Yugoslavia can partly be attributed to the fact that most Western European countries were reluctant to actively participate in burden-sharing (Loescher, 1993: 120). So far however, the main flows to Hungary have come from specific refugee crises, mainly those in Romania and in former Yugoslavia, and no significant flows have emerged from further afield.

Hungarian ethnic minorities in the region

The second major external precondition for Hungary's immigration and refugee policy involves the political and security concerns about Hungarian ethnic minorities in the neighbouring countries, which are intertwined with the broader foreign policy goals (Szöke, 1992: 316; interview with Sándor). There are substantial Hungarian minorities in Romania, Ukraine, Slovakia and former Yugoslavia. There have been recurrent instances of restrictions on the freedom of speech, assembly and association on the local level in Transylvania against the estimated 1.6 million ethnic Hungarians living in Transylvania, Romania (Refugee Survey Quarterly 1994: 41). A Hungarian university and several high schools have been closed down, and Hungarian schools have been the victims of harassment by local Romanian school inspectors. An agreement reached in July 1993 on the rights of minorities in Romania did not seem to put any end to this ethnic discrimination (UNHCR, 1994). The November 1996 elections paved the way for a more cooperation-oriented government with the head of the Democratic Convention of Romania, Emil Constantinescu, assuming the presidency. Hungarian minority representatives from the Hungarian Democratic Federation of Romania (RMDSZ) were given two ministerial portfolios in the new Cabinet, the Ministry of Tourism and the Office for National Minorities. This move like other appointments on regional level, has, however, been criticized and tensions between the ethnic groups are expected to continue (OMRI, 19 November 1996).

Some 150–200,000 ethnic Hungarians live in a part of western Ukraine. This group has in general not been discriminated against, and there have been no major migrant flows into Hungary. There have, nevertheless, been concerns that in the case of political unrest, a large number of ethnic Hungarians might head towards Hungary (Bugajski, 1991: 52–3). In June 1991, Ukraine and Hungary signed a declaration of basic principles and a joint statement on guaranteeing the rights of national minorities, which might contribute to a more stable development (Larrabe, 1992: 16).

The Hungarian government has more reasons to fear nationalistic sentiments in Slovakia and the negative attitudes towards the Hungarian minority there. The Magyar minority in Slovakia amounts to over 600,000 people, or 10 per cent of the population. In some counties in southern Slovakia there are up to 50 per cent ethnic Hungarians. In the period before the separation from the Czech Republic, emerging Slovak nationalism gave rise to concerns about the position and safety of the Hungarian minority. Some extremists demanded that Hungarians and other minority groups should be expelled from the country in order to establish a purely Slovak state (Bugajski, 1991: 77–8). In the autumn of 1996, the Slovakian prime minister Vladimir Meciar discarded growing demands for recognition of the Hungarian minority, alleging that half of them would actually be Roma (OMRI, October 31). Later in that year, the Slovak nationalities council rejected a minority language act proposed by representatives of the ethnic Hungarians (OMRI, November 22).

Concern for the ethnic Hungarian minorities in neighbouring countries has also been felt in Hungarian domestic politics. Since 1993, there is an Act on National Minorities in Hungary. Thirteen minority groups including the Roma have been recognized as national minority groups (none of which are immigrant groups). Many have alleged that the main reason for this liberal law has been the concern for Hungarian ethnic minorities abroad, rather than the national minority groups living in Hungary. Another reason is allegedly the eagerness to become accepted among the EU member states and in other Western international fora. As noted by Human Rights Watch/Helsinki (1996: 112 quote and 114–5) 'Hungary's first post-communist government hoped to both provide a model for neighbouring countries in their treatment of Hungarians and to put pressure on those countries by demonstrating to Western countries that Hungary was willing, not only to tolerate its minorities, but to foster their growth and well-being to positively integrate them in society.' The minorities Act, with its delineated system of local and national representation through self-government for national minorities, has been criticized for being very liberal on paper, but not functioning well in reality due to a lack of resources and practical political guidelines.

The external border control

Hungary is attempting to build up strict external border controls. As noted, the country's geographical location makes it a gateway between the East (and indirectly the South) and the West. During the short recent history of Hungarian immigration policy, border controls have been made stricter several times. Measures were initiated in early 1996, for example, with more rigorous controls at Hungary's non-EU borders against the traffic of illegal immigrants (Mozaik, 1996). It has also become increasingly evident that the control policies of neighbouring countries do have an impact on Hungary's policy choices. The Austrian decision in mid-1992 not to accept refugees from Bosnia, for instance, substantially increased the number of refugees from the region coming to Hungary. A few days after the Austrian move, the Hungarian Minister of Interior, Peter Boross, pleaded for assistance from the Council of Europe to open more refugee camps. Hungary's counter measure in terms of control was to deny entry to all Bosnians who wanted to transit through the country but who did not have Austrian visas. Only those applying for asylum directly in Hungary were accepted (Pataki, 1994: 36).

Border control of refugees and asylum seekers is perceived as problematic as such migrants are still a novelty. The border guards have still very limited information and training, if any, in refugee matters. Until 1995, ordinary soldiers patrolled the borders. More recently professional border guards have been trained through a newly established institution, and several Western countries such as Austria, France, Germany and USA, have provided occasional training assistance (interview with Sándor). UNHCR regularly monitors the performance of border guards to check whether they act according to convention rules and recommendations. There is, however, a lack of capacity and resources from the UNHCR or NGOs to examine on which grounds people, some of whom may be asylum seekers, are turned back at the borders (interview with Ambrus). Pataki has observed and argued that '[i]n the absence of adequate legislation, border guards and the police are often forced to act on their own initiative [. . .]. Mistakes are often made' (Pataki, 1992: 37; Amnesty International 1993).

It could be argued that spontaneous solutions, and inconsistent and random handling of asylum seekers by border guards and police, are a result of the vagueness of the regulations (interview with Juhász). In addition, the discretionary powers conferred on officials may foster abusive treatment. Police have been reported to frequently stop Roma and foreigners in the streets, checking for identification and there have been allegations of harassment and police brutality (Human Rights Watch/ Helsinki, 1996: 25, 31–2).

Hungarian border control is still not efficient in the sense that illegal border crossings do continue (interview with Vég, 1996). To balance the lack of capacity to check borders, the Minister of Interior, Peter Boross, has declared that measures against illegal migrants must consist of both strict border controls and internal controls, i.e. regular police checks (Szöke, 1992: 316). There is thus an awareness of the external and internal duality of control. As some of the unwanted migration consists of legal commuters on tourist visas, and by visa overstayers, it is clear that entry cannot be controlled solely by external control instruments.

Context for Internal Control

Two broad categories of migrants are central for internal control policies, namely refugees and asylum seekers on the one hand, and labour migrants on the other. I will attempt to show that explicit policy is underdeveloped within both these areas, thereby leaving room for implicit and ad hoc solutions. Hungary is trying to grapple with a situation of specific refugee flows, and with labour migrants who are drawn into the informal labour market. As no long-term planning exists, management by trial and error is still applied, something that can be expected from new policy areas, and which has also been common at earlier stages of migration policy making in the Western European countries.

Refugees and the Geneva Convention

During the Cold War, the regimes in socialist countries had opposed the Geneva Refugee Convention as a tool in the hands of Western states. Refugee policy in Hungary before 1989 was primarily favouring those refugees who shared the ideology of state socialism. The determination procedure was highly political and secretive (Szöke, 1992: 307). The influx of ethnic Hungarian refugees from Romania at the end of the 1980s posed a foreign policy problem for Hungary in relation to the socialist 'brother country' Romania. The reception of refugees from Romania was seen as a direct critique against the Romanian government. Hungarian experts were sent to Geneva to study the UNHCR and possible ways to set up an institutional and procedural framework for refugee reception in Hungary (Ministry of Foreign Affairs 1993). Hungary acceded to the Geneva Convention of 1951 and the New York Protocol of 1967 in March 1989, which came into force in June the same year. Soon thereafter a Decree governing the recognition and status of refugees was introduced and entered into force in October 1989 (Nagy, 1995: 44–5). The new Refugee Act was presented in the end of 1997.

The Geneva Convention and the New York Protocol had been signed with the reservation that Hungary would only accept refugees originating from events taking place in Europe. The reason for this limited responsibility has, according to official argumentation, been the economic problems as well as already existing tensions between refugees and Hungarians (Ministry of Foreign Affairs 1993). The geographic limitation, initially intended to be lifted in 1992, was postponed several times, among others in 1994, when the parliamentary elections again for some time placed this issue to the side of the main agenda. The delays were also motivated by the government's fears about potential difficulties for Hungarian society in accepting and integrating 'culturally different' refugees. Large numbers of Asian and African refugees are perceived to increase negative attitudes towards all foreigners in Hungary. There was also a fear that the economic costs would be too overwhelming as long as the economic transformation had not progressed further. The geographic reservation was finally lifted with the new Refugee Act in late 1997.

The ambivalence towards the Geneva Convention has also lead to some inconsistencies between the Geneva Convention and Hungary's interpretation of it, and the Hungarian Constitution as laid down in the constitutional amendments adopted in October 1989. According to the Geneva Convention, anyone *in fear of* persecution should have the right to enjoy protection, whereas the Hungarian Constitution only recognizes a *real* and actual threat. This could result in an essential change of the meaning of the text, requiring absolute proof of persecution for the right of asylum. 'Language' has been added to the causes of persecution in the constitution, probably with the ethnic Hungarians in Transylvania in mind (Office of Refugee and Migration Affairs, 1995; Nagy, 1995: 47).

Before the new Refugee Act in 1997, when non-Europeans applied for asylum, they were sent to the UNHCR representative in Budapest, who investigated their status. The procedure for regulating the status of an asylum applicant was defined by a government Decree. The parameters for UNHCR's work were only formulated in very general terms (Pataki, 1994: 35; interview with Ambrus). The lack of regulation posed problems both for the UNHCR and for the Hungarian authorities (Office of Refugee and Migration Affairs, 1995: 15). The UNHCR had to cater itself for those non-Europeans it recognized as mandate refugees. The number of these refugees was, however, very low and assistance and housing were also provided by the Red Cross. In 1994, only 15 of 231 applicants, and in 1995 62 out of 460 applicants were recognized by UNHCR for mandate refugee status (UNHCR and interview with Ambrus).

The status of temporary protection was regulated merely through ad hoc decision-making and informal procedures on a lower administrative level. The lack of transparent and discernible regulation for this category had wide-ranging effects as most refugees came to Hungary with this status (some 75,000 between mid 1991 and 1996 from former Yugoslavia) (Jungbert, 1996; Nagy, 1995: 47). As in all Western European countries adopting the instrument of temporary protection, criticism has been received from the UNHCR, arguing that: '[f]or all its benefits as a pragmatic response to situations of compelling humanitarian urgency, there are fears that temporary asylum, while broadening refugee protection, may also weaken it . . . (as it) eases the pressure on governments to apply the Convention along with its wide range of economic and social rights' (Láczkó, 1995: 173). Temporary protection gives a less favourable legal status than Convention status, and from the point of view of the government it is bound with less obligations. Asylum seekers are also handled under the Aliens Act, which, for example, makes it more difficult for them to find employment. The asylum seekers from former Yugoslavia have in fact been able to apply for convention status, but very few, and mainly ethnic Hungarians have succeeded in receiving it (Láczkó, 1995).

The lack of a formal, direct and explicit procedure to process manifestly unfounded applications, led in effect to a more restrictive policy. In 1992 it was estimated that about 90 per cent of the asylum applicants were screened out in an early informal pre-screening procedure (UNHCR 1993). According to the Office of Refugee and Migration Affairs, in the first half-year of 1996, 742 arrivals were registered by the local authorities, and 73 procedures for Refugee Status were started (Office of Refugee and Migration Affairs, Refugee Statistics, 1996: 21). Officials in charge of the first encounter with the asylum seeker often lack sufficient knowledge of legislation or they are insufficiently trained, and often the asylum seeker is not provided with legal aid (Nagy, 1993: 205). A common perception is that ethnic Hungarians are informally preferred or receive preferential treatment by officials in this process (interview with Szekely). There is an implicit attitude among border guards and police that people not of Hungarian ethnicity are unlikely to want to stay in Hungary, or that the main task of the police or border guards should not be to aid asylum seekers. There is little information on foreign languages about what rules apply, and lack of communication might be a reason why many do not succeed in launching an application for asylum (interview with Ambrus). Similarly, asylum seekers who want to appeal against a negative decision might face problems. The judges in the appeal courts do not seem to be sufficiently oriented about the Geneva Convention, and about the regulations and decrees that apply (interviews with Szekely and Köszeg).

Labour migration

Hungary's experience of a socialist planned economy has shaped the particular characteristics of its labour market. In the planned economies, unemployment was unheard of and it was even illegal, but there was some hidden unemployment or underemployment (Jackman and Rutkowski, 1994: 134). Soft budget constraints in state enterprises gave no incentives to cut labour costs and there had always been some on-the-job inactivity. Gradual economic reform had started in 1968, introducing small-scale private enterprise. More-or-less open unemployment emerged at the end of the 1970s, although officially unemployment remained illegal much longer. During the 1980s the most inefficient large state enterprises were facing cuts and redundancies. The demand for unskilled and semi-skilled labour decreased (Sciráczki, 1990: 138). The characteristic large informal labour market, made up of both formal and informal jobs outside the system of taxation and regulation, had developed in Hungary during this long period of the planned economy. Towards the end of the socialist rule, many worked on their free time with a second or even third job in the informal labour market.

The present process of economic transition is dominating the political and economic scene. The transition has become much more difficult and costly than most economists had assumed. Open unemployment as a percentage of total labour force increased from 2 per cent in 1990 to a peak of 12 per cent in 1995 and stabilized at 10 per cent in 1996 (IMF, 1994: 68; OECD, 1997; Portes, 1994: 1178). Leaving the initial, traditional gradualist reform path, Hungary later introduced measures closer to shock therapy. This was symbolized by an austerity programme announced in March 1995 by the Hungarian finance minister Bokros, which has been widely criticized and which has led to massive and repeated demonstrations.

In this context there has not been room for any public discussion about labour migration, and no formal or consistent policy of importing labour has developed. The limited labour immigration that takes place has three different characteristics: (a) skilled professionals from the West, (b) 'legal' labour migration, and (c) 'illegal' labour migration. There is also considerable local commuting and trade over the Hungarian borders, which effects the labour market (cf. Hárs, 1995: 91). It is possible here to identify a clear (albeit unofficial) distinction between wanted (encouraged) and unwanted (discouraged) categories of labour. In total, between 15,000 and 30,000 formal work permits have been issued per year in the early 1990s, representing less than 1 per cent of the total Hungarian labour force. More than half of the legally employed aliens have been of Hungarian ethnicity (IOM, 1994: 26).

The granting of work permits to the first category of migrants (highly skilled professionals) started to grow in 1991. The economic transition requires a certain amount of skilled professionals who are not available in the domestic workforce and who may bring in capital and investments. Investors, entrepreneurs and managing directors of foreign enterprises are especially encouraged categories and have been exempted from work permits (Nyiri, 1995: 207; Juhász, 1995: 211). The growing number of Western firms that invest in Hungary tend to bring their own staff, for example, in management, marketing, finance, public affairs, for which there are not enough graduates from Hungary (Rédei, 1995: 110; IOM, 1994: 26). Around one quarter of work permits are issued to people from Western countries, and half of these permits cover white collar positions (OECD/SOPEMI, 1995b: 144). The second and third categories of labour migrants originate to the main part in the East. Most of the total number of the work permits have benefited manual workers. Half of these have been Romanians, mostly of Hungarian ethnicity (Hárs 1995:89). The term 'illegal' is here used to cover both those who cross the borders in a clandestine or illegal manner with an intention to work, and those who enter the country legally, but take on work 'illegally' in the informal labour market.

The employment and work of foreigners is regulated both by the Employment Act from early 1991, and the Aliens Act. Work permits are issued to the employer, but the employee needs a special employment visa. In order to enter the country for employment purposes, employment visas must be obtained from abroad through a Hungarian embassy or consulate. An alien can only fill a vacancy after it has been properly advertised and if there is no Hungarian citizen who qualifies for the job (Juhász, 1995: 211). In practice, a large proportion of the work permits have been issued on applications from within Hungary. There are also several ways around the formal procedures. Employers may, for example, demand qualifications that they know Hungarians will not have, such as specific language skills, in order to hire cheap foreign labour. Another problem is that it is very difficult to control whether the foreigner who has been granted a work permit for a particular job will actually stick to that or if he will do completely different work (interview with Rédei). It has been alleged that many Chinese start businesses and invest in Hungary in order to gain immigration status, in order to settle in Hungary or to use Hungary as a base near Western European countries, or to do business in Central and Eastern Europe (interview with Dobos; cf. Hárs, 1995: 95). The limited control in this area may be caused both by a lack of resources for intervention or by inefficient control instruments. This question may be illuminated by a focus on the informal labour market, which is of increasing concern for Hungarian control policy.

Illegal labour migration and the informal labour market

Illegal labour migrants do play an important role in the informal labour market. These migrants may have entered the country legally or illegally. What they have in common is that their employment status is not regulated or that they take on jobs in the secondary economy. This sector mainly consists of unskilled temporary labour with limited chances for advancement. There is a market for those who are willing to work under poor conditions with low pay (Hárs, 1995: 95). As the informal labour market in Hungary is very significant, estimated to account for more than 30 per cent of the GDP, it is an immense problem for the government to control it. The informal economy is so large both due to the low returns from formal income sources in the primary economy, and as it becomes a safety net against unemployment and poverty when an adequate social security system is not available. Opinion surveys between November 1993 and March 1994 showed that almost 70 per cent of the population in Hungary were involved in second income activities (IMF, 1994: 84). Other surveys indicate that poverty rose from 10 per cent of households in 1990 to 27 per cent in 1992. If private transfers and hidden incomes from second jobs are taken into consideration, poverty is still more than twice as high as before the transition started (Sipos, 1994: 236).

Illegal work is thus not a problem that is specific to migrants, but is more common among Hungarian citizens in general. Control policies in this case would therefore have to be targeted at citizens as well as aliens and progress within this area has as yet been slow. There are substantial numbers of illegal migrant workers in, for example, construction and agriculture (Migration News 1996). Recently it was estimated that 100,000 illegal immigrants were residing in Hungary (Office of Refugee and Migration Affairs 1995). According to some estimates the number of yearly illegal border crossings amounts to 15,000 (Szöke, 1992: 313). Such estimates should be regarded with caution, however, as there is no way to reach any sufficient level of certainty.

It is disputed whether labour migrants are competing for jobs or supplementing for the lack of certain types of labour on the domestic labour market. Various interest groups disagree according to their political and economic stakes in the matter. The Union of Hungarian Construction Entrepreneurs' representatives have expressed the view that foreign labour force is needed in the industry, and that there should be legally controlled ways to hire foreigners (Hárs, 1995: 95). This argument is probably guided by the need for lower labour costs, or for foreign experts, but similar viewpoints were expressed in a recent study that pointed out that there is 'a manifest need of the Hungarian economy and society for labour migrants, despite of public and political opinion to the contrary' (IOM, 1994: 24).

There has not, however, been any formal discussion among politicians and political parties about whether to introduce immigration quotas for foreign labour. Neither have amnesties ever been discussed as a means to 'legitimize' illegals on the labour market (interview with Juhász). The labour unions, being concerned about high unemployment, would resist formal labour import if it would reach any significant volume. The employer sanctions that are used against employers who do hire illegal labour, are still quite impotent and are only used sparingly. Police raids against employers take place, but costs are still too high for these to be comprehensive. In 1996, the fines to be paid by the employer if an employee is caught working without a valid work permit, were increased. The fines go into the Hungarian Unemployment Fund (Migration News 1996). This seems, again, to link immigration with the question of economic transition and unemployment, and such a policy linkage may have been chosen due to the perceived sensitivity of this issue.

The fact that the government increasingly perceives illegal labour as a problem has been shown by several 'clean-up' operations, the first major one in October 1991, against illegal trading or illegal migrants. More-or-less frequent checks of employers are undertaken by the regional police authorities (interview with Dobos). Attempts are made to establish a clearer distinction between various categories of migrants. Tourists and visitors can no longer receive work permits. This measure does not, however, influence cross-border commuting and trade. It is quite common that Romanians come to Hungary as tourists for the period of one month, which they can do without a visa. During this stay they are involved in trade or other work. Their intention is not to stay, only to do business or work, and as their visas expire they leave the country, often to come back on repeated occasions. This form of illegal migrant labour has been very difficult to control or take sanctions against (IOM, 1994: 41).

Police searches for illegal migrant workers are often characterized by discretionary and erratic handling. Nyiri has argued in the case of the October 1991 clean up operation that 'a negative or positive decision [whether a migrant could stay or not] was essentially up to the personal preference of the official dealing with the case and was rather unpredictable' (Nyiri, 1995: 208). Some of this implicit, internal control has a deterrent effect. Also some migrants with official work permits have been the target of ambiguous control measures, as for example, when around 70 per cent of the Chinese in Hungary had to renew their residence permits monthly, some even weekly (Nyiri, 1995: 209). On the other hand, persons who stay or work illegally in Hungary, when apprehended by the authorities, are in general not very often sent back home (interview with Hárs).

To sum up, the existence of a very large informal labour market reveals that the problems of control involve much more than control directed at illegal, foreign labour. Despite successes with occasional 'clean-up operations', side costs are prevalent, but do not seem to be influencing policy makers to any significant extent. The lack of action can be explained by the overwhelming costs that more comprehensive control would entail.

Integration and Control

The lack of an integration policy

As has been demonstrated already by some examples, Hungarian internal control mechanisms are often ambiguous and haphazard. Control is therefore to a large extent implicit. Furthermore, Hungary has no formal integration policy, although the new Refugee Act of 1997 lists integration as one of the responsibilities of the refugee reception centres. As other Central and Eastern European countries, Hungary is mainly regarded as a transit country. Two thirds of all illegal migrants caught by the police in early 1994 were on their way to leave Hungary. Most of them were apprehended at the Austro-Hungarian border, attempting to get into Austria (Juhász, 1995: 208). Both refugees and labour migrants have been regarded as temporary, and as most migrants are ethnic Hungarians, integration comes very low on the agenda.

Another reason for not giving high priority to the establishment of an integration system is that most of the government's attention has been focused on the economic transition. Neither time nor resources to develop an integration policy have been available since the late 1980s, as efforts have instead been pooled into short-term management of the two recent refugee flows (interview with Erdelyi). There are almost no integration programmes such as language training, vocational training, or housing policies, as these would be too costly, and as the authorities have not perceived the temporary migrants as wanting them (Láczkó, 1995: 173).

Most ethnic Hungarians who came with the first refugee wave from Romania between 1988 and 1991 and stayed, have received citizenship or have been formally recognized as immigrants (Nagy, 1995: 43). Many of them were relatively well educated with limited problems in finding jobs and integrating into society. There were, however, Hungarians who disapproved of their presence on the labour market. The refugees were often willing to work for lower wages than native Hungarians. Nevertheless, in this first period there was a great deal of tolerance and acceptance of these refugees on the part of the Hungarian population. As the ethnic Hungarians from Transylvania speak the same language, and share substantial cultural components with the population in Hungary, their cultural integration was mainly unproblematic. The fact that the media dealt extensively with their fate also contributed to the public support and solidarity towards them (Pataki, 1994: 34–5).

The second wave of refugees, from the conflicts in former Yugoslavia, have faced a different challenge in terms of integration. Many of the refugees who arrived from Croatia and Vojvodina/Serbia in 1991 were ethnic Hungarians and those who stayed on could be integrated in the local communities in the southern parts of Hungary. Most of the refugees from former Yugoslavia gained only temporary protection in Hungary and the majority originally planned to return as soon as possible. According to one poll among ex-Yugoslav refugees conducted after two years of stay in Hungary, 74 per cent still wanted to return home, seven per cent intended to move on to the West and only 15 per cent wanted to remain in Hungary (Láczkó, 1995: 179). The refugees from Bosnia who came later on had more difficulties in integrating due to lack of contacts, language and cultural or religious differences, some of them being Muslim. Most of these refugees have stayed in refugee camps, and due to the unpredictability of the war their stay has become much longer than expected (Horváth, 1995: 147). Life in the refugee camps has segregated the refugees from the rest of the Hungarian society. There have been six major refugee camps in Hungary mainly for refugees from the former Yugoslavian conflicts. Several camps, including the largest camp, Nagyatád, which housed up to 1,100 refugees, were closed down as the numbers of remaining refugees diminished considerably.

Refugees with temporary protection have only been allowed to work outside the camps if jobs were first advertised and offered to Hungarian citizens. With high unemployment rates, many refugees have instead turned to the informal labour market, with seasonal jobs in agriculture, picking fruits, work on construction sites as handymen and other unqualified work. Incomes have still not been sufficient and camp life has lead to dependency and inactivity (Horváth, 1995: 149). As an application for immigrant status is bound to a viable income and guaranteed housing, refugees living in camps have in general not been accepted, despite having fulfilled the time criteria for an immigration application after years of residence (interview with Szekely).

It has been problematic to find affordable private accommodation for refugees without family, relatives or friends to stay with. About 2,700 registered refugees stayed in private accommodation in the summer of 1994 (Láczkó, 1995: 177–8). Almost 90 per cent of these refugees lived below the official Hungarian minimum subsistence level, although many may have incomes from the informal economy. As temporary protection status does not include a right to the limited social security available in Hungary (Láczkó, 1995: 180–1, 184), refugees in private accommodation are also far from enjoying conditions that would be conducive to political and social integration. While Convention Refugees enjoy the same legal status as citizens, apart from voting rights, the overwhelming majority of refugees are only temporarily protected. Their lack of prospects for economic, political and social integration in Hungary may have preserved these refugees' hopes to return or transit to a Western country. This has constituted an indirect, implicit form of control in the Hungarian society.

The legal protection of aliens is also undeveloped in the case of those asylum seekers and 'illegal' migrants who lack sufficient documentation, visas or permits. These migrants may face detention, which is the most extreme form of internal control. Illegal migrants and asylum seekers whose status cannot be determined are often held for very long periods in custody and conditions at the detention centre or prison at Nagyfa may be very harsh. It often takes several months for the Hungarian authorities to find the necessary information and to confirm the citizenship of the detained persons, and some people have been detained for years (Pataki, 1992: 36; UNHCR 1993).

Another problem with the integration of migrants has grown out of the political history of Central and Eastern Europe. The authoritarian system did not leave any room for a civil society, which has led to the lack of independent voluntary organizations, charities and NGOs that would cater for the welfare of refugees. There are only a few such organizations, still with underdeveloped routines and infrastructure. International organizations such as the Red Cross, Amnesty and the UNHCR find it difficult to establish cooperation with local counterparts. Legal counsel for asylum seekers is still rare. There is also a lack of qualified and impartial interpreters with skills in non-European languages. Moreover, there is a problem with the secrecy or lack of transparency of the asylum processing routines, which remains outside public scrutiny and therefore beyond the control of NGOs, refugee lawyers, and the concerned public (Nagy, 1995:50). The limited scope for a civil society as well as the lack of transparency in Hungary can also be regarded as an implicit dimension of control, which has a bearing on migration issues and which distinguishes Hungary from most of the Western European countries.

This lack of a civil society may explain that government authorities hesitate to organize refugee reception in co-operation with charities and NGOs. In the early 1990s the government authorities attempted to build up and consolidate a state-run system of refugee reception and refugee camps. The attitude is however slowly changing and NGOs and charities are becoming more established. The Hungarian Interchurch Aid is among the first to run a private refugee camp that receives some state support.

Party Politics and Public Opinion

Political discourse and ethnic Hungarians in the region

On the whole, migration has been rather low on the political agenda in Hungary. None of the political parties has had any clear programme or position on migration. There has been no apparent difference between the political parties on migration issues. The Young Democrats (FIDESZ) emphasized international co-operation and the need for an early warning system of potential and emerging mass migration flows. The Hungarian Democratic Forum (MDF) stressed that Hungary must avoid becoming the main transit country of the region, but it also underlined commitments to international norms and human rights. The two ruling parties from the 1994 elections, the Hungarian Socialist Party (MSZP) and the Alliance of Free Democrats (SZDSZ), were trying to balance between more populist, restrictive policy demands and the more liberal, human rights objectives. There has been one minor party that has been openly xenophobic and populist, the Truth and Life Party (MIEP), which did not gain any seat in the Parliament after the 1994 elections. Although that party has been quite marginalized and despite the absence of overt racist parties or groups, support for such groups may increase as xenophobic attitudes and signs of intolerance towards Roma are common among the broader public. One of the larger parties, the populist Independent Smallholders Party (11 per cent of the vote in the 1994 elections), has repeatedly exploited nationalistic and intolerant sentiments. The party has also provided financial, administrative and technical support to skinhead groups. Human Rights Watch has argued that '[s]upport for skinhead organizations from one of Hungary's major political parties extends legitimacy and tacit approval to the overtly anti-Roma position of these organizations and their members' (Human Rights Watch, 1996: 44–9).

The Kadar regime had initially tried to ignore the first refugee flow from Romania due to the sensitivity of the matter. Refugees were sent back, but reports of abuse by the Romanian authorities influenced public opinion against the Hungarian return policy. Public opinion in favour of change became increasingly difficult to disregard (Kutch, 1989). As the first necessary step had been taken, great emphasis in public discourse was soon given to the solidarity links with ethnic Hungarians in Romania and elsewhere (although many ethnic Romanians were also among the refugees). Hungarian politicians found that this was a popular standpoint. MDF had made the issue of supporting ethnic Hungarians in Transylvania one of its first profile issues in 1987. During 1989–90 this solidarity was both an expression of the empathy with those who suffered under the totalitarian regime in Romania, and a part of the euphoria when Ceaucescu was removed from power. Many also remembered 1956 when Western countries had received Hungarian refugees with open arms. The multiparty elections in Hungary in 1990 led to a government more outspoken on the topic of ethnic Hungarians in the region, and especially in Transylvania (Bugajski, 1991: 77–8; Kutch, 1989: 27).

The socialist-liberal government from 1994 chose a lower profile approach. Possibly due to the economic problems during the transition, cross-border solidarity as well as solidarity with refugees in Hungary has decreased. This change in attitude might have contributed to the loss of support for the MDF in the 1994 elections, whereas the socialists could benefit from it. The government of Gyula Horn seemed to have abandoned the ethnic solidarity theme as a political platform (Brown, 1996). Migration and refugee issues in Hungary can be characterized as apolitical. No Cabinet member has wanted to gain a profile on migration issues. On the other hand, the government does not want to hand over responsibility for migration and refugee issues on NGOs and charities, or to the civil society. The message that may be read into this is that the government wants to maintain control over migration issues, but with little political division or debate (interview with J. Tóth). Political discourse and party politics also show that there is more concern for the foreign policy aspects of migration issues rather than the integration aspects. Juhász has pointed out that 'the political discourse on migration is mainly one regarding migration control and regulation and not one of integration' (Juhász, 1995: 215).

Xenophobia and exclusion

Ethnic nationalism was in general regarded with very negative sentiments during the period of state socialism in the Central and Eastern European countries. Since the end of the Cold War, nationalism underwent a revival in this region. This may have affected the trans-border collective identities of Hungarianness. On the domestic level though, with the dominance of ethnic Hungarian migration to Hungary, one would assume that xeno-phobia (as one ingredient in nationalistic sentiments) would not constitute such a dominant problem as in many Western European countries. However, discrimination and xenophobic attitudes are present in Hungary and have also been prevalent during the communist years and before, mainly directed against the Roma and Jews (see, for example, Sciráczki, 1990: 137). There is still recurrent discrimination against the Roma in the workplace, in education, in housing, by the police and government institutions (Human Rights Watch/Helsinki 1996). Although many gener-ations of Roma have been living in Hungary, the negative attitudes towards them are more widespread and well established than towards any group of immigrants or refugees (Csepeli and Sik, 1995: 124).

Xenophobic attitudes are often based on negative stereotypes, on feelings of cultural and 'ethnic' distance and according to phenotypic markers. Ideas of what constitutes the nation and the historical process of nation building in Hungary are important for the explanation of attitudes towards both newcomers and national minorities. Hungarian language, ethnicity and culture (despite the difficulty in defining the latter two) have been central features of national identity, and for the definition of belonging and exclusion. As shown above, this cultural ingredient has also formed the basis of legislation on citizenship and immigration.

Attitudes towards the temporarily resident asylum seekers from former Yugoslavia have in general been positive and accepting. The solidity of such attitudes depends, however, on the promise of their eventual return and that they will not become a burden on Hungarian society (Juhász, 1995: 218). We may compare this 'elasticity' of attitudes with the change in public opinion regarding the ethnic Hungarians from Transylvania. In 1989 the attitudes towards this group were mainly positive and optimistic.

In the early 1990s, the economic hardships that accompanied the economic transition became more and more obvious. Hungarians turned increasingly negative also towards other ethnic Hungarians living in the neighbouring countries or coming to Hungary as asylum seekers (Csepeli and Sik, 1995: 122–4). Sik and Tóth (1991: 126) has pointed out that '[i]n December 1990, close to half of the population already regarded refugees [mainly ethnic Hungarians from Romania] as traitors (having let down their homeland and those who stayed behind) and almost the same percentage blamed refugees for the worsening conditions on the Hungarian labour market (taking away the job opportunities from Hungarian nationals)'. This attitude may partly be explained by the authoritarian policies during state socialism portraying 'exit' as a form of disloyalty to the state and society. On the other hand, Juhász argues that

> [t]he public opinion polls prove that there was a strong feeling of solidarity towards ethnic Hungarian refugees, but the fact that the refugees also had economic needs had an opposite effect. The resonance of economic rivalry was heard from the very beginning. The results of four countrywide surveys show that conflicts of economic interests have gradually reduced public sympathy towards ethnic Hungarian refugees. (Juhász, 1995: 217)

Negative attitudes have thus become increasingly common during the 1990s. Csepeli and Sik argue that '[x]enophobia toward immigrants has been overwhelming, no matter which country the refugees fled' (Csepeli and Sik, 1995: 123). In order to explain why there is also a certain degree of xenophobia against ethnic Hungarians from Romania, one should look at the economic factors – these migrants have been regarded as competitors for scarce job opportunities and as consumers of welfare benefits without having contributed as much as persons born in Hungary (Csepeli and Sik, 1995: 122–5). Unemployment and hardships during economic transition are important influences on both public opinion and government policies towards immigrants and refugees. Nevertheless, it is important to underline that ethnic Hungarians from Transylvania are still favoured and receive preferential treatment by a majority of the population (Juhász, 1995: 217).

The role of mass media is important here, particularly as the coverage of migration does not seem to be totally neutral in Hungary. A newspaper survey has indicated that most newspaper articles describe migration as an 'undesirable phenomenon both for Western Europe and, particularly, for Hungary'. Most articles are generalizing and one-sided in their report-ing. The government's position is referred to more often than opposing viewpoints. Integration issues are hardly touched upon (Juhász, 1995: 216).

Bearing in mind that the foreign population in the country is relatively limited, xenophobic reactions and intolerance call for concern. Political parties and decision makers do explicitly and implicitly acknowledge this public opinion. Public opinion therefore also constitutes an important influence on the internal and implicit control, discouraging political parties from seeking to establish an integration policy and permanent settlement of non-Hungarian migrants.

Conclusions

Analysis of the contexts of migration control in Hungary, has suggested a number of general conclusions. External control has been found to be more crucial than internal control, partly due to the fact that Hungary is a new country of immigration and that the size of the settled foreign population is still limited (see also Tamas 1996). Very limited immigration and emigration took place in Hungary during the Cold War. A new democratic Hungary in transition has turned into a transit country, and into a country of immigration for migrants from the east and the south who cannot or do not want to proceed further westward. Foreign policy considerations have had an important influence on how the new immigration control policy has developed. The main determinant has been the large number of ethnic Hungarians in neighbouring countries due to historical developments and border reshuffles, for which there is great concern. Together with Hungary's aspirations to become an EU member state and to be recognized as a liberal European democracy, these external factors have shaped the early policy choices within the control policy area.

Due to Hungary's geographical position, external control is crucial and it is approached both through physical border controls and via an externalization of control, such as visa regimes and bilateral readmission treaties with countries in the region. This restrictive control is in line with the restrictive, externalizing measures taken by Western European countries. Despite these and other preventive measures, illegal migration over the green borders takes place. Attempts to check borders are combined with control measures internally, through police checks and campaigns and through legislation. Internal control involves frequent police checks and officials often act erratically, on their own initiative and without clear rules of conduct. The rights of asylum seekers and migrants are often endangered in this implicit daily practice. Moreover, efficiency of internal control is reduced by the importance of the large informal labour market in Hungary, in which surveillance of illegal labour is complicated. The informal labour market is more a general problem than one specific for foreign labour. Comprehensive counter-measures have remained wanting as the costs involved would be too high. To a large extent, the limitations of internal control are due to that Hungary's attempts to manage migration are still quite young. Legislation and the institutional framework are still only in a rudimentary state, with lack of co-ordination, *ad hoc* solutions, haphazard improvizations and not clearly defined rules. These shortcomings make the implicit aspects of control an important feature.

The lack of internal control has been based on the assumption that migrants will stay only temporarily, making neither internal control, nor integration policies necessary. A large number of the temporarily protected refugees have lived isolated from the rest of society in refugee camps. Although it has formally been possible for them to live in private accommodation, this option has been untenable for many due to lack of funds and contacts. In general, ethnic Hungarian refugees have fared better both in this regard and in general. Concern for ethnic Hungarian minorities abroad has led to an ethnic preference in legislation, where the principle of *jus sanguinis* has guided legislation both for immigration and naturalization. This ethnic preference has also been obvious in the informal, implicit routines of officials. Ethnic Hungarians have been able to integrate culturally, without the need for any public programmes, but more recently they too have been the target of growing xenophobic attitudes. This intolerance in the Hungarian society is partly due to the problems endured during the process of economic transition with high unemployment, and the perception that refugees and migrants add to the competition for scarce resources without having contributed. Despite such sentiments, and despite media and party focus on the specific refugee flows, migration has not yet become as politicized as in Western European countries. On the other hand, Hungary has started to establish its immigration and refugee policies at a time when the general trend in Western Europe is increasingly restrictive. Notwithstanding the particular situation of this country, it is clear that Hungary has followed suit with the restrictiveness of migration control.

References

Amnesty International (1993), *Hungary: Torture and ill-treatment of foreigners*, London.

Barr, N. (ed.) (1994), *Labour Markets and Social Policy in Central and Eastern Europe: The Transition and Beyond*, Oxford: Oxford University Press, for the World Bank and LSE.

Bibó, István (1991), *Democracy, Revolution, Self-Determination; Selected Writings*, ed. by Károly Nagy, Boulder: Westview.

Bonoli, G. (1993), *The Integration of a New Country in the European Refugee Regime: the Case of Hungary*, Leeds: University of Leeds, MA dissertation.

Brown, J. (1996), 'Estranged in a familiar land', *The Hungary Report*, 10 April.

Bugajski, J. (1991), *Nations in Turmoil: Conflict and Co-operation in Eastern Europe*, Boulder: Westview.

Collinson, S. (1996), 'Visa requirements, carrier sanctions, safe third countries and readmission: the development of an asylum buffer zone in Europe', *Transactions of the Institute of British Geographers*, 21: 76–89.

Csepeli, G. and Sik, E. (1995), 'Changing Content of Political Xenophobia in Hungary – Is the Growth of Xenophobia Inevitable?' in Fullerton, M. et al. (eds), *Refugees and Migrants: Hungary at a Crossroad*, Budapest: Hungarian Academy of Sciences, Political Science.

Dövényi, Z. (1992), 'The Role of Hungary in the European Migrations of the Twentieth Century', *Conference on Mass Migration in Europe*: Implications in East and West, March 5–7, Vienna.

—— (1995), 'Nemzetközi Vándorlás', *Magyar Nemzeti Atlasz*.

ECRE, (1994), *Asylum in Europe: Review of refugee and asylum laws and procedures in selected European countries*, ECRE 2.

Erdös, A. (1995), 'Statement' to *Conference on refugees, returnees, displaced persons and related migratory movements in the CIS and relevant neighbouring states,* December, Budapest.

Fullerton, M., Sik, E. and Tóth, J. (1995), eds. *Refugees and Migrants: Hungary at a Crossroad*, Yearbook of the Research Group on International Migration, Budapest, Hungarian Academy of Sciences, Political Science.

Giorgi, L., Pohoryles, R., Pohoryles-Drexel, S. and Schmid, G. (1992), 'The Internal Logic and Contradiction of Migration Control; An Excursion into the Theory and Practice in Relation to East-West Migration', *Innovation*, 5: 3.

Hárs, Á. (1995), 'Migration and the Labour Market: Evidence, Misinterpretations, Lessons', in Fullerton, M., et al., (eds) op. cit.

Horváth, L. (1995), 'Asylum Seekers at Nagyatád', in Fullerton, M., et al. eds., op. cit.

Hovy, B. (1993), 'Asylum migration in Europe: patterns, determinants and the role of East-West movements', in King, R. (ed.) *The New Geography of European Migrations,* London: Belhaven.

Human Rights Watch/Helsinki, (1996), *Rights Denied: the Roma of Hungary*, New York.

IMF (1994), *World Economic Outlook*, October, Washington DC.

IOM (1994), *Transit Migration in Hungary*, Migration Information Programme, Budapest.

Jackman, R. and Rutkowski, M. (1994), 'Labour Markets: Wages and Employment', in Barr, N. (ed.) op. cit.

Juhász, J. (1995), 'International Migration in Hungary', *Innovation*, 8: 201–19.

Jungbert, B. (1996), *Háttéranyag,* Budapest: Office of Refugee and Migration Affairs.

Kutch, K.A. (1989), *Summary Report on Romanian Asylum-Seekers in Hungary*, Refugee Studies Program, University of Geneva, Geneva: Webster.

King, M. (1992), 'The Impact of EC Border Policies', *Innovation* 5: 3.

Láczkó, F. (1995), 'Temporary Protection and Ex-Yugoslav Refugees in Hungary', in Fullerton, M., et al. (eds), op. cit.

Larrabe, S.F. (1992), 'Down and Out in Warsaw and Budapest: Eastern Europe and East–West Migration', *International Security*, 16: 5–33.

Loescher, G. (1993), *Beyond Charity: International Co-operation and the Global Refugee Crisis*, Oxford: Oxford University Press.

Magyarország Menekültpolitikájának Föbb Elemei, 1996-05-14.

Migration News (1996), *Hungarian Immigration*, 3: 2.

Ministry of Foreign Affairs (1993), *Activities of the Republic of Hungary Regarding International Refugee Matters and Migration*, Fact Sheet on Hungary, Budapest.

Mozaik, (1996), 'Hungary to set up Serious Fraud Office by June', *Mozaik* 1: 302.

Nagy, B. (1993), 'The Refugee Situation in Hungary: Where Now?', *Acta Juridica Hungarica*, 35: 193–210.

—— (1995), 'Changing Trends, Enduring Questions Regarding Refugee Law in Central Europe', in Fullerton, M., et al. (eds), op. cit.

Nyiri, P.D. (1995), 'From Settlement to Community: Five Years of the Chinese in Hungary', in Fullerton, M., et al. (eds), op. cit.

OECD (1995a), *Economic Outlook*, 57, Paris.

—— (1994 and 1995b), SOPEMI: *Trends in International Migration*, Annual Report 1993–4, Paris.

Office of Refugee and Migration Affairs (1995), (1996a and b), *Refugee Statistics* (Menekültügyi Statisztika), Budapest.

OMRI Daily Digest (1996), Numbers 48, 211, 227 and 244.

Pataki, J. (1992), 'Increasing Intolerance of Foreigners', München: *Radio Free Europe (RFE/RL) Research Report*.

—— (1994), 'The Recent History of the Hungarian Refugee Problem', München: *Radio Free Europe (RFE/RL) Research Report*.

Portes, R. (1994), 'Transformation Traps', *The Economic Journal*, 104.

Rédei, M. (1994), 'Hungary', in Ardittis, S. (ed.) *The Politics of East-West Migration*, New York: St. Martin's Press.

—— (1995), 'Internal Brain Drain' in Fullerton, M., et al. (eds) op. cit.

—— (n d), Migration and its Regulation in Hungary, unpublished memo.

Romania: Selected Issues (1994), *Refugee Survey Quarterly*, 13: 4.

Sik, E. and Tóth, J. (1991), 'Hungary – Loss of Innocence: The Socio-historical Aspects of the Hungarian Refugee Policy', *Migration*, 11–2.

Sipos, S. (1994), 'Income transfers: family support and poverty', in Barr, N. (ed.) op cit.

Sziráczki, G. (1990), 'Redundancy and Regional Unemployment: A Case Study in Ózd', in Hann, C.M. ed., *Market Economy and Civil Society in Hungary*, London: Frank Cass,

Szöke, L. (1992), 'Hungarian Perspectives on Emigration and Immigration in the New European Architecture', *International Migration Review*, 26: 305–23.

Tamas, K. (1996), *The Politics of Migration Control: a case study of Hungary*, MA dissertation, Sussex: University of Sussex, European Institute.

Tóth, J. (1995), 'Who are the Desirable Immigrants in Hungary under the New Adapted Laws?' in Fullerton, M., et al. (eds), op. cit.

Tóth, P.P. (1995), 'Refugees, Immigrants and New Citizens in Hungary 1988–1992', in Fullerton, M., et al. (eds), op. cit.

UNHCR (1993), *Legal Fact Sheets on Asylum Procedures in Central and Eastern Europe*, Geneva: UNHCR.

—— (1994), *Background Paper on Romanian Refugees and Asylum Seekers*, Geneva: UNHCR, Centre for Documentation on Refugees,

Interviews in 1996:

Conducted *A. in June and B. in November with:*

Ambrus, Agnes, national legal training officer, UNHCR, Budapest, Hungary, A and B.

Erdélyi, István, Refugee and Migration Policy Unit, Ministry of Interior, Budapest, A and B.

Dobos, Görgyné, head of department. for aliens and immigrants, National Police Commander's Office, B.

Haraszti, Katalin, deputy director, Refugee and Migration Policy Unit, Ministry of Interior, Budapest, A.

Hárs, Ágnes, Institute of Labour Studies, Budapest, A.

Holló Miklosné, National Headquarters of the Border Guards, Budapest, B.

Juhász, Judith, Central Statistical Office, Budapest, A.

Köszeg, Ferenc, Hungarian Human Rights Protection Centre, B.

Láczkó, Frank and Tass, Thomas, IOM, Budapest, B.

Lehel, Lászlo, Szekely, Judith, and Kovács, Béla, Hungarian Inter-Church Aid, Budapest and refugee camp at Eröpuszta, B.

Rédei, Mary, REG-INFO Ltd., A.

Sándor, István, head of Department and Lakatos, István, Ministry of Foreign Affairs, A.

Sik, Endre, Institute of Political Science, Budapest, B.

Szilagyi, Zoltánné, and Nagy, Sándor, Debrecen Refugee camp, B.

Tóth, Judith, Institute of Political Science, Budapest, B.

Vég, Zsuzsanna, head of the Schengen Unit, Ministry of Interior, B.

–10–

Controlling Immigration in Europe
Grete Brochmann

'The more fiercely a civilisation entrenches itself, the less it is left with to defend'. This statement by Hans M. Enzensberger (1993: 18) embodies the nemesis of control in our societies: the process in which the 'control with others' recoils and turns against oneself. It touches the edge of meaning in the realm of control as such. Who is controlling what for which aims and with which consequences? Even though these ultimate thresholds seem far on the horizon, the dynamics in the statement are present in many decisions – big or small – at different levels in society. How we act and relate to immigrants or 'foreigners' based on ways of thinking, social definitions and ideology of nationhood basically reflects what kind of society we want. Ethnically segmented surroundings influence the normative basis of the welfare state. Racism is a threat to not only ethnic minorities, but also against democratic traditions and the general social climate. In liberal societies there is no clear cutting edge where control turns into repression.

Through the eight case studies we wanted to draw attention to a broader tableau of control dimensions. Beyond the traditional approach to studies of immigration regulation, where border control and alien control are the two major targets of analysis, we wanted to study the terrain in between and around these control positions. This means studying the mechanisms operating in the interplay between external and internal immigration control, the way in which more subtle or implicit forces may counteract and undermine, or support and strengthen intentional policies, and trigger and reinforce or obstruct formation processes in the realm of public opinion. As we saw in the introductory chapter, there is basically an interaction between the exercise of sovereignty in terms of territorial control, and internally – the consolidation of national identity and integration. The case studies reveal national variations within Europe along these lines in the midst of policy convergence. Some explanations for this variation are given in the historical accounts. Different kinds of state systems develop different modes of control over the years, which in turn means that the national historical approaches – judicially and politically – gain their own momentum.

These national distinctions are embedded in an international context, which increasingly provides premises for national policies. A study of immigration control in today's Europe must necessarily have European Union policy as a central dimension. The impact of the European scene is therefore taken into account in all the case studies.

Despite national variations there are nevertheless two conclusions to be drawn as to the general tendencies. There is no significant *control crisis* present in Europe today in relation to immigration. On the contrary, our case studies reveal steadily higher sophistication in terms of flow control and internal surveillance. The other tendency is that externalization of control – as defined in the introductory chapter – has become an efficient instrument for reduced immigration. We also suggest that externalizing the control measures is one way of coping with the basic welfare state dilemma spelled out in this book – the trade off between humanitarian obligations and the national need for *realpolitik*.

What Decides Policy Formation?

The most basic rationale behind the formation of a country's immigration control – territorial protection and internal cohesion – was broken down into more detectable factors in the introductory chapter: *national security* – maintenance of peace and stability; *national economy* – labour market consideration, sustainability of public budgets etc.; *demography* – population density, fertility rates, the age pyramid etc.; and *social and cultural cohesion* – the preservation of national traditions, identity etc. On top of this, we should add the international – or the EU dimension, partly influencing all the former factors, partly being a factor in itself. This is true in broad outline for all the countries studied, even for the ones without membership of the EU. Common to all the factors mentioned is that they may represent both substantial interests and ideological legitimations.

Let us now start by asking two questions: under which conditions are different material interests and legitimizations activated? And which of these have been the most important preoccupations that European states have tried to satisfy through actual policies of immigration control?

Our case countries hold very different positions when it comes to preconditions for immigration control. In today's Western Europe, all receiving countries want to limit immigration from non-OECD countries, and all the countries would explain and legitimize this standpoint with reference to the factors mentioned above: the economy (structural changes and restraints on the welfare budgets); security issues and the question of national cohesion. Of these themes, the economy is the prime public argument against immigration in all the countries, even though investigations in some of the receiving countries reveal that the economic impact of immigration by and large has been favourable. Demographic arguments, which in some countries have been used in favour of immigration (except in the Netherlands where the opposite is true), are mostly neglected or rejected.

This is a general picture in our case countries. What varies, though, is the urgency of this control preoccupation, and the consistency and concern with which it is implemented. This variation has to do with a number of factors influencing the *control setting* – the preconditions for each and every country's control endeavour. Geographical location; territorial matters; history of immigration and traditions in handling influxes; labour market considerations; administrative and management systems; national history, particularly in relation to civic and political culture, collective identities, the nationhood question and so forth.

Preconditions for Control

Geographical location certainly constitutes a factor that creates preconditions for immigration control. A territorial position directly bordering sending areas does increase the likelihood of being affected. There is, however, no mechanical relationship between geographical location and inflow intensity. The way in which geography becomes relevant depends on a number of other variables. To a large extent we may speak of a *political geography* in this realm. West Germany's borders with the former East bloc countries were for many years not major gateways due to the rigid emigration policy of the communist regimes. There is necessarily a foreign policy component in this political geography. There is of course also an *economic geography* present: immigrants may bypass the closest country to enter a more distant, but more attractive, destination country to amplify life chances. This mechanism partly explains why a peripheral country like Sweden has received a disproportional high number of immigrants despite its geographical position.

Looking at our case countries in a context of current European politics and economics, there is no doubt that geography is 'interacting' with other factors in a significant way. The combination in Italy of a long territorial coastline, proximity to a major sending area and a labour market with a large informal component, makes it a candidate for substantial immigration. This is even more so if we add 'short experience of handling influxes' to the Italian list. Norway, at the other end of Europe, has had a relatively low immigration rate, partly due to its distant placement in the cold northern periphery, not surrounded by any major sending area (the Kola Peninsula of Russia may change this in the future). The contrast to Sweden is interesting, Norway not being markedly less attractive in terms of economics and welfare, but at the same time holding a very similar geographical position, at least in relation to the kind of flows witnessed since the 1980s. Differences in policy with succeeding cumulative effects basically account for this contrast. In the Swedish case, geography was outclassed by economic performance and welfare provisions. Among our case countries, Germany has nonetheless been the largest magnet – the preferred end station for the majority of Europe's immigrants so far. The geographical component in this seems to be mixed. West Germany also had this magnet position before the fall of the Wall in relation to migrants coming from distant geographies. With the end of the old regime in Eastern Europe, it was quite evident that a unified Germany would also constitute an attractive destination for prospective migrants from the east.

Both Germany and Austria – the two countries with possibly the most strategic location in relation to today's land based immigration – have recently tried to neutralize the geographical factor through more rigid implementation of control, through less generous conditions for immigrants who have arrived and through claims for burden sharing with other countries.

History of immigration is important in two major ways. Firstly, tradition in terms of streams from particular areas or countries that have created migration 'bridges', do have a tendency to nurture itself. This takes place through various mechanisms, the most important ones being bilateral foreign relations on state level – foreign policy – and through the so-called network effect within the migrant communities. Certain migration connections are thus subjected to cumulative causation through historical processes. Some of our case countries even have what they consider parts of their own ethnic population living abroad – like the *Aussiedler* in the German case and the *ethnic Hungarians* in Hungary.

Secondly, the length of a country's immigration history might have implications for the ability of the state to handle immigration. This applies both to the level of sophistication of the juridical instruments and to general experience. Legislative traditions may represent both an asset and a restriction from the authorities' point of view. On the one hand, well-developed regulation may be easy to activate when circumstances require quick reaction; on the other hand well-established legislation may be difficult to move in new directions, particularly if this legislation has been embedded in popular consensus. *Ad hoc* legislation in Norway concerning the Bosnian war refugees was easily introduced and presented few difficulties in terms of political opposition. The new 'Bosnian Law' was incorporated in the existing Aliens Law shortly afterwards. At the other end of the scale, the change of the asylum paragraph in the German Basic Law was not easily achieved, due to historical factors and established legislation.

Among our case studies Hungary and Italy represent examples of countries without much experience of immigration regulation, and which have quickly – and flexibly – adopted new restrictive legislation from the start. Both countries have – to different degrees – bought the whole restrictive package, as it were, from the more experienced receiving countries.

Historical experience of immigration may also have various implications for attitudes and climate for tolerance in the population. The causal connections are difficult to come by. It is nevertheless obvious that historical experiences do have an impact, although possibly in different ways, on distinct social segments of society. Besides, 'historical experience' needs to be broken down by other variables to make sense in a comparative exercise.

The labour market constitutes one of the most important factors when it comes to conditions for control, being one of the prime attractions in receiving OECD countries, generally speaking. By and large Western labour markets appeal to potential migrants throughout the world. The *structure* of the labour market plays a role, however, as to the scale of the attraction and to the kind of labour in question. The regular labour market is currently of minor relevance, due to limited demand for low skilled/unskilled labour. *Contract labour*, particularly in the way Germany has organized it since 1991, is here an exception. This kind of labour is – as the term indicates – regulated in terms of contracts, and it has been brought about by a *de facto* demand for foreign labour in the German market. However, it is not *immigration*, as the contracts are only temporary, not containing any rights in terms of settlement facilities. Apart from contract labour, it is the size and, to a certain extent, the quality of the informal labour market that constitute the most important comparative aspects: the ease with which one may operate in the black and the grey markets as an illegal immigrant. Here we find significant variations. Earlier, it was possible to trace a south-north axis in this respect – placing Italy and Sweden/Norway at the edges. Even though there is still some sense in this approach, the picture has become more nuanced. Firstly, the dismantling of the iron curtain has had implications for the central and northern flank, in particular for Germany, Austria and Hungary. The impact on Hungary is here markedly different from the other countries due to its position as a former East bloc country, now holding a transit role for East–West migration. Secondly, the tendency towards deregulation throughout Europe has opened up some segments of the labour market even in the formerly highly regulated Sweden, and increasingly made it a target for illegal migration.

The interplay between these various preconditions for control will form a basis for analysis throughout the comparative analysis. Territorial matters, the historical heritage in all its complexity as well as various labour market parameters together make up the ground for policy making in today's Europe.

Stages of Immigration Control – Modes of Refugee Reception

Migration control is exercised at different points along the migration route, which starts at the origin, goes through possible transit stations and leads to entry, settlement and possible naturalization in a destination country. The migrant can be subject to control at different stages of this route. In the introductory chapter we divided this control into two broad categories: external and internal control, depending on where, territorially speaking, the control is exercised. After having gone through the eight cases, it is now feasible to refine and extend this dichotomy into stages or phases in a process. These stages may sometimes represent grey zones in terms of the external/internal divide. The various stages or phases may also be viewed differently for labour migrants as compared to refugees/asylum seekers. It can be useful to relate *control policies* to these different stages and make a distinction between labour migrants and refugees/asylum seekers.

For documented labour migration we may identify five major types of policy: first, policies directed towards the areas of origin, aiming at influencing the development of an emigration *potential* (for the time being the aim is to reduce this potential, but it is also possible to stimulate emigration); second, policies directed towards countries of origin with the aim of controlling the size of an emigration *flow* (promotion of immigration by recruitment, control of flows through visa requirements, deterrence of unwanted immigration by information campaigns and so forth); third, control at admission to the territory of the receiving country (such as border checks of visas, residence permits); fourth, control of access to the labour market and employment (work permits); fifth, return migration policies (by financial incentives or enforced in case of unemployment, lack of independent income or due to criminal record). The repertoire of immigration control is thus geared towards splitting up migration flows into components accepted for permanent settlement and components destined for return. There are, however, some phenomena that tend to escape this dichotomy. Increasing numbers of voluntary migrants tend to go back and forth periodically between countries of origin and of immigration, or create transnational households, which send their members to different destinations and pool their income (Basch et al., 1994). Permanent resident status facilitates such two-way flows, and dual citizenship exempts some groups from regular control altogether.

In the admission of refugees, we may distinguish between *active* policies of taking in groups fleeing from persecution, war or famine, and situations where destination countries are rather passively exposed to refugee-producing crises in neighbouring or other countries and become a natural target for those seeking shelter. Asylum seekers or the so called spontaneous refugees also belong in this category. In both kinds of admissions receiving countries will generally try to establish systems of control that make sure that only the welcome and 'deserving' refugees can benefit from asylum. Normally the loci and instruments of control will be different in relation to the two categories. In the former case, external control will prevail with countries of asylum being actively involved in the selection of admissible refugees in camps abroad, and often determining quotas for specific groups or for total numbers per year. In the latter case, control used to be mostly internal with a thorough checking of asylum claims and with policies of ensuring transit or return of those who are not accepted for permanent settlement. Most countries are mixed cases and apply both strategies at different points in time or towards different groups of refugees. Recent developments have, however, externalized the control of even spontaneous refugees or asylum seekers, as we will see.

In between these two kinds of control, there are cases of countries that have consciously opened themselves to inflows of people seen as belonging to the national population in terms of ethnic origins or religious affiliation. Some of the largest migration flows fall into this category. In our context, Germany and Hungary in particular have adopted more-or-less open admission policies for their ethnic kin coming from other countries. Normally such loosening of control for a specific group of immigrants is not only justified by common origins but also by their need for protection from ethnic and political discrimination or persecution. The basic element of control in such admission policy is, of course, the determination of membership in the group entitled to immigrate and to immediate or quick access to citizenship. Once the inflow comes to be seen as a burden, control will normally be extended first towards the external side with attempts to improve conditions in countries of origin or the establishment of quotas for a yearly intake, as is now witnessed in relation to the *Aussiedlers* in Germany.

Preventive and Externalized Control

The immigration policies of our case countries were for a long time *ad hoc*, reactive, short term and pragmatic. Despite the fact that immigration was a significant economic and social phenomenon – at least for France, Germany, Austria, Sweden and the Netherlands – systematic policy generation was limited for many years – possibly with the exception of Sweden. With the increased immigration from the South, with the dismantling of the Berlin Wall towards the East and with the establishment of the EU internal market, the need for planning and co-ordination became pressing. If we look at the gates above, the three last ones – located at the receiving end of the labour migration chain – have been (intentionally) closed or highly restrictive since the early 1970s. Migrants have nevertheless kept coming – a fact that in turn, has directed more attention to the sending side; the conditions in the countries of origin. This new focus partly reflects a realization of the fact that *development* in the end is necessary to reduce the need to move, or to affect the causes that make people want to move; partly it represents a step to tighten control at the source to prevent people from reaching the border of the potential destination country. This twofold externalization can be seen to accommodate both the short- and long-term need to prevent people from coming, at least in theory. It also represents a strategy that is less controversial *internally* in the receiving countries, as it often does not directly challenge powerful 'pull' forces.

Most of our case countries have embarked upon a policy line that includes preventive and/or externalized measures in one way or the other. These measures can be seen as *indirect*, according to our chart in the introductory chapter. There are various degrees of sophistication, however, both in terms of rhetoric and practical implementation. The Scandinavian countries and the Netherlands were first within our sample of countries to formulate a so-called *comprehensive approach*. This policy shift addresses the 'root cause analysis', and it should ideally accommodate both the source of labour migration and refugee flows. It is based on an understanding that the economic and political causes of emigration are linked, and that a development-cum-democratization process would eventually lead to a removal of the root causes of 'unwanted international migration'. Another novelty of the comprehensive approach, was that it aimed to handle the migration complex as a whole – both substantially and in some places (Sweden and the Netherlands) even administratively. All policy areas with relevance for migration should be formulated and implemented together, including development aid/emergency aid, foreign policy, diplomacy, trade politics, and human rights questions. This new approach should be seen as enriching the traditional control policy, not replacing it. In fact the comprehensive approach was sometimes introduced in a rhetorical framework, where a reinforced border control was legitimized by long-term preventive measures in the countries of origin (Sweden and Norway). On a European level, the agreement between the EU and the Maghreb region contains elements of the same thinking: trade agreements and economic transfers should compensate for tighter immigration control on the European side.

Consequently, if we consider the field of labour migration, the two most external gates or stages in our system have been re-emphasized during the last ten years, not at the expense of, but in addition to the traditional gates. In real terms, however, it is hard to tell what priority is given to preventive or 'root-cause' measures when it comes to the pinch. Transfers are limited, and the target – economically speaking – is often unclear. Critics even claim that the underlying assumption is wrong – at least in the short run – in the sense that development triggers more migration rather than stemming it (Teitelbaum 1991).

When it comes to refugees, preventive measures are even less clear. There is an assumption present that economic development also fosters the generation of democratic institutions, and that development will therefore eventually contain the need to flee. Beside these complicated and highly uncertain propositions, a number of innovative concepts are suggested in the political realm: 'early warning systems', 'flight prevention', 'right to stay', 'the creation of safe areas' and so forth – concepts that have appeared in a context where containment of flows outside the territory of receiving countries is on the agenda. Most of these concepts remain quite abstract, mostly appearing in international settings where existing or potential far-reaching crises are discussed. The Gulf War and in particular the Bosnian crisis induced some of these new ways of thinking in Europe.

As far as the process of externalization of control in relation to spontaneous refugees is concerned, two very tangible developments are taking place. Firstly, the new notion of 'safe countries' adds a collective 'flow' dimension to what used to be individual refugee protection – a notion that has clearly been introduced for control purposes. A person coming from a 'safe country' will nearly automatically be labelled as having a 'clearly unfounded case', and will consequently be refused directly at the border without any further investigations. Secondly, the 'first country rule', which implies that any asylum seeker can be returned to the first 'safe' country he or she has passed through on the way, constitutes an effective filter for countries not bordering conflict areas, and with limited direct flights or boat connections to turbulent regions. These two instruments have been introduced and implemented very effectively in nearly all our countries, with little *formal* co-ordination. (The Dublin Convention, which contains the formalization of the first country rule for the EU countries was not ready for implementation until 1 September 1997, yet the member countries as well as Norway have nevertheless since long started practising this rule.)

There is, however, important bilateral co-ordination taking place, in particular between Germany and Austria respectively, and the bordering Eastern countries in terms of readmittance agreements for asylum seekers and illegal migrants. Some of the other countries have signed similar, yet less comprehensive agreements (Sweden and the Netherlands). These new measures are targeted towards the most important and most problematic flows, seen from the point of view of the authorities in the receiving countries, and they have had a significant impact. The agreements have diminished the major flows of asylum seekers coming via land-based transportation from the east. The reduction in numbers of asylum seekers wanting to enter countries such as Germany and Sweden after 1993 is mainly attributed to this new control system.

The quota system in Austria is another external control invention with a strong impact. By fixing a yearly quota of immigration from all non EU/EEA countries, and independent of actual pressure, Austrian authorities have managed to introduce a strict limitation to some of the few entry possibilities in Europe today. Through the new externalized methods, most of our countries have – to different degrees – compromised on traditional human rights agreements among European countries.

Border Control – Visa Policy

We have already touched upon the third stage – the actual border control – through the new practices of refusing some asylum seekers *at* the border who earlier would have been let into the territory and had their asylum case processed. The *visa* policy is of a similar kind; partly externalized way beyond the territorial border, partly being operated *at* the border. People will either never succeed in obtaining a visa from their country of origin, and consequently give up, or people can manage to reach the border, but are refused entry. The visa policy may have the same deterrence effect as the new asylum practice of 'clearly unfounded cases'. There are costs involved, and if the probability of being refused is high, more people will probably not even try. On the other hand, the visa restrictions may force people into illegal activities. People in need of protection sometimes cannot escape to other countries without assistance, which in many cases means using traffickers who increasingly profit from the restrictions. Thus, intensified use of visa regulations in combination with other methods of control is the beginning of a vicious circle.

There are different kinds of visas, however, and an important loophole in the tight system is the tourist visa. All our countries want tourism, and for some, particularly Italy and Austria, tourism is a major income earner. Consequently, this loophole will be most likely to remain. Nevertheless, it is often difficult to acquire a tourist visa if the immigration authorities consider the likelihood of 'overstaying' as being high. It is thus more difficult to travel as a tourist from what is considered a sending region.

The visa policy is clearly an effective instrument within the whole control complex. It is by no means a new mode of control, but it has recently been activated more extensively in relation to refugee-producing areas. The Bosnian case is the most striking example of how a fear of being the preferred target for war refugees turned into a 'domino effect' of visa conditions in the receiving countries throughout Europe.

Visa policy was, until the Amsterdam Summit in 1997, the only relevant immigration policy field that was fully integrated into the EU supranational structure. This means in practice that all member countries subscribe to the same number of countries (now 130) being subject to visa requirements for their nationals. The list basically includes countries outside the OECD – and hereby all countries of relevance when it comes to current refugee flows. The visa policy as an instrument in relation to refugee crises is included in the Maastricht Treaty (Article 100c): *'In the event of an emergency situation in a third country posing a threat of a sudden inflow*

*of nationals from that country in the Community, the Council may ...
introduce a visa requirement for nationals from the country in question.'*
The combination of visa requirements and *carrier sanctions* has proven
effective in the hands of the receiving authorities in trying to reduce major
inflows of asylum seekers and some kinds of illegals. Apart from being
an effective external method of control, *carrier sanctions* are an externalized instrument in another sense as well: they place the responsibility for
control on actors external to the political authorities – the transportation
companies. Even Norway and Hungary – not being member countries –
are by and large following the same visa policy as the European Union
(Hungary with exceptions for some of the neighbouring countries). There
is, however, no general agreement on which criteria should be used in
deciding on the list, a fact that the European Parliament has criticized on
different occasions.

The Schengen Agreement

The whole border control issue went into a new stage with the implementation of the Schengen Agreement in 1995. According to this
agreement – being initiated as a 'pilot–project' for the European Union
as regards border control issues – national border control between the
signatory countries should be abolished. As a consequence of this 'lost
control' at national borders, entry control is supposed to be reinforced at
the external Schengen borders (Schengen states bordering third countries)
and, besides, so-called 'compensatory measures' should be developed
internally in each and every signatory country. 'Compensatory measures'
is here another term for increased mobilization of security and internal
control systems.

The reason why the original Schengen countries (Benelux, France and
Germany) initiated an alternative process to the general European integration was the disagreement on the interpretation of article 8A in the
Single European Act (see introduction): the question of free movement
of persons within the internal market. Since Great Britain, Ireland and
Denmark wanted to maintain national border control, and to exclude third
country nationals from the right to free movement internally in the
Community, they functioned as a break block on the European integration
on a central issue. The countries in favour of a more rapid integration
process – France and Germany in particular – therefore saw the possibility
of stepping up the pace by introducing an alternative structure, which in
turn could serve as a catalyst in the broader European process. The
countries most energetic in the Schengen structure calculated that it would

be easier to progress in policy making on sensitive issues like transnational police cooperation, immigration and asylum policy among countries which also shared position on the border control issue. The aim was then gradually to include the Schengen arrangements into the Community structure, hereby making the Schengen Agreement redundant as such. In the development of the internal market, cooperation in the field of justice and home affairs became much closer, a fact that was first confirmed by the inclusion of this area in the Maastricht Treaty in the so called 'third pillar', and after the Amsterdam Treaty the full inclusion of the Schengen system into the EU structure. The transitional unanimity requirement of five years may however still limit more controversial integration efforts.

Ironically the Schengen 'pilot project' – which was intended to be realized far in advance of the internal market – was blocked several times by internal problems and disagreement, so that it took more than two years after the opening of the Internal Market before the Schengen Agreement was ready for implementation, on 26 March 1995. Even after this date, however, France quickly signalled that the 'compensatory measures' were not good enough for France to abolish border controls. Late in the spring 1995 France imposed a halt in the process, and announced delays in abandoning border checks. A basic problem all along has been the question of drug traffic. In France the major stumbling block has been what are perceived as liberal drug laws in the Netherlands, Spain, and possibly also Italy. Besides, the bomb explosions in Paris that spring made the government even more alerted to the border-control question. French politicians have been clear in their message: there will be no suppression of internal frontiers unless the Schengen partners apply the same restrictive external border control as France (Cruz 1993). *Trust* is generally speaking a central ingredient in Schengen; to accept the abolition of national border control, one has to rely on the countries supervising the common external borders. There are also costs involved: the signatory countries with external borders have to cover the expenses of a reinforced border control towards third countries.

The Schengen Agreement has had an inconsistent impact on immigration control in Europe. On the one hand it introduced the right to free movement for third country nationals having entered the Schengen area legally. It also substantiated the responsibility of the 'first country' to handle asylum applications (unless they are 'clearly unfounded' and therefore refused directly at the border). On the other hand, entry into the Schengen area was (at least intentionally) made even more restrictive, and not least, the internal control within the different nation states have been stepped up, through the SIS system and through physical units on the ground. Through the Schengen system, migration has been handled as a *security* issue.

The case countries of this study have different positions – both objectively and politically – in relation to Schengen. There seems to be little disagreement among the Schengen countries on the intentional side as concerns the *external* control: all countries have the ambition of combating illegal immigration more effectively, as well as reducing the asylum pressure. The variation in this respect is therefore more on the operational level: the capacity and skills to effectuate the policy. All the factors mentioned initially in this chapter here of relevance are: geographical location, history of immigration, administrative systems and so forth.

Italy is again seen as the major problem child in this respect – often labelled the 'soft underbelly' of Europe, but Austria has also been addressed (mainly from Germany) with concern in relation to the irregular inflow, particularly from the East. Austria officially supports the EU enlargement to the East, even though Labour politicians have expressed strong reservations against the free movement of labour migrants from former socialist countries. By extending the EU border further east, Austria would be relieved from the complicated and costly task of controlling an external EU/Schengen border.

It seems that Sweden has had only minor objections to Schengen affiliation: it is in the interest of Sweden to attach to an area of free movement. More restrictive external control has also been on the agenda for a while, and collective action with EU partner countries makes this endeavour more easily acceptable to public opinion.

France, Germany and the Netherlands were among the initiating countries of the Schengen Agreement. France has nevertheless been a major stumbling block along the way, as we have seen, due to distrust in relation to efficiency of other countries' external control as well as internal drug control/policy. Germany used to be – and still is – a major gateway to Western Europe. The number of (registered) immigrants has been higher in Germany in the 1990s than in all other Western European countries taken together. 'Burden sharing' has consequently been a more pressing concern for the German government than for others. When the German Basic Law was to be changed to facilitate a more restrictive line on asylum, adjustment to the Schengen regime was an important card to play for the authorities. In the Netherlands Schengen has not been a major public issue, although it has contributed to a stronger focus on internal control mechanisms.

The two non-EU countries in our group – Norway and Hungary – have had different positions in relation to the Schengen issue. Hungary with its clear aspiration for EU membership, needs to adjust as much as possible to the control regime that predominates among the EU member countries. This is the case, even though the incentives for introducing an external control of the Schengen order are not obvious. Knowing that most migrants do not want to settle in Hungary, the motivation to invest large resources in the control system is limited. This trade-off constitutes Hungary's position for the time being. Norway, on the other hand, jumped off the EU wagon in 1994 after a national referendum. EU membership is consequently not on the agenda in the foreseeable future. Schengen imposed itself on the Norwegian public when Sweden and Finland joined the European Union and subsequently prepared for negotiations with Schengen together with Denmark. The historic Nordic Passport Union was thus in danger unless Norway also joined Schengen in some way or another. The Norwegian government started negotiations with Schengen together with the other Nordic countries, and finalized an agreement in December 1996. This agreement provided Norway with a position as an observer with access to all meetings and arrangements, yet without the right to vote. Disagreement meant exit. At the same time Norway was responsible for the adjustment of the national legislation to the Schengen rules. The Schengen affiliation caused a heated debate in public, partly due to the EU connection – which has strong symbolic significance in Norway – and due to substantial parts of the agreement, related to the internationalized control through the information system SIS. Ironically, this – politically speaking – rather dearly bought agreement was endorsed in parliament only days before the Amsterdam Summit made it virtually valueless, as Norway's status as non-EU member conflicted with the integration of the Schengen Agreement into the EU structure. In 1998 Norway started new negotiations with Schengen.

The Bosnian Crisis as a Trigger for a New Refugee Policy

The war in former Yugoslavia has been a significant marker in all our countries for a more restrictive asylum policy – possibly with the exception of Italy. In Hungary the Bosnian question in fact served to introduce migration as a political issue. The conflict in the Balkan states confronted Europe with the most complex and extensive refugee crisis since the Second World War. The Yugoslavian crisis thus injected urgency into the process of restructuring the Western European refugee strategy. The refugee exodus from Bosnia arose on top of an existing concern in Western Europe over increasing migration from various parts of the world, and served as an impetus for tendencies that were already present. The majority of national economies in Western Europe have been under pressure during recent years with high unemployment and structural adjustments. In the light of this, financially demanding asylum procedures have been viewed with increasing anxiety, particularly after the number of 'ad hoc refugees' started to increase in the mid 1980s. Individual verification of each application is one of the factors that have led to considerable administrative and financial expense, increasing along with the growth in the number of asylum applicants. Due to the fact that a large proportion of asylum applicants have been allowed to stay despite being refused refugee status (acceptance on humanitarian grounds), existing refugee policy has gradually developed into a costly and time-consuming system in which questions of fairness have also been raised. In most Western European countries, the formation of asylum laws has been connected with the development of the UN/Geneva Convention. As a result, asylum laws in the respective countries have been formulated on the basis of assumptions that are not necessarily applicable to today's situation.

The Bosnian crisis was a marker both in terms of border control and in relation to internal conditions in the recipient country. Whereas refugee policy in principle belongs in the realm of human rights, it turned out to be a border control issue where the (in this case obviously legitimate) right for refugees to seek protection was discarded. For the refugees who were actually accepted, the novelty *temporary protection* was supposed to cater to the fear of permanent immigration, seen from the authorities' point of view. The majority of Western European countries discarded their normal practice of considering each case individually, and introduced temporary protection on a collective basis.

As to the active versus passive mode of reception, the war refugee exodus placed the destination countries in an overwhelmingly passive role from the beginning. When this made the recipients play the visa card, policies turned into a more active mode. The visa introduction was presented – at least in Sweden and Norway – together with an aid package to be implemented in the sending region, as well as a quota policy in co-operation with UNHCR. The Bosnian case was thus another manifestation of the externalization of control in Europe.

Some of our countries were major recipients of the Bosnian refugees, partly due to geographical location. Austria, Germany and Hungary all received substantial numbers, but even Sweden – being located quite far from the war area – accommodated around 80,000 before visas were introduced. Only Sweden and the Netherlands granted permanent residency from an early stage, cutting short the possibility of utilizing forced return at a later stage. Norway kept this door open until the end of

1996, when all Bosnians were accepted on a permanent basis. Germany and Austria have been the most rigid countries in this respect in our group – insisting on the impermanence of the protection.

Italy's position is somewhat surprising. Being located very closely to the conflict area, and at the same time not having very severe restrictions on entry for asylum seekers, one would expect a major inflow in this country. When this has not been the case, it probably has to do with a number of more subtle mechanisms being active in Italy. Highly discretional policy implementation at the borders despite the liberal outline of policies may have deterred part of the flows. Besides, Italy has been known for very limited allowances for asylum seekers in a comparative European sense. As we saw in the Italian chapter, Italian policies in this realm have been characterized as being a mix of liberal provisions, restrictive practices, discretional acceptance at the border and low priority treatment.

The Bosnian case revealed very clearly the interdependence of the European countries in relation to immigration policy. The flows of people started going to areas in the vicinity of the former Yugoslavia as well as to areas with some existing tradition or some networks of Yugoslavians. When these doors started closing, flows were directed elsewhere. Norway experienced this position as a latecomer recipient country until visa restrictions were imposed even there. The Austrian decision in mid 1992 to stop accepting refugees from Bosnia directed large numbers to Hungary. The desperation of the situation in the war zones partly explains this rather clear pattern. Italy is the only country not fitting into this picture.

The role of the European Union in the refugee crisis has primarily been an indirect one. Although the EU, as an supranational body has not played an active role in terms of defining new approaches to the refugee situation, it is clear that the EU countries keep abreast of each others' national policies in order to minimize differences, and avoid any single country becoming a more 'liberal haven' than the others. All the EU countries, with the exception of the Netherlands and Sweden, introduced temporary protection for refugees from Bosnia-Herzegovina. The question of 'burden sharing' has concerned (and still concerns) the EU, but due to a lack of genuine authority, the concept of sharing the burden evenly between the member countries has remained wishful thinking on the part of those most affected.

All the countries have one way or the other tried to externalize controls, at the same time making them more efficient during the 1990s. For Italy and Hungary it has been a question of *establishing* a control policy in the first place. These two countries have tried to assume the same control package as the experienced receiving countries in Europe. This has, however, presented difficulties economically and administratively. The legislation in both Italy and Hungary has proved to be ambiguous, hindering a responsible management at the borders. Border control has both places suffered from discretion and random handling.

This externalization and effectivization (intentional or actual) is a response to the realization that if migrants manage to enter a territory, the states will be less likely to stay in control. The population must have confidence that protection against uncontrollable influxes is effective, otherwise the government's capability will be called into question. This has been a rising problem as the gap between official (closed door) policies and *de facto* increases in immigrant communities has widened since the 1970s. The rigidity is partly motivated by a genuine ambition of limiting immigration for economic reasons, partly a fear of losing control of popular reactions; the fear of *le Pen-izing* new areas. This latter point can, of course also be used rhetorically – legitimizing stricter control. This points to the intricate interplay between the border control issue and the *internal* dimension.

Internal Control

In the introductory chapter we divided internal control into an explicit and an implicit (direct or indirect) dimension. The further we move away from the explicit, the more problematic becomes the term 'control'. The *actor* then has a tendency to disappear, and we are left with entities *having a control function* or control *implications*. This involves subtle mechanisms which are hard to trace empirically, but which might nevertheless have a bearing on the whole control complex the way we have dealt with it in this book.

The explicit or direct internal control measures are, however, more tangible, and easier to detect in documents and in reality. Some of the elements we labelled 'explicit internal' may nevertheless seem puzzling to some readers. We have, for example, placed welfare arrangements, social benefits, and various sorts of public allowances into our internal control scheme. As we will argue below, where public arrangements are developed into a part of a comprehensive welfare state system, there exists an element of structural control through these arrangements in different ways. On the other hand, if public welfare in itself is not well controlled – where the transparency of the system, as it were, is not present – it may turn into a pull factor for potential migrants. This in turn can be seen a factor that serves to weaken immigration control.

Internal Explicit Control

The explicit part of internal control has developed partly as a consequence of the imperfections of external control. Immigrants who have managed to gain entry to the territory illegally can be detected internally and treated according to the rules. Since there is also the possibility of entering a country *legally* (for example, as a tourist, student or seasonal worker) internal surveillance is also a method for catching 'overstayers' – those who fail to leave the country when their permits expire.

There are also explicit internal mechanisms that can be seen more as a part of the general national regulation system. Control of access to various facilities – such as ID cards, housing, schooling, social benefits – means that irregular foreigners can be located. These mechanisms do not *prevent* illegal sojourn, but they make life as an illegal resident in an advanced state more difficult.

Sanctions against employers are both a preventive and a remedial means for attacking illegal employment – a means sometimes also targeted at irregular employment of *nationals*.

Union policies can have both a direct and an indirect impact on alien control. With varying force, unions may serve as a 'structural police' against social dumping caused by irregular work undertaken by natives or by foreigners. In Scandinavia, where unions have traditionally repre- sented a considerable political force, this 'police function' has been quite marked. Immigrant workers thus tend to find work in branches where union influence is weak, like certain sections of the service sector (catering and domestic work). Unions may in some societies, due to their central role in the corporate state, also play a more general role in terms of securing higher standards as to working conditions and living conditions. Unions may therefore support a generous line towards foreigners (when these are registered as residents) to avoid the creation of a systemic 'under-class'.

National labour unions thus find themselves in a dilemma: their interests will often direct them to maintain a restrictive line on *entry*, but a generous/ integral attitude towards legal foreign residents. This is clearly the case in Norway and Sweden. The dilemma of the unions turn them into a position where they tend to favour regularization or 'amnesties'. The Austrian unions represent a contrast here by being strictly opposed to amnesties. For the Austrian unions the dilemma was perceived differently: either control overall immigration through social partnership, or represent immigrant workers at the shop floor level and more generally in society. So far the first option has been preferred.

Amnesties have increasingly become an internal control mechanism, particularly in southern Europe where illegal entries represent a considerable problem. Illegals are invited to register and become legals, subjects to official regulations of various kinds. Among our countries, Italy is the one having used amnesties most significantly. Apart from the fact that amnesties represent an ambiguous mechanism as both being an active inclusive instrument and at the same time reflecting a resignation in terms of external control, amnesties may increase the image of the examination process as unpredictable. The 'lottery' aspect of immigration is reinforced. The amnesty dimension is related to the need of advanced states to manage central forces in the economy – and the social consequences thereof. Developed welfare states cannot live with an uncontrolled inflow of foreigners – both due to the limited inclusive capacity of the welfare systems, and due to the adverse effects on regulated markets.

The welfare state connection affects the various countries in this study quite differently. The countries have developed welfare state structures to different degrees. Hungary, being the youngest state in this respect, barely has provisions for immigrants. Italy also represents a weak case in terms of welfare arrangements. Among all the other more established welfare states in our group the traditional welfare approach has come under pressure, and a tendency to privatize services is prevalent. This is the case even in Norway, being the only country within the group with a booming economy in the late 1990s. When public budgets are cut back, however, legitimacy becomes an issue: who should benefit and who should care for themselves. Then it becomes clearer which *implicit* obligations society attaches to the 'welfare contract'. The problem of solidarity towards poorly situated groups becomes particularly salient when newcomers arrive, people who have not 'invested in society' over a lifetime. Two basic principles of the welfare state conflict in these matters: the value of humanitarian obligations is contested by an internal distributive logic. Generally speaking, this points to a central dilemma for Europe's welfare states today. The norms and values that define the democratic welfare state may be violated by excluding immigrants, either at the border or internally by not giving them access to social, economic and political benefits. On the other hand, including them in the system could challenge people's sense of fairness and national belonging when it comes to the divisions of burdens and rights.

The real or perceived welfare crisis of the Western European countries has allowed rightist parties to capitalize on discontent, and it has been used to legitimize cutbacks in benefits for asylum seekers and immigrants.

These cutbacks are partly motivated by the idea that welfare arrangements function as a pull force in relation to potential migrants.

The ultimate explicit internal control mechanism is the option of naturalization – of gaining full citizenship. This innermost and sometimes most attractive gate represents the formal and symbolic cutting edge between life as a 'foreigner' and life as a 'national'. It embodies the moment when one leaves the statistics of aliens and (at least ideally) escapes alien control. There are different approaches to naturalization in our countries. The pair of states most often referred to in the literature in this context is France and Germany. More writers have used the two to constitute a contrast – as France and Germany used to represent opposite poles on the scale from *jus soli* to *jus sanguinis*. As we have seen from the respective chapters, the naturalization policies of the two countries have come closer lately: Germany has loosened its rigid *jus sanguinis* policy somewhat and France has turned more restrictive.

Internal Implicit (Indirect) Control

Implicit *internal* control pertains to the *clôture sociale* – the invisible social barriers that often present themselves in terms of lack of access rather than offensive prohibitions. Foreigners are often made to feel that they do not *belong,* and therefore cannot take part, through subtle mechanisms that need not be explicitly hostile. These non-formal control mechanisms can, of course, also be more openly and at times system-atically unfriendly and excluding. In addition, more-or-less systematic discrimination and marginalization belong in this domain. Here we have entered the nebulous terrain of the *control functions* and *implications of control*, where it is the interaction effects of external and internal control mechanisms that represents the axis of analysis. To trace the various control mechanisms at work in a given country fully is a complex, if not impossible endeavour, as it involves analysing complicated social processes not always openly linked to the migration complex. The notion of 'general social control' is unwieldy in itself, as is its causal connection to the migration question. The interaction between the explicit policy and the more subtle mechanisms is also difficult to trace empirically. We will nevertheless introduce two partly contradictory hypotheses, which are often implicitly present in different forms in discussions on the inter-connections between border control/external control and popular reactions and attitudes towards immigrants or foreigners. On the one hand there is an underlying assumption that border control is a necessary (yet not sufficient) precondition for the integration of immigrants in society. Actual control, and not least the confidence within the population in the government's capability of having control, will – according to this hypothesis – contribute to an open and tolerant climate in relation to newcomers. Michael Walzer (1983) has, in this respect, claimed that societies can be open only if borders are at least potentially closed, or the other way around; that society has a tendency to close itself in, if borders are open.

The other – and partly conflicting hypothesis – claims that a restrictive immigration control contribute to the stigmatization of immigrants. If there is erratic handling of entry restrictions or unforeseen consequences of entry control policy with new and/or unexpected categories of migrants appearing, hostile and excluding attitudes towards *all* foreigners may develop. These attitudes may be directed generally towards foreigners independent of their status as residents. The heavy emphasis on immigration *control* since the 1970s, combined with the subsequent increase in asylum seekers as well as illegal immigrants, has made it difficult to avoid a rising stigmatization of immigrants in society. The immigration 'stop' was meant to put an end to new ethnically 'visible' immigrants, apart from a very few traditional *bona fide* refugees as well as family members of established migrants. 'Immigrant' thus became synonymous with 'unwanted', a fact that feeds back into attitudes towards legitimately integrated immigrants. Public opinion has become 'confused' as to who is whom. A similar confusion is also illustrated by the 'amnesties' in southern Europe: the migrants are not wanted in the first place, and yet, once they have managed to get in, they may gain legal status. Aside from the signals these 'regularizations' send to potential regions of *emigration*, what they communicate to citizens of the receiving country is quite double-edged: the authorities are providing the right to stay for the already-established immigrant, while identifying the new immigrant as a potential danger.

It is difficult to determine which of the hypotheses that accords best with facts. Different parts of the population will react differently, dependent on individual biographies and position in the socio-economic topography. Opinion polls undertaken at different points in time can nevertheless indicate tendencies over time. These results may be confronted with possible changes in the control policy or practice, but it is nevertheless problematic to draw conclusions as to causal connections.

It is nevertheless quite clear that the xenophobic or hostile reactions towards foreigners or people who are visibly different represent a strain on immigrants in many places in Europe today. This strain may in turn serve as a hindrance to integration and it may eventually also reduce the attraction of certain areas. Xenophobia and potential direct hostility towards newcomers or ethnic minorities are also used, in different ways, by authorities as an argument for continuous restrictions. The psychological elements in this are different from case to case. There is a complicated interplay with the 'national biography', geographical location, economic performance and so forth.

Germany is in a particularly delicate situation here, having to cope with the fact that narratives from the past intermingle with present conditions, even though these may not be significantly worse, in terms of xenophobic reactions, than other places in Europe. The racist attacks at the beginning of the 1990s thus turned into what chancellor Kohl labelled a 'state crisis'. Anticipating public reactions to 'foreign looking' refugees, Hungary originally placed a limitation on the Geneva Convention, giving protection only to refugees originating in Europe. This specific clause was later (1997) removed, however.

Control Through Welfare and Integration

The integration policy of a country refers to efforts or actions directed towards legally established immigrants to promote their inclusion into society. This policy can address a whole series of fields that influence the situation of immigrants in a receiving country, like the labour market, housing, social care and welfare generally, education, and language training.

Usually, this policy only addresses immigrants with permanent residence status. As we have seen in the Norwegian case, however, even refugees with temporary protection have been subject to integration policy lately: the Bosnian war-refugees obtained temporary protection on a collective basis, but were simultaneously testing a political novelty – 'integration in a return perspective'.

The concrete integration policy that a state conveys can both directly and indirectly influence both the number and the characteristics of the immigrants who arrive or attempt to arrive. Sometimes generous conditions of integration may constitute a *pull*-factor for potential immigrants. Or the other way around: insignificant integration support may make potential immigrants try another country. Integration of established immigrants may be strained by a restrictive stand on family reunification. If we assume that having family members join in the receiving country is an important precondition for individual well-being and integration, the refusal of family members may have negative consequences for adjustment or integration. Thus there are connections between the integration policy of a country and the preconditions for entry control and vice versa. Seen this way, the integration policy indirectly becomes a part of the national control complex.

Today there is more variance between the European countries in integration policy than in border control policy. There is a tendency for specific state systems to engender different models for integration: border control policy, the degree of liberality regarding naturalization and the tolerance for cultural/ethnic heterogeneity will affect how foreign individuals or groups are received in the receiving country, and thus also on the conditions for the adjustment to new surroundings. These factors will, in other words, constitute important premises for the immigrants' adaptation to society and society's ability to include immigrants: will they form accustomed ethnic milieus within a multicultural context; will the receiving society include them in ways that make their ethnic attributions disappear over time; or will they constitute lasting ethnic minorities, more or less marginalized in society? The result of these different political paths, combined with the popular interpretations of them, will again feed back on the government's formulation of the external control policy. Right from the inception of the 'stop'-policy in the 1970s, governments have argued that it is necessary to restrict the inflow to avoid marginalization and anxiety between ethnic groups and the receiving society.

Beyond these connections to the external control, the integration policy may serve as a more subtle control mechanism in itself, exerting the implicit control that follows from attachment to and dependency on welfare provisions. The structural paternalism epitomized by the welfare state does have social control as a side effect.[1] These mechanisms have probably been most discernible among asylum seekers and refugees who are dependent on special assistance upon arrival. Often they remain in a client situation, either because they are not allowed to work or they are not capable of finding a job. This 'clientalization' or generation of dependence can also be seen among legal foreign residents who for various reasons may have greater problems than the average national in finding appropriate work or adjusting to local conditions. Social exclusion and marginalization based on ethnic background represent *processes* we can locate in all the countries of the study, and it has become a major concern in some of the more advanced welfare states like Sweden, Norway and the Netherlands.

1. See Ian Culpitt (1992) for a general discussion on the welfare state and control mechanisms.

Three Models of Immigration Reception

In a way, the development of integration policy reflects differences in socio-political structure, for example, in terms of degree of centralization of decision making and the involvement of the state in social fields; historical factors and experience with immigration over time as well as variation in the conception of the phenomenon of *integration* as such.

Roughly speaking, there have been three models for handling immigration in Western Europe. Firstly, there is the German approach, in which we can also include Austria, where the concept *'Gastarbeiter'* indicates the basic attitude to immigrants: they are *labour* and they are *guests*, in the sense that they are expected to return to their place of origin when they have completed work, and when there is no demand of their labour power anymore. Meanwhile they have some social rights, yet they are not expected to acquire citizenship. This sketchy model has increasingly been in conflict with reality, as hundreds of thousands of immigrants have decided to remain in Germany, and due to the fact that the *Länders* and the state have developed a range of public initiatives to ease the integration of immigrants. There are, all the same, strikingly few immigrants who have naturalized in Germany after several years of residence.

In societies where the *Gastarbeiter* ideology predominates, there is paradoxically some leeway for cultural heterogeneity. Immigrants may even be encouraged to maintain their ethnic identity, so that the return scenario is preserved. The German reluctance to grant citizenship has even been supported by the argument that pressure to assimilate is immoral and unjustified.

The other major model is represented in the French republican approach. In this model all individuals should have the same access to citizenship independent of ethnic and national heritage. This approach implies, at the same time, that ethnic and cultural distinctions are hardly encouraged, and that the pressure to assimilate is significant. The model has, however, been adjusted to conform with reality. It has proven impossible to handle social problems as if the ethnic dimension is non-existent in certain contexts. Not least during the 1980s and the 1990s, political changes have brought ethnicity and cultural differences into focus. The question of integration has been pushed forward partly through the fact that individuals from ethnic groups are more systematically marginalized in society, and partly through the repatriation movement headed by the nationalist Jean-Marie le Pen. In the beginning of the 1990s the so called Pasqua laws were introduced to modify the rights of immigrants in terms of naturalization. Immigration has been 'securitized' in the public, and has been related to a series of social ills like terrorism, narcotics, criminality and violence.

The third model, is the one most often called *multiethnic* or *multicultural*. In its simplest form, this approach contends that it is possible (and advisable) to integrate immigrants to the degree necessary for the functioning of a society with members from different ethnic groups. This approach allows for the maintenance of ethnic group identity as long as it does not basically collide with the norms and culture of the 'majority society'. This approach, which has been increasingly contested (see Ålund and Schierup, 1991) has been brought forward, and proclaimed as guiding policy in Sweden, Norway and the Netherlands. The model is inspired by social democratic thinking, where the *ethos of equality* has a strong case. Integration should take place in a context where the state arranges the scene through highly developed schemes in most fields of society, without putting 'too much' pressure on the immigrants. Sweden has probably been the most advanced case in this respect. The Swedish state took an explicit stand of not following a guest worker policy at an early stage. Sweden accepted (or wanted) permanent immigration, the process was highly planned, and was not very controversial among the public.

Hungary and Italy do not belong in this set of models, as none of the two countries – being novel receiving states – have developed an integration policy of significance so far. Thus, apart from Hungary and Italy, all the countries of this study have carried out integration policies of some kind since the middle of the 1970s. It has become clear that groups that are conceived as being distinctly different from the majority population as to language, religion and/or ethnic identity, have settled permanently. These groups have consequently challenged the traditional (and in most places ideological) understanding of nationhood as being based on a common ethnic heritage and a cultural, religious and linguistic unity.

Even though it is obviously possible to trace national distinctions in terms of discourse and concrete integration policy, there is even here a tendency to convergence – although weaker than in the external control area. Precisely due to the (implicit) control dimension of integration, each state has an interest in not deviating too much from the other receiving countries in terms of generosity. This understanding is based on the assumption that excessively benevolent arrangements serve as a *pull* factor, and hereby lead to less control. In most of our countries there have been cutbacks in welfare for asylum seekers lately, to discourage them economically. In Italy, asylum seekers who appeal against their cases lose public assistance and may not work. In Hungary there is not much welfare for asylum seekers in the first place. Due to the communist past there are also very few NGOs providing alternative care. This may be the reason why there are very few asylum seekers in these two countries altogether. Norway is a possible exception as there have been few significant cutbacks in welfare benefits for asylum seekers and refugees lately (if we ignore the rather drastic, but unclear, change in terms of making *temporary protection* the general rule). This makes it even more urgent to keep up external and preventive control, as well as to effectuate deportations vigorously. It should be added that there could be other, substantial reasons for the changes in welfare policy towards asylum seekers and immigrants in general than the economic interests and the question of deterrence. In the countries with a *multicultural* approach, there are arguments for a revision of the 'kindness'-design, but this is outside the scope of this book.

The question of access to work has been a shuttlecock in different countries: When Germany ended sanctions upon work during the asylum procedure in 1991, France was in the process of introducing them. Indecisiveness in this respect may be explained by conditions and fluctuations in the labour market. Given the restrictive labour immigration policy, the authorities may consider the stock of asylum seekers as a reservoir in situations where labour is in demand. The unintended consequence of raising restrictions on work for people under investigation is, of course, that the illegal market becomes the only option.

The welfare connection of the control complex points to an important dilemma for the receiving states. It is pertinent for the immigration countries not to make welfare policies an incentive for new migration, thereby reducing capacity for control. At the same time it is necessary for advanced welfare states to provide unfortunate groups with assistance to avoid the generation of systemic marginalization, with dumping problems, the undermining of the system of tripartite negotiations, the expansion of a shadow labour market and possibly increased criminality.

Control Efficiency and the Labour Market

It seems, based on most of the countries in this study, that *efficiency* of immigration policy is more a question of the ability to supervise the labour market than of policing the national borders: it revolves on the state's ability to prevent employers from hiring undocumented workers and its ability to maintain generally high standards of employment conditions. The capacity to control inflows depends largely on how the labour market is organized and structured. In other words, the specific migration setting is the ongoing result of a combination of policy and market forces, so the control aspects discussed so far are in a constant interplay with labour market parameters as well as social forces attached to the blending process of cultures.

The labour market plays a decisive (although not all-embracing) role in the *integration* of immigrants. Absorption of the immigrant population in the regular labour force also disburdens public budgets and may contribute to economic growth. Both for the immigrants and for the national population the labour market can serve as a stepping stone for social integration. Thus, the efficiency of control is related to the labour market in different ways

Yet, control of immigration and of the labour market are related in a complicated manner. As labour immigration is now basically restricted to qualified personnel from OECD countries (apart from contract labour), significant connections between control and the labour market are found in the shadow market – in other words through illegal labour. The term 'irregular/illegal immigrant worker' covers a whole range of categories: An immigrant worker may be 'regular' in terms of residence but not in regard to work, or the other way around. There is the seasonal worker who moves to another sector in which he or she does not have a permit; then there is the temporary resident who has paid work but only a tourist visa; the legal temporary resident who stays on after the permit has expired; there is the regular student who works without a permit; the asylum seeker who works irregularly while the case is being examined and processed; the asylum seeker whose application has been turned down, yet who stays on, and so forth (Commission, 1992).

The labour market plays a key role in relation to illegal immigration. An illegal worker implies an illegal employer – unless the immigrant is provided for by close relatives or others. The size of illegal immigration depends to a large extent on how employers can use their labour. Access to work is a central attraction in relation to the establishment and maintenance of irregular immigration. Insofar as work exists for these migrants when they arrive, the system will continue to function. An important lesson from the 'amnesties' given to illegal immigrants in various places in Europe, is that it is impossible to control irregular immigration without attacking structural aspects of the labour market. Entry control, ID checks, as well as various sanctions against employers and possible mediators can thus be only *a part of* a policy to curtail illegal immigration.

Yet, the structural aspects of the labour market are difficult to come to grips with. The presence of unauthorized immigrants indicates there are internal (unofficial) contradictions in the various receiving countries when it comes to the influx of cheap labour. Many people have an interest in illegal labour. Middle-class households are increasingly hiring domestics; the higher the official wage level, the greater is the temptation to do it 'unofficially'. There exist, among groups of employers within the various EU countries, several more-or-less open pressure groups concerning access to cheap foreign labour. Experiences from Italy reveal that restrictive legislation can co-exist with *de facto* lenience towards illegal labour in some contexts. Variation between EU countries – in terms of labour market structure, size, and composition of the black labour market and hence variation in the patterns of the vested interests in foreign labour – are an important factor in the process towards harmonization of the European immigration policies.

The increase in illegal immigration has been an unforeseen consequence of the end to recruitment of foreign labour introduced in the 1970s. The more complicated it becomes to enter Western Europe *legally,* the more illegal trafficking grows. Furthermore, the higher the risks involved, the more lucrative is the business undertaken by traffickers. Irregular migration today represents a wide-ranging yet unwieldy terrain, where data are necessarily scarce and unreliable. The issue has become highly sensitive in the public debate, partly due to its magnitude (at least some places) and partly because of the discrepancy between the authorities' proclaimed continuous devotion to combating the traffic, and their *de facto* incapacity/incapability to do so.

Irregular immigration in itself leads to insecurity and instability in the labour market, which again may mean greater difficulties for already resident immigrants to achieve integration into society. The 'hidden economy' and irregular immigration tend to reinforce each other (see, for example, Commission, 1990), in the sense that a continuous incentive exists to hire illegally, as the supply is there. In the Italian chapter it is argued that, in Italy, the basic reason behind ethnic tensions is the interaction between the various segments of the labour market – between the official and the shadow market. A concentration of illegal immigrants is encouraged where semi-criminal labour brokering already operates. Thus the matching of cultural stereotypes and individual behaviour is mutually reinforcing through the labour market.

It can be argued that a similar relationship exists between the welfare state and the immigrants in areas where there are more asylum seekers than illegal immigrants. The 'stop' has channelled immigrants into routes that are more costly for the authorities, and this in turn gives grounds for opinions that they come 'to exploit our welfare state', resulting in increased hostility.

However, even if scholars would agree as to the 'objective' functioning of immigration in receiving economies, the market forces of migration, as well as the ineffective control systems, would have an independent momentum beyond the planning procedures of governments. One reason for this is that there are inconsistencies in the market needs of receiving countries. Despite recurrent unemployment, certain sectors of the European economies seem to be short of labour, both seasonally and more permanently. This applies particularly to agriculture, hotel and catering, construction, small sub-contracting firms, maintenance and cleaning, as well as various other services. This seems to be true for more-or-less all the states in this study. Even though all EU member countries are overwhelmingly in favour of restricting immigration from outside the EU, certain states (Germany, France and Italy in our context) nevertheless want to keep the door open for a policy of labour immigration. Through arrangements like short-term contract work and quotas, these governments hope to keep some flexibility in relation to needs in the labour market, while at the same time retaining a restrictive general immigration policy.

Thus, the question of efficiency in the relation between immigration control and the labour market is highly complex. Besides, the question of efficiency itself is somewhat entangled: Efficiency in one sense may become inefficiency in another. The 'immigration stop' introduced in many European receiving states in the beginning of the 1970s was 'efficient' in the sense that organized and market-regulated (legal) labour immigration by and large came to a halt. It was 'inefficient' in the sense that flows (partly as a consequence of the policy) changed character and found new legal routes – as family reunification for established immigrants, or later as asylum seekers – and irregular channels. The change in character of the flows has in turn prompted authorities to readjust their policies. Gradually more sophisticated instruments are used to curtail illegal immigration. The criteria for family reunification have been tightened; an increasing share of the asylum-seeker flows are being defined as 'economic refugees' not qualifying for asylum; the term 'temporary protection' is invented to create more flexibility in handling larger flows like war refugees, even visa schemes are introduced in trying to reduce the number of asylum seekers reaching the borders, as we have seen. In this respect we might almost speak of an 'unintended efficiency', if we were to take the basic humanitarian principles of democratic states seriously. The quest for control of what is seen as an illegitimate flow of asylum seekers may undermine the institution of asylum as such. A related question to raise in this respect is in whose interest 'full efficiency' of the control systems would be. Complete control has been the aim in some

Arab Gulf states. Such control is, however, nearly impossible in the Western democracies of today, given the social and political consequences of imposing such a rigid all-embracing system.

The Control of Control in Liberal Democracies

In democracies, characterized by parliamentary systems, independent judicial systems and civic freedoms and rights, immigration is restrained. Our analysis has shown that if immigration remained uncontrolled, the implications would be negative on two counts: on one hand with regard to the immigration of foreign citizens, and on the other hand with regard to the status and rights of alien residents in the receiving country.

Internal control often involves direct infringements upon the integrity of individual foreign citizens, who may, for example, be ordered to report to the police every day, who may be taken into custody for a few days or even for weeks or months. Resident and work permits can be refused to them, and if granted, later revoked. The legislation is in all project countries implemented with a large amount of discretion, and the tolerated space seems to be somewhat broader both in young immigration countries like Hungary and in old ones as, for example, France, but the opposite trend is also important to note. In European aliens legislation the residential status, including permanent resident permits and the rights of non-citizens, has increasingly been made as explicit as possible, specifying the conditions, under which non-EU citizens (or citizens of third countries), can be refused work or stay, taken into custody, deported and so forth.

Immigration control is constrained not only by rules in the state's own aliens legislation, but also in several international human right principles, developed in the UN and in the European Council. The integrity of a person must not be violated, if this is not explicitly permitted by law or in a court decision. A due process of law must be given to anyone, independent of citizenship. No one may be arrested for more than a few days without a court decision. In spite of this, immigration control often implies imprisonment, handcuffing, transportation with police escort, and so forth, which otherwise apply only to criminals or suspects of criminal acts. Some observers may therefore ask: 'Is it a crime not to be a citizen?' Others want to know, whether it would change anything, if the regular police were replaced by a special immigration authority, or if fingerprinting was abandoned. The core dilemma in any policy of immigration control seems to be how to strike the balance between respect for personal integrity and national interests.

Many foreign citizens are long-term residents or denizens. For them a deportation may involve severe consequences, out of proportion to an offence against the aliens legislation. The longer the time they have spent in the country, and the more integrated they are in the society, the less fair it may be to deport them in the interest or for the security of the state, or even for trespassing the aliens legislation. In most states, foreigners with very long residence periods are therefore normally not deported.

Now this is not an argument against all deportations or in favour of less immigration control. Induced from the comparison of eight European systems, this is instead a reminder that control of immigration and residency should be considered both from the state's perspective and from that of the individual alien. The states are actors with the power to pursue their policy interests as far as given constraints allow them. The individual immigrants and alien residents can apply, argue, plead but finally have to obey. Some among them try to evade enforcement of the law by entering or working illegally, overstaying their visas or going underground to avoid deportation. While economic interests obviously restrain states in combating circumventions of immigration control, commitments to respect individual rights of immigrants tend to be less efficient in constraining their methods of control.

Symbolic Control

In almost all our project countries, immigration control has recently been politicized. Populist parties (like for example the National Front in France, the Progress Party in Norway and the Freedom Party in Austria) have gained unexpected success, campaigning on anti-immigrant or xenophobic platforms, and heavily criticizing the countries' immigration policy. The Republican Party in Germany has been more restricted and less successful, partly because the German unification deprived right-wing nationalists of a major theme around which to rally. More recent examples are the 'New Democracy' Party in Sweden, and the Lega Nord in Italy, whereas attempts of this kind so far have failed in Hungary, and been rather unsuccessful also in the Netherlands.

The traditional parties have incorporated large parts of the new populist parties' arguments for an end to immigration and more restrictive policies into their own campaigns. The entire political climate has moved towards protectionism and nationalism, and not only conservative parties, but also labour parties favour tough measures. Exceptions are not all but some Christian and most Green parties, and it is mainly groups within these parties that warn against excessive restrictions, claiming that fundamental democratic values set limits to a state's control policy and its implementation.

The symbolic quality of immigration politics has been enhanced in the period analysed in this book. The economic depression, the long-lasting unemployment and the budgetary deficits have had an impact on party sympathies and trust in politicians. These great social problems cannot be easily solved by political decisions, but symbolic politics may offer a diversion, and migration control may be a suitable issue, especially as foreign workers are often seen as unwanted competitors, who take those jobs native workers should have got, or who live on social benefits which others have paid for – and so forth.

The same mechanism may also be reinforced when fundamental changes in the world at large generate a basic insecurity about the future. After the Cold War, severe political and ethnic conflicts and open warfare have brought about mass refugee movements. In Europe the plans for a reconstructed and strengthened EU with new roles for its member states are also grounds for a new national uncertainty. Not least, a number of major global or international problems remain hopelessly unsolved and even neglected (poverty, environmental protection, pollution, and population development). Politicians can offer little but symbolic gestures, and even if the fear for this unknown future is not clearly expressed most of the time, it is shared by many. The conclusion is that the future is not under control, and that politicians must reassure their voters. They may promise to do their best, but the audience is sceptical and suspicious and not easy to convince.

The symbolic value of immigration control may furthermore be enhanced by the fact that neither the efficiency of control, nor the size of future immigration flows can be accurately measured. In all our project countries, politicians have exaggerated the numbers of potential immigrants. The arrival of a few hundred people is blown up into imminent invasions. Even more serious forecasts, based on the expected increase of the population and the workforce in potential countries of origin, have been doubtful. The causal relationships between population growth, future unemployment levels, and future international migration are most complex, and the prognoses have not considered adequately the many factors which make people stay where they are, instead of emigrating. As the forecasts can neither be proved nor disproved, the claims that more control is needed have seldom been critically examined. By playing safe, emphasizing efficient control, politicians can hope to attract political support. In this sense, the policy of immigration control has become a field for symbolic policies, in which the liberal democratic limits of control are much too often forgotten.

General Tendencies – Concluding Remarks

International migration represents a dynamic system, where cumulative processes of actors, groups of actors, institutions, as well as political and economic structures interplay in a complex web. Economic, social, and cultural changes generated in both areas of origin and destination through international migration, equip the flows of people with a forceful inherent momentum not easily regulated by governments.

It is nevertheless one of the major conclusions of this book that European governments have become steadily more concerned to control immigration since the early 1980s. Paradoxically, one may say that the successively more sophisticated and inventive ways of circumventing the control systems on the part of the immigrants is an indication of an elaborated functioning apparatus. At the same time, there is no doubt that loopholes in the systems, as well as increased criminal activities in relation to illegal immigration, represent a major impediment on policy implementation. Control strategies imposed by the authorities of receiving countries have given rise to counter-strategies or strategies of circumvention by actual and potential migrants. Immigrants are *actors* who will react to restrictive policies by utilizing whatever channels are available. Thus, effectivization of control gives rise to another tendency, namely *clandestinization*. This is a tendency all our countries experience to different degrees.

There is, however, another – more intrinsic – nemesis in the efficiency domain: the tendency to over-administration and bureaucratization. This way success in imposing restrictions may lead to costly ineffectiveness in implementation. This tendency may have different implications in different settings, yet the German case is probably the most striking example of a huge control apparatus not necessarily resulting in clear implementation. The tendency to over-administration due to the increased range of categories and – partly as a consequence of this – the increased complexity of legislation has in turn lead some states to introduce yearly quotas. These quotas sometimes do not ask which category migrants belong to, so the acceptance or refusal becomes a numerical question, requiring much less in terms of administration. (The major objective of the quota system is nevertheless its impact on the control of the total numbers accepted.) Within this efficiency realm we may also sort out a move from short-term and *ad hoc* measures to more long-term planning. This tendency is to a large degree a function of the level of development and the length of experience of immigration policy-making in the receiving countries.

Another significant tendency in most receiving countries is the increased focus on *flows* rather that individuals. This tendency is most marked in relation to refugees who used to be, by definition, individuals who needed protection, but who currently more and more are treated as parts of collectives. Categories like 'safe third countries' and 'war refugees' disregard the original meaning of refugee protection, and make humanitarian traditions be reinterpreted as control.

The perception of immigrants as representing flows rather than individual human beings, reinforces the threat images of immigration, and has contributed to a tendency of *politicization* of immigration. Metaphors like 'flood', 'invasion', 'hungry hordes' play on people's fear and insecurity in the receiving countries. This fragile landscape has become a seedbed for rightist or populist forces in a number of receiving countries.

The realism in these threat scenarios may be discussed; among experts there is near consensus that both politicians and the media tend to dramatize the prospects. Historical parallels are drawn to show that the *de facto* flows of today by no means are alarming compared with earlier times in Europe. Besides, immigration 'pressure' is obviously also a function of how strictly border control is enforced. As long as foreign labour was in demand, immigration pressure was not an issue in the West. However, if immigration is perceived as a threat, it *becomes* a threat, until the public can be convinced of the contrary. It is in the end the *feeling* of being swamped, as well as worries in relation to the unpredictability of the future that substantiate general anxiety over immigration.

One of the most profound tendencies we have analysed in this study is the inclination to *externalize* control. It is possible to trace a twofold externalization in this respect: the emphasis on *preventive* measures way beyond the national borders of the receiving country, and the more acute externalized control measures like visa requirements alone or in combination with carrier sanctions. This tendency unfolds simultaneously with a stronger sophistication and diversification of internal control mechanisms. One of the major tasks of this study has been to analyse how the external and the internal control mechanisms interact and influence the scope of operation in the respective field.

The dynamic interplay between external and internal control mechanisms has been more pregnant and visible through the Schengen Accord. This agreement is based on the assumption that there are central interconnections between the two control dimensions. On the national level there is, all the same, significant variation in the way in which this interplay operates, as we have seen. The operation of this interplay is influenced by a *setting* in which the national labour market on the one hand, and several international parameters on the other, have a strong impact.

The structure of the labour market (in terms of factors such as composition of demand, unemployment, size of unofficial market) will influence the size and composition of actual immigration, whereas this structure is in turn influenced by immigration. Thus, directly and indirectly, entry control and internal control mechanisms have an impact on labour market factors, as the structural labour demand will set important pre-conditions for effective control.

Labour market facilities are furthermore a central variable in the matter of *integration*. Wage labour opens up other doors to society. Conversely, lack of integration will easily imply marginalization, which might, in turn, affect the structure of the labour market. The tendency of *deregulation* of the labour market in Western Europe has had control implications, in the sense that irregular employment has expanded, hereby providing structural incentives for irregular immigration.

Concerning the interaction between *integration* and immigration *control,* one rather obvious relation has been discussed in the sense that lack of entry and internal control hampers planning, and thus complicates integration into advanced welfare states. Deficient integration of immigrants would therefore tend to influence entry control policies in more restrictive directions. A more subtle mechanism, between control and integration related to the ambiguous implicit messages is contained in restrictive control policies: having heavy restrictions on immigration could be interpreted as official authorization of the insider/outsider 'us'/'them' thinking, which contributes to worsening the climate rather than alleviating relations between already established immigrants and nationals.

These complex internal dynamics in the respective nation states impede coherent planning and policy formulation. Furthermore, any total 'fencing out' of third-country immigrants is untenable, for many reasons. Apart from control aspects – the 'hole in the fence' problems – and inconsistent market needs, basic humanitarian or moral aspects are involved in the issue, which has here been discussed in terms of welfare-state dilemmas. Normative obligations present receiving states with limitations as to the formulation of control policies. The basis for legitimization of control varies. Here national narratives play a part, in terms of symbolic codes, myths and historically generated discourses. National distinctions in this realm give each country different grounds for mobilizing political support when it comes to policy formulation on migration control. Long-term targets of immigration control are generally determined by perceptions of national interests and national identities. Yet, control policies are often contradictory – arising from difficulties in aggregating conflicting interests in society into one single set of national interests.

International migration – in itself a phenomenon that transcends national borders – will have to be politically addressed beyond the nation state, if it is an aim for decision makers to have more sophisticated control over people's movements. The European Union today plays a role in Europe partly as a force in itself and partly as a frame of reference for member countries – and for non-member countries as well. On the one hand, the immigration policy of any European country may affect the policy of other European countries and also that of the European Community. On the other hand, the European integration process has an indirect and direct impact on the national momentum.

As we saw in the introductory chapter, the European Union has not yet developed a fully harmonized immigration policy. It nevertheless functions as a premise for national decision making through its mere existence. It is a question of mutual expectations that might become self-fulfilling prophecies. The existence of the European Union implies that central actors *assume* (even without supra-national competence) that the EU countries as a group will end up with a clearly restrictive line on immigration. This 'anticipatory harmonization' is based on the fact that everybody is afraid of the 'magnet effect', which in practice means that the policy of the most restrictive state will set the tone.

Individual governments may use the EU process as a shield against their own public opinion; arguing that a certain policy is necessary to conform with the other member countries, and with the expected future policy of the Community. This EU mechanism is functioning even in the non-member countries in our group – Norway and Hungary.

Nevertheless, the nation state in Europe still matters in relation to immigration control, a fact which is amply illustrated throughout this book. The process of harmonization witnessed in today's Europe, can more precisely be labelled *conditional convergence*. The basic reason for this is variation in national traditions in immigration policies and practice and, partly as a consequence of this, opposing *interests* on the side of the governments: The wide gap in terms of numbers received is a disincentive for burden sharing among the countries that are *less* affected. This seems to be the crude rule of the game, and position in relation to EU membership is *not* a significant variable in this. Norway's 'outsidership' does not suggest a drastically different policy line from the actual member countries of the Union, neither in entry control matters nor in practising asylum policies.

The tendency towards *conditional convergence* witnessed throughout our case studies will most likely develop further in the years to come. The transitional period sparked off by the Amsterdam Treaty gives openings in different directions, but the overall trend is towards a successively more co-ordinated and restrictive immigration policy.

References

Commission of the European Communities (1990), *Policies on immigration and the social integration of migrants in the European Community,* Brussels: SEC(90) 1813 final, 28 September.

—— (1992), *Immigration and employment,* Brussels: Working Paper, SEC(92) 955, 7 May.

Cruz, A. (1993), *Schengen, ad hoc immigration group and other European Intergovernmental bodies*, Brussels: Churches Committee for Migrants in Europe, Briefing paper 12.

Culpitt, I. (1992), *Welfare and citizenship. Beyond the crisis of the welfare state?,* London: Sage.

Enzensberger, H.M. (1993), *Den store vandringen, Treogtredve markeringer med en fotnote: 'Om noen særegenheter ved menneskejakten',* Oslo: Cappelen.

Teitelbaum, M. (1991), 'The effects of economic development on out-migration pressures in sending countries', *OECD Conference on Migration,* Roma.

Walzer, M. (1983), *Spheres of justice: Defence of Pluralism and Equality.* New York: Basic Books.

Ålund, A. and Schierup, C.-U. (eds) (1991), *Paradoxes of multiculturalism.* Aldershot: Avebury.

Index

absorption capacity, 14, 60, 195
administrative discretion, 14, 225, 244,
   267, 270, 276, 313, 316, 327
admission, 8–9, 100, 124, 139, 211, 239,
   242, 268, 303
Afghanistan, 154
Africa, 24, 46, 83, 92, 144, 216, 236, 256,
   263
agriculture, 282, 286, 326
Albania, 30, 240, 246, 250, 267
Algeria, 61, 63–4, 81, 242–3
aliens legislation, 113, 119, 124, 172, 186,
   190, 200, 205–7, 211, 237–40, 281,
   313
amnesty, 14, 21, 65, 186, 234, 239, 244,
   252, 257, 283, 315–8
Amnesty International, 191, 197, 287
Amsterdam Summit, 19, 179, 228, 307–9
anti-immigrant vote, 21, 99, 110, 179,
   228, 247, 307, 309
anti-Semitism, 67, 104
apolitical issue, 124, 178, 197, 241, 265,
   288, 292
appeal procedure, 120–1, 173, 183, 187,
   197
application from abroad, 125,147, 173, 213
Asia, 39, 145, 216, 256, 263
assimilation, 11, 72, 92, 172, 267, 321
Assyrians, 178
asylum, 239, 277, 291, 326
   application, 47, 196, 264, 309
   crisis, 33, 42, 47, 55
   first country, 43, 103, 306, 309
   legislation, 45, 89, 119, 121, 129, 150,
     187, 264–8, 284, 301, 312, 323
   procedure, 51, 122, 150, 153, 184, 214,
     222, 235, 312
   seeker, 20, 74, 78, 83, 108, 118–20,
     130, 140, 145, 150–1, 176–8, 184,
     189–91, 210, 217–19, 228, 244, 265,
     276–7, 286, 308, 325, 326

unfounded case, 120, 307
attitudes of (in)tolerance, 117, 146, 158,
   209, 223, 227, 240, 273, 319, 331
attractions/pulls, 48, 117, 120, 228–9,
   237, 272–3, 301, 323–4
Aussiedler, 33, 36, 55, 300
Australia, 12, 13, 143
Austria, 24, 51,100, 262, 276, 284, 300,
   302–15, 320–1, 328
Austro-Hungarian empire, 99, 262, 284

Balkan countries, 243
Balladur, E., 64, 74, 78–80
Baltic states, 180–2, 193
Bangladesh, 211
Bavaria, 34, 41, 50
Belgium, 91, 146
Benelux, 308
Berlin, 29, 41, 264, 271, 304
big city, 157
boat people, 42
Boross, P., 276–7
Bosnia, 33, 41, 44–9, 117, 122–4, 154,
   182, 199, 205, 215, 285, 301, 306–7,
   311–13
Brubaker, R., 54, 256
buffer zone, 273
burden sharing, 313

California, 75–9
Canada, 12–13, 45, 91, 108, 143
carrier sanction, 14, 23,154, 308, 331
Catholic organisation, 104, 234–6, 241,
   246, 250
ceiling decision, 243–4
Central European Initiative CEI, 272
chain migration, 11, 54, 100
Chevénement, J-P., 72, 87–90
children unaccompanied, 54
children's rights, 192
Chile, 31, 208, 235, 263

Index

Index

early warning system, 23, 219, 230, 305
Economic and Monetary Union, EMU,
    84–5
EEC, 31, 53, 209, 247
efficiency, 2–3, 20, 55, 99, 121, 127, 145,
    170, 194, 239, 244, 256, 270,291, 307,
    310, 326, 329
elections, 67, 158, 203–4
electoral rights, 33, 215, 255
emigration, 7–8, 99, 135, 143, 207, 233,
    235, 254, 261, 263, 290, 302
    control, 85, 246, 263
employer sanction, 14, 148, 164, 188,
    238–9, 253, 283, 315
employment centre, 236–7, 243
equal treatment, 53, 84, 215–6
Eritrea, 208
Estonia, 183
ethnic,
    cleansing, 41, 122, 221
    community, 11, 14
    German, 30, 36–40, 45–6, 104
    Hungarian, 263, 266–8, 274, 279,
        284–7, 290–1, 300
    minority, 11, 178, 274
    network, 11, 49, 208, 229, 300
ethnicity, 255, 261, 288–9, 292, 303
EU, 9, 17–8, 23–5, 43–7, 51–2, 63, 73,
    114–5, 130, 139, 144, 163, 171, 179,
    181–2, 193, 199, 203–5, 227–9, 242,
    246–7, 255–7, 261, 270–2, 291, 298,
    304–5, 308–11
EU borders, 180, 203, 272, 308
European Economic Area, EEA, 115, 24–5
Evian Agreement, 63
externalization, 23, 46, 55, 90, 92, 164,
    170, 193, 241, 273, 298, 303–4, 308,
    312–4, 325, 329, 331, 333
extreme right, 157–9

family reunification, 2, 46, 55, 61, 64, 78,
    86, 93, 99, 101, 126,148, 150, 157,
    179, 210, 214, 237, 244, 266, 326
fascism, 235, 241, 250
fingerprint, 83, 193
Finland, 170–1, 178, 180, 203, 207
flight prevention, 219, 230, 305
foreign policy, 4, 212–3, 242, 246, 256,
    271, 288, 291, 299

France, 24, 43–4, 51, 129–30, 135, 146,
    174, 276, 304, 308–10, 317, 321,
    326–7
free movements, 9, 28–9, 139, 170–1,
    207, 309
Freedom Party, FPÖ, 97, 109, 125–9,
    328
freedom, negative/positive, 76, 327
Front National, 66–8, 71, 74, 80–4, 87,
    92, 159, 328
fundamentalism, 81

Gambia, 243
Geissler, 41
Geneva Refugee Convention, GRC, 4,
    122–5, 140, 150, 182, 186, 207, 221,
    264, 277–9, 312
geographic reservation, 278
geopolitical location, 160, 169, 247, 299
German Democratic Republic, GDR,
    29–30, 38, 117, 181, 199, 264
Germany, Federal Republic, BRD, 13, 24,
    60–4, 76–8, 91, 97, 100–5, 117, 122–4,
    129–31, 135–8, 146–9, 161, 173–4,
    180–1, 207, 233, 256, 262, 276,
    300–12, 317–21, 326–30
Ghana, 145
Giscard d'Estaing, V., 63–4, 87
GISTI, 69, 76
government of cohabitation, 70, 74, 84
Greece, 171, 263
guest-worker, 97, 100, 175, 321
Gulf states, 305, 327
Gypsy see Roma

Habsburg empire, 98–9, 103
Haider, J., 109–10, 125, 128–9
harmonization, 17, 203, 333
Haut Conseil à l'Intégration, 71
Heimatrecht, 100, 104
Hindu school, 156
housing standard, 89, 147, 155, 211, 268
human rights, 4, 20, 69, 124, 200, 220,
    271, 287, 327
Human Rights Watch, 197, 275, 288
humanitarian principles, 55, 131, 137,
    151, 182, 186, 200, 209–10, 217, 231,
    242, 244, 298, 312, 316, 331–2
Hungarian Interchurch Aid, 287

Index

Hungary, 24, 29, 33, 45, 108, 117–8, 122, 171, 300–3, 308–16, 319, 322, 327–8
hunger strike, 80, 191
hyphenated Italians, 256

Iceland, 180, 207, 228
identity,
    card, 12–3, 76, 88, 161, 187, 194, 217, 315
    check, 68, 161, 164, 184, 187
    document destruction, 22, 183, 189, 250
    forged, 158, 185
    uncertain, 184–9
illegal,
    employment, 43, 128, 147, 160, 171, 176, 187, 237, 248, 257, 324
    entrance, 121, 154, 161–4, 171, 180, 240, 271, 281, 315
    immigration, 79–83, 86, 194, 217, 234, 237, 325
    residency, 140, 142, 181, 245, 249
    trafficking, 2, 14, 125, 158, 180–3, 193, 245, 276, 307, 325
    worker, 65, 79, 142, 187–8
immigrant organisations, 156, 159
immigration,
    authority, 35, 47, 49, 61, 114, 120, 172–3, 211, 235, 269, 327
    country, 34, 233, 291
    history, 59, 137,204, 234, 297, 300
    legislation, 211, 235, 241, 267, 303
    stop, 205, 209
    temporary/permanent, 101, 124, 147, 170, 175, 178
    welfare paradox, 15
immigration policy, 60, 68, 74, 85, 112, 171, 175, 210, 215, 224, 234, 257, 267
    comprehensive and active, 177, 193, 213, 219–20, 304–5, 330
    reactive, 136, 194, 291, 303–4
income requirement, 211, 248, 267–9
Indonesia, 143,
integration, 97, 136, 151, 210, 217, 224, 231, 254, 289, 332
    policy, 15, 48, 66, 71, 85, 90, 151, 155, 172, 175, 241, 271, 284, 319
    return perspective, 175
    social/cultural, 11, 144

integrity personal, 196–200, 327
international co-ordination, 170, 198, 271
international obligations, 3–4, 116, 212, 231, 235, 271, 298, 332
International Organization for Migration, IOM, 41, 182–3, 187
international trade, 14, 136, 169
invasion, 240, 331
Iran, 46, 68, 154, 176, 183, 197
Iraq, 46, 154–5, 176
Ireland, 43, 308
Islam, 72, 81, 92, 156, 158, 285
Israel,108
Italy, 24, 49, 51, 61, 91–2, 109, 171, 262, 299, 301, 307–16, 322, 325–8
ius domicilis, 254
ius sanguinis/soli, 60, 68, 70, 77, 85–7, 129, 137–8, 217, 254–5, 268, 317
ius soli double, 64

Japan, 45, 91, 141
Jew, 41, 59–60, 91, 104, 173, 205, 262, 289
Jewish community, 33, 43
    emigration, 33, 40–1, 45, 55, 108
Jospin, L., 72, 80, 85, 87, 89, 91
judicial review, 31, 49, 53, 78, 83, 111
judiciary,63, 79, 99, 111, 124, 327
Juppé, A., 80–1, 84

Kasakhstan, 38
Kurdistan, 158, 176, 183, 192, 245

labour market,21, 102, 123, 127, 156, 206, 217, 228, 230, 301, 323, 326, 332
    deregulation, 23, 332
    dual/secondary, 103, 251–2
    informal, 53, 56, 65, 169, 176, 188, 194, 228, 253, 277, 324–5
    supervision, 102, 223, 253
language test, 34, 40, 130, 189, 217,
Latin America, 154, 216, 256, 263
Le Pen, J-M., 66–7, 71, 80–1, 86, 314, 321
Lebanon, 176
Lega Nord,328
legge Martelli, 239
liberal, 34, 36
Lichterketten, 34, 43, 97, 128

Index

Index